STUDIES IN THE HISTORY OF ART ·78·

Center for Advanced Study in the Visual Arts

Symposium Papers LV

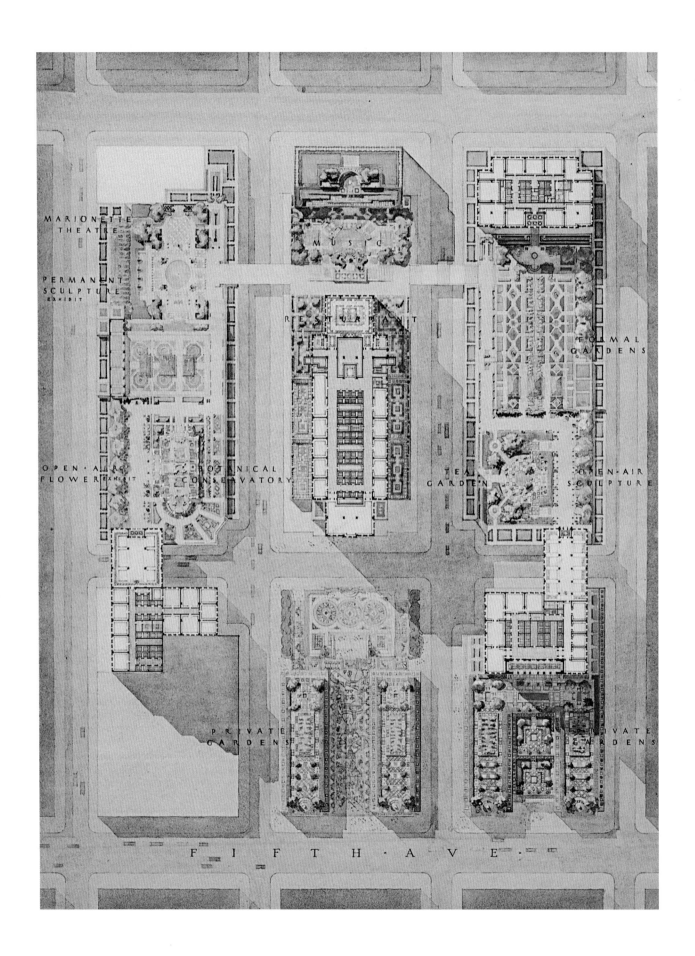

MARIONETTE
THEATRE

PERMANENT
SCULPTURE
EXHIBIT

MUSIC

RESTAURANT

FORMAL
GARDENS

OPEN·AIR
FLOWER EXHIBIT

BOTANICAL
CONSERVATORY

TEA
GARDEN

OPEN·AIR
SCULPTURE

PRIVATE
GARDENS

PRIVATE
GARDENS

FIFTH·AVE·

Modernism and Landscape Architecture, 1890–1940

Edited by

THERESE O'MALLEY AND JOACHIM WOLSCHKE-BULMAHN

National Gallery of Art, Washington

Distributed by Yale University Press
New Haven and London

This volume was produced by the Center for Advanced Study in the Visual Arts and the Publishing Office, National Gallery of Art, Washington
www.nga.gov

Editorial Board
JOHN OLIVER HAND, *chairman*
SUSAN M. ARENSBERG
SARAH FISHER
THERESE O'MALLEY

Editor in Chief
JUDY METRO

Deputy Publisher and Production Manager
CHRIS VOGEL

Series Editor
THERESE O'MALLEY

Managing Editor
CYNTHIA WARE

Program Assistants
BAILEY SKILES
CATHERINE SOUTHWICK
SARAH WILLIAMS

Design Manager
WENDY SCHLEICHER

Assistant Production Manager
JOHN LONG

Assistant Editor
LISA SHEA

Typeset in Sabon and Whitney by Princeton Editorial Associates, Inc., Scottsdale, Arizona
Separations by Prographics, Rockford, Illinois
Printed in China on 157 gsm FSC-certified Gold Sun by Asia Pacific Offset

Distributed by Yale University Press
New Haven and London
www.yalebooks.com

Abstracted and indexed in BHA (Bibliography of the History of Art) and Art Index

Proceedings of the symposium "Modernism and Landscape Architecture, 1890–1940," co-organized by the Center for Advanced Study in the Visual Arts, National Gallery of Art, and the Zentrum für Gartenkunst und Landschaftsarchitektur, Leibniz Universität Hannover, and sponsored by the Arthur Vining Davis Foundations. The symposium was held March 7–8, 2008, in Washington and October 16–18, 2008, in Hannover.

The Center for Advanced Study in the Visual Arts was founded in 1979 at the National Gallery of Art to foster the study of the history, theory, and criticism of art, architecture, urbanism, and photographic media, through programs of meetings, research, publication, and fellowships, and through the formation of a community of scholars.

Library of Congress Cataloging-in-Publication Data

Modernism and landscape architecture, 1890–1940 / edited by Therese O'Malley and Joachim Wolschke-Bulmahn.
    pages   cm
(Studies in the history of art, ISSN 0091-7338; 78. Symposium papers; 55)
Includes index.
ISBN 978-0-300-19639-9 (hardcover : alk. paper)
1. Landscape architecture—History—19th century.
2. Landscape architecture—History—20th century.
3. Modernism (Art)—Influence. I. O'Malley, Therese.
II. Wolschke-Bulmahn, Joachim.
SB470.5.M63 2015
712—dc23
                                    2014038065
ISBN 978-0-300-19639-9
ISSN 0091-7338

Frontispiece: Rockefeller Center, roof gardens, plan rendered by Associated Architects, 1932, ink and watercolor. © 2014 The Rockefeller Group Inc./ Rockefeller Center Archives

Contents

Preface

This volume of Studies in the History of Art has been long in the making. The twenty years or so over which it has evolved have seen many shifts in focus in the relatively young field of the history of landscape design. Modernism, especially in architecture, has also been placed under deep scrutiny in these decades. The symposium from which this volume results, dedicated to the discussion of landscape design and modernism from the end of the nineteenth century to the beginning of World War II and including developments in Europe, Latin America, and North America, recognized an opportunity for genuine interdisciplinary and international collaboration.

In the mid-1990s close ties between Steven Mansbach, then an associate dean of the Center for Advanced Study in the Visual Arts, and Joachim Wolschke-Bulmahn of Leibniz Universität Hannover were consolidated in a pair of roundtable meetings held under the auspices of the Center and Dumbarton Oaks. In 1994, during Wolschke-Bulmahn's tenure as director of garden and landscape studies, "Hostility towards Nature: Avant-Garde and Garden Design" was organized at Dumbarton Oaks in collaboration with Mansbach. In December 1995 Henry Millon, then dean of the Center, and Associate Dean Therese O'Malley convened "The Design and Management of the Environment under Authoritarian Regimes: 1920–1950" at the National Gallery of Art. Mansbach and Wolschke-Bulmahn subsequently published a selection of their material in a special issue of *Centropa* (2004), to which Gert Gröning, formerly professor of urban horticulture and landscape architecture at the Universität der Kunste, Berlin, also contributed. Discussions among Mansbach, Wolschke-Bulmahn, and Gröning, joined by Therese O'Malley, continued over the years, leading to a symposium held in two parts, in Washington and Hannover, in which several lifetimes of scholarship were brought together in the context of recent and new developments. Environmental concerns, gender issues, and questions of political ideology, for example, were less prominent in the field some fifty years ago than they are now, and yet the pioneering work of the earlier generation of scholars in laying the ground for a cultural, political, and institutional history of landscape design in the broadest sense remains vital and relevant. The symposium, organized by Steven Mansbach, Joachim Wolschke-Bulmahn, and Therese O'Malley, recognized the essential continuity in this rapidly expanding field, and we are especially grateful to Gert Gröning, one of its founders, for his contributions to these meetings.

The two parts of the symposium, each two days long, took place seven months apart, with the organizers attending both. In Hannover we were honored by a welcome from Professor Dr.-Ing. Erich Barker, president, Leibniz Universität Hannover. The staff of the Zentrum für Gartenkunst und Landschaftsarchitektur, especially Lidia Ludwig, gave tremendous support to the events, including arranging visits to the historical gardens at Wörlitz and to the Stiftung Bauhaus Dessau, with tours of Walter Gropius' masters' houses and his housing estate in nearby Törten, as well as of Leopold Fischer's settlement houses in Knarrberg. In each of these sites the historical, political, and cultural implications of landscape design are now seen as essential to the understanding of the built environment as a whole, not as additional or peripheral to it.

The sense of shared values and design ideas that characterized earlier definitions of modernism has given way to more complex and even contending sets of visions and expectations. We hope that this publication will contribute to a deeper understanding of changes both in the field of landscape architecture and in approaches to its history over the long term. Special thanks are due to Cynthia Ware for her editorial work in preparing this volume for publication, and especially to Therese O'Malley for her enormous contribution as scholarly editor, together with Joachim Wolschke-Bulmahn. A grant from The Andrew W. Mellon Foundation made this publication possible.

ELIZABETH CROPPER
Dean, Center for Advanced Study in the Visual Arts

Foreword

As director of the Zentrum für Gartenkunst und Landschaftsarchitektur (CGL) at Leibniz Universität Hannover, I was pleased to co-organize and jointly host the two-part symposium at which the contributors to this volume originally presented their essays. Founded in 2002, the CGL is dedicated to conducting and promoting research on garden art and garden memorials and to engaging with the current practice of landscape architecture.[1] The CGL's mission includes the exchange of information and experience among scholars nationally and internationally and presenting research findings to the public through publications, lecture series, and exhibitions. Since its founding, the CGL has dedicated particular attention to questions of modernism and garden design in Germany, a topic addressed in several volumes of the CGL-Studies publication series.[2] A German edition of the present volume will be published as part of that series.

As Elizabeth Cropper notes in the preface to this volume, Steven A. Mansbach, Therese O'Malley, and I organized the symposium "Modernism and Landscape Architecture, 1890–1940" in order to expand the international parameters of a scholarly discourse dating back to the 1990s.[3] When I began to study the history of modern landscape and garden design, what had been written was largely from the perspective of fine arts, graphic and applied arts, and architecture.[4] Neglect of landscape design and garden history had become deeply entrenched and seemingly little questioned. This disregard can be explained historiographically. Historians of modernism attributed to the arts a profound suspicion of nature and of the natural landscape. In the early twentieth century many "modern" artists and architects banished nature from their "new society." Nature, they claimed, was inconsistent with their utopian project for a world founded on universal laws. For them, nature was guilty of promoting arbitrariness, encouraging emotion, and sanctioning history. They promoted a focus on man, rather than nature, as the necessary approach for the future. They installed rationalism in the place of emotionalism and internationalism in place of chauvinism. As Steven Mansbach said in his opening remarks at the symposium, "Nature was perceived by the makers of modernism as incompatible with a projected, man-made world of pure, rational, and transparent relationships."[5]

In an environment so inhospitable to nature, garden design was rarely considered. And yet throughout the period of modernist art, landscape architecture and garden design offered fertile grounds on which to work out new definitions and practices of this art. Particularly after World War 1, garden architects in Europe searched for new models for "modern," meaningful garden designs. Regarding modernism and garden design in Germany, these developments have been investigated since the 1980s. Given this volume's chronological focus on the years 1890 to 1940, it is worth reflecting on an essay of that period, "The Modern German Formal Style," which appeared first in 1917 (with subsequent editions in 1929 and 1931) in Henry Vincent Hubbard and Theodora Kimball's still remarkable book on the tasks of landscape architecture, *An Introduction to the Study of Landscape Design*. They wrote that before "the very modern national consciousness of the German empire," there was nothing in Germany that could be said to be an independent historical style of landscape design:

The modern German conscious seeking for national expression in every field has had its influence on German landscape architecture notably in the production of a formal style of landscape design, intentionally different from any style which has gone before. In many another style the artist has consciously adapted his means to his ends to express the ideal which seemed to him of most worth, but here for the first time landscape designers have gone deliberately to work to determine what their national ideal ought to be and then logically deduced what means should be employed for its attainment.[6]

In all aspects of landscape design concerned with aesthetics, according to the authors, "the modern German feeling that a German must be different from other men in his nature and in his needs has found an interesting expression."[7] Hubbard and Kimball thus assigned the concept "modernism" in Germany to the "Modern German Formal Style," a mode of geometric formality that, from 1900, under the influence of English theorists, was propagated by architects such as Hermann Muthesius and Peter Behrens.[8]

It is notable that Hubbard and Kimball did not mention Willy Lange (1864–1941) in their book, for he was one of the landscape architects who were trying at that time to develop a national and modern style in Germany. Developments in the modern natural sciences during the late nineteenth century—particularly in such disciplines as ecology, plant geography, and plant sociology—stimulated Lange's efforts.[9] He was perhaps the first German landscape architect to take up the concept of ecology, which he understood not in the sense of preserving nature (a motivation that is captured by several essays in this volume), but rather as "the science of communal living among entire groups" of similar species, or, in other words, as a "physiognomic understanding of the plant world within nature."[10] This approach to landscape garden design would, Lange claimed, be "the truly modern garden, the garden for our time."[11] But Lange's concept of the *Naturgarten* was highly influenced by his racist ideas about a close and harmonic relationship of the German people to nature. In his book *Reactionary Modernism: Technology, Culture and Politics in Weimar and the Third Reich* (1984) Jeffrey Herff coined the term "reactionary modernism" for "the mixture of 'great enthusiasm for modern technology with a rejection of the Enlightenment and the values and institutions of liberal democracy' which was characteristic of the German Conservative Revolutionary movement and National Socialism."[12] Lange's "modern" ideas about garden design fit well under this umbrella.

With the advantage of our historical perspective we know, in fact, that the first three decades of the twentieth century in Germany saw developments in garden design that lie outside the parameters of the formal style and that their relationship to concepts such as modernism and nature warrant discussion. Indeed, the introduction of formal modes of garden design in Germany after 1900 and the rejection of the landscape style (or, as it was then also called in Germany, the "Lenné-Meyersche" style) heralded the beginning of modern trends in garden design. But attempts were also undertaken in that period to develop aspects of the Jugendstil (art nouveau), expressionist, and

Dutch De Stijl art movements. In those cases, designers objectified gardens to an extreme degree, seeking to exclude both nature (in the form of naturalistic design and plantings) and—particularly—romanticism. These developments were linked in Germany above all to garden architects such as Leberecht Migge (1881–1935), Hans-Friedrich Pohlenz (1896–1960), and Georg Pniower (1896–1960), who pioneered the introduction of the most advanced technology into the garden and its culture.[13]

These efforts toward modern garden design in the Weimar Republic were vilified under National Socialism; blacklisting and other Nazi persecution measures terminated the professional careers of most practitioners. José Tito Rojo describes parallel political obstacles to modernism in landscape design in Spain in an essay that brings that historical episode to light for the first time.

The search for a modern national expression in landscape is a theme taken up by many of the essays in this volume. Spain, Argentina, the United States, and Italy all produced rhetoric proclaiming their attempts to define progressive—even avant-garde—landscape design, whether formal or naturalistic, as an expression of cultural modernity. Scholarly discussions and publications have explored the theme of modernism in Germany since the 1980s; yet, as demonstrated by Michael Lee's essay in this volume, new methodological approaches to the topic are yielding important results.

The contributors to this volume address important questions that have not previously been raised and that will shed new light on the relations between modernism and garden design. It is to be hoped that many of these questions can be answered; we can be sure that from them, new ones will arise.

JOACHIM WOLSCHKE-BULMAHN
Director, Zentrum für Gartenkunst und
Landschaftsarchitektur
Leibniz Universität Hannover

NOTES

I thank Therese O'Malley for an extremely fruitful and enjoyable collaboration, and particularly for carrying by far the major burden of preparing this volume for publication.

1. For information on the Zentrum für Gartenkunst und Landschaftsarchitektur, one of seven research centers at Leibniz Universität Hannover, see Hubertus Fischer, "Angekommen in der Mitte der Gesellschaft: Die eindrucksvolle Erfolgsgeschichte des Zentrums für Gartenkunst und Landschaftsarchitektur (CGL)," *Unimagazin*, no. 3/4 (2013): 4–7.

2. Relevant examples in the CGL-Studies series (published by Martin Meidenbauer, Munich) include Gert Gröning and Joachim Wolschke-Bulmahn, eds., *Naturschutz und Demokratie!?* (2006); Eberhard Eckerle and Joachim Wolschke-Bulmahn, eds., *Landschaft, Architektur, Kunst, Design: Norbert Schittek zum 60* (2006); Andrea Koenecke, Udo Weilacher, and Joachim Wolschke-Bulmahn, eds., *Die Kunst, Landschaft neu zu erfinden: Zu Werk und Wirken von Bernard Lassus* (2009); Andrea Koenecke, *Walter Rossow: "Die Landschaft im Bewusstsein der Öffentlichkeit"* (2014); Gert Gröning, *Zwischen Dangast und Colorado Springs: Irma Franzen-Heinrichsdorff 1892-1983; Leben und Werk der ersten Absolventin eines Gartenarchitekturstudiums* (2014).

3. In addition to the scholarly collaborations with the Center for Advanced Study in the Visual Arts mentioned in the preface, during my term as director of landscape architecture studies (1991–1996) Dumbarton Oaks organized several other scholarly gatherings and publications either partly or wholly dedicated to topics relating to modernism and landscape. See, for example, Therese O'Malley and Marc Treib, eds., *Regional Garden Design in the United States* (Washington, 1995); Joachim Wolschke-Bulmahn, ed., *Nature and Ideology: Natural Garden Design in the Twentieth Century* (Washington, 1997); Joachim Wolschke-Bulmahn, ed., *Places of Commemoration: Search for Identity and Landscape Design* (Washington, 2001).

4. The following remarks are based on Steven Mansbach and Joachim Wolschke-Bulmahn, "Introduction," *Centropa* 4, no. 2 (May 2004). I thank Steven Mansbach for the inspiring collaboration in guest editing this special issue and for his outstanding contributions to it.

5. The symposium was preceded by many years of research into questions of modernism in the arts by Mansbach, whose focus has been on central and eastern European countries. His publications include *Graphic Modernism from the Baltic to the Balkans, 1910–1930* (New York, 2007); *Modern Art in Eastern Europe: From the Baltic to the Balkans, ca. 1890–1939* (New York, 1999); *Standing in the Tempest: Painters of the Hungarian Avant-Garde, 1908–1930* (Cambridge, MA, 1991); *Visions of Totality: László Moholy-Nagy, El Lissitzky, and Theo van Doesburg* (Ann Arbor, MI, 1980).

6. Henry Vincent Hubbard and Theodora Kimball, *An Introduction to the Study of Landscape Design* (New York, 1929), 51–53.

7. Hubbard and Kimball, 1929, 53.

8. Joachim Wolschke-Bulmahn, "Nature and Ideology: The Search for Identity and Nationalism in Early 20th-Century German Landscape Architecture," *AICGS (American Institute for Contemporary German Studies) Seminar Papers*, no. 17 (February 1996): 1–31. Regarding Muthesius and his impact on garden design, see Uwe Schneider, *Hermann Muthesius und die Reformdiskussion in der Gartenarchitektur des frühen 20. Jahrhunderts* (Worms, 2000).

9. See Joachim Wolschke-Bulmahn, "Political Landscapes and Technology: Nazi Germany and the Landscape Design of the *Reichsautobahnen* (Reich Motor Highways)," *Selected CELA Annual Conference Papers: Nature and Technology* 7 (September 1995): 157–170; Gert Gröning and Joachim Wolschke-Bulmahn, "The Ideology of the Nature Garden: Nationalistic Trends in Garden Design in Germany during the Early Twentieth Century," *Journal of Garden History* 12, no. 1 (1992): 73–80; Gert Gröning and Joachim Wolschke-Bulmahn, "Some Notes on the Mania for Native Plants in Germany," *Landscape Journal* 11, no. 2 (1992): 116–126; Joachim Wolschke-Bulmahn, "The 'Wild Garden' and the 'Nature Garden': Aspects of the Garden Ideology of William Robinson and Willy Lange," *Journal of Garden History* 12, no. 3 (1992): 183–206.

10. Jost Hermand, "Rousseau, Goethe, Humboldt: Their Influence on Later Advocates of the Nature Garden," in Joachim Wolschke-Bulmahn, ed., *Nature and Ideology: Nature and Garden Design in the Twentieth Century* (Cambridge, MA, 1997), 48–51

11. Willy Lange, *Gartengestalung der Neuzeit* (Leipzig, 1909), 28.

12. *Wikipedia*, s.v. "Reactionary Modernism," accessed September 15, 2014, http://en.wikipedia.org/wiki/Reactionary_modernism.

13. Regarding Migge, see David Haney, *When Modern Was Green: Life and Work of Landscape Architect Leberecht Migge* (London and New York, 2010). Pohlenz presented his avant-garde and provocative garden design under the title "Sonderbarer Garten" (peculiar garden) at the Juryfreie Kunstschau Berlin in 1925; see Joachim Wolschke-Bulmahn, "The Avantgarde and Garden Architecture in Germany: On a Forgotten Phenomenon of the Weimar Period" in *Gartenarchitektur und Moderne in Deutschland im frühen 20. Jahrhundert: Drei Beiträge*, ed. Joachim Wolschke-Bulmahn and Andrea Koenecke (Hannover, 2005), 8–24. Pniower, one of the outstanding modernists in German garden design, also tried to develop expressionist approaches to garden design. See Peter Fibich and Joachim Wolschke-Bulmahn, "'Garden Expressionism': Remarks on a Historical Debate," *Garden History* 33, no. 1 (2005): 106–117.

Introduction

More than twenty years ago, Marc Treib opened his influential book with the assertion, "The story of modern landscape architecture remains to be told."[1] Since then, a generation of scholars has risen to the challenge of documenting the history of design from the late nineteenth century onward with publications, conferences, and exhibitions that have greatly enriched the field. Whereas early histories sought to define the formal characteristics of landscape design and concentrated on single periods, sites, or designers, our writing now is informed not only by social, geopolitical, and environmental issues but also by histories of institutions and exhibitions and by the imperative to conserve and restore the gardens and landscapes of this period.

For years historians had studied a few master designers and architects, creating a narrow picture of modernism, devoid of real understanding of the teams and collaborations involved and leaving many aspects of modernism neglected. This, too, has changed. Scholars are beginning to understand the significant roles played by figures such as the Prairie School designer Alfred Caldwell, who designed the grounds for Ludwig Mies van der Rohe's Lafayette Park in Detroit (begun 1940), and Marjorie Cautley, who worked with Clarence Stein at Radburn, New Jersey (1928–1930).[2] Even the masters of the modern movement have been revisited, as in recent important exhibitions at MoMA. Curator Barry Bergdoll, in "The Nature of Mies's Space," his catalog essay for the exhibition *Mies in Berlin*, wrote that interpretation of Mies' work has overlooked the complex layering of outdoor and indoor space fundamental to his architecture.[3] More recently, the curators of *Le Corbusier: An Atlas of Modern Landscapes*, argued for a dramatic reassessment of Le Corbusier's life work in terms of its condition upon the land, revealing the ways in which he observed and imagined landscapes throughout his career.[4] The exhibition *Frank Lloyd Wright and the City: Density vs. Dispersal* presented Wright's model for Broadacre City, his concept for fundamentally reorganizing the American landscape and social economy with a radically dispersed network of private homesteads, high-rise dwellings, and shared highways.[5] Scholars have begun to write histories of the built environment that reinsert the elements of garden design, extending a vision of the environment as a whole, and—as did these pioneers of modern landscape design—recognizing the garden as an integral component of the residences and parks that are critical parts of the modern city.

The growth of an international community of scholars engaged in the study of twentieth-century landscape design has resulted in a rich cross-disciplinary conversation. A decade or two ago our discussion tended to be far more discipline-bound, segregated according to the traditional fields of art and architectural history and literary studies. We now find ourselves engaged in an exchange that spans the full history of culture.

Steven Mansbach and Joachim Wolschke-Bulmahn proposed this project following a fruitful discussion held ten years previous in a seminar sponsored jointly by the Center for Advanced Study in the Visual Arts (CASVA) and Dumbarton Oaks, which was later published in a special issue of the journal *Centropa* under the title *Modern Central European Landscape Design*.[6] The motivation for the first meeting was their observation that, although scholars had challenged the modernist paradigm in art and architecture, comparatively little attention had been paid to landscape architecture and garden design. This volume continues the groundbreaking work of these historians as it addresses new areas, figures, and topics that preceded the now well-understood monuments of post–World War II landscape architecture.

The tripartite title—modernism, landscape architecture, and the time range 1890–1940—deserves explanation. Several scholars have written that the term *modernism* indicates a place for architecture and landscape architecture within the more general history of twentieth-century culture and contemporaneous movements in art, music, literature, and dance.[7] However, K. Michael Hays, in *Modernism and the Posthumanist Subject*, gives a nuanced definition that is more useful for our purposes:

Modernism, whatever else we may mean by the term, has something to do with the emergence of new kinds of objects and events and, at the same time, new conceptualizations of their appearance, of the changed event structures and relationships between objects, their producers, their audiences and consumers…. Modernism itself… forces the recognition that modern aesthetic practice aims to bring into being new meanings and new subjectivities, seeking to figure not only what *is* but what *could be*.[8]

Each of the authors in this volume has attempted to identify the definition and significance of the concept of modernism in a place and period.

For a contemporaneous definition of landscape architecture, we can look back to Henry-Russell Hitchcock's introduction to the catalog for the San Francisco Museum of Art exhibition *Contemporary Landscape Architecture and Its Sources* (1937; fig. 1). It opens with these words:

Adequate discussion of a theory of modern gardening would run to many pages. For the modern garden, in theory, may be either an entire forest or a mere roof terrace, a national park including several counties, or a few square yards of concrete tiles with shrubs and flowers in built-in beds.[9]

Hitchcock's definition of landscape and garden design, one that embraces all scales, has guided us in defining the parameters of this volume: from regional projects to new urban forms to domestic environments. This sense of breadth and inclusiveness also helped determine the time range. In the last years of the nineteenth century, with the founding of societies and associations for landscape architecture internationally, the foundation for an exclusive profession was laid. Specialization within the profession into areas such as town planning or landscape engineering would not happen until World War II, instigated by landscape architects such as John Nolen, who founded independent city and regional associations. Thus this transition in practice was occurring at different rates and in different ways in countries around the world.

The professionalization of landscape design (in the United States in 1899; Argentina, 1918; the Netherlands, 1922; Britain, 1929) coincided with new conditions for practice, teaching, and training. For example, 1900–1901 saw the creation of the first degree program in landscape architecture in America at Harvard University, a program whose influence on the development of the profession has been chronicled

in several recent studies.[10] During this period, women entered the workforce to an unprecedented degree and were instrumental in shaping the practice of landscape architecture. This phenomenon has been studied in several important books and is the subject of a recent exhibition at the New York Botanical Garden, *Groundbreakers: Great American Gardens and the Women Who Designed Them.*"[11]

Scholars have shown that after the first three decades of rapid growth, the profession collapsed along with the stock market in 1929. Ethan Carr has noted that by 1930, 90 percent of the profession was unemployed. However, by 1932, those numbers were reemployed, with newly defined roles in government agencies devoted to public service, recreation, and planning.[12] The country house era was over, and middle-class housing, garden cities, and park systems dominated the field.

The contributors to this volume describe the period under study as one of technological and social revolution as they document the myriad responses to a changing world. The essays represent a breadth of approaches and an international range of subjects dealing with more than a dozen countries in Latin America, North America, Africa, and Europe, reflecting the variety and texture of the field's methodological approaches, from the biographical, to the hotly debated theme of ecological imperatives, to gender issues, nationalism, and critical theory.

The increase in number of professional landscape organizations throughout Europe engendered a need to achieve legitimacy through public recognition of expertise. Two strategies arose: one in which architects claimed the outdoors, promoting architectonic gardens; the other in which landscape architects distanced themselves from architects. In her essay Dorothée Imbert argues that, even as they set themselves apart, landscape architects co-opted architecture's theoretical credentials and adapted notions of functionalism and modernity. She discusses how two garden designers, the Dane G. N. Brandt (1878–1945) and the Belgian Jean Canneel-Claes (1909–1989), espoused current architectural arguments to validate stances on modernization that were similar in spite of the formal oppositions of their designs. Brandt, who had a wide knowledge of plants and history, stressed spiritual experience and unconscious associations through the narrative of plants. Activating the architectural promotional machine to define and defend the profession of landscape design, Canneel formulated the "functional garden" as a rational space with structures for physical exercise and the production of food as a solution to social and hygienic requirements.

In his essay on new concerns of hygiene and fitness emerging in avant-garde social theory, Johannes Stöffler argues that in the course of the popularization of the modern movement, "the designed landscape acquired a central role as mediator between architecture and people, and between functional needs and sentimental preferences." This position is manifested in the evolution of the public outdoor swimming pool and its landscaped environment in Switzerland.

A fundamental debate in landscape discourse generally, and specifically during the Weimar period, was whether the abstraction and geometrization of the architectonic garden came closer to a higher, more essential nature than the banal imitation represented by the nature garden. Michael Lee in his consideration of gender suggests that classic narratives of modernism—even as "progressive art"—expressed some deep-seated hostility toward the feminine. Lee examines the "classic narratives" by which modernism "enunciates its discourse through the heroic figure of the genius (male) architect, disseminates its ideal form via the icon of the (phallic) skyscraper, and carries out its rational (male) operations within the denatured (defeminized) space of the metropolis." He asks if Weimar modernism—"arguably the quintessential modernism"—displayed such tendencies, and whether they "ultimately were animated by a more comprehensive negation of nature itself, coded as female."

Several essays in this volume respond to John Dixon Hunt's exhortation that "we need to recover a sense of gardens as expressions or representations of a culture's position vis-à-vis nature."[13] In addition to shifting programmatic demands on the professional practice of landscape design, the period covered here was marked by growing interest in the conservation of natural resources. Again, to use the American situation as an example, the federal Division of Forestry, the National Conservation Commission (under President Theodore Roosevelt), and the National Park Service were all created in the decades around 1900. In an essay about the emerging profession of landscape architecture, Anita Berrizbeitia and Karen M'Closkey present case studies of projects in which landscape architects led a "national conversation on issues of resource utilization and conservation." They argue that specific projects (including certain national parks and metropolitan park systems) together with their new design approaches and work methods exemplify the model of critical practice articulated around 1930 by the Frankfurt School of critical theory. Underlying these designs was a motivation and desire to break with convention in order to bring about change in practice while questioning the interaction of capitalism and environmental values.

Alan Powers in his essay identifies an expression of modernism in England that he calls "romantic regeneration," in which he sees a return to the potential of the countryside in order to heal the devastation of development, pollution, and industrial growth. This movement coincided with a general recovery of national pride based on British culture, especially in relation to country life. His approach makes it possible to interpret the aesthetics of landscape in the context of conservation movements internationally, clarifying the shaping of sensibilities as both ecological awareness and the wilderness debate emerge.[14]

In the period under study in this volume, some landscape and garden designers departed from the paradigmatic model of rationalism, internationalism, and antihistoricism that remains the legacy of the idealistic pioneers of modern design. Jože Plečnik (1872–1957) is well known as an architect and interior designer but is rarely studied for his landscape and garden designs. Steven Mansbach presents two projects by Plečnik: first, the gardens of Prague Castle, built to mark a transition from monarchy to liberal democracy; and second, a city park for the new Slovenian capital at Ljubljana. Mansbach claims that Plečnik was a modernist whose overt reverence for nature, both

materially and symbolically, was matched by his use of the past "as a valued support of the present."

Since the 1980s scholars (notably Joachim Wolschke-Bulmahn and Gert Gröning in Germany) have demonstrated the explicit connection between politics and the representation of nature in designed landscapes and gardens. While some Germans conceptualized the distinctive mode of a national German style to be the nature garden,[15] the Italians saw the architectonic garden—geometric, rigid, and regular—as distinctly Italian. In his essay on Italy during the 1920s and 1930s, Franco Panzini illustrates how landscape architecture was used under the Fascist regime to shape a regionalist context for buildings designed by architects who shared the rigorous and simplified vocabulary of the international modern movement. He identifies three tree species—pines, palms, and holm oaks—as design elements that reveal a preference for an idealized landscape, which served as a romantic counterpart to the rationalist expression of architecture. The species were selected not for their "aesthetic qualities or functional suitability" but for their "capacity to evoke a heroic past." The same iconic trees were used in colonial North Africa as well, where, as exotics, they were clearly used to connect outpost or periphery to the center.

Both Panzini and Sonja Dümpelmann assert in their essays that the preservation of historic sites and gardens in Italy played a critical role in promoting the ideology of nationhood that began with reunification in the late nineteenth century and continued into the Facist period. Dümpelmann examines how cultural nationalism not only lay at the heart of the first initiatives in Italy to protect and revive gardens in rural areas such as Capri; it also furthered the promotion of gardens in the urban context and in the art world. Since most commentators envisioned the Italian garden of the future as a geometric, "architectural" construction—repeatedly asserting that "the Italian garden is a work of architecture"—architects were considered the most appropriate garden designers.

In Spain, Santiago Rusiñol's *Jardins d'Espanya*, published in 1903, precipitated a regionalist movement and offered a suitable remedy to ills facing urban districts. José Tito Rojo argues in his essay that the appearance of nationalism at the beginning of the twentieth century was accompanied by the desire to define a Spanish garden style. The new regional and official style, based on Andalusian/Arabic precedents and as manifested in Seville and Granada, was, paradoxically, defined by the internationally active French landscape designer Jean-Claude Nicolas Forestier. Simultaneously, Tito Rojo argues, a movement of resistance can be found in the work of several Spanish landscape architects, who sought personal styles, sensitive to new architectonic trends that synthesized tradition, history, and environmental characteristics.

Whereas indigenous plants or forms may define national or regional schools of design in one place, exotic plants and obvious geometries may do so in others. Sonia Berjman's essay is an effort to recover a figure who has been under the shadow of the ubiquitous Forestier. Berjman presents Benito Javier Carrasco (1877–1958), who spent his career in Argentina inserting green space as a basic aspect of urbanism. Politically left leaning, he practiced park design as an instrument of social reform, a science, and a fine art. Carrasco established the first university chair in garden art and landscape in Argentina in 1918. His landscape theory was rife with the rhetoric of utopian socialism, promoting design's potential for economic, democratic character.

The City Beautiful Movement provided the modern foundations for urban planning and design in which spacious and orderly landscaped cities were designed with open spaces that showcased public buildings and monuments. Although the history of this urban transformation is well known for Chicago and Washington, in smaller cities (such as Cleveland, Detroit, San Francisco, Kansas City, Harrisburg, Seattle, Denver, and Dallas) campaigns were also undertaken to develop urban centers with ambitious public gardens, boulevards, and monumental spaces. Lance Humphries' essay documents this important history for the city of Baltimore, where ambitious plans were undertaken to link sites of historic, governmental, and cultural significance with a system of parks, monuments, and public buildings dating from the first years of the twentieth century.

In the same period, such figures as Sigfried Giedion and José Luis Sert hailed multilevel urban design as town planning in three dimensions, praising it for decongesting the city core. This movement was exemplified by Rockefeller Center in New York City, which Giedion claimed was equal to the large-scale parkways and engineering works of the modern world and expressive of open planning on a new, monumental scale. Mardges Bacon opens her history of Rockefeller Center, in midtown Manhattan, a project carried out between 1927 and 1940, with the proposal of two views of modernism: one pragmatic and traditional (interpreting the thin high-rise slabs of the ensemble as expressive of the capitalist city) and the other, spontaneous and expressive of the self and the social nucleus. The collective force of buildings, the cohesive character of landscaped terraces, rooftop "sky" gardens, and the vitality of social space at the heart of the city would serve, she argues, as a model for the urban core in postwar reconstruction and planning.

In closing, we return to the 1937 exhibition *Contemporary Landscape Architecture and Its Sources*, for which the architect and landscape architect Richard J. Neutra wrote a brief essay. In it he identified what it meant to design for modern life and the modern world:

Our generation, more than any one ever before, is attracted by nature, landscape, the out-of-doors. City park systems, metropolitan green belts, national forests, recreation camps, nature resorts of all kinds bear witness to this.

The keynote of modern architecture has become a friendliness to the out-of-doors, a generous opening to the health agents and primary esthetic offerings of nature, radiation, sun and air. Roofdecks, balconies, solaria, flower windows, pools, are frequent ingredients of truly contemporary design....

Our relation to the natural setting is a biologically minded appreciation of the soil, in which all life is rooted and must remain rooted, to succeed....

The garden ... is laid out for the enjoyment of bodily exercise and mental relaxation in a setting that is an ensemble of plants which can keep natural company — which are not arbitrarily assembled like a masquerade party, in opposition to climate, exposures, soil conditions and biological decency.[16]

This volume is an effort to document and examine the cultural contributions of landscape architecture as it evolved into a profession distinctly different in history, intent, and procedure from its sister fields of art and architecture. At the same time, modernism in landscape design is revealed to have been like modernism in architecture, which, according to Sigfried Giedion, Sarah Goldhagen, and Rod Barnett, was not a style or single movement, but a discourse or conversation about the role of technology, tradition, and nature in the human approach to living.[17] Our contributors hope to illuminate the complexity of the decades surrounding the turn of the twentieth century, during which landscape architecture assumed professional status while struggling to express a contemporary aesthetic and purpose responsive to startling changes in society, politics, and perceptions of both built and natural environments.

NOTES

I thank the following research associates of the Center for Advanced Study in the Visual Arts for their help in preparing this volume for publication: Robyn Asleson, Kathryn Barush, Malcolm Clendenin, and Emily Pugh.

1. Marc Treib, *Modern Landscape Architecture: A Critical Review* (Cambridge, MA, 1993), viii.

2. Caroline Constant, *The Modern Architectural Landscape* (Minneapolis, 2012), 169–190; Thaisa Way, *Unbounded Practice: Women and Landscape Architecture in the Early Twentieth Century* (Charlottesville, VA, 2009); and Judith Major, *Marianna Van Rennselaer: A Landscape Critic in the Gilded Age* (Charlottesville, VA, 2013). See also Kristine F. Miller, *Almost Home: The Public Landscapes of Gertrude Jekyll* (Charlottesville, VA, 2013); Louise A. Mozingo and Linda Jewell, *Women in Landscape Architecture: Essays on History and Practice* (Jefferson, NC, 2012); Catherine Phillips, "'Connecticut Motive': Beatrix Farrand and the Marsh Botanic Garden of Yale University, 1922–1939," *Studies in the History of Gardens and Designed Landscapes* 27 (January 2007): 1–30; and Judith Tankard, *Gertrude Jekyll and the Country House Garden: From the Archives of Country Life* (New York, 2011) and *Beatrix Farrand: Private Gardens, Public Landscapes* (New York, 2009).

3. Terence Riley and Barry Bergdoll, eds., *Mies in Berlin* (Museum of Modern Art, New York, 2001). Mies' inclusion of sunken gardens and an orchard-like copse of trees in relationship to the house point to his early coupling of landscape and architectural design. Better known, however, are his designs that were edited through actual erasure and redrawing prior to their appearance in the vastly influential *Modern Architecture — International Exhibition* at MoMA in 1932.

4. Jean-Louis Cohen with Barry Bergdoll et al., *Le Corbusier: An Atlas of Modern Landscapes* (Museum of Modern Art, New York, 2013).

5. *Frank Lloyd Wright and the City: Density vs. Dispersal*, exhibition, Museum of Modern Art, New York, February 1–June 1, 2014; see http://www.moma.org/visit/calendar/exhibitions/1448.

6. *Centropa: A Journal of Central European Architecture and Related Arts* 4, no. 2 (May 2004). Joachim Wolschke-Bulmahn was director of studies in landscape architecture, Dumbarton Oaks (1991–1996).

7. Steven Krog associated modernism with art movements that addressed issues such as immediacy, simultaneity, individuality, and planarity in "The Language of Modern," *Landscape Architecture* 75, no. 2 (March/April 1985): 56–59. See also Catherine Howett, "Modernism and American Landscape Architecture," and Marc Treib, "Axioms for a Modern Landscape Architecture," in Treib 1992, 18–35 and 37–39.

8. Hays adds, "A history of modernism ... must involve the concept of the producing, using, perceiving subject as well as the object.... Modernism defeats

the view that meanings and subjectivities are already formed and existent somewhere outside the work of art and that the critic's and historian's business is to locate them." K. Michael Hays, *Modernism and the Post-humanist Subject: The Architecture of Hannes Meyer and Ludwig Hilberseimer* (Cambridge, MA, 1992), 4.

9. Hitchcock set down certain ideas based on the relationship of modern gardening to modern architecture "as they affect the gardens of the individual house." An asterisk leads to a note connecting these ideas to houses built by such important modern European architects as Le Corbusier, Mies, Berthold Lubetkin, and many others in the preceding ten years. The exhibition catalog, however, includes illustrations reflecting the full range of projects encompassed by the category of contemporary gardening and landscape as Hitchcock defined it. See *Contemporary Landscape Architecture and Its Sources* (San Francisco Museum of Art, 1937), 15–20.

10. See Anthony Alofsin, *The Struggle for Modernism: Architecture, Landscape Architecture, and City Planning at Harvard, 1900–1999* (New York, 2002), and Melanie Simo, *The Coalescing of Different Forces and Ideas: A History of Landscape Architecture at Harvard, 1900–1999* (Cambridge, MA, 2000). Simo identifies the movements for social and environmental improvement at the opening of the twentieth century as a base of support for the emergence of landscape architecture as a profession.

11. *Groundbreakers: Great American Gardens and the Women Who Designed Them*, exhibition, New York Botanical Garden, Mertz Library, May 17– September 7, 2014.

12. Ethan Carr, *Wilderness by Design: Landscape Architecture and the National Park Service* (Lincoln, NE, 1998), 249–251.

13. John Dixon Hunt, *Gardens and the Picturesque: Studies in the History of Landscape Architecture* (Cambridge, MA, 1994), 299.

14. See also Melanie Simo, *Forest and Garden: Traces of Wildness in a Modernizing Land, 1897–1949* (Charlottesville, VA, 2003).

15. On the nature garden, see Joachim Wolschke-Bulmahn, "The 'Wild Garden' and the 'Nature Garden': Aspects of the Garden Ideology of William Robinson and Willy Lange," *Journal of Garden History* 12, no. 3 (1992): 183–206; Gert Gröning and Joachim Wolschke-Bulmahn, "The Ideology of the Nature Garden: Nationalistic Trends in Garden Design in Germany during the Early Twentieth Century," *Journal of Garden History* 12, no. 1 (1992): 73–80; Gert Gröning and Joachim Wolschke-Bulmahn, "Some Notes on the Mania for Native Plants in Germany," *Landscape Journal* 11, no. 2 (1992): 116–126; and Joachim Wolschke-Bulmahn, ed., *Nature and Ideology. Natural Garden Design in the Twentieth Century* (Washington, DC, 1997).

16. Richard J. Neutra, "Landscaping—A New Issue," in San Francisco Museum of Art 1937, 21–22.

17 Sarah Williams Goldhagen, "Something to Talk About: Modernism, Discourse, Style," *Journal of the Society of Architectural Historians* 64, no. 2 (June 2005): 144–167. See also Rod Barnett, "Gardens without Meaning," *Landscape Review* 3, no. 2 (1997): 23–24.

DOROTHÉE IMBERT

The Form of Function:
Theorizing Modernity in the Garden,
1920–1939

This essay examines the discourse of landscape architecture in relation to architectural theory during the 1920s and 1930s through the work and writings of two garden designers: G. N. Brandt (1878–1945) from Denmark and Jean Canneel-Claes (1909–1989) from Belgium.[1] Though seemingly antithetical, the positions of Brandt and Canneel in fact reflected a common desire to establish professional expertise by simultaneously drawing and distancing landscape architecture from architectural trends.

Brandt advocated for sensory relaxation and illusory seclusion in a lush garden that was rooted in the Danish cultural landscape (fig. 1). At the other end of the formal spectrum, Canneel's garden archetype aimed to achieve harmony and rhythmic equilibrium through rigorous geometric composition (fig. 2).[2] However, it is possible to discern in both Brandt's and Canneel's writings the influence of the contemporary debate on the relation of function to aesthetics and to emotion. This debate was intimately tied to the perceived impact of industrialization and modernization on twentieth-century living and the impetus to develop a theoretical discourse for landscape architecture.

The early twentieth century saw a tremendous rise in the creation of professional organizations for landscape architecture across northwestern Europe: the French, British, Belgian, Danish, Norwegian, Swedish, Dutch, French, and Swiss associations were all created between 1920 and 1930.[3] (The German association, the Deutsche Gesellschaft für Gartenkunst, had been founded in 1887 as the Verein deutscher Gartenkünstler.) This common drive to organize answered the need to increase the visibility of landscape architecture as a specific and modern profession and to resist its annexation by architects.

Different practitioners—whether landscape architects, garden architects, or horticultural architects—used different means to establish expertise. Some situated their practices within a historical context, claiming entitlement as heirs to a tradition. Others argued for superiority in technical and aesthetic matters: knowledge about plants and an artistic sensibility separated them from architects and nurserymen. Yet others equated the modern profession with a new practice and theoretical stance. Landscape architects shared this struggle for legitimacy with architects, themselves aiming for the status of the more established medical and judicial professionals. The definition of a modern profession rests on, among other things, a specialized education, a title, a professional organization, a code of ethics, and what the sociologist Magali Sarfatti Larson defines as "cognitive exclusiveness," or the public recognition of expertise.[4] Furthering the notion of cognitive exclusiveness is the implied condition of a specific language. Landscape architects and architects had to differentiate their professions from trades by developing a theoretical discourse. To increase their cultural capital, twentieth-century landscape architects aligned themselves with the older and more established architectural profession. By joining the much-publicized architectural debates, landscape architects sought a readymade connection to modernism and a common language with architects. This discourse offered both the opportunity for collaboration and the claiming of professional territory. Latecomers to the professional design scene, few in number,

England—was one that occupied designers well into the twentieth century. Writing in the 1880s and 1890s Blomfield and Robinson based their arguments for stylistic suitability and professional attribution on notions of Englishness, whether formal, in Blomfield's case, or horticultural, in Robinson's.[5] Shortly thereafter Willy Lange (1864–1941), the vocal proponent of the German *Naturgarten*, or natural garden, claimed design rights through the artistic understanding of plant associations, thus taking the garden away from the architect (fig. 3).[6] Conversely, French author André Vera (1881–1971) wrote his 1924 exhortation to architects to design gardens on the grounds that landscape architects lacked the formal rigor necessary to shape the geometric *jardin régulier*.[7] Thus landscape architects not only needed to define their practice in a new social and economic context; they also had to contend with the byproduct of the garden as extension of the house: that is, the garden as extension of architectural services.

1. G. N. Brandt, cemetery, Ordrup, Denmark, 1910–1927
Author photo

2. Jean Canneel-Claes, Heeremans garden, Liedekerke, Belgium, 1937–1963, photographed c. 1939
Courtesy Karl Heeremans

and frequently lacking formal training, landscape architects vied to gain legitimacy.

The question of authorship for the garden—widely publicized in the debate between William Robinson (1838–1935) and Reginald Blomfield (1856–1942) in

Witness to this trend was the German architect Hermann Muthesius (1861–1927) with his espousal of the so-called architectural garden of the early twentieth century. A member of the Deutscher Werkbund and a prolific author, Muthesius became the cultural ambassador for a very selective view of Englishness. Borrowing his arguments from Reginald Blomfield, he promoted the garden as a series of outdoor rooms and as the domain of architecture and the rational antidote to the decadence of mock miniaturized nature he saw in the natural garden.[8] To Muthesius, the garden should be *regelmässig*, the German equivalent to Vera's *style régulier*, and as such was to be designed by the architect.[9] In his treatment of the country house and garden, *Landhaus und Garten* (1907), he declared that "the house and garden are so intimately related in their nature, that it [is] simply impossible that two people unknown to one another, an architect and a gardener, give form to the house and its surroundings," concluding that "if the house is architecture, then the garden must

also be architecture."[10] To illustrate his position, the first edition of *Landhaus und Garten* promoted the architectural gardens of architects Peter Behrens and Josef Maria Olbrich, neatly compartmentalized outdoor rooms furnished with trellises and other structures (figs. 4 and 5). By the second edition of 1919, Muthesius appeared to relent in his stance on architectural exclusivity in the residential environment to include the work of fellow Werkbund members and garden architects Harry Maasz (1880–1946) (fig. 6) and Leberecht Migge (1881–1935).[11] Maasz envisioned a garden that was programmed with modern functions and whose plantings promoted relaxation and health. Migge shared Muthesius' desire to reform domestic culture through rational design but did not tie function to a specific aesthetic. His vision for the *kommende Garten*, or garden of the future, remained formally neutral, as he considered the type and style of gardens to be dictated by the "economic-ethical demands" of the masses rather than aesthetics (fig. 7).[12]

6. Harry Maasz, garden, Lübeck

Hermann Muthesius, Landhaus und Garten: Beispiele kleinerer Land-häuser nebst Grundrissen, Innen-räumen und Gärten *(Munich, 1919); Frances Loeb Library, Harvard Graduate School of Design*

7. Leberecht Migge, Selbst-versorger Type A garden, bird's-eye view

Leberecht Migge, Jedermann Selbst-versorger! *(Jena, 1918); Frances Loeb Library, Harvard Graduate School of Design*

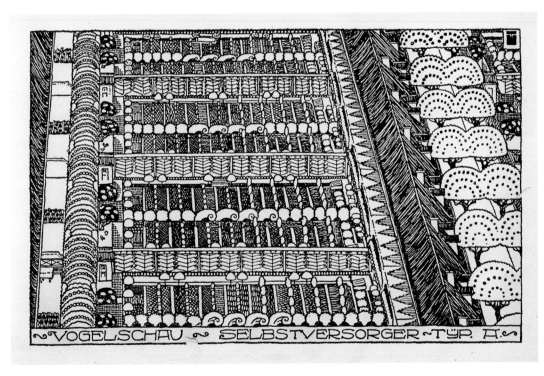

8. G. N. Brandt, Mariebjerg Cemetery, children's burial quadrant, Gentofte, Denmark, 1925–1936
Author photo

Style and function were contentious notions in the debate on landscape modernity. Inasmuch as style provided a convenient mechanism for refuting the past and introducing garden reform, it became itself a trope for conservatism, as if style were inherently historicist. Similarly, G. N. Brandt swayed between modernism and the so-called *Naturgarten* when advocating for the appropriate garden for contemporary needs. His vehement argument against the literal application of architectural elements and principles to the garden was on economic grounds. His was not a reaction to the intrusion of architects into the garden per se: he fostered a vital dialogue with architects as the first lecturer in landscape design at the Danish Academy of Fine Arts, where he educated scores of architecture students on the design, reading, and planting of gardens and landscapes. Not unlike Muthesius, he was strongly influenced by English garden design, albeit as a fervent supporter of William Robinson rather than Reginald Blomfield.[13] But if Brandt did not reject a rigorous structure in garden design—as witnessed in his ordered layout for Mariebjerg Cem-

etery (fig. 8)—he was a staunch defender of perceptual ambiguity.[14] To him, ambiguity was the much-needed opposite of clarity and of the utmost importance in garden design. Ambiguity bypassed style to build on the emotions and childhood memories evoked by plants. Brandt best expressed this position in his own articles on the *kommende Garten*, published in 1927 and 1930 in German periodicals, shortly after Migge's.[15] Brandt took both Muthesius and the architectural garden to task, deeming "incomprehensible how Muthesius and his contemporaries nearly rejected the garden cultures of both the eighteenth century and Japan in order to introduce their grossly expensive architectural garden." Alas, Brandt continued, "many landscape architects were influenced by the architectural garden style that has dominated the last 25 years, forgetting their own true calling, and acting as second-rate architects."[16] In this condemnation, he pointed to the importance of landscape roots (horticulturally, historically, and culturally), economy, truth, and the need to differentiate between architecture and garden design, all arguments

9. G. N. Brandt, garden for his own residence, Ordrup, Denmark, 1914–1945
Author photo

10. G. N. Brandt, June Garden (Junihave), Svastika, Rungsted, Denmark, 1925

Die Gartenkunst 40, no. 6 (June 1927); Frances Loeb Library, Harvard Graduate School of Design

supporting the specificity of the landscape architect.

Brandt saw no contradiction in drawing from a multiplicity of historical sources to shape his garden of the future. He invoked as influences the Japanese garden, the landscape style, the architectural Neues Bauen movement, the *Naturgarten*, and even the architectural garden. In fact, the garden of the future was of its time: looking ahead while recognizing the past. Instead of advocating modernism's typical rupture with the past, Brandt focused on current conditions to shape the garden. Unlike architecture, the "garden of the future will not be the product of a revolution," wrote Brandt, but instead "crystallize gradually, under the pressure of new social conditions."[17] Ultimately what made Brandt's garden modern was the function it served in terms of emotional release in contemporary life, through greenness.

The garden of the future was to be "100% grün," one hundred percent green, Brandt stated, as a cure to a gray urban life. It was to be quiet, free of noisy gravel paths. It would be small (eight by eighteen meters), enclosed, and protected from neighbors, and yet have a "feeling of boundlessness" achieved with layered vegetation and reflecting water.[18] As examples, Brandt selected views of his own experimental garden in Ordrup, begun in 1914, and of the so-called June Garden (Junihave) at Svastika, an estate in Rungsted, Denmark (1925)—although, as

Lulu Salto Stephensen pointed out, the modesty of Svastika belied the socioeconomic status of its owner, one of the richest men in Denmark (figs. 9 and 10).[19] Formally simple, these gardens offered a wealth of imaginary readings, triggered by ambiguous boundaries. A reflecting pond, an allée, a concave lawn, and implied continuity removed the garden user from rational city life, all the while triggering connections to beyond. In Ordrup, Brandt distilled the Danish collective landscape into the elements of ditch, stone wall, hedge, meadow, and grove. From the house (now gone), one entered a garden room furnished with an apple orchard and a meadow. The ditch and marsh flower garden, for all its rustic character, was entirely constructed. An outlet hole in the brick-clad wall allowed the gaze to continue as if following a stream. Brandt described "the feeling of ambiguity [as] deliberate—to provide space for the imagination" (fig. 11).[20]

Brandt's concept of greenness (*Grünheit*) appeared neutral, eschewing all stylistic allegiances. Conversely, the sensory and the poetic were subjective notions applicable to a wider geographic context. He specified that "the garden [should be] shaped more by the subjective than the rational [*Sachlich*] ... and influenced by emotion and aesthetics."[21] His use of the word *Sachlich* called attention to one of the main debates in landscape modernism: the question of function and its relation to beauty. The terms *Sachlich* and *Sachlichkeit* were widely used at the time. Though at the onset of the twentieth century *Sachlich* had originally described simple, practical architecture, it later became synonymous with "rational," "functional," and "modernist," as in the 1920s concept of *neue Sachlichkeit*.[22]

A contentious concept in architectural circles, functionalism formed an ambiguous one in garden design. For some, it entailed spaces in which to practice gymnastics, play, sunbathe, or grow vegetables and fruits, as in Migge's or Canneel's gardens. For others, like Brandt, it stood as a misguided transfer of architectural language onto the landscape. Critical of the architectural functionalism that had

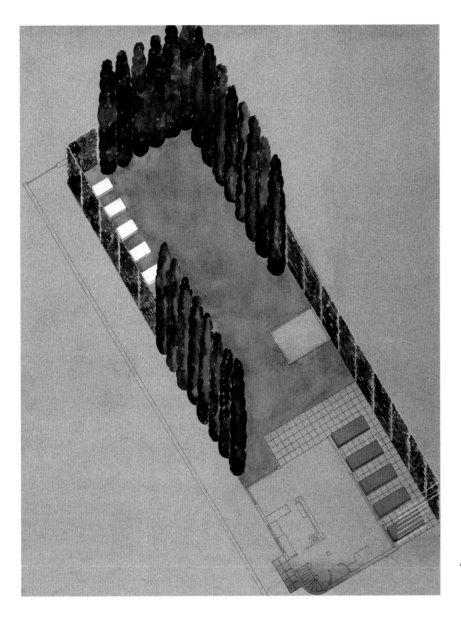

12. Jean Canneel-Claes, garden for his own residence, Auderghem, Belgium, axonometric view, 1931

Archives d'architecture moderne, Brussels

the experience of the contemporary with the poetry of plants. In turn, this maneuver entrusted the landscape architect with the necessary expertise for designing the garden. He considered that architectural modernism and new materials bore little influence on the garden of the future—a plant was a plant was a plant, to paraphrase Gertrude Stein—which remained the domain of the landscape architect.[25] In this respect, he stood in clear opposition to Muthesius and Vera, who assigned the design of the garden to the architect.

Ultimately, Brandt's response to modernization was manifold: to establish the historical continuity of landscape architecture; to stress the timelessness of vegetation; to address changes in lifestyle; and to resist *Sachlichkeit* with calm, escapism, and illusion. The garden was to counter the constructed and the functional with spiritual experiences and unconscious associations, best expressed through the narrative value of plants. His was not a nostalgic plea for romanticism, nor was it a negation of modernity, but a scientific experiment in psychological comfort and free association, in other words, a modernized permanence. But Brandt's position also expressed a reaction to contemporary architecture, specifically functionalist architecture. To him, the "cleaner" and simpler architecture became, the greener and lusher and more ambiguous the garden should be.

Opting for a different conceptual stance, Jean Canneel-Claes argued for the functionalist garden (fig. 12). Canneel himself embraced modernity through architecture. Educated in Brussels at La Cambre, the decorative arts school headed by Werkbund founding member Henry Van de Velde (1863–1957), Canneel was well aware of the contemporary architectural discourse on functionalism. He promoted a new brand of designer equally versed in landscape, architecture, and urbanism. Barely twenty years old, he commissioned a house from Le Corbusier in 1929. Although the project did not materialize, it revealed Canneel's drive to position him-

turned the architect into an "unrefined constructor," Brandt urged the landscape architect to consider the intangible rather than the rational and act as a "subtle psychologist."[23] In his view, function had a place in the garden only as a means to relax and rest—a shelter against the ills of modernization. "The more the world becomes mechanized, rationalized, standardized, and organized," he wrote, "the more gardens will provide relaxation through seclusion" and romantic associations.[24] Rather than addressing the new architecture through formal mimesis, Brandt balanced

self as the quintessential modernist garden designer. Less than two years later, he would test his functionalist principles on his own residence in Auderghem, outside Brussels, and use its garden as a vehicle to advance his theoretical views.

The house itself, designed by Louis-Herman de Koninck (1896–1984), was a modest cube with terraces facing the south and the garden (see fig. 12). With interior spaces flowing smoothly outward, the house and garden read as shorthand for simple, healthy domestic living. The solarium on the rooftop featured gymnastic equipment and curtains for privacy when sunbathing. The bedroom opened onto a sleeping terrace. A much-published photograph of the living room opening up to the garden advertised the contemporaneity of reinforced concrete and plate glass (fig. 13). The placement of De Koninck's tubular armchair at the threshold of the room held the promise of a benign climate and outdoor living. However, Canneel went beyond the typical

modernist construct of a minimalist terrace displayed against a vegetated background to propose instead a relationship of equivalence between inside and outside.

The garden fit contemporary needs with a children's play area and sandbox, an expanse of lawn for sunbathing and exercise, and simple decorative plantings for minimal maintenance (fig. 14). This functional apportionment of the site was implied but not outlined, much in the same way the studio, living, and dining areas flowed into one another. Although this conceptual mirroring of interior spaces could be interpreted as echoing Muthesius' architectural garden, Canneel's vision was one that relied equally on the rigor of composition and the reading of the site.

The functionalist garden was to be styleless. Avoiding both the "sentimental" wild garden and the "intellectual" French formal garden, Canneel favored a "social conception of the garden" that satisfied the needs for exercise, leisure, and sustenance.[26] Pro-

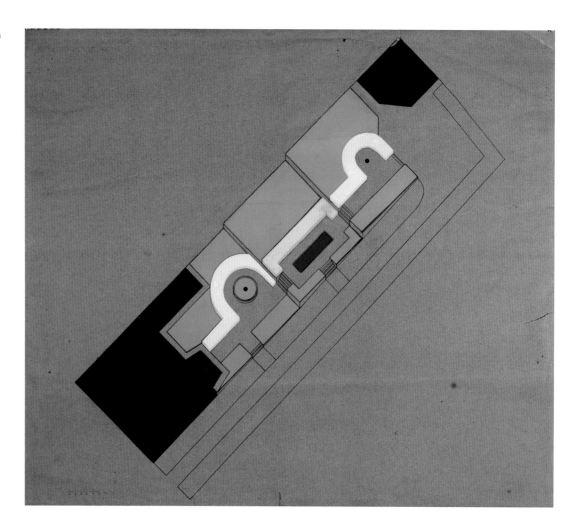

gram and architectural elements structured the site functionally and perceptually and highlighted landscape characteristics. For instance, in his garden for J. P. Buzon in Schaerbeek, a series of plinths articulated an incline and allowed for showcasing two massive existing beech and linden specimens (fig. 15). Similarly, in the garden for Fernand Danhier in Uccle (1933), he inserted plateaus within a sloping matrix of trees, stressing the progression from ornamental to physical and productive with a living terrace, an exercise and sunbathing room, and, at the toe of the incline, a vegetable garden (fig. 16). Although Canneel's functionalism relied on the organizing principles of geometry and asymmetry, it nevertheless responded to specific conditions with a gradient of formalism.

The theoretical stances behind Canneel's and Brandt's gardens had substantial simi-larities despite their differing formal outcomes. Both sought emotional well-being in the garden and adapted architectural key words and concepts to landscape applications. Brandt's five points for the garden of the future referred to Le Corbusier and Pierre Jeanneret's five points for a new architecture and closely matched Canneel's own manifesto.[27] Of Brandt's points—that the garden be inexpensive, easy to maintain, functional, and flexible and allow for the cultivation and enjoyment of flowers—four matched Canneel's own design principles. Whereas Canneel determined function in the use of the garden for exercising, playing, or raising fruit trees, Brandt did so in terms of sitting and resting, making quiet places the measure of practicality. In other words, Brandt's garden did not reflect a change of lifestyle as in the pursuit of physical health, but rather as a need for moral health.

16. Jean Canneel-Claes, Fernand Danhier garden, Uccle, Belgium, c. 1933, axonometric view
Archives d'architecture moderne, Brussels

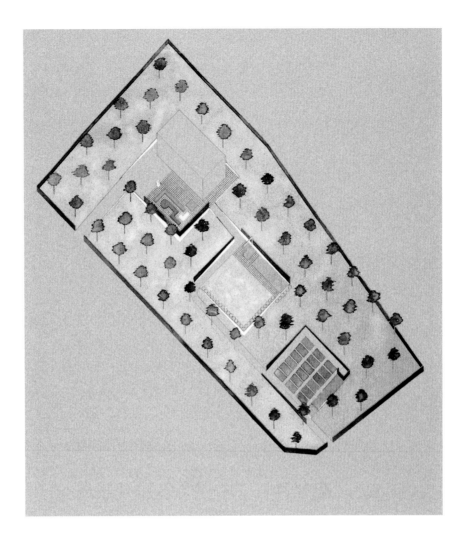

Instead of Brandt's calculated ambiguity, Canneel favored structural clarity, whether in relation to, or in spite of, the house. Canneel's garden expressed modernity in addressing current architectural concepts: free plan, space, order, hygiene, and exercise. Although Canneel's and Brandt's end results differed, namely in the ratio of plants to architecture, their respective co-opting of function underscored the struggle to define modern aesthetics.

In a sense, Brandt's and Canneel's positions on functionalism reflected the tension between proponents of *Sachlichkeit* and *neue Sachlichkeit*. As architectural historian Eve Blau has demonstrated, there was a significant shift from the prewar vision of *Sachlichkeit*—exemplified by Adolf Loos' cultural reading of modernity—and the rationalized and standardized "anti-aesthetic aesthetics" of the 1920s.[28] Architects such as Josef Frank argued for a tradition-rich modernity against the "total environment" and standards of the Bauhaus and other "radical modernists."[29] His declaration that "every human being has a certain measure of sentimentality which he has to satisfy" and that industrial workers required "sentimental surroundings" to provide distraction from the rational workplace applied equally to Frank's interiors and to Brandt's hundred-percent-green garden.[30]

Brandt's use of collective memory, desires, and emotions to counter standardization and industrialization resonated with the defenders of a human-feeling-based *Sachlichkeit*. The garden did not need to look modern (whether in drawing or reality); it simply *was* modern—styleless and restful. Canneel was a little harder to place. On one hand, his enlisting of modern architectural tropes—axonometric representation, photography, architectural publications, and international associations—cited the avant-garde architecture and art of Le Corbusier, the Congrès Internationaux d'Architecture Moderne (CIAM), and De Stijl.[31] On the other hand, Canneel's attention to the physical and psychological needs of modern dwellers suggested a more flexible attitude than the *neue Sachlichkeit* mimetic equation of function and beauty.

Canneel's and Brandt's theoretical stances reflected the need for landscape architects to posit themselves as equals to architects. They both addressed the needs of modern dwellers through their own versions of functionalism. They simultaneously claimed professional expertise: Brandt, through a wide knowledge of plants, a broad understanding of architectural and landscape history, and a high regard for the past; Canneel, by addressing an architectural audience as both design and theoretical interlocutor. Well aware of the short-lived nature of styles, neither designer sought to establish a prescriptive formal language. Following the impetus of modernization in the reform of architectural thought, they strove to mark the place of professional garden designers in shaping the environment.

NOTES

1. For G. N. (Gudmund Nyeland) Brandt, see Lulu Salto Stephensen, *Garden Design in Denmark: G. N. Brandt and the Early Decades of the Twentieth Century* (Chichester, UK, 2007); for Jean Canneel-Claes, see Dorothée Imbert, *Between Garden and City: Jean Canneel-Claes and Landscape Modernism* (Pittsburgh, 2009).

2. On Canneel's twinning of geometry and rhythm, see his letter to architect Huib Hoste, Brussels, August 17, 1934, Hoste Archives, Katholieke Universiteit Leuven (hereafter KUL). See also Huib Hoste, "Een vraagesprek met Canneel," *Opbouwen*, no. 15 (October 1934): 210–214, and Jean Canneel-Claes, "Le Jardin fonctionnel," *Bâtir*, no. 5 (April 1933): 179. Canneel would synthesize his views in the manifesto of the Association Internationale des Architectes Jardinistes Modernistes (AIAJM). See specifically point 2, which states: "Aesthetics will focus on the search for harmony and rhythmic equilibrium, and 'pure form.'" Hoste Archives, KUL. For a discussion of the role played by Canneel in the association, see Imbert 2009, chap. 4.

3. For a discussion of the professional associations of garden designers and landscape architects, see Dorothée Imbert, "Landscape Architects of the World, Unite! Professional Organizations, Practice, and Politics, 1935–1948," *Journal of Landscape Architecture* 2, no. 1 (2007): 6–19.

4. On the creation of professional markets, see Magali Sarfatti Larson, *The Rise of Professionalism: A Sociological Analysis* (Berkeley, CA, 1977), particularly xv, xvii, 14, 17.

5. Blomfield, fierce advocate of garden design as a purview of the architect, was the author of *The Formal Garden in England* (1892). Robinson, proponent of the wild garden, wrote *The English Flower Garden* (1883). For a discussion on the battle of words between the camps of Blomfield and Robinson and on the associated notions of Englishness, see Anne Helmreich's excellent analysis in *The English Garden and National Identity: The Competing Styles of Garden Design, 1870–1914* (Cambridge, 2002).

6. On Willy Lange and William Robinson, see Joachim Wolschke-Bulmahn, "The 'Wild Garden' and the 'Nature Garden': Aspects of the Garden Ideology of William Robinson and Willy Lange," *Journal of Garden History* 12, no. 3 (1992): 183–206. Reiterating Robinson's position, Lange declared: "Enough, I do not accept the definition of the garden as an enlarged dwelling." Willy Lange, "Meine Anschauugen über die Gartengestaltung unserer Zeit," *Die Gartenkunst* 7 (1905): 114, cited in Wolschke-Bulmahn 1992, 195.

7. André Vera, "Exhortation aux architectes de s'intéresser au jardin," *L'Architecte* 1 (1924): 68–71, and "Nouvelle exhortation aux architectes de s'intéresser au jardin," in *L'Urbanisme ou la vie heureuse* (Paris, 1936), 169–182. For a discussion on Vera and the French garden during the interwar years, see Dorothée Imbert, *The Modernist Garden in France* (New Haven, 1993).

8. Muthesius was in London, where he was sent by the German ministry of commerce, from 1896 to 1903. During this time he familiarized himself not only with questions of trade and education but also with contemporary architecture and gardens. Upon his return to Germany he published the three-volume *Das englische Haus* (1904). Uwe Schneider traces Blomfield's *Formal Garden in England* as the main source for Muthesius' survey of English gardens. See "Hermann Muthesius and the Introduction of the English Arts and Crafts Garden to Germany," *Garden History* 21, no. 1 (summer 2000): 57–72. See also Schneider's *Hermann Muthesius und die Reformdiskussion in der Gartenarchitektur des frühen 20. Jahrhunderts* (Worms, 2000).

9. In the introduction to his translation of Leberecht Migge's *Gartenkultur des 20. Jahrhunderts* (originally published 1913), David Haney points out that Muthesius' term *regelmässig* should be interpreted as "regular" and "functional" rather than "formal." See David Haney, translator's introduction, *Garden Culture of the Twentieth Century*, Dumbarton Oaks, Ex Horto (Washington, DC, 2013), 8, 39.

10. Hermann Muthesius, *Landhaus und Garten: Beispiele neuzeitlicher Landhäuser nebst Grundrissen, Innenräumen und Gärten* (Munich, 1907), xxv–xxvi.

11. See the essay by Michael Lee in this volume. The Deutscher Werkbund also included garden architects Max Bromme and Hermann König. See Inge Maasz, "Public Parks," in *The Werkbund: History and Ideology, 1907–1933*, ed. Lucius Burckhardt (New York, 1980), 57.

12. Leberecht Migge, "Der kommende Garten," *Gartenschönheit* 8, no. 3 (March 1927): 64–65.

13. Brandt apprenticed in England, France, Belgium, and Germany in the first years of the twentieth century.

14. Brandt laid out Mariebjerg Cemetery, to the north of Copenhagen, from 1925 to 1936.

15. G. N. Brandt, "Vom kommenden Garten," *Die Gartenkunst* 40, no. 6 (June 1927): 89–93, and "Der kommende Garten," *Wasmuths Monatshefte für Baukunst und Städtebau* 14 (April 1930): 161–176. For an English translation of the latter, see G. N. Brandt, "The Garden of the Future," trans. Claire Jordan, *Oase*, no. 56 (summer 2001): 15–33.

16. Brandt 1930, 169. Migge's and Brandt's writings on the *kommende Garten* were responses to Gustav Allinger's eponymous design for the Jubiläums-Gartenbau-Ausstellung, held in Dresden in 1926. For Allinger's proposal, see O. Völckers, "Jubiläums-Gartenbau-Ausstellung Dresden 1926. Der 'kommende Garten.' Natur und Garten. Entwurf G. Allinger," *Gartenkunst* 39 (1926): 168. See also Stephensen 2007.

17. Brandt 1930, 161.

18. Brandt 1930, 162–164.

19. See the description of the June Garden, designed for Vagn Jacobsen, the owner of the Carlsberg brewery, in Brandt 1927, 92.

20. See Brandt 1930, 161, 164, and Brandt 1927, 89–93.

21. See Brandt 1930, 161.

22. Muthesius began employing the term *Sachlichkeit* at the beginning of the twentieth century in relation to English and American architecture—using it to mean fit for purpose, modest, and nonornamental. See Adrian Forty's discussion of *Sachlichkeit* (literally, thingness) in *Words and Buildings: A Vocabulary of Modern Architecture* (London, 2000), 105–109, 181, and, on functionalism, Tim Benton, "Building Utopia," in *Modernism: Designing a New World, 1914–1939* (London, 2006), 155–159.

23. Brandt 1930, 164.

24. Brandt 1927, xx. Canneel's functionalist garden and German landscape architect Harry Maasz's economical garden promoted similar concepts. See Harry Maasz, *Dein Garten—Dein Arzt: Fort mit den Gartensorgen* (Frankfurt, 1927). To Brandt, the main function of the garden was to provide amenities for sitting and resting. See Brandt 1927, 92.

25. Brandt made his point by stating that *Phlox Hindenburg* and *Delphinium Mussolini* (a rather symbolic choice of cultivars) were not construction materials. As noted earlier, he also virulently condemned the "grossly expensive" architectural garden promoted by Hermann Muthesius and Max Laeuger in the 1900s–1910s: Brandt 1930, 169–170. For examples of architectural gardens see Günter Mader, *Gartenkunst des 20. Jahrhunderts: Garten- und Landschaftarchitektur in Deutschland* (Stuttgart, 1999), 10–33. Gertrude Stein's often-quoted "a rose is a rose is a rose" is from her poem "Sacred Emily" (1913).

26. See Canneel, "La Leçon au fond du jardin: Le jardin fonctionnel," interview conducted by Pierre-Louis Flouquet, *Bâtir* 3, no. 24 (November 1934): 27. Almost four years later, Christopher Tunnard would state: "The functional garden avoids the extremes both of the sentimental expressionism of the wild garden and the intellectual classicism of the 'formal' garden; it embodies rather a spirit of rationalism and through an aesthetic and practical ordering of its units provides a friendly and hospitable milieu for rest and recreation. It is, in effect, the social conception of the garden." Christopher Tunnard, "The Functional Aspect of Garden Planning," *Architectural Review* 83, no. 497 (April 1938), 199, and *Gardens in the Modern Landscape* (London, 1938), 81. Even though Tunnard's version came years after Canneel's, it was widely acknowledged as his own with the broad dissemination of *Gardens in the Modern Landscape*. For instance, Lance Neckar discussed the notion of functionalism and a "social conception of the garden" as merely Tunnard's. See Lance Neckar, "The Garden in the Modern Landscape," in *Modern Landscape Architecture: A Critical Review*, ed. Marc Treib (Cambridge, MA, 1993), 146.

27. See "Les 5 Points d'une architecture nouvelle," in *Le Corbusier et Pierre Jeanneret: Œuvre complète de 1910–1929*, 4th ed. (Zurich, 1946), 128–129.

28. Eve Blau, "Isotype and Architecture in Red Vienna: The Modern Projects of Otto Neurath and Josef Frank," *Austrian Studies, Journal of the Modern Humanities Research Association* 14 (2006): 237–245.

29. See Christopher Long, *Josef Frank: Life and Work* (Chicago, 2002), 120–125.

30. See Blau 2006, 240.

31. Canneel's interest in Le Corbusier's theory and work, first manifested with the commission of a house in 1929, was long lasting. He positioned himself in relation to the architect specifically on the question of roof gardens and the landscape of the radiant city. Canneel described the AIAJM as loosely resembling CIAM. Finally, Canneel's axonometric representations and his call for an environment governed by geometry, asymmetry, and occult balance cited the 1920s architectural and artistic avant-garde of De Stijl. See Yve-Alain Bois, "Metamorphosis of Axonometry," *Daidalos* 1, no. 1 (September 1981): 41–58, and Theo van Doesburg, "Towards a Plastic Architecture," 1924, reprinted in *Programs and Manifestoes on 20th-Century Architecture*, ed. Ulrich Conrads (Cambridge, MA, 1970), 80. On Canneel's use of axonometry, see Dorothée Imbert, "Skewed Realities: The Garden and the Axonometric Drawing," in *Representing Landscape Architecture*, ed. Marc Treib (London, 2007).

MICHAEL G. LEE

Landscape and Gender in Weimar Modernism

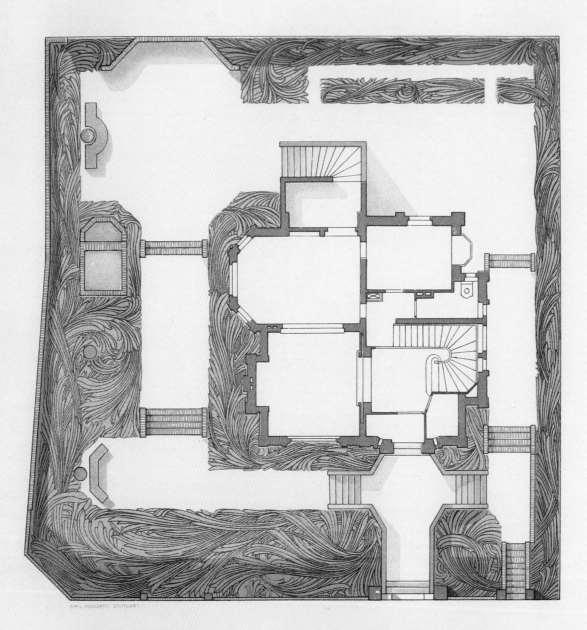

GARTENPLAN
DES HAUSES BEHRENS

Architectural modernism has almost universally been construed as a masculine project. The sociologist James C. Scott, for example, describes it as a "muscle-bound" practice tied to an unfettered faith in scientific and technical progress.[1] Moreover, the classic narratives recite a similar formula: modernism enunciates its discourse through the heroic figure of the genius (male) architect, disseminates its ideal form via the icon of the (phallic) skyscraper, and carries out its rational (male) operations within the denatured (defeminized) space of the metropolis. Several influential studies of modernist visual culture have explored the darker implications of these gendered formulations, suggesting that for Weimar Germany in particular the consequences were acute.[2] Such studies demonstrate that, despite its avowed progressive politics, the same culture that gave birth to vertiginous ecstasies of a liberated avant-garde also harbored a fascination with images of misogyny and sexual violence. If Weimar modernism—arguably the quintessential modernism—displayed such an entrenched hostility toward the feminine even in its "progressive" art, one must wonder whether such tendencies ultimately were animated by a more comprehensive negation of nature itself, coded as female.

It is to this question of modernism's gendered relationship to nature that landscape design in Weimar Germany offers valuable insights. Because its practice ranged from the reform parks of social democracy to the nature gardens of National Socialism's "reactionary modernism," the opportunities for gauging modernism's encounter with nature are unusually diverse. A number of studies have already demonstrated the profound differences separating its poles, emphasizing their political-ideological content.[3] An even more complex picture emerges, however, when this analysis is augmented through a consideration of gender, for it reveals unexpected and troubling commonalities. For whether designers were implicitly espousing the old Wilhelmine slogan "children, kitchen, church" (*Kinder, Küche, Kirche*) or the nominal sexual equality of an envisioned socialist state, the agent of reform was invariably a masculine rationality acting upon a compliant natural and social order.

In order to understand the emergence of this gendered framework, it is necessary first to sketch the primary debate that structured landscape discourse during the Weimar period: the contrast between the "architectural garden" (*Architekturgarten*) and the "nature garden" (*Naturgarten*). The emergence of these opposing types was the result of dissatisfaction with what was generally termed the Lenné-Meyer school, which had dominated German garden design throughout the second half of the nineteenth century. This picturesque orthodoxy was derived from the work of Peter Joseph Lenné and Gustav Meyer and was typically governed more by visual and decorative considerations than functional concerns. It was this perceived frivolity that came under attack in Germany around 1900. Hermann Muthesius' book *Das englische Haus* (1904–1905) was the first of increasingly strident calls for an integration of house and garden that would make the garden essentially an architectural extension of interior living space. Far from being a merely formal, or even functional, concern, however, this polemic was pointedly a struggle over professional turf.

1. Peter Behrens, garden plan of the Behrens residence, Darmstadt, 1902, an example of an *Architekturgarten*

Deutsche Kunst und Dekoration 9 (October 1901–March 1902): [161]

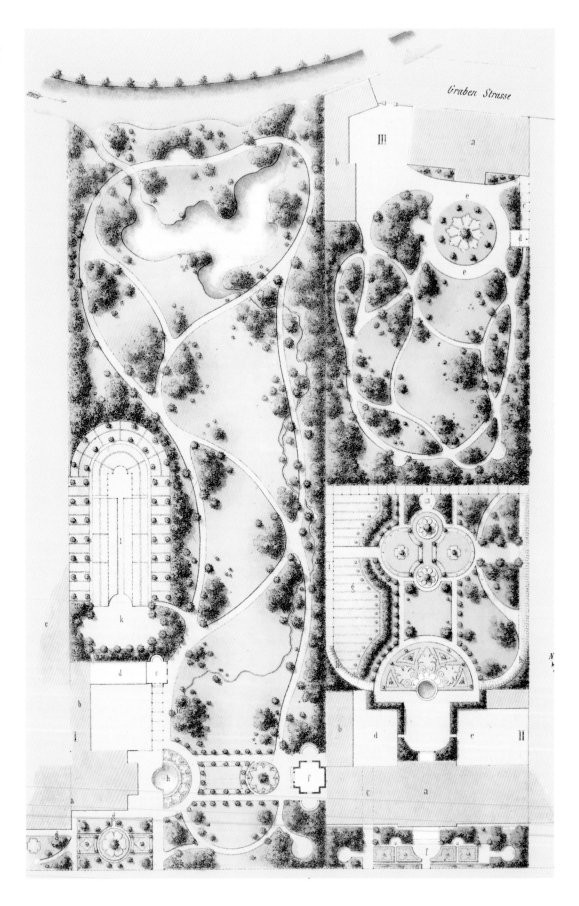

2. Gustav Meyer, villa garden

Gustav Meyer, Lehrbuch der schönen Gartenkunst *(Berlin, 1860), plate 19;* National Gallery of Art Library, Washington

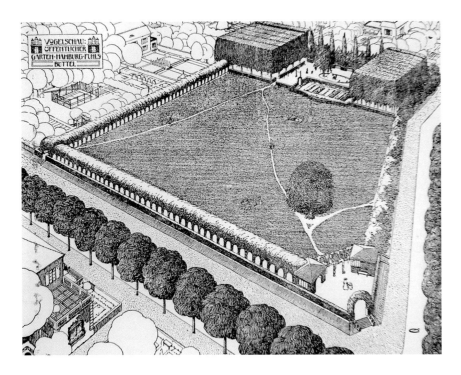

3. Leberecht Migge, public garden in Hamburg-Fuhlsbüttel, bird's-eye view

Leberecht Migge, Die Gartenkultur des 20. Jahrhunderts *(Jena, 1913), 75; private collection*

During these years it was trained gardeners who defended the status quo, while architects led the charge for extending their influence over the entire composition of the dwelling. At the symbolic core of this debate stood plants, and, more broadly, nature itself. For the traditionalists, the plant world signified what was both unique and unchanging about landscape design. The laws of plant growth also suggested for these designers an inherent conservatism. Carl Heicke encapsulated this view in a 1906 article in *Die Gartenkunst*, where he wrote: "We are bound by the expressive means and possibilities of our materials; our material determines our style."[4] A landscape modernism derived from architecture, then, would have to uproot this recalcitrant nature (figs. 1 and 2).

In brief, this is how the participants in this debate saw the issues. In what follows, I would like to explore the debate's gender implications, for they are crucial to understanding the development of landscape modernism during the Weimar period. These will be organized under two umbrellas. The first is an examination of the actual place of men and women in these spaces. That is,

how were public parks, domestic gardens, and other open spaces designed with gender differences in mind? The second is an attempt to locate these concrete concerns within a more symbolic field, looking at gendered expressions of landscape within the broader discourse of Weimar culture.

I will begin by considering public parks because of their close ties to reform movements that were widespread both before and after World War I. One of the leading voices in this charge was Leberecht Migge (1881–1935), whose *Die Gartenkultur des 20. Jahrhunderts* (1913) paved the way for some of the most progressive German work during the 1920s. Migge's prescription for the new century's public parks, as seen in his design for a park in Hamburg-Fuhlsbüttel, is squarely within the design language of the architectural garden, employing long alleys of trees, clipped hedges, and vast lawns for exercise and sport (fig. 3). Migge's writings are filled with descriptions of the life he envisions in these spaces, particularly the fields of turf. He specifically mentions that both girls and boys would populate these parks with their games and organized sports.[5] His equal treatment of the sexes in this regard is consonant with many of the progressive movements of the era, and one senses that the visual tabula rasa of these green planes was equally that of a social tabula rasa upon which a new order would express itself. It is less clear, however, if this vision of equality extended beyond the stages of youth, for the play areas for younger children—such as those in his park design for Hamburg-Fuhlsbüttel—are described as the province of mothers, rather than of parents more generally.[6] More to the point, Migge's description does not consider the possibility that adult women might appear in these parks unaccompanied by offspring.

This ambivalence is expressed even more clearly in Migge's domestic work. His design for the Wegmann garden in Rhede exemplifies his architectonic approach, which differentiates outdoor rooms according to designated uses (fig. 4). As Migge explains,

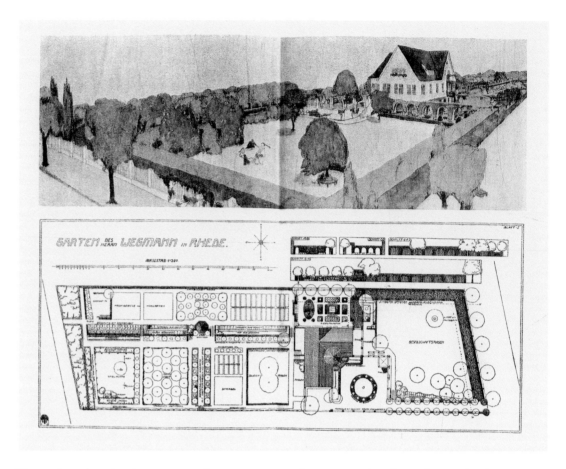

"A good garden simply *reiterates* the customary habits of domestic life, *amplifies* them, and transplants them into garden life."[7] The garden space on the right of the plan was intended as the most public zone, with a raised terrace and clipped vegetation framing a large open space, labeled the "social lawn" (*Gesellschaftsrasen*). It was to accommodate "the romping about of children, adult sports, and social gathering on festive occasions."[8] What is especially noteworthy, however, is the equal attention given to the other zones of the garden, one of which is described as the housewife's realm. This utilitarian garden "contains everything that the heart of an economically minded housewife could wish for. Every available parcel is maximized for use."[9] Elements include orchards, vegetable plots, and a laundry yard. Separated from the more public spaces, and thus discreetly shielded from view, this zone could be claimed by the woman of the house as her own, subject to her authority

alone. Immediately to the south of the house is a rose garden, a type of outdoor room that Migge elsewhere in the text equates with a "garden boudoir" that typically adjoins the "ladies' room" of the residence.[10] Migge notes condescendingly that the "ladies of the house" have a weakness for showy flowers and finery, and he further opines that this tendency often leads to indiscretion.[11] Whether this indiscretion is taken to be aesthetic, amorous, or of a different nature, such musings tend to undercut Migge's otherwise progressive stance in designing a semi-autonomous feminine sphere in the garden.

At the opposite end of the political spectrum, the so-called conservative revolution, or "reactionary modernism," was expressing its own ideology in landscape terms.[12] The domestic garden was a major focus, and this emphasis reflected the far right's broader interest in portraying the traditional family as the foundation for German

5. Lilies in the front garden of
Willy Lange's villa, Wannsee

Willy Lange, Gartengestaltung der
Neuzeit *(Leipzig, 1922), 441 (figure
294); Frances Loeb Library, Harvard
Graduate School of Design*

as "domestic" and "foreign," and human organizations could be justified in terms of a natural order.[14] One sees this elision in his description of the front garden of his Wannsee villa, where he praises the "pious white lilies, gentle and content like good women!" (fig. 5).[15] Considering that Lange based these plantings on the motif of a traditional German farmhouse garden, the equation of pious lilies with German farm-wives, "gentle and content" in their traditional roles, speaks to conservative fears of the new forces challenging patriarchy. Like many other conservatives, Lange located these forces in the public realm, casting the private garden as a counterbalancing site for renewing the traditional order. In fact, he went so far as to claim, contra Migge, that the private garden, rather than the public park, was ideally suited for music, exercise, and sport.[16] In this, he saw little or no role for large parks, which he deemed fit only for the anonymous masses. He was clearly taking a swipe at proponents of the architectonic reform park, which he termed "impersonal and boring, un-Nordic and un-German" (fig. 6).[17] But one must also wonder whether his assessment of these parks as "impersonal" betrays a deeper fear of the relative sexual equality inscribed in those spaces.

renewal. Within design circles, most proponents of these views, such as Willy Lange, Alwin Seifert, and Hans Hasler, favored the so-called nature garden as the proper landscape setting for this "natural" family. Although Lange sometimes employed concepts that were identical to Migge's, such as treating the garden as extended living space, his vision for both the design and the social life of these spaces was different.[13] For Lange, human sociology and plant sociology were coextensive; thus plant groupings could be modeled after social concepts such

6. Erwin Barth, *Sketch for the
Redesign of the Reichskanzler-
platz, Berlin: View of a Modern
Metropolis,* reproduction on glass
slide of lost original, c. 1924

*Institut für Landschaftsarchitektur
und Umweltplanung, Technische
Universität Berlin, Diasammlung
Barth*

7. Fritz Köhler, *Siedlung in Unterrath*, 1934, oil on canvas
Landeshauptstadt Düsseldorf–Stadtmuseum, B 1422

The *Siedlung*, or settlement, movement in Weimar Germany serves as a special case for structuring these issues, for not only does the *Siedlung* form address the level of the individual garden, but it also takes into account a collective social existence that includes public and semipublic spaces. The settlement movement had its roots in utopian thinking in the prewar period, and its adherents spanned the political spectrum. Regardless of the particular political agenda of the group, these independent associations sought to achieve relative economic self-sufficiency, a reformed social organization, and varying levels of engagement with modern technology.[18] Settlements created by those on the far right, such as Siedlung Thewissen in Düsseldorf-Unterrath, employed an architectural language of the traditional German farmhouse. The front gardens were modest and used primarily for food production. They figure prominently in a painting from 1934 by Fritz Köhler, which also emphasizes the pseudorural simplicity of the scheme by depicting children playing in the street (fig. 7).[19] Willy Lange included images of such vegetable gardens in his book on settlements, even going so far

as to stipulate that the design guidelines of these neovernacular residences be enforced by "aesthetic police."[20] After the National Socialist takeover in 1933, settlements like these became the norm, and the propaganda of the Third Reich often made use of this backdrop. The German family, each a miniature version of the national patriarchal order, was visually conflated with this ideal landscape. Whether the background image was the traditional German farm and village or the enveloping wings of the party, the link between the nuclear family and the landscape was thoroughly naturalized.

The settlements developed by the left are perhaps better known because of their prominence within narratives of architectural modernism. Some of these, such as Bruno Taut's Horseshoe in Berlin and the Siedlung Bruchfeldstraße in Frankfurt, were especially innovative, both architecturally and in their integration of functional gardens. Because of their progressive political orientation, it would be easy to assume that one would find evidence here of equally progressive efforts to promote gender equality or even neutrality. But this is not so. Attitudes toward family life remained quite conservative in most of these settlements, as can be seen in Migge's *Siedlung* proposal in his manifesto *Jedermann Selbstversorger!* (1918). Not only were single adults and single parents excluded from candidacy as members, but childless couples as well.[21] In a very real sense, then, these "landscapes of productivity" were about the production not just of fruits and vegetables, but of German babies. Contemporary photographs drive home this point, for they typically depict mothers and children working the gardens (fig. 8). Men, although sometimes shown, are generally far less visible. Given the conditions of massive population loss during World War I, it is understandable why these attitudes would have been broadly shared. Nevertheless, one must keep in mind the decidedly conservative bent of these policies and their eventual distortion during the years of National Socialism.

8. Siedlung Praunheim, Frankfurt am Main, 1929

Die Gartenkunst 42, no. 5 (May 1929): 70; Frances Loeb Library, Harvard Graduate School of Design

The question of female agency in these garden spaces naturally arises, and again one can turn to Migge for insight. His suggestions, however, are less than satisfying. For even though he promotes the idea of women expressing themselves more fully in the tending of domestic gardens, he is reluctant to assign them the leading role of designer. He maintains rather that the woman's "specific field of work" is the spiritual revival of the garden: "Here, in the *conscious spiritualization* of the new garden, lies a natural task for the woman which remains unfulfilled." He goes on to note that "the gardening profession now has a good number of positions that intelligent women could easily fill with a high degree of satisfaction."[22] Nevertheless, his few practical suggestions echo those of Carl Staehle, writing in November 1918: "Even today in our women's home economics schools we have divisions for gardening and household economy suited to outstanding young girls who wish to put their knowledge to use in the service of the community. Small garden and *Siedlung* ventures offer the woman a viable sphere of work."[23] The status of women in these positions remained low throughout the

Weimar era, however, and often produced self-doubt. For example, in her essay of 1932, "Die Frau und ihr Garten," the female director of the Gartenbauschule Düsseldorf-Kaiserswerth, Ilse Dieckmann, twice interrupts her argument to protest modestly, "I would like to state my opinion here only as a woman, not as a garden designer, for in this I have no training."[24]

The experience of female students at the Bauhaus, founded in 1919, is perhaps the most telling example of the gendered structure of Weimar's design world. Although from its inception the official position of the school was to respect gender equality, the reality of its practices was quite different.[25] In her extensive research on this topic, Anja Baumhoff has shown that the Bauhaus systematically limited the number of women admitted into its programs and also directed those admitted to fields of study that were perceived as suitable for them, such as weaving. In fact, the sole woman among the Bauhaus instructors was Gunta Stölzl, head of the weaving workshop. While male students were being groomed in the so-called higher arts of architecture and painting, female students were effectively barred from these areas of study. Personal accounts by these women show that the barriers were often psychological as well as institutional.[26] Käthe Brachmann complained in 1919 that male students often asked her why she did not follow her "natural calling." Her response was: "The ultimate creation, the bearing of children, will come in time. And if it does not, this woman still owes humanity another kind of creation." Her fellow female students typically shared these positive views of deferred childbearing, but many also expressed doubts regarding the ultimate status of women's abilities. Resi Jäger-Pleger's reservations, for example, belie an acceptance of gender stereotypes when she writes: "But how far we can go in art with our feminine feelings depends on each individual." Helene Schmidt-Nonne's internalization was even more pronounced:

The vision of a woman is to some extent childlike, for like a child she sees the singular and not the universal.... [B]ut one should not deceive oneself that this characteristic will change, in spite of all the accomplishments of the women's movement. Indeed there are even signs that a woman looks at her limitations knowing that this is a great advantage. The lack of intellect results out of a greater originality and harmlessness that is much closer to life itself.

The sentiments expressed in this passage have deep roots in psychological stereotypes: men as cool and rational, women as warm and emotional. But within both the German aesthetic tradition and its guild system, we can also observe an implicit gendering of art forms that was carried forward into the very heart of modernism. Kant, for example, equates garden design with "the decoration of rooms by the aid of tapestry, bric-a-brac [*Aufsätze*], and all beautiful furniture which is merely available to be looked at," along with "the art of tasteful dressing" and "ladies' finery" (*Putz der Damen*). When he claims further that garden art is a mere "adornment of the soil" (*Schmückung des Bodens*), he implies that it is nothing more

than the application of makeup to a topographic surface. There is more than a subtle put-down in this talk of surfaces and superficiality, for it is ultimately Kant's gendering of garden art as feminine that justifies its low status in his system.[27]

This Kantian legacy was still clearly at work in the valuation of the decorative arts, and by extension of women, in Weimar modernism. Seen in this light, the early twentieth-century diatribes against the Lenné-Meyer school take on another cast. For the arguments between gardeners and architects over professional status were as much about the gendering of the professions as their claims to expertise. One notices this bias, for example, in the journal *Die Gartenkunst* after the change in editorship in 1906 from Emil Clemen to Carl Heicke.[28] Close examination of the polemics reveals the frequent use of implicitly gendered terms to paint opponents in a bad light. Proponents of the architectural garden referred to their own works as "sober" and "resolute" but dismissed those of the landscape school as "whimpering," "frilly," "capricious," "fickle," "delicate," and "coquettish."[29] Further, they claimed that the gardeners' imitation of nature made them "weak" and led to a fascination with "baubles" and "trinkets."[30] The tables could be turned, of course, and often were. When the historian Franz Hallbaum wrote his dissertation on the gardener Ludwig von Sckell during the mid-1920s, he did so in part to rehabilitate the reputation of the landscape garden. In both the preface and the conclusion he explained that the basis of the landscape garden's appeal lay in its subsumption of the "heroic" qualities of paintings by Nicolas Poussin and Claude Lorrain. In other words, Hallbaum (who later espoused National Socialism) sought to demonstrate that the landscape garden, if properly understood, was in fact even more masculine than the new architectural gardens.[31] Richard Rothe, in a racially tinged essay in *Die Gartenkunst* condemning the architectural garden as an invention

of southern peoples, referred to it simply as "effeminate" (*verweichlicht*).[32]

The contingency of these gender associations needs to be emphasized, especially given that landscape modernism in Germany begins with a negative appraisal of horticulture as decorative and feminine.[33] Images of gardens throughout this era, even the new architectonic ones such as that designed by Max Laeuger for the Internationale Kunst- und Grosse Gartenbau-Ausstellung, held in Mannheim in 1907, register this correspondence among the garden, decoration, and women (fig. 9). Flower gardens in particular were often photographed with women serving as the central ornament, a human flower growing among her own kind. The woman as ornament was also a favorite motif among conservative designers such as Willy Lange, whose publications frequently included such images. Moreover, one sees this tendency even among artists usually classified as modernists, such as Max Liebermann, whose paintings of his Wannsee garden typ-

ically included women as central elements. So what are we to make of this seemingly natural correlation between women and ornamental gardens when one can find counterexamples in other cultures, such as the rich association between masculinity and floriculture in the Ottoman Empire?[34]

One clue to the cultural specificity of this connection lies in the history of the German notion of *Gemütlichkeit*, usually translated as "coziness."[35] The term conjures up images of the nineteenth-century interior, the Biedermeier and Wilhelmine parlor in particular, as a retreat from the "coldness" of public life (fig. 10). Walter Benjamin, for example, derided the cozy interior as a cocoon, a separation of public and private life that feeds the illusions brought on by capitalist forms of consumption. Le Corbusier described coziness as "sentimental hysteria," managing in one pithy phrase to fuse the most notorious concept in Freud's female psychology, hysteria, with a central theme of the landscape garden tradition, sentimentalism.[36] Max Brod, in his essay

10. "Das Kunstgewerbe in Anwendung auf Zimmereinrichtung," after a watercolor by G. Rehlender, frontispiece of *Die Erfindungen der neuesten Zeit: Zwanzig Jahre industrielle Fortschritte im Zeitalter der Weltausstellung* (Leipzig, 1883), a typical Wilhelmine interior later reproduced as a negative example by Bruno Taut

Bruno Taut, Die neue Wohnung: Die Frau als Schöpferin *(Leipzig, 1924); Frances Loeb Library, Harvard Graduate School of Design*

"Women and the New Objectivity" (1929), sums up the gender implications matter-of-factly, stating that under current conditions "love, women, hearth, soul have no place."[37]

Under the banner of modernism, then, the domestic sphere was to become part of the new objective culture, detached from emotional needs and approached as a rational, technical problem. One aspect of this agenda was to embrace the coldness of functionalism and formal purity in the private garden. A number of cultural historians, including Helmut Lethen, have interpreted this coolness and distance as a response to the outcome of World War I. In part a loss of faith in traditional authority and social structures, it was also a compensation for what many perceived to be the demasculinization of German culture resulting from military defeat. The new attitude included the exhilaration of feeling liberated, not only from the constraints of historical precedent but also from the constraining sentimental attachments of bourgeois family life.[38] The implications of the latter have been explored perhaps most fully by Klaus Theweleit. In an analysis of the German Freikorps during the Weimar period, he has shown that for its members the disavowal of emotional attachment and the armoring of the body were prerequisites for the construction of masculine identity.[39] In landscape terms, one might draw a comparison between pre–World War I gardens, where proliferating pergolas, arbors, and summerhouses serve as vestigial markers of an interior coziness, and the private gardens of modernists such as Sepp Rasch, where austerity of form leaves little room for intimacy. In the latter, even the most private spaces feel exposed despite being armed with stiff hedges and other boundary structures.[40]

Perhaps the most paradoxical aspect of this war on coziness is that its proponents understood it as the path to women's emancipation. That is, in order for the world to eventually become hospitable for everyone, including women, it must first be made

equally cold for all.[41] To understand why
progressives during this era would embrace
such a paradox, it is helpful to consider the
conservative position. As early as 1907, the
pages of *Die Gartenkunst* were applying
the terms "gemütlich" and "Biedermeier" to
the neovernacular gardens of Paul Schultze-
Naumburg, who later in his career notoriously embraced National Socialism.[42] Willy
Lange argued in his book *Gartengestaltung
der Neuzeit* that *Gemütlichkeit* is precisely
what enables the property owner and his
family to enjoy "country and garden life."[43]
In a slightly later work, *Gartenpläne*, Lange
takes the idea a step further and writes
that "degenerate architectonic gardens
are un-German because [they are] uncozy
[*ungemütlich*]."[44] One photograph in particular from *Gartengestaltung der Neuzeit*
makes his desire to connect the cozy interior
and the nature garden explicit, and the caption reads, in part, "full of warmth [*gemüt-
voll*], therefore German." A similar image
from that book reveals the gender implications of this connection, showing a nature
garden opening directly off a traditional
kitchen, the proper place of the German
wife (figs. 11 and 12).

Given such associations, it is understandable why progressives of the Weimar era
shunned cozy warmth and embraced the
new objectivity. But for many, purity of
form was not enough. The new sobriety
demanded a more committed asceticism, a
reduction of garden form to its "skeleton,"
a level of self-denial frightfully close to
anorexia.[45] Walter Benjamin described this
discipline as the "new poverty," a stripping
away of the superfluous through a desire
for "nakedness."[46] But did this naked transparency mean the erotic exhibitionism of
Josephine Baker's cabaret striptease, the
celebration of virility in the cult of the male
body, the innocence of unclothed children
depicted in Hermann Mattern's manifesto
Freiheit in Grenzen (1938), or something
else entirely? If, as Benjamin maintained,
the cozy interior was the last refuge of

personality because its traces could still be found in the folds of drapery and creases of cushions, then modern architecture had revealed the significance of glass as a trace-resistant transparency.[47] It was only under such conditions that Harry Maasz could design a garden space defined by glass walls, and Leberecht Migge could proclaim, "The coming garden will be a useful garden. It will be a working garden. It will be—a glass garden" (fig. 13).[48]

This notion of a "coming garden" (*kommende Garten*) marks the most contentious moment in the Weimar debates over landscape modernism.[49] From Gustav Allinger's design of 1926 (best known as the setting for a *Vogue* fashion shoot) to diverse offerings from both the political left and right, designers attempted to distill the forces of the present as articulations of a possible future. Allinger's design tries to broker a truce between architecture and horticulture, but the tension between their masculine and feminine coding makes this peace tenuous (figs. 14 and 15).[50] At the same time, an equally contentious gender image had emerged in German media and advertising. Termed the New Woman, this modern urban female was young, attractive, confident, and financially independent.[51] Embodying two of the most significant social outcomes of World War I, women's suffrage and the dramatic rise of female employment, she was an object of both fear and desire.[52] She was knowledgeable of the latest fashion trends and put that knowledge to use for her own pleasure. A clever verse describing the New Woman appeared in the magazine *Die Dame* in 1925:

What is the modern woman?
A charming "bobbed head" [*Bubikopf*][53]—says the hairdresser
A model of depravity—says Aunt Klotilde
A complex of sexual problems—says the psychoanalyst
Comrade and soul friend—says the youth
Miserable housewife—says the reactionary
Expensive—says the bachelor
The best customer—says the stockings dealer
An unhappiness for my son—says the mother-in-law
The center of the sanitorium—says the doctor
The same since the dawn of history—says the wise man.[54]

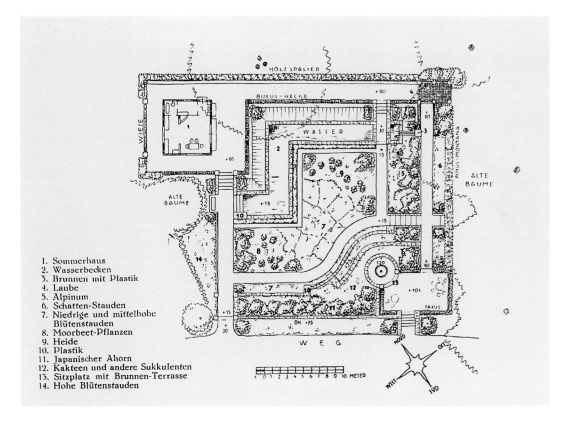

1. Sommerhaus
2. Wasserbecken
3. Brunnen mit Plastik
4. Laube
5. Alpinum
6. Schatten-Stauden
7. Niedrige und mittelhohe Blütenstauden
8. Moorbeet-Pflanzen
9. Heide
10. Plastik
11. Japanischer Ahorn
12. Kakteen und andere Sukkulenten
13. Sitzplatz mit Brunnen-Terrasse
14. Hohe Blütenstauden

Advertisements during these years drew a direct link between the modern woman's lifestyle and modern architecture, often pairing her with icons such as the Weissenhofsiedlung in Stuttgart. Other advertisements extended the comparison with modernist architecture to include the sleek lines of automobiles, a visual strategy strongly reminiscent of Le Corbusier's argument in *Vers une architecture* (1923) (fig. 16).

Because she disdained traditional female roles, the New Woman quickly became a lightning rod. Although a significant number of young women embraced the image, many critics homed in on the New Woman's most egregious failing: a reluctance to embrace motherhood. The National Socialist organ *Völkischer Beobachter*, for example, drew the following contrast in 1928:

Natural, unpretentious and modest, in harmony with their way of life, was how the German [women previously] dressed themselves.... With their intimate closeness to nature and because of their pronounced sense of duty, they had little or no use for luxury and trinkets.[55]

Party ideologue Engelbert Huber was even more emphatic about traditional gender norms:

The intellectual attitude of the [National Socialist] movement ... is opposed to the political woman. It refers the woman back to her nature-given sphere of the family and to her tasks as wife and mother.... The German resurrection is a male event.[56]

This reaction from the right was to be expected, but mainstream opinion was often equally hostile. A 1921 newspaper article entitled "Die Mode als Kampfmittel," for example, made the same point by lamenting the New Woman's "sterile frailty."[57] Even more alarming to respectable society was the pronounced androgyny of the new look, with women's clothing and hairstyles often parodied as excessively masculine (fig. 17). Conversely, the New Woman's androgyny produced fears running in the opposite direction, with many observers worried that men's fashion was becoming increasingly feminized, even homosexual. Otto Dix's portrait of the

16. "The Spirit of Modern Fashion Reflects the Spirit of Modern Architecture," fashion advertisement showing the New Woman with modern architecture and an automobile, 1929

Das neue Berlin 8 (1929): 151; Frances Loeb Library, Harvard Graduate School of Design

17. Caricature of the androgynous New Woman, 1925

Lustige Blätter (Berlin, 1927), as cited in Friedrich Wendel, Die Mode in der Karikatur (Dresden, 1928), 280 (Abb. 367)

18. Otto Dix, The Jeweler Karl Krall, 1923, oil on canvas

Von der Heydt-Museum, Wuppertal, KMV 1954–55/1; © 2010 Artists Rights Society (ARS), New York/VG Bild-Kunst, Bonn

jeweler Karl Krall certainly speaks to this anxiety (fig. 18).

The nearly synchronous appearance of the New Woman and the "coming garden," then, was no accident. For the uncertain negotiation between architecture and horticulture found in Allinger's design is symptomatic of the gendered discourse running throughout Weimar culture. But do we really find in the coming garden an equal encounter between the masculine agency of architectonics and rationality and the feminine world of horticulture and nature?

Perhaps the key to an answer lies in the following quotations. Returning to the gendered world of the Bauhaus, one may consider Bauhaus painting master Paul Klee as he explains to the female weaving students why they do not possess genius:

You [women weavers] were industrious: but genius is not industry…. Genius is genius, is grace, is without beginning and end. Is begetting.

Genius as formal movement is the essential in a work of art. At the beginning, a motif switching on energy, sperm. Art work as forming in the material sense: originally female. Art work as form-determining sperm: originally male.[58]

That is, women are passive receptacles for reproduction, but men of genius provide the form-giving sperm.[59] In a similar vein, Leberecht Migge describes his own experience of the creative process:

How often, when my staff and I are immersed over our heads in garden plans, have I wished for feminine assistance, to lend to us hopelessly form-obsessed, rational men her light touch in the weaving together of flowers and other things, her sensitive soul, and her God-given serenity.[60]

For Migge, the male architect's excessive formalism can always be mitigated after the fact with a woman's soft touch.

But if this is how it goes for progressive modernism, then what about the reactionary nature garden?[61] At first glance, its emphasis on horticulture might suggest a more generous attitude toward the feminine, and some of Willy Lange's writings seem to say as much. He feared, for example, the reduction of nature to "mere material for technology," an attitude he saw expressed in the "materialist worldview" of the French-Italian garden.[62] (As contemporary reference points, both Fritz Lang's *Metropolis* and Sigfried Kracauer's analysis of the Tiller Girls speak to the mechanization of the female body.) Further, Willy Lange argued for a relationship to nature based on "harmony," rather than either dependence or dominance.[63] But exactly how was this harmony to be conceived?

Was feminine nature to be his equal partner in the nature garden? The following passage explains why the answer was an emphatic "no," and why the visual result so easily disguised this fact.

Penetration — not side-by-side adjacency — is the highest aim for relating the architectonic and natural motives of garden design on the whole. In this regard, one should always consider the architectonic motive as the stronger, the natural motive the weaker. One could also speak of these as masculine and feminine motives … in the sense of a polarity spanning our entire perceptual and sensible being.[64]

In Lange's ideal nature garden, then, harmony is not the same thing as equality. Female nature is completely suffused with, and literally penetrated by, the male formative principle. What appears to be an elevation of nature is nothing but a thinly disguised version of the old patriarchy.

One can trace this shared image of masculine creativity to Hermann Muthesius, who, as noted earlier, essentially set the terms of the debate in 1904. Commenting on the responsibilities of the domestic architect, Muthesius writes,

Just as he has taken this art of interior design from out of the hands of the stylistically wayward decorator, so he has realized that he must take possession of the garden in order to rescue the house from the state of degeneration into which it sank in the nineteenth century and to impose on it the stamp of artistic unity.[65]

It is not clear whether the "wayward decorator" is a woman, or more stereotypically a gay man, but the situation must be righted in any case by a straight male architect forcibly taking possession of the garden turf. The implied violence of this image is echoed in a book by Bruno Taut, whose title — *Die neue Wohnung: Die Frau als Schöpferin* (The new dwelling: the woman as creator) — suggests that its pages contain a robust account of female agency (fig. 19).[66] On the contrary, Taut recounts how his noble efforts

19. Bruno Taut, *The Living Room Undressed*, before (above) and after (below)

Bruno Taut, Die neue Wohnung: Die Frau als Schöpferin *(Leipzig, 1924); Frances Loeb Library, Harvard Graduate School of Design*

to "undress" the cozy bourgeois interior are met with resistance by the housewife.[67] Although Taut's forcible undressing might be downplayed as mere metaphor, it nonetheless shares a disturbing affinity with images of sexual violence that were prevalent in Weimar avant-garde painting, such as Otto Dix's *Lustmord*.[68]

The coming garden, then, registers ambivalence within the project of modernism. Although, like its predecessors, it relies on a model of masculine creativity, its visual balance suggests that a different engagement with nature and the feminine might be possible. One final example, Hans Friedrich Pohlenz's so-called *sonderbarer Garten,* might prove instructive in this regard (fig. 20).[69] Although not classified by Pohlenz as a coming garden, his design of 1925 nonetheless shares the context and ambitions of these proposals, especially in its orientation toward the future.[70] But rather than translate *sonderbarer Garten* properly as "peculiar garden," I suggest that we take some liberties and call Pohlenz's project a "queer garden."[71] The attractiveness of this proposal lies in its "outsider" status, in the possibility that it might undo some of the gender oppositions that underlie Weimar garden design.[72] For what Pohlenz's queer garden puts on display is the desire of the progressive wing of Weimar modernism, at least in theory, to create a gender-neutral space. But the results are clearly not neutral. Instead, this work and others like it belie a fundamentally masculine organization of that void. From this perspective, Reinhold Hoemann's exhortation to his fellow designers to refashion the German garden from a "poor Cinderella" into a "stunning princess" has to be one of the queerest moments in Weimar modernism.[73] For what else are we to make of this image of male architects acting as fairy godmothers? The ultimate failure of such androgynous constructions to alter significantly the gendered foundations of modernism invites a reassessment of progressive

20. Hans Friedrich Pohlenz, *The Peculiar Garden*, 1926

Fritz Wilhelm Schönfeld, "Kritische Betrachtungen über drei Hausgärten (Pohlenz–Hübotter–Valentien)," Die Gartenkunst 39, no. 3 (1926): 37; Frances Loeb Library, Harvard Graduate School of Design

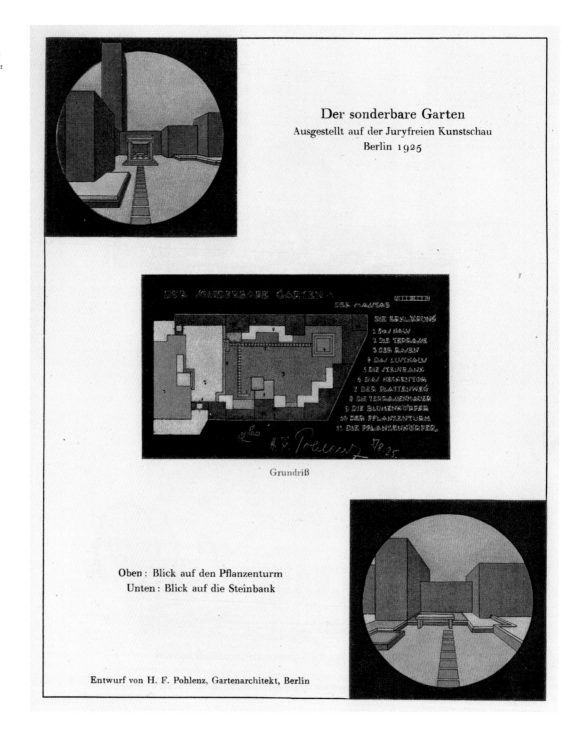

culture's eventual uncritical embrace of its aesthetics. Nevertheless, these constructions do succeed in illuminating modernism's logic of negation, if only to indicate its limits when confronted by the agency of nature and the feminine. It is to this question of the articulation of feminine agency and the androgyny of modernist space that the categories of "queer modernism" and "queer nature" may be useful. It is an aspect of the modernist legacy that still needs to be investigated, and I would like to suggest that Weimar is the most promising place to begin.

Translations are mine unless otherwise indicated.

1. James C. Scott, *Seeing Like a State: How Certain Schemes to Improve the Human Condition Have Failed* (New Haven, 1998), 89. Conversely, Scott credits the insightfulness of Jane Jacobs' critique of modernist urban planning to her "woman's eye," which, unlike the viewpoint of masculine modernism, does not reduce the notion of purpose to linear instrumentality (Scott 1998, 138–139).

2. Two studies that have been especially influential for my research are Maria Tatar, *Lustmord: Sexual Murder in Weimar Germany* (Princeton, 1995), and Klaus Theweleit, *Male Fantasies*, 2 vols., trans. Stephen Conway (Minneapolis, 1987–1989).

3. Gert Gröning and Joachim Wolschke-Bulmann have analyzed this theme in numerous articles, several of which are coauthored. These include Joachim Wolschke-Bulmann and Gert Gröning, "The Ideology of the Nature Garden: Nationalistic Trends in Garden Design in Germany during the Early Twentieth Century," *Journal of Garden History* 12, no. 1 (January–March 1992): 73–80, and Joachim Wolschke-Bulmann, "The 'Wild Garden' and the 'Nature Garden': Aspects of the Garden Ideology of William Robinson and Willy Lange," *Journal of Garden History* 12, no. 3 (July–September 1992): 183–206.

4. "Wir sind an die Ausdrucksweise und an die Ausdrucksmöglichkeiten unseres Materials gebunden, unser Material bedingt unsern Stil." Carl Heicke, "Die Nachahmung der Natur in der Gartenkunst [part 2]," *Die Gartenkunst* 8, no. 12 (1906): 229 (cited subsequently as Heicke 1906a).

5. Leberecht Migge, *Die Gartenkultur des 20. Jahrhunderts* (Jena, 1913), 25. Migge suggests later in the text that in the case of large sports parks it might be preferable to separate the sexes (Migge 1913, 31). He also praises the Chicago park system in part because its swimming facilities accommodate both sexes (Migge 1913, 23). On Migge's life and career, see Martin Baumann, "Freiraumplanung in den Siedlungen der zwanziger Jahre am Beispiel der Planungen des Gartenarchitekten Leberecht Migge" (PhD thesis, Universität der Künste, Berlin; Halle, 2002); and David H. Haney, *When Modern Was Green: Life and Work of Landscape Architect Leberecht Migge* (New York, 2010).

6. Migge 1913, 73.

7. "Ein guter Garten *wiederholt* einfach die Gepflogenheiten des Hauslebens, *erweitert* sie und setzt sie in Gartenleben um." Migge 1913, 62.

8. "Er dient dem Tummeln der Kinder, den Sporten der Erwachsenen und geselliger Vereinigung in festlicher Stunde." Migge 1913, 68.

9. "Sie enthalten alles, was sich das Herz einer wirtschaftlichen Hausfrau wünschen kann. Jedes verfügbare Plätzchen ist ausgenutzt." Migge 1913, 70.

10. Migge 1913, 62.

11. Migge 1913, 67–68.

12. On the use of the term "reactionary modernism" in German cultural history, see Jeffrey Herf, *Reactionary Modernism: Technology, Culture, and Politics in Weimar and the Third Reich* (New York, 1984). On its relation to garden history, see Joachim Wolschke-Bulmann, "'The Peculiar Garden'—The Advent and the Destruction of Modernism in German Garden Design," in *The Modern Garden in Europe and the United States: Proceedings of the Garden Conservancy Symposium Held March 12, 1993 at the Paine Webber Building in New York, New York*, ed. Robin Karson (Cold Spring, NY, 1994), 17–30.

13. Lange uses the phrases "Wohnen im Freien" and "erweiterte Wohnung" in Willy Lange, *Gartengestaltung der Neuzeit*, 5th ed. (Leipzig, 1922), 307 (cited subsequently as Lange 1922a).

14. See, for example, Wolschke-Bulmann 1994, 23–25; Joachim Wolschke-Bulmann and Gert Gröning, "Der kommende Garten: Zur Diskussion über die Gartenarchitektur in Deutschland seit 1900," *Garten + Landschaft* (March 1988): 50–52; Willy Lange, *Der Garten und seine Bepflanzung* (Stuttgart, 1913), 29; and Lange 1922a, 168.

15. "... jene frommen weißen Lilien, mild und wohlig wie gute Frauen!" Lange 1922a, 306.

16. Willy Lange, *Gartenpläne* (Leipzig, 1927), 16.

17. "... unpersönlich und langweilig, unnordisch und undeutsch." Lange 1927, 18.

18. Thomas Rohrkrämer, *Eine andere Moderne? Zivilisationskritik, Natur und Technik in Deutschland, 1880–1933* (Paderborn, 1999), 124–126.

19. Theweleit 1987–1989.

20. Willy Lange, *Land- und Gartensiedelungen* (Leipzig, 1910), 26.

21. David H. Haney, "Leberecht Migge's 'Green Manifesto': Envisioning a Revolution of Gardens," *Landscape Journal* 26, no. 2 (2007): 207.

22. "Denn hier, in der *bewußten Verinnerlichung* des neuen Gartens liegt eine natürliche Aufgabe der Frau noch unerfüllt.... Dabei gibt es im gärtnerischen Wirtschaftsleben schon jetzt eine ganze Anzahl von Positionen, die von intelligenten Frauen gut und mit hoher Befriedigung ausgefüllt werden könnten." Migge 1913, 89–90.

23. "Schon heute haben wir aus den weiblichen Haushaltungsschulen einen Stamm für den Gartenbau und die hauswirtschaftlichen Aufgaben vorgebildeter junger Mädchen, die ihre Kenntnisse in den Dienst der Allgemeinheit stellen wollen. In den Kleingarten- und Siedlungsbestrebungen liegt für die Frau ein entwicklungsfähiges Arbeitsgebiet." Carl Staehle, "Aufgaben der Garten- und Friedhofverwaltungen während des Kriegs und nach Friedensschluß," *Die Gartenkunst* 31, no. 11 (1918): 138.

24. "Ich möchte hierzu Stellung nehmen, nur als Frau, nicht etwa als Gartengestalter, wozu ich nicht berufen bin" and "Ich spreche nicht als Gartengestalter, was ich nicht bin, sondern als Frau mit einiger Kenntnis der Einstellung weiterer Kreise zu diesem Problem." Ilse Dieckmann, "Die Frau und ihr Garten," *Die Gartenkunst* 45, no. 2 (1932): 25.

25. Women did not receive the right to vote in Germany until 1918, so it is unrealistic to expect that gender equality would have been achieved immediately. What is striking, however, is that an institution that billed itself as progressive made so few strides during the ensuing years of its existence.

26. The following are quoted in English translation in Anja Baumhoff, *The Gendered World of the Bauhaus: The Politics of Power at the Weimar Republic's Premier Art Institute, 1919–1932* (Frankfurt am Main, 2001), 54–57.

27. Immanuel Kant, *Critique of Judgement*, trans. J. H. Bernard (New York, 1951), §51. I have explored the systemic significance of Kant's gendered language at greater length in *The German "Mittelweg": Garden Theory and Philosophy in the Time of Kant* (New York, 2007), 188–189.

28. Marie Luise Gothein, *Geschichte der Gartenkunst*, 2 vols. (Jena, 1914), 2:454–455. Gothein cites essays by Alfred Lichtwark and Ferdinand Avenarius, both published in 1892, as the first written polemics against the landscape style.

29. "Sober" (*nüchtern*): Migge 1913, 64; "resolute" (*resolut*): Leberecht Migge, as quoted in Günter Mader, *Gartenkunst des 20. Jahrhunderts: Garten- und Landschaftsarchitektur in Deutschland* (Stuttgart, 1999), 22; "whimpering" (*Stilgewinsel*), "frilly" (*Mätzchen*): Leberecht Migge, as quoted in Mader 1999, 18; "capricious" (*Laune*), "fickle" (*Inkonsequenz*): Heicke 1906a, 233; "delicate" (*anmutig-feinen*), "coquettish" (*kokketiert*): Carl Heicke, "Zeitschriftenrundschau," *Die Gartenkunst* 8, no. 3 (1906): 49.

30. "Weak" (*schwach*): Carl Heicke, "Die Nachahmung der Natur in der Gartenkunst [part 1]," *Die Gartenkunst* 8, no. 11 (1906): 212. Heicke does allow, however, that a slavish adherence to straight lines can also be seen as a form of weakness. "Baubles" (*Spielereien*), "trinkets" (*Kleinigkeiten*): Heicke 1906a, 233.

31. Franz Hallbaum, *Der Landschaftsgarten: Sein Entstehen und seine Einführung in Deutschland durch Friedrich Ludwig von Sckell, 1750–1823* (Munich, 1927). Shortly after the publication of Hallbaum's book, Willy Lange noted with satisfaction that it was a "sign of the renewed inclination toward the (Nordic) feeling for nature in garden art" (Lange 1927, 95). Joachim Wolschke-Bulmahn has provided an analysis of Hallbaum's relation to National Socialism in "The Search for 'Ecological Goodness' among Garden Historians," in *Perspectives on Garden History*, ed. Michel Conan (Washington, DC, 1999), 166.

32. "... dass jene pomphaften, architektonischen Schöpfungen der Schauplatz und die Bühne einer grenzenlosen Verschwendung, Verweichlichung und Genusssucht waren, die das Lebensmark von Nationen aufzehrte." Richard Rothe, "Die deutsche Gartenkunst aus weiter Perspektive," *Die Gartenkunst* 8, no. 7 (1906): 128. The perennial appeal (and effectiveness) of this strategy is apparent even today. One need look no further than efforts to discredit former U.S. presidential candidate Senator John Edwards by labeling him "The Breck Girl."

33. In listing terms, I have included only those that are most obviously coded as feminine. There are many others, however, that could also be interpreted in this light. Two of the more interesting include the charge that garden design during the second half of the nineteenth century had grown "slack" or "limp" (Otto Bernhardt, "Gärtner oder Künstler: Unmaßgeblich Meinungen eines Laien," *Die Gartenkunst* 9, no. 4 [1907]: 69), and the description of these nineteenth-century designers as having been mired in the "swamp" of nature imitation (W. Singer, "Über künstlerische Gestaltung des Hausgartens," *Die Gartenkunst* 9, no. 10 [1907]: 200). I include the latter in light of Klaus Theweleit's provocative reading of swamp and marsh imagery as a visceral, negative reaction to the female body's emissions.

34. Nurhan Atasoy, *A Garden for the Sultan: Gardens and Flowers in the Ottoman Culture* ([Istanbul], 2002). See also Maria Subtelny, "Visionary Rose: Metaphorical Application of Horticultural Practice in Persian Culture," in *Botanical Progress, Horticultural Innovation and Cultural Change*, ed. Michel Conan and W. John Kress (Washington, DC, 2007), 13–36. Subtelny addresses this theme in the Persian context, but with an emphasis on its spiritual associations. I am grateful to Michel Conan for bringing this reference to my attention.

35. This theme has been thoroughly explored by Karina Van Herck in her article "'Only Where Comfort Ends, Does Humanity Begin': On the 'Coldness' of Avant-Garde Architecture in the Weimar Period," in *Negotiating Domesticity: Spatial Productions of Gender in Modern Architecture*, ed. Hilde Heynen and Gülsüm Baydar (London, 2005), 123–144.

36. Van Herck 2005, 124–126. This rhetoric of "coldness" also frequently found its counterpart in garden literature, where it was usually directed against the new architectural garden. Examples include members of the Lenné-Meyer school accusing garden architects of having "hearts of stone" (Gothein 1914, 2:455) and W. Singer contrasting the "cold stones" of architectonic elements with the warmth of plants (Singer 1907, 204).

37. Max Brod, "Women and the New Objectivity (1929)," in *The Weimar Republic Sourcebook*, ed. Anton Kaes, Martin Jay, and Edward Dimendberg (Berkeley, 1994), 206.

38. Van Herck 2005, 132–135.

39. Theweleit 1987–1989.

40. This paradoxical aspect of modernist privacy echoes earlier recommendations by Migge, who stated that the enclosed space of a private garden should not differ from that of a house interior (Migge 1913, 62).

41. Van Herck 2005, 125.

42. Singer 1907, 204.

43. Lange 1922a, 33.

44. Lange 1927, 10.

45. For "skeleton," see Mader 1999, 14, 28. Within the design rhetoric of this period, the term could carry either a positive or a negative connotation.

46. Van Herck 2005, 130.

47. Van Herck 2005, 127.

48. "Der kommende Garten wird … ein Nutzgarten sein, er wird ein Arbeitsgarten sein und wird—ein Glasgarten sein." Leberecht Migge, "Der kommende Garten," *Gartenschönheit* 8 (1927): 65. Although Migge is referring to greenhouses used for the production of fruits and vegetables, I include this quotation to underscore the symbolic resonance of glass as a preferred material within modernism, even when it was directed toward explicitly utilitarian ends.

49. Other contemporary proposals for the "coming garden" included Leberecht Migge, "Der kommende Garten," *Gartenschönheit* 8 (1927): 64–65; G. N. Brandt, "Der kommende Garten," *Wasmuths Monatshefte für Baukunst* 14 (1930): 161–176; and Alwin Seifert, "Der kommende Garten," *Deutsche Bauzeitung* (1933): 367–371. See also Joachim Wolschke-Bulmahn and Gert Gröning, "Der kommende Garten: Zur Diskussion über die Gartenarchitektur in Deutschland seit 1900," *Garten + Landschaft* (March 1988): 47–56, and Gert Gröning, "Der kommende Garten: Anmerkungen zu einer europäischen Diskussion um Gartenkultur im ersten Drittel des 20. Jahrhunderts," *Die Gartenkunst* 7, no. 2 (1995): 268–281.

50. Although not speaking of gardens, one of Lange's fellow reactionary conservatives, Ludwig Klage, put the matter bluntly, stating that the masculine principle was the "shape of what is coming [*Gestaltung des Kommenden*]" (Rohkrämer 1999, 203).

51. Irene Guenther, *Nazi Chic? Fashioning Women in the Third Reich* (Oxford, 2004), 53–88.

52. After the attainment of women's suffrage in 1918, the 1920s saw the election of many women to political offices. There were also modest gains in women's professional lives. During World War 1, many women out of necessity took jobs in what had previously been considered male-only professions. With the loss of a substantial percentage of the male population during the war, many of these women remained in the workforce despite social pressures to return to more traditional roles in the household. These pressures would intensify during the early 1930s with the rise of mass unemployment, when women were accused publicly of "taking away men's jobs," but for a time during the 1920s there was a new space for female employment. This would accommodate, to a limited degree, women designers who had trained in art academies and new design schools such as the Bauhaus.

53. In what might reasonably be interpreted as a swipe at the New Woman, Willy Lange criticizes the practice of shearing plants as a passing fashion for "Bubiköpfe." He argues that these clipped plant forms rob the garden of its spiritual dimension by reducing its maintenance to a series of mindless, repetitive tasks. Lange 1927, 77.

54. Quoted in English translation in Guenther 2004, 67.

55. Quoted in English translation in Guenther 2004, 75.

56. Quoted in English translation in Guenther 2004, 95.

57. "Die Mode als Kampfmittel," *Münchner neueste Nachrichten* (August 27/28, 1921). See Guenther 2004, 63.

58. Quoted in English translation in Baumhoff 2001, 155–156.

59. Otto Bernhardt draws upon a contrasting set of gender values when he argues that the art of the gardener is superior to that of the architect. By emphasizing that the gardener "brings forth" his work and is involved in "lifelong nurturing," Bernhardt relies on traditional feminine virtues to make the case for the gardener's superiority. Otto Bernhardt, "Gärtner oder Künstler: Unmaßgeblich Meinungen eines Laien," *Die Gartenkunst* 9, no. 4 (1907): 67.

60. "Wie oft habe ich mir schon, wenn ich mit meinen Getreuen so recht bis über den Kopf im Gartenplanen steckte, weibliche Hilfskräfte gewünscht, die uns hoffnungslosen Form- und Verstandesmenschen bei der Zusammenfügung von Blumen und anderen Dingen ihre leichte Hand, ihre einfühlende Seele und ihre gottgegebene Ruhe liehen." Migge 1913, 89–90.

61. On the relation of the nature garden to reactionary political cultures in early twentieth-century Germany, see Wolschke-Bulmahn and Gröning 1992 and Wolschke-Bulmahn 1992.

62. "Der Sport sieht immer nur 'Ziele,' die Jugend muß wieder 'Wege' finden lernen, besonders in die Natur mit ihrem unerschöpflichen Reichtum an geistigen, seelischen Werten. Andernfalls ist alles, was wir von der Natur wissen, nur Material für Technik. Der geistig hochstehende, darum naturnahe Mittelstand leidet jetzt Not—und stirbt aus; hier liegen Aufgaben für Lehrer der Jugend. Ist der Materialismus als Weltanschauung überwunden—ihm entspricht der gebaute Garten südalpinen Stils—, dann wird der Idealismus in künstlerisch gesteigerter Natur sein Gartenziel suchen." Lange 1927, 13.

63. Lange makes this argument in a number of places, but a good summary can be found in Lange 1910, 5–6.

64. "Durchdringung—nicht ein Nebeneinander—von Bau- und Naturmotiven ist auch das höchste Ziel bei

der Gestaltung des Garten im ganzen. Dabei ist das Baumotiv immer als das stärkere, durchdringende Motiv zu denken, das Naturmotiv als das schwächere. Man könnte auch in männlichen und weiblichen Motiven, von allerlei anderen Gegensätzlichkeiten sprechen, die im Sinne eines Widerspiels (Polarität) das Ganze unseres Wahrnehmungs- und Empfindungswesens umspannen...." Willy Lange, *Gartenbilder: Mit Vorbildern aus der Natur* (Leipzig, 1922), 91–92. Lange's elevation of the "architectonic motive" over the "natural motive" here appears to be unique within his body of written work. My interpretation of this passage attempts to render it consistent with the views stated elsewhere in his books and essays.

65. Hermann Muthesius, *The English House*, 3 vols., ed. Dennis Sharp, trans. Janet Seligman and Stewart Spencer (London, 2007), 1:218.

66. Taut outlines a program for improving the efficiency of what he considers "woman's work" by streamlining residential spaces for modern lifestyles. He writes, "[New dwellings will provide] the woman with a way to improve her performance. She will adopt a new organization for her work and, with due consideration to the given circumstances, arrange to perform individual chores—tending the children, cooking, serving meals, washing up, cleaning, laundry, shopping, etc.—according to a plan. Sufficient time for going on walks and sleeping will be calculated into it, as the new home economics teaches, which amounts to the application of the Taylor System to the household. All the members of the household, the man and the children, will contribute to making the beds, cleaning the washstand, etc., as necessary." As translated in *The Weimar Republic Sourcebook*, ed. Anton Kaes, Martin Jay, and Edward Dimendberg (Berkeley, 1994), 461–462. Despite the thoroughness of Taut's treatment, however, the garden does not figure for him as a significant component of the dwelling.

67. Van Herck 2005, 130–131. One noteworthy passage in Taut's text maintains that while the woman is responsible for organizing the house, it is the man who organizes the office and the factory (Taut 1926, 104). Taut further suggests that because the (male) architect's practical and technical arguments are "masculine," they will not convince a woman, whose judgment relies on warmth and feelings (Taut 1926, 107).

68. Tatar 1995.

69. The design was prepared in 1925 for a nonjuried art exhibition in Berlin, the Juryfreie Kunstschau. Images and a review of Pohlenz' proposal can be found in Fritz Wilhelm Schönfeld, "Kritische Betrachtungen über drei Hausgärten (Pohlenz–Hübotter–Valentien)," *Die Gartenkunst* 39, vol. 3 (1926): 36–43. For a discussion of the design's significance see Wolschke-Bulmahn 1994, 17–30, and *Gartenarchitektur und Moderne in Deutschland im frühen 20. Jahrhundert: Drei Beiträge*, ed. Joachim Wolschke-Bulmahn and Andrea Koenecke (Hannover, 2005), 14–17.

70. In his review, Schönfeld recognized that Pohlenz' design shared its orientation to the future with many contemporary proposals, including those of Gustav Allinger, although he remained noncommittal with regard to their ultimate efficacy: "Ganz gleich, ob der 'Sonderbare Garten' der der Zukunft ist oder nicht: ein Mensch, der ohne Vorurteil an die Erzeugnisse seiner Umwelt geht, wird den feierlichen Eindruck empfinden, den dieser Entwurf macht." Schönfeld 1926, 41.

71. This play on words is not unique to my analysis. Many gay bars in Germany have used the names Sonderbar or Sonder Bar.

72. "Peculiar—*sonderbar*—has in modern German a negative connotation. To be labelled as peculiar means to be an outsider, to be odd and strange. And to be a stranger in a society such as the present German society may involve disadvantages, and may even include a threat to one's health or life. But to be peculiar, to be strange and different, can also be interpreted as stimulating, thought-provoking, remarkable, and enriching for one's culture." Wolschke-Bulmahn 1994, 17. In referring to the "outsider" status of the *sonderbarer Garten*, I also have in mind Peter Gay's classic work *Weimar Culture: The Outsider as Insider* (New York, 1968).

73. "Fassen wir unseren Beruf so auf, wie jene Männer den ihren, und die Gartenkunst, die jetzt oft ein armselig Aschenbrödel ist, wird sich dem Volke noch einmal zeigen als schmucke Prinzessin, die jeder liebt und achtet und verehrt." Reinhold Hoemann, "Neuzeitliche Bestrebungen auf dem Gebiete der Gartengestaltung," *Die Gartenkunst* 8, no. 11 (1906): 210.

JOHANNES STOFFLER

Modernism for the People:
Swimming Pool Landscapes in Switzerland

In 1934 the Zurich architectural historian Sigfried Giedion saw the Neues Bauen movement as standing at what he called a "remarkable crossroads."[1] Just six years previously, the Congrès Internationaux d'Architecture Moderne (CIAM) had been founded in La Sarraz, Switzerland, and Giedion appointed its secretary general. Now, as a committed propagandist of the art and architecture of modernism, Giedion paused for a moment to analyze the state of the movement. He was convinced of modernism's enduring international triumph, which, in his view, the new political situation in Germany and Russia would not affect in the long term. The crossroads of which Giedion wrote was more specifically pertinent to the question of how the "limited specialist circle" of architects should formulate its "claim on general public interest."[2] Giedion's sober pronouncement was:

The balance — or if one prefers, the inner equilibrium that is essential to a meaningful life — does not depend on the number of inventions or high production figures but on the ability to internalize what has been invented and produced — emotionally, economically, and politically.[3]

In other words, Giedion was posing the question of the everyday usefulness of 1920s avant-garde ideas. The previous phase of "puritan attitudes" among the avant-garde was flowing, as he saw it, into a new stage of modernism in which not only issues of form and economics but also individual emotional needs and political feasibility would play important roles.[4]

More explicitly but also more polemically formulated was the architect and art historian Peter Meyer's critique of the avant-garde

in modernism in the years that followed. Meyer (1894–1984) was, along with Giedion, one of the great protagonists but an equally energetic critic of Neues Bauen in Switzerland, and, from 1930, editor of the influential magazine *Das Werk*, organ of the Schweizerischer Werkbund, the Swiss artists' association. Meyer was quick to distance himself from what he called the "histrionic German emotional *Weltanschauung*" of the Bauhaus and ascribed to its followers a high level of narcissism and remoteness from ordinary life.[5] The Neues Bauen movement, Meyer held, could survive only if it evolved and if its representatives ceased "preaching to the converted."[6] Meyer called for a modernism in which people's needs for tradition, sentimental attachment, and coziness should also have their place. Neither bleak functionality nor rustic "masquerades and decorative shows" in architecture should be the aim, but rather a lively coexistence and interweaving of a restrained modernism on the one hand and vernacular built form on the other.[7]

Such an appeal reflected a broad-based reorientation of modernism in Switzerland in the 1930s that could finally make it an effective force in the larger society.[8] Progressive and conservative forces entered into a pragmatic and constructive dialogue that consciously sought to take account of popular needs and preferences, and that became an integral part of Switzerland's democratic culture.[9] This essay argues that in this popularization of modernism the designed landscape acquired a central role as mediator between architecture and people, between functional needs and sentimental preferences, and that this is clearly apparent in the development of the public outdoor swimming pool.

Crazy paving paths and luxuriant planting, Letzigraben public baths, Zurich, c. 1952

Nachlass Ammann, gta Archiv (NSL-Archiv), Eidgenössische Technische Hochschule, Zurich

1. *Kastenbad* (Belvoir women's baths), Zürichsee, Zurich, c. 1900
Baugeschichtliches Archiv Zürich

2. *Ausdruckstanz* by Mary Wigman, reformist colony of Monte Verità, Lake Maggiore, Ascona, 1913
Photograph Johann Adam Meisenbach; Monacensia Literaturarchiv und Bibliothek, Munich

From the *Kastenbad* to the Early Neues Bauen Lido

As early as the end of the nineteenth century, the public outdoor swimming pool had become an indicator of swiftly changing social conventions and ideas about hygiene in Switzerland. The predominant type around 1900 was still the *Kastenbad*, which made use of the country's numerous natural water features, a box fixed to pilings or floats in a river or anchored in a lake and equipped with changing cubicles and with separate facilities for men and women (fig. 1). Lingering at the pool was discouraged; its principal purpose was physical hygiene and brisk swimming. The common characteristic from which these pools derived their name (literally, box pool) was the high wooden wall that for reasons of propriety obscured the view into the pool but conversely prevented any contact with the surrounding landscape.

In the course of the turn-of-the-century movement known as *Lebensreform*, expectations of swimming in the open air also shifted away from the mere washing of the

body.[10] Numerous natural health associations in Switzerland propounded a more wholesome way of life, and in particular teetotalism, vegetarianism, regular outdoor gymnastics, sunbathing, and air baths.[11] They followed the precepts of natural healers such as the Swiss Arnold Rikli (1823–1906), also known as the Sunshine Doctor, who treated his patients with fresh air, showers, intensive sunbathing, and a vegetarian diet. Rikli's ideas were enthusiastically taken up at Monte Verità, a reformist colony in the mountains above Lake Maggiore in Italian Switzerland. Nudism and *Ausdruckstanz*, or dance in the open air, were firm features of a new, utopian way of life intended to offer an escape from rampant industrialization and bourgeois society (fig. 2).[12] In the course of this shift in social values the *Kastenbad* came to symbolize a bygone age, unhealthy and both spatially and morally constrictive. Moreover, the relatively few older public baths were quickly insufficient to meet the new enthusiasm for recreational bathing. *Wildes Baden*, or bathing—clothed or unclothed—in unspoiled lakes and rivers, thus grew in

3. Bathing in the wild (*wildes Baden*), Lake Constance, near Arbon, c. 1920

Photograph Max Burkhardt; Museumsgesellschaft Arbon

4. Geiselweid open-air pool, Winterthur, 1911

Winterthurer Bibliotheken, Sondersammlungen

popularity during the first two decades of the twentieth century; enthusiasts relished the socially dégagé and unconstrained sojourn in the open countryside (fig. 3). The many lidos that were established in these years, often at those unofficial bathing places, were intended to bring bathing back to "orderly" circumstances and ensure the separation of the sexes. For many, however, unofficial bathing in natural rivers and lakes was still immensely more pleasurable.[13]

In places lacking such natural features, engineering and technological inventions were applied. But the first baths to use the newly invented water filtration techniques, for example, were still deeply rooted in the nineteenth century in their spatial structures. Geiselweid swimming pool in Winterthur, built in 1910–1911 to designs by architects Rittmeyer & Furrer, was the first reinforced concrete pool with modern filtration technology in Switzerland (fig. 4). The needs of a nascent modern leisure society for extensive recreational areas were only partly gratified with a beachlike *Sandplatz* beside the pool. The newly awakened attraction to the open countryside also had to be subordinated to traditional morals and proprieties: the high fence enclosing the pool, which at first could never be used by men and women together, excluded the outside world completely.

The early Neues Bauen lidos were an initial response to the new public demand for more space for sports and games away from

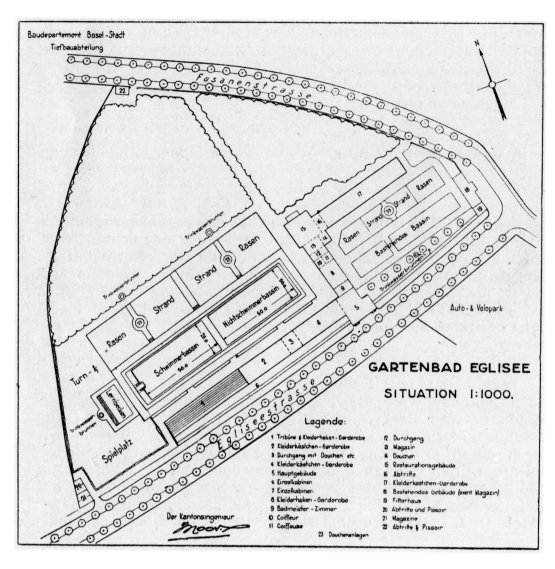

the swimming pool itself. This was clearly expressed at Gartenbad Eglisee in Basel, designed by the city's building inspector Theodor Hünerwadel (1864–1956). It opened in 1931 after two years of planning and construction as the largest and most important example of these early Neues Bauen public baths in Switzerland (figs. 5 and 6).[14] The public bath should be, in the words of Hans Hunziker (1878–1941), lecturer in hygiene at Universität Basel, a "place of physical culture that, along with swimming, offers extensive opportunity to enjoy fresh air and sunshine, that along with a sandy beach has green play areas and sports grounds where people can play and exercise—where happy, healthy people can take pleasure in their

lives."[15] The name *Gartenbad* indicated that the pool was complemented with generously proportioned sports facilities. Initially, these areas had little to do with a notion of garden design in which the elaborate use of plants played a major role; Gartenbad Eglisee was much more a manifestation of "hygienists' and technicians' knowledge and abilities."[16] In the double right angle of the long, flat-roofed building, everything required at a modern public pool was housed, from sanitary facilities to a restaurant and hairdresser to spectator stands. The building contained pools of various functions and depths: one smaller women's pool in the east separated from three sports and family pools for both sexes in the west. The pool water was

6. Gartenbad Eglisee, Basel, c. 1932, view across the lawn and beach to the swimmers' and non-swimmers' pools and building containing (left to right) restaurant, changing rooms, entrance hall with tower, changing rooms, spectator stands

Photograph H. Ochs-Walde; © Basler Denkmalpflege

filtered and chlorinated by the most modern German circulation systems. Next to the two long main pools was a rectangular, bordered sandy area with a sunbathing lawn and large outdoor showers. The adjacent wood to the north was thinned on its southern edge to form groves and otherwise left in its original state.

The distinctive quality of Gartenbad Eglisee was the way in which "it was designed, both outdoors and indoors, as an emphatically functional construction."[17] The primary task for this project lay in the logistical challenge of operating a public bath for up to five thousand visitors, or sports events with as many as two thousand spectators. The aesthetic of the complex celebrated this functionality, appearing to provide a techni-

cally perfected solution for all the visitor's needs. Even so, although Eglisee attracted the expected masses of visitors on hot days, it had two drawbacks. One was the forthrightly monumental architectural setting of a public pool for the masses, in which the individual was seen as part of a system. A brochure published for the opening made this clear:

The clothes lockers are consecutively numbered; this runs into four figures.... Visitors wishing to use the communal changing rooms would therefore, in order to spare themselves any inconvenience ... do well to mark the number of their locker very carefully.[18]

The other factor was that Eglisee did not fulfill the evidently still widespread yearning for a more natural setting. For many inhabitants of Basel, nothing could replace bathing in the Rhine, as described in 1944 by Basel writer and painter Johanna Von der Mühll:

[T]he real Basler, man or woman, goes to the new swanky public baths near the Badischer Bahnhof railway station only occasionally. They despise the still water in the artificial pools of Eglisee and stay true in their affection for being carried along by the strong, cold current that seeks its impetuous course below the Pfalz.[19]

The Invention of the *Parkbad*

The experience gained by planners of early Neues Bauen projects was of substantial significance for the further development of modernism in Switzerland and the subject of public debate. Critical reflection on what had been achieved so far was an important part of various exhibitions staged in Zurich between 1929 and 1935 on the issues of housing settlements, schools, and public baths.[20] The exhibition *Das Bad heute und gestern*, which opened in the spring of 1935 at Zurich's Kunstgewerbemuseum,

7. Herbert Matter, exhibition poster, *Das Bad heute und gestern*, Kunstgewerbemuseum Zürich, 1935
Museum für Gestaltung, Zürich

addressed the construction of public baths as a pressing issue because the city's *Kastenbäder* and public baths were chronically overcrowded (fig. 7). Furthermore, for many residents of the swiftly expanding suburbs of Zurich, the lakes and rivers at the centre of the city were unreasonably distant. The Social Democratic government of "Rotes Zürich" (1928–1949) therefore planned new open-air baths for outlying districts. The moving spirits of the exhibition were Sigfried Giedion and young architects and CIAM founding members trained at the Eidgenössische Technische Hochschule: Werner Max Moser (1896–1970), Rudolf Steiger (1900–1982), and Max Ernst Haefeli (1901–1971). Many other Werkbund members contributed to the exhibition, among them the Zurich garden architect Gustav Ammann (1885–1955). The exhibition called for public baths that, unlike Gartenbad Eglisee, which solely served the purposes of personal hygiene and sport, provided more places for leisure and relaxation. The exhibition proposed that a visit to a public bath should also be an experience of landscape. Rudolf Steiger set out the idea:

From closed, floating baths to the structurally rigid and geometrically organized family pools of today, there will have to be a further development to informal, loosely arranged facilities with a very strong inclusion of landscape values [*landschaftliche Werte*].[21]

The swift response to these demands was Freibad Allenmoos, the first municipal district baths in the north of Zurich and the prototypical *Parkbad*.[22] Just a few months after the exhibition closed its doors, Zurich's city council staged a public pool design competition in which architects Max Ernst Haefeli and Werner Max Moser carried off the laurels for their joint project. The jury particularly commended their design for "striving for informality," which distinguished it markedly from the geometrical organization and layout of comparable facilities (fig. 8).[23] The grounds of the winning project were, however, only schematically represented; what was clear was the

8. Max Ernst Haefeli and Werner
Max Moser, winning design,
Freibad Allenmoos competition,
Zurich, 1935

Schweizerische Bauzeitung *54, no. 21
(1936): 232*

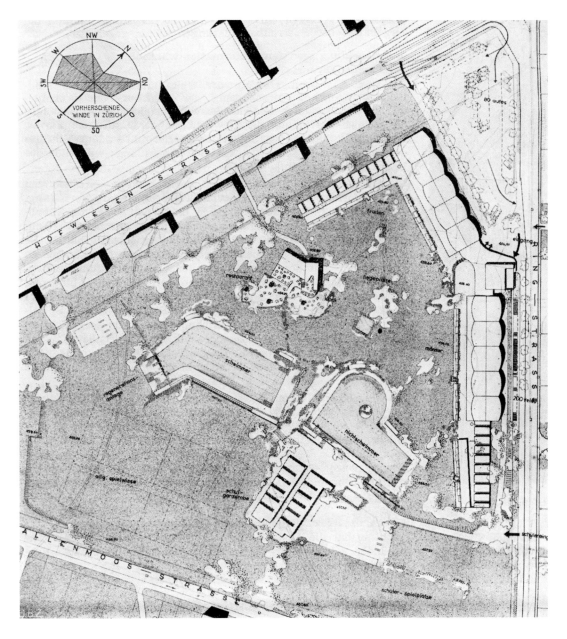

architects' intention to set the pools in a broad
expanse of lawn and informal shrubbery.

To remedy this weakness in their treatment of the grounds, the winners invited the
garden architect Gustav Ammann to rework
the project. Ammann was the natural choice
for the team; they had cooperated successfully just a few years earlier, in 1930–1932,
on the Werkbundsiedlung Neubühl, a Zurich
housing settlement. Ammann had not
only established a reputation as an enthu-
siastic experimenter and forward thinker
of his profession in Switzerland; he also

called for a consistently informal, "natural"
(*natürlich*) design style for gardens, something that made him an ideal partner for the
architects who wished to give more weight
to landscape values (*landschaftliche Werte*),
as Steiger had called them.[24]

Ammann had in fact entered the design
competition with another team, which had
finished second. In planning that submission
he had advocated an informal, natural design
for the grounds but had not been able to
overcome the opposition of his architect partners. A surviving sketch plays with the idea

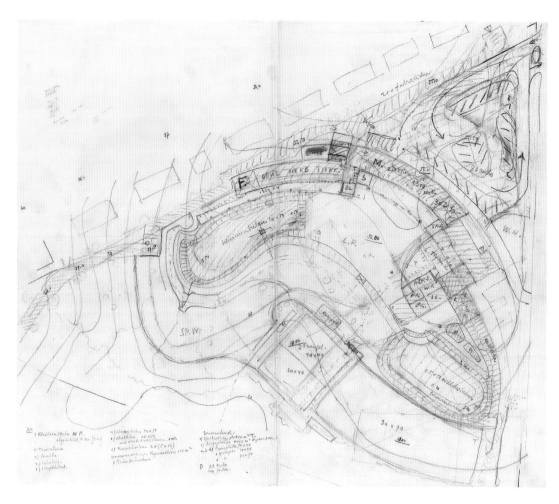

9. Gustav Ammann, topographical sketch plan, Freibad Allenmoos competition, Zurich, 1935

Nachlass Ammann, gta Archiv (NSL-Archiv), Eidgenössische Technische Hochschule, Zurich

10. Model of Freibad Allenmoos as built, Zurich, c. 1939

Werk 34, no. 7 (1947): 213

of organically shaped pools set like natural ponds, as low as possible in the terrain (fig. 9). Ammann also embedded the buildings in the gently undulating site and developed them along the contour. This alignment of open-air baths with the existing topography was comparable to that of Haefeli and Moser's winning project, and thus Amman played an important role in the subsequent reworking of their design. He assumed the entire responsibility for the planning and layout of the grounds, from pathways to landscaping and planting schemes.

After construction delays caused by an economic crisis, Freibad Allenmoos opened in 1939. At its center lay the adults' pool, for swimmers, and the children's pool, for nonswimmers, both of which deviated from the conventional rectangular form, enclosed in abundantly blooming flowerbeds that

11. View across mixed border to nonswimmers' pool, Freibad Allenmoos, Zurich, c. 1945
Baugeschichtliches Archiv Zürich

the open countryside. Nevertheless, it was not a perfect imitation of nature, based on ecologically correct plant societies, that interested him, but rather the "vegetation picture" (*Vegetationsbild*) of the landscape and its free, artistic interpretation.[25] For example, he used the moisture-loving poplar as a quotation from riparian vegetation close to the pools while integrating these trees in a mixed border whose numerous ornamental shrubs and herbaceous cultures bloomed throughout the bathing season (fig. 11). Moreover, Ammann's gardenist interpretation of the riverbank landscape found space not only for indigenous species but also for such exotics as Caucasian wingnut and Chinese silvergrass. He used well over a hundred species and varieties of woody plants and an equally rich assortment of herbaceous perennials in the planting design for Freibad Allenmoos, which is popularly known today as Arboretum Zürich-Nord.

Ammann drew his primary inspiration for this form of plant use from the "wild gardening" of the English reform garden[26] and particularly the creations of Gertrude Jekyll (1843–1932), whose approach he also discerned and valued in the work of the German herbaceous perennial breeder Karl Foerster (1874–1970). Ammann explained his approach: "Now the new English garden reenters in triumph, with loosely arranged masses of shrubs and flowering herbaceous perennials, with crazy paving paths, drystone masonry overgrown with cushion plants and other motifs."[27] Repeatedly and euphorically, Ammann spoke of the "English spectacles" (eyeglasses) that he put on in order to design and which, since the end of the 1920s, had markedly influenced modernist garden architecture in Switzerland.

Above and beyond such garden finesse, the landscape vision in which the *Parkbad* was founded evoked a backward-looking critique of civilization; the new bathing landscape artistically staged a better world that was believed lost. This had been ideal-

restricted access to the water to a few points with footbaths. On the lawn around the pools, loosely arranged clumps of trees provided shade while creating separate park spaces and framing the baths and their activities in a picturesque setting (fig. 10).

Public Bath Landscapes: Between Nostalgia and Progressive Convictions

Ammann's planting designs for the *Parkbad* incorporated numerous references to

12. "Ideal" preindustrial riparian landscape

Paul Schultze-Naumburg, Kultur-arbeiten, *vol. 8,* Die Gestaltung der Landschaft durch den Menschen *(Munich, 1916), 240*

evident have become consciously relished delights."[30]

Yet the Freibad Allenmoos landscape was on no account intended as a museum piece, a return to a long-lost world. Rather, it was to reshape suitable images from the past for modern Swiss society. This meant that such landscape images had to be reinterpreted to meet the requirements of urban mass activity and its specific needs for play, sport, and recreation. Functionality and economy were thus the crucial criteria on which not only the buildings but especially the grounds of the *Parkbad* would have to be judged. Notwithstanding the "casual," park-like design, the baths therefore had a clear system of visitor management by which up to thirty-six hundred bathers were guided, though they may not have been aware of it. The layout determined at which places visitors should change, shower, rest, eat, play ballgames, enter the pools, and swim. As these were family baths, various areas were reserved for adults, young people, and children, separated by loose plantings of trees. At other places, too, the plantings reinforced the functional requirements of the baths' operations. The blooming herbaceous borders enclosing the pools also included thorny plants and were intended to prevent barefoot visitors from taking the shortest way to the water. Instead the thorns compelled them to walk through one of the footbaths in the gaps between herbaceous beds, to prevent soiling the pool. Nor were considerations of function and economy excluded from the planting plans; to keep the costs of planting and maintenance as low as possible, improved, hardy, and long-blooming varieties were bred, which were adapted to the conditions of the location and could form durable plant groupings.

ized by conservative reformists like Paul Schultze-Naumburg (1869–1949), one of the founders of the Bund Heimatschutz (homeland conservation association) as early as 1901 in his *Kulturarbeiten* (fig. 12). Its leitmotif was the aesthetic configuration of preindustrial natural and cultural landscapes that had apparently been spared the "appalling devastation of our land in all areas of visual culture."[28] During his training, from 1905 to 1911, Ammann was influenced by Schultze-Naumburg's early writings, and he joined the Zürcher Heimatschutz in 1923; that he was concurrently working successfully with leading architects in the avant-garde of modernism in Switzerland is a clear indication of the broad consensus that reigned in both the traditionalist and the progressive camps with regard to such landscape values.[29] In 1939 Peter Meyer traced this consensus to an all-embracing phenomenon of modern society, nourished by a deep sensibility of the loss of tradition and nature: "The exponential industrialization of Europe and intensification of agriculture ... have lent untouched tracts of land the quality of an exception, of rarity. Beauties that formerly went unnoticed because they were self-

"Romantic" Modernism

In contrast to the grounds, the architecture of the baths at Freibad Allenmoos offered a self-confident showcase of the new style consistent with the sculptural possibil-

ities of reinforced concrete. The restaurant building referred, moreover, to the motif, so popular in modernist architecture, of the ocean liner, complete with railings, which was suited both to the aquatic context and to the wide-ranging enthusiasm of the avant-garde for the aesthetics of machinery (fig. 13). But apart from its display of function and technology, the architecture, when compared to works such as the Gartenbad Eglisee, was notably small-scale and non-monumental, appearing to have been sited around the park landscape in a reserved fashion. The elegant structures were framed by and interspersed with vegetation and were subordinated to the sentimental setting of the grounds. Together with the landscaping, they formed a complementary unity; architecture and park landscape created a common space in which functionality and emotion, enthusiasm for technology and yearning for nature, modernism and tradition were all interwoven. Nature became the substructure within which these contradictions of the age could be resolved harmoniously and, for the public, comprehensibly. Thereby a conception of modern-

ism was manifested that completely refuted the "rejection of nature" that had partly shaped the avant-garde of the 1920s.[31] In 1938 Werner Max Moser himself characterized the joint achievement at Allenmoos as "romantic" in the best sense of the word. Romanticism, according to Moser, was "in no way the opposite of modern, as Neues Bauen wishes most strongly to take account of, and to express emotional values— through and arising from function."[32] And Gustav Ammann had already propounded six years earlier: "The garden for our times is, then, along with a pure fulfillment of purpose, perhaps also an unfulfilled dream country for many who wish once again to gaze upon blades of grass, leaves, flowers, and fruits."[33]

Inaugurated in 1939, Allenmoos was a tremendous success. At the opening, a reviewer in the *Neue Zürcher Zeitung* remarked that it had proven possible "to create an integrity of form within which the human being can live in harmony with the physical and spiritual influences of earth and water, air and light."[34] Progressivism allied with sentiment marked this new and particular construct

of modernism. No less important, the splen-
dor of the flowers must have made a strong
contribution to the public bath's popularity.
What Giedion had called for in 1934 had
finally come to pass: Neues Bauen had—at
least as far as public baths were concerned—
stepped out of its "limited specialist circle"
and been enthusiastically received by the
general public.[35]

Counterworlds for the Individual

Even neutral Switzerland was not spared
the trauma of World War II. With Hitler's
breach of the Treaty of Versailles in 1936,
an invasion by German forces became a
conceivable threat, and on the "Schwarzer
Tag," as the country's media called it, of
the outbreak of war, September 1, 1939,
Switzerland mobilized. Just one year later
the Alpine land found itself surrounded
by fascist countries and their new provinces, while internal tensions arose between
Switzerland's own political extremes.[36]

Against this background, the role of the
Parkbad also shifted. Whereas Freibad
Allenmoos was above all intended to promote equilibrium between body and spirit,
sport and recreation, the subsequent generation of public baths foregrounded the
individual's yearning for comfort and security. The baths also served the social organism in the sense that they created jobs and
offered an innocuous leisure activity. In an
era when cities were regarded as politically
unstable, and, by contrast, the countryside
and rural Switzerland were viewed as the
redoubt of the democratic Swiss Confedera-
tion, park baths became a political instrument serving as rural implantations in the
city; they offered the diverting, flowery
scenery of an unsullied world far from the
brutal realities of world war.[37]

This was especially apparent at Freibad
Letzigraben in Zurich, built in 1942–1949
as a joint project by Gustav Ammann
and the architect and writer Max Frisch
(1911–1991).[38] Frisch's strictly functional

architecture drew its charm from emphatically filigree constructions and whimsical
details. Not only did the restaurant pavilion
reflect a newly awakened desire for ornamentation that was carried almost seam-
lessly into the outdoor spaces; new design
emphases were apparent in the grounds
themselves, laid out for a substantial forty-
two hundred visitors a day (fig. 14). Along
with an emphatically diverse planting
scheme, Freibad Letzigraben differed from
Allenmoos in its extensive use of the most
varied natural stonework in winding paths
of crazy paving, as well as edging and rustic stone walls (fig. 15). The grounds were
intended, in their emphatically modest proportions, to distract visitors from everyday
cares and woes and to offer places of refuge
in the midst of the massive communal baths.
The decisive criterion in the design of the
grounds was a sense of intimacy. Thus the
magazine *Das Werk* remarked:

To a far greater extent than at Allenmoos, Letzigraben
exemplifies a striving for the greatest possible dis-
aggregation of all the built structures.... The numerous,
constantly varying garden sections and plant groupings
in combination with the architecture, pools and terrac-

ing engender in the visitor a feeling of being, rather
than part of a crowd, in an intimate setting.[39]

The *Parkbad* in the Postwar Era

After 1945 Allenmoos and Letzigraben
attracted international attention. In a war-
ravaged Europe these baths were seen as
shining examples illuminating a new dawn
of modernism, promising escape from the
ruins of everyday life and conveying a feeling of personal comfort and security. In
the postwar years, in fact, there was a
lively general interest in Swiss city planning, architecture, and landscape architecture, which had been pursued throughout
the war because of the country's neutrality
and which now offered an abundance of
demonstration material for European reconstruction. The *Parkbad* was understood as
an integral part of decentralized "organic
urban development" (*organischer Städtebau*) with its widely spaced ribbon developments, green corridors, and generously
proportioned school grounds. "Helvetia
docet," proclaimed German architect Rudolf
Schwarz (1897–1961) admiringly on the
occasion of an exhibition on Swiss architecture shown in Cologne in 1948. Numerous international publications documented
reawakened interest during the postwar
era in Swiss architecture and garden design,
among them *Switzerland Builds* (1950)
by American architect and commentator
George Everard Kidder Smith, who offered
Parkbad Allenmoos as an exemplar of the
high regard for the social value of open-air
baths in Switzerland (fig. 16). He wrote
that "almost every Swiss town has some
sort of outdoor pool."[40] A further example,
presented in *Schweizer Architektur* (1951)
by German architect Hans Volkart, eluci-
dated the Swiss "object lesson" through
numerous descriptions of projects, including Letzigraben and Allenmoos (fig. 17).[41]
Switzerland itself also contributed to the
dissemination of *Parkbad* ideas, whether
in gardening books, such as *Landscape
Gardens*, by Gustav Ammann, or the Swit-

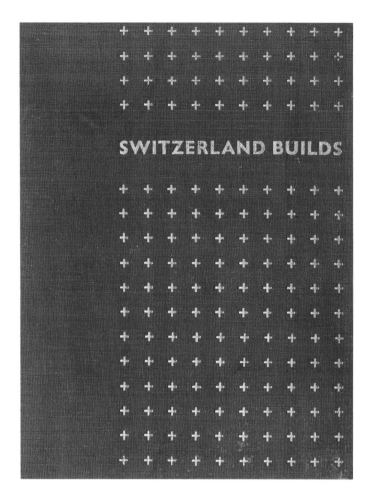

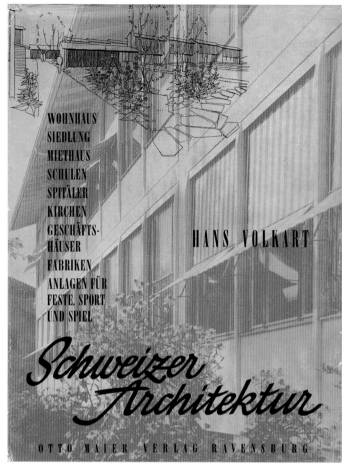

16–19. Exports of Swiss building
and garden culture after World
War II

16. G. E. Kidder Smith, *Switzerland Builds: Its Native and Modern Architecture* (New York and
Stockholm, 1950), cover

17. Hans Volkart, *Schweizer
Architektur: Ein Überblick über
das schweizerische Bauschaffen
der Gegenwart* (Ravensburg, 1951),
cover

zerland Planning and Building Exhibition,
staged in London in 1946 at the invitation
of the Royal Institute of British Architects
and subsequently shown in Copenhagen
(figs. 18 and 19).[42] In 1956, when the fifth
congress of the International Federation
of Landscape Architects (IFLA) was held in
Zurich, it was astonishingly well attended:
more than 250 participants from 25 countries gathered impressions of Swiss landscape architecture from the preceding 25
years in lectures and tours. The resounding
success of the congress, according to the editorial of the German magazine *Garten und
Landschaft*, could also be ascribed to "the
congress venue, Zurich, which in the postwar era exercised a particular fascination
for garden architects."[43]

Sigfried Giedion also contributed to
the further dissemination of the *Parkbad*.

Although he reproached Swiss architecture
of the 1940s for offering the public too
much "coziness" and saw it as "endangered
by sentimental trends," he appeared to
welcome thoroughly the same sentimentality in landscape design, and he never
fundamentally questioned the *Parkbad*
concepts of design and content.[44] In his
documentation of the CIAM 6 congress,
which assembled, under the title *A Decade
of New Architecture*, a selection of "visionary" constructions designed between 1937
and 1947, he therefore praised Freibad
Allenmoos as a felicitous combination of
landscape and architecture: "Special care
was devoted to the development of the trees
and flowers and to the unobtrusive character of the buildings."[45] For the new editor
of *Das Werk*, Alfred Roth (1903–1998),
a former employee of Le Corbusier and

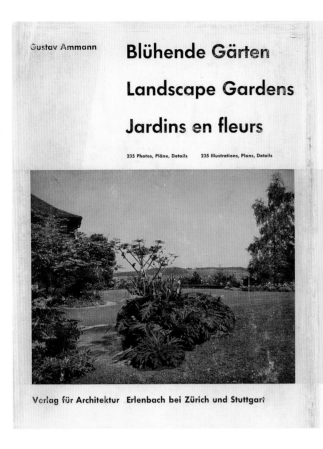

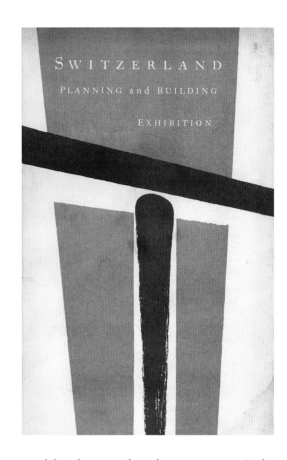

18. Gustav Ammann, *Blühende Gärten / Landscape Gardens / Jardins en fleurs* (Zurich-Erlenbach, 1955), cover

19. *Switzerland Planning and Building Exhibition* (Royal Institute of British Architects; Zurich, 1946), cover

friend of Giedion, Freibad Allenmoos "set the direction for future amenities."[46] Roth underlined the "natural" composition of the *Parkbad*:

The character of public baths should, wherever possible, be close to that of a natural park, assimilated organically in the city district, the local prospect or the landscape. Following such considerations, pools too should resemble natural ponds and be liberated from the rigidity of the conventional rectangular shape. Natural features such as elevations in the terrain should be utilized to lend the park as free and lively a form as possible.[47]

Designs resulting from the open-air bathing boom that began after World War II in Switzerland and continued into the 1970s were in their essentials based on Freibad Allenmoos, the prototypical *Parkbad*, although with variations following contemporary taste: for one, the pool shape, which increasingly departed from the natural-pond

model and returned to clear-cut geometrical forms, and for another the renaissance of concrete, which, after wartime shortages, became more readily available at the beginning of the 1950s and superseded stone walls and crazy paving. In Switzerland, this development also brought a long-drawn-out leavetaking from the internationally popular motifs of the Edwardian garden, whose "miles of dreary dry-walling and crazy paving" were so sharply criticized by architect Peter Shepheard in his *Modern Gardens* (1953).[48] What remained unchanged, though, were the picturesque, parklike aesthetic of the plantings and the interpenetration of architecture and landscape. The idea of a municipal open-air bath in a naturalistic setting as it first found a practical form to meet the public's needs at Freibad Allenmoos was enduringly popular. It was held up as a model of design even in 1959 in the guidelines for green space in local communities published by the Schweizerische Vereinigung

für Landesplanung.[49] From Dübendorf to Delémont, from Bern to Basel, up and down the country new public baths were built, in Gustav Ammann's words, as "a haven of felicity amid the toil and moil of the workaday world," expressing the great longing of modern society for a life close to nature (fig. 20).[50] The widespread popularity of sentimental images of nature was unabated—even though these natural images were highly artificial and functional products.

NOTES

Translated from the German by Mic Hale

I thank Christophe Girot, Eidgenössische Technische Hochschule, Zurich, who has generously and energetically supported my research into modernist landscape architecture in Switzerland. My thanks also go to Anette Freytag and Sibylle Hoiman for their constructive criticism.

1. Sigfried Giedion, "Leben und Bauen," in *Sigfried Giedion: Wege in die Öffentlichkeit; Aufsätze und unveröffentlichte Schriften aus den Jahren 1926–1956*, ed. Dorothee Huber (Zurich, 1987), 119. Architectural historians use the term *Neues Bauen* to denote the avant-garde school of modernist architecture between 1918 and 1933 in the German-speaking world. See Vittorio Magnago Lampugnani, ed., *Lexikon der Architektur des 20. Jahrhunderts* (Ostfildern-Ruit, 1998), 263. Neues Bauen architects in Switzerland, however, also applied it to modernist architecture after 1933 (see n. 32 below).

2. Giedion 1987, 119.

3. Giedion 1987, 119.

4. Giedion 1987, 121.

5. Peter Meyer, "Vom Bauhaus Dessau," *Schweizerische Bauzeitung* 45, no. 25 (1927): 334.

6. Peter Meyer, "Die Architektur der Landesausstellung-kritische Besprechung," *Das Werk* 26, no. 11 (1939): 322.

7. Peter Meyer, "Situation der Architektur 1940," *Das Werk* 27, no. 9 (1940): 248.

8. Sonja Hildebrand et al., eds., *Haefeli Moser Steiger, die Architekten der Schweizer Moderne* (Zurich, 2007).

9. Michael Koch and Bruno Maurer, "Zauberformeln," in *Architektur im 20. Jahrhundert: Schweiz*, ed. Anna Meseure et al. (Munich, 1998), 35–44.

10. Kai Buchholz et al., eds., *Die Lebensreform: Entwürfe zur Neugestaltung von Leben und Kunst um 1900*, vol. 1 (Darmstadt, 2001).

11. Eva Büchi, *Als die Moral Baden ging: Badeleben am schweizerischen Bodensee- und Rheinufer 1850–1950 unter dem Einfluss der Hygiene und der Lebensreform* (Frauenfeld, 2003), 106.

12. Simon Baur, *Ausdruckstanz in der Schweiz: Anregungen, Einflüsse, Auswirkungen in der ersten Hälfte des 20. Jahrhunderts* (Wilhelmshaven, 2010); Martin Green, *Mountain of Truth: The Counterculture Begins, Ascona, 1900–1920* (Hannover and London, 1986).

13. Büchi 2003, 65.

14. The design has hitherto been attributed to Hünerwadel's successor, Julius Maurizio (1894–1968); see Dorothee Huber, *Architekturführer Basel: Die Baugeschichte der Stadt und ihrer Umgebung* (Basel, 1993), 285. However, Maurizio first took up his post as Hünerwadel's assistant on November 15, 1929, and

the application for a building permit was submitted on January 3, 1929. Furthermore, all the plans for the construction project bear Hünerwadel's signature. I thank Erwin Baumgartner of the city of Basel heritage conservation authority for pointing this out.

15. Hans Hunziker, "Das neue Basler Gartenbad Eglisee," separate offprint of *Technische Hygiene*, nos. 4–5 (1932): 1.

16. Hunziker 1932, 1.

17. Sanitätsdepartement Basel-Stadt, ed., *Das Gartenbad Eglisee* (Basel, 1931), 13.

18. Sanitätsdepartement Basel-Stadt 1931, 39.

19. Johanna Von der Mühll, *Basler Sitten: Herkommen und Brauch im häuslichen Leben einer städtischen Bürgerschaft* (Basel, 1944), 93.

20. These included an exhibition on school buildings, *Der neue Schulbau*, shown in 1932, and one on the Werkbundsiedlung Neubühl housing development (built 1928–1932).

21. Rudolf Steiger, "Das öffentliche Bad," in "Weiterbauen: Zusammengestellt durch die Schweizergruppe der Internationalen Kongresse für Neues Bauen," supplement, *Schweizer Bauzeitung* 2, no. 4 (1935): 27.

22. Alfred Roth, "Freibadeanlagen," *Das Werk* 34, no. 7 (1947): 210.

23. Stadt Zürich, "Bericht des Preisgerichts über den Wettbewerb zur Erlangung von Plänen für eine Freibadeanlage im Allenmoos in Zurich 6/7. Februar 1936," 11, Nachlass Ammann, gta Archiv (NSL-Archiv), Eidgenössische Technische Hochschule, Zurich (hereafter abbreviated ETH).

24. Gustav Ammann, "'Vom Naturgarten zum natürlichen Garten,'" *Neue Zürcher Zeitung*, no. 1674 (September 1, 1929), 1st Sunday edition; Johannes Stoffler, *Gustav Ammann: Landschaften der Moderne in der Schweiz* (Zurich, 2008), 82.

25. Gustav Ammann, "Freibad Allenmoos: Die Grünanlagen," *Neue Zürcher Zeitung*, no. 1132 (June 22, 1939), evening edition.

26. David Ottewill, *The Edwardian Garden* (New Haven and London, 1989), 5. See also W[illiam] Robinson, *The Wild Garden, or, Our Groves & Shrubberies Made Beautiful by the Naturalization of Hardy Exotic Plants: With a Chapter on the Garden of British Wild Flowers* (London, 1870).

27. Gustav Ammann, "Vom Naturgarten zum natürlichen Garten," *Neue Zürcher Zeitung*, no. 1674 (September 1, 1929), 1st Sunday edition.

28. Paul Schultze-Naumburg, *Kulturarbeiten*, vol. 1 (Munich, 1901), foreword, n.p.; see also Celia Applegate, *A Nation of Provincials: The German Idea of Heimat* (Berkeley, CA, 1990); William H. Rollins, *A Greener Vision of Home: Cultural Politics and Environmental Reform in the German Heimatschutz Movement 1904–1918* (Ann Arbor, 1997).

29. Steiger 1935, 27.

30. Peter Meyer, "Garten, Landschaft, Architektur," *Schweizerische Bauzeitung* 57, no. 18 (1939): 209.

31. Steven A. Mansbach, "Introduction to the Round Table on Avant-Garde and Garden Design," Center for Advanced Study in the Visual Arts, National Gallery of Art, and Garden and Landscape Studies, Dumbarton Oaks, Washington, DC, February 1994, manuscript, quoted in Joachim Wolschke-Bulmahn, "The Avant-Garde and Garden Architecture in Germany: On a Forgotten Phenomenon of the Weimar Period," *Centropa* 2, no. 2 (2004): 102.

32. Werner Max Moser, lecture manuscript, January 29, 1938, Nachlass Moser, gta Archiv, ETH.

33. Gustav Ammann, "Der zeitgemässe Garten," in "Zeitgemässes Wohnen," supplement to the *Tages-Anzeiger*, Nachlass Ammann, gta Archiv (NSL-Archiv), ETH, Belegbuch 2, 66.

34. Anonymous, "Freibad Allenmoos: Rundgang durch die Anlagen," *Neue Zürcher Zeitung*, no. 1132 (June 22, 1939), evening edition.

35. Giedion 1987, 119.

36. Jean-François Bergier, ed., *Die Schweiz, der Nationalsozialismus und der Zweite Weltkrieg* (Zurich, 2002).

37. Bergier 2002, 75–78. On the political significance of the landscape, see Stoffler 2008, 126.

38. Johannes Stoffler, "Eine blühende Badelandschaft," in *Freibad Letzigraben: Von Max Frisch und Gustav Ammann*, ed. Ulrich Binder and Pierre Geering (Zurich, 2007), 121–124.

39. Alfred Roth, "Freibad Letzigraben in Zürich," *Das Werk* 37, no. 9 (1950): 274.

40. G. E. Kidder Smith, *Switzerland Builds: Its Native and Modern Architecture* (New York and Stockholm, 1950), 193.

41. Hans Volkart, *Schweizer Architektur: Ein Überblick über das schweizerische Bauschaffen der Gegenwart* (Ravensburg, 1951). The Letzigraben lido is discussed on 214–216.

42. Gustav Ammann, *Blühende Gärten / Landscape Gardens / Jardins en fleurs* (Zurich-Erlenbach, 1955); *Switzerland Planning and Building Exhibition* (Royal Institute of British Architects; Zurich, 1946).

43. Ernst Cramer and Gerda Gollwitzer, "Schweizer Gartengespräch," *Garten und Landschaft* 26, no. 12 (1956): 357.

44. Sigfried Giedion, *A Decade of New Architecture* (Zurich, 1951), 2.

45. Giedion 1951, 155.

46. Roth 1947, 210.

47. Roth 1947, 210.

48. Peter Shepheard, *Modern Gardens: Masterworks of International Garden Architecture* (London 1953), 15.

49. Schweizerische Vereinigung für Landesplanung, ed., *Die Grünflächen in den Gemeinden: Richtlinien* (Zurich, 1959).

50. Ammann 1955, 22.

ALAN POWERS

*Modernism and Romantic Regeneration
in the English Landscape, 1920–1940*

A modernist approach to landscape design existed in England before World War II, but if we consider it only as a movement in the visual arts, it involved a small group of people, smaller even than those concerned with modern architecture.[1] It was the period in which a profession of landscape architecture began to take shape in the practice and writing of Geoffrey Jellicoe and Christopher Tunnard, following the foundation of the Institute of Landscape Architects in 1929, with the significant figures Brenda Colvin and Sylvia Crowe already at work but less publicly visible. Tunnard's book *Gardens in the Modern Landscape* (1939), the sole attempt at a manifesto for modernism in landscape, illustrated only a handful of his own projects for the gardens of modern houses, not all of them executed, and a proposal for replanning Claremont Park, an eighteenth-century estate in Surrey, with slab block housing, but surprisingly little else to show what modernism in landscape might mean (fig. 1). Although Geoffrey Jellicoe later became a leading practitioner, before 1939 his landscape work, as opposed to his architecture, had barely begun to develop a specifically modernist visual language.[2] Only during and after World War II did the landscape design profession achieve an independent identity and take its place among garden design, architecture, and planning, with some overlap into all these categories.

In architecture, modernism is identifiable by certain clear signifiers such as flat roofs. In landscape, nothing so obvious can be assumed. The continuity between modernism in landscape and its precursors is greater than any sense of contrast. Argu-

ably, the difference comes less from a new aesthetic than from a new articulation of landscape's role in a continuum of practices extending from planning to agriculture, oriented toward some conscious ideal of a better future. Even here, the difference between modernism and the early garden cities is far from absolute. It therefore seems fruitful to look beyond the profession literally defined to examine the many things landscape signified to many people—the nostalgic, the ecological, the touristic, the national, and the political—while also representing a sphere for creative design. The related activity was largely polemical and voluntary, but it was highly visible in books and other publications, forming the basis for later developments and engaging the attention of opinion-formers and the large number of lovers of the countryside who lived mostly in cities and suburbs. I have chosen the term "romantic regeneration" to convey two aspects that were fused during the 1930s and help characterize the momentum in landscape activity that carried through World War II to become much more visible and effective after 1945.

It could be said that for most of the twentieth century, the English countryside was cast in the role of victim. It had suffered from long-term change caused by agricultural decline since the 1870s, leading to depopulation, and was subject to threats from advancing modernity such as penetration by cars and the commercial opportunities for ramshackle services and advertising that they afforded; uncontrolled building development; overhead power lines; and much else besides. Some commentators greeted these immediate problems only with

1. Christopher Tunnard, drawing by Gordon Cullen, proposal for redevelopment of Claremont Park, Esher, Surrey, 1938

Architectural Review 54, no. 502 (1938): 114

pessimism, but others became active in seeking ways of dealing with them and considered longer-term strategies to mitigate the effects of change. The different responses that the plight of the countryside evoked then remain a subject of study and fascination, while the sense that modernity poses risks to a natural and social order outside cities is as strong as ever.

In the eyes of some commentators, however, the countryside is less the victim than the perpetrator of decline. This idea is particularly associated with one book, *English Culture and the Decline of the Industrial Spirit, 1850–1980*, by the American historian Martin J. Wiener, published in 1981, proposing that, but for a misguided sentimentality about the land and a life free from the taint of commerce and industry, Britain might have enjoyed more enterprise and greater prosperity.[3] Wiener's work was in the neoconservative spirit of its time, although he was not the first to take an unsentimental view of the ruralists' imagined past and future. Since 1981 a number of historians have scrutinized the way in which the countryside was constructed by writers between the wars, finding their vision bizarre and detached from reality; yet arguably some of these ideas deserve more sympathetic attention.[4]

Between these two positions lies a field of ideas in which the definition of modernism in landscape can be tested against various evidence provided by activities and writings of the period. In 1997 Peter Mandler contested the terms in which the debate had been constructed, suggesting instead that "across Europe the historical impulse and modernisation often went hand in hand in the nineteenth century, causing little cognitive dissonance." Mandler proposed that in the interwar period "England did become a kind of 'post-urban' culture, but not in the backward-looking way so often assumed, and, still, less tempted by true rural nostalgia than other European countries."[5]

The question of what constitutes modernism in twentieth-century landscape is addressed in the conclusion of David Haney's study of Leberecht Migge, *When Modern Was Green*.[6] In his career in Germany between 1900 and 1935, Migge collaborated as a landscape designer with several leading modern architects, but his ideas about self-sufficient agriculture based on traditional principles, similar in many respects to those of some of the English organicists, who were a principal target of much later criticism, might put him in a different category. This example calls into question the reliability and usefulness of the standard categories of modernism. Haney quotes Bruno Latour:

Modernism — like its anti- and post-modern corollaries — was only the provisional result of a selection made by a small number of agents in the name of all. If there are more of us who regain the capacity to do our own sorting of the elements that belong to our time, we will rediscover the freedom of movement that modernism denies us — a freedom that, in fact, we have never really lost.[7]

This possibility of reconsidering the past is particularly relevant to understanding the never very clear definition of modernism in landscape (especially in its English context), whether as a design practice or as a more broadly based cultural activity. The assumption that the country is by nature conservative and antimodern appears in contrast with the strong concern among the modernist design community in England in the 1930s about preserving landscapes and the livelihoods that went with them, uniting the more traditional architects and designers with modernists in the Campaign for the Protection of Rural England (CPRE) and the Design and Industries Association (DIA).[8] Arguably, their commitment stemmed less from an alignment with a particular design language than from a shared background of class, education, and culture at the beginning of the century, as a result of which they held in common a belief that the countryside was under threat and could be protected if the right measures were taken.

The modern movement in architecture was not just about buildings and their ability

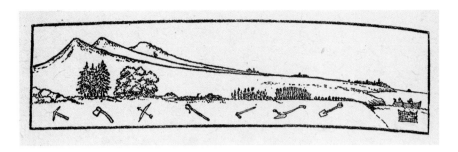

2. Patrick Geddes, *The Valley Plan of Civilization*, showing the valley section and the basic occupations

Victor Branford and Patrick Geddes, The Coming Polity: A Study in Reconstruction (London, 1919), 86

3. Patrick Geddes, *The Association of the Valley Plan with the Valley Section*

Victor Branford and Patrick Geddes, The Coming Polity: A Study in Reconstruction (London, 1919), 87

from Ruskin's similar insights into a wider field of academic evidence and practical implementation. In his scope and persuasiveness, as a thinker and doer, Geddes was the prime example of a modern concept of romantic regeneration, although his activity was so widely dispersed that it is hard to grasp. As with the romanticism of a hundred years before, biological research and the scientific study of nature created a holistic vision of the unity of human and material worlds. From the beginning of the century, there was a major shift in understanding of the underlying principle of existence, from the mechanistic to a form of vitalism prompted by new discoveries in physics that destroyed the Newtonian paradigm. As a reviewer wrote of J. C. Smuts' *Holism and Evolution* in 1926,

The mechanistic theory of the universe, which has reigned for three centuries, is on the point of being superseded.... The little billiard balls, as ultimates, have gone never to return. The matter, and even the space and time, of the old physics are so far from being ultimate constituents of reality that they are not even adequate for the purposes of physics itself.[11]

Geddes' influence was particularly felt in relation to his *Cities and Town Planning Exhibition*, held in London in 1911, where a young architect, Patrick Abercrombie, came under his spell. Geddes overcame the conceptual division between city and country through his influential conceptual schemas, such as the "valley section," showing the interdependence between a city and its hinterland, and the need to achieve balance between them (figs. 2 and 3).[12] When Geddes and Abercrombie met, Abercrombie was enrolled at Liverpool University in the first town planning course in Britain. He went on to become a leading academic in the field and the most prolific author of development plans for English cities and regions before and after World War I.[13] He was a founder of CPRE, whose manifesto he wrote in 1926.[14] Books by Geddes' pupil Lewis Mumford (1895–1990), such as *Technics*

to perform a function with elegant efficiency, but also about people and society. Landscape was an integral part of the thinking of all the international leaders of the movement, especially those associated with the Bauhaus.[9] In most minds, not only was the countryside a victim of change, but so was the city, which, after a hundred years of industrialization, represented an unnatural and noxious environment. Richard Overy's *The Morbid Age: Britain between the Wars* (2009) is a valuable insight into concerns of the period about eugenics, political extremism, and the fall of capitalism. Against this background, nearly all forms of belief in a better future could be seen as having common cause.[10]

The career of Patrick Geddes (1854–1932), biologist, sociologist, planner, and thinker, represents the complex cluster of issues at work in many progressive minds, in which an interpretation of biology as a clue to action and as a metaphor carried forward

and *Civilization* (1934) and *The Culture of Cities* (1938), were key texts for the first generation of modernists in Britain, who built a new world after the war. The conclusion of *Technics and Civilization* was explicit about the limitations of a machine culture divorced from nature, seeing its outcome and self-destruction in fascism. Instead, Mumford called for "the rebuilding of the individual personality and the collective group, and the reorientation of all forms of thought and social activity toward life."[15] This was the forthcoming "Neotechnic" age, in which, as Mumford foresaw it, "form, pattern, configuration, organism, historical filiation, ecological relationship are concepts that work up and down the ladder of the sciences; the esthetic structure and the social relations are as real as the primary physical qualities that the sciences were once content to isolate." He saw this change as part of "the general resurgence of life—the care of children, the culture of sex, the return to wild nature and the renewed worship of the sun."[16] We would be wrong, then, in Mumford's view, to see the 1930s as the culmination of a period of modernism in these general areas of thought and attitude toward nature; rather, we should understand those years as the beginning of a second phase in which, as Smuts' reviewer indicated, earlier assumptions about the mechanistic basis of the world and of humanity would give way to belief in a life principle.

The interwar years saw a reappraisal of romanticism in literature and the arts. Indeed, modernism had hardly taken hold in the visual arts in Britain before it was inflected by the romantic revival.[17] Although there had been a brief moment of mechanistic modernism in the visual arts before World War I, linked to enthusiasm for American doctrines of efficiency, the effect of the war was to return attention to the healing potential of the countryside. Increasing devastation inflicted by development, pollution, and industrial growth after 1920 pushed writers from the wistful regret about the suburban invasion of the home counties,

evident in E. M. Forster's *Howards End* (1910), to more extreme expressions, such as the passages in works of D. H. Lawrence that describe the postindustrial landscape as a "mining camp" and call for the destruction and rebuilding of English towns.[18]

While much of the turn toward rural subjects in literature and painting was conservative in style, the theme also became a vehicle for a different kind of modernism. Paul Nash (1889–1946) made his name first as a war artist and then as an interpreter of dreamlike and increasingly surreal visions of English landscape. Samuel Palmer's work of a hundred years before in the Shoreham "Valley of Vision" was presented in a major exhibition at the Victoria and Albert Museum in 1926, and this inspired a new generation of artists, especially Graham Sutherland (1903–1976), who found in Palmer's work formal attributes of compressed space and Picasso-like vigor of drawing as well as spiritual inspiration for a reenchantment of nature (fig. 4). Art critics such as Herbert Read and Geoffrey Grigson (both also poets) interpreted these connections for a wide public. One result was a

4. Graham Sutherland, *Clegyr Boia*, 1938, etching and aquatint on paper
Author collection; © The estate of Graham Sutherland

recovery of national pride in British artists, following a long period in which France was assumed to be superior in every respect, focused on the popular exhibition *British Art* at the Royal Academy (1934).[19] The new media of broadcasting and documentary film were important in promoting a renewed interest in British culture, especially in relation to country life.

"Regeneration" describes the political act springing from the romantic impulse to choose life over death. In the interwar decades, the opportunities to practice regeneration were limited, and those who carried it out were rarely themselves visual artists or landscape designers. There were, nonetheless, several landowners who were also engaged in cultural projects. The most outstanding and durable example was Dartington Hall, Devon (discussed below), where Leonard and Dorothy Elmhirst regenerated a decayed house and estate while creating an educational program in the arts, including patronage of architects and garden designers. Dartington was famous for its modernist outlook, yet its alliance of farming with a social and cultural program makes it comparable to Rolf Gardiner's activities at Springhead in Dorset, which aspired to reunify work, singing, music, and dance on folk-revival lines. At Portmeirion, Wales, the architect Clough Williams-Ellis was not involved in farming but saw his creation of a holiday village as an educational project that would inspire visitors with the possibility of building appropriate architecture to beautify the landscape. Like many country landowners before them, they cared deeply about the lives of the people on their land, translating this concern into personal visions of future society, establishing models for propagation elsewhere. In these two cases, different in many ways but similar in their broad intentions, there was an aesthetic aspect to the work of regenerating landscapes, while the arts (especially the communal arts of music and acting) were valued for restoring significance and meaning to being a rural worker in a secular industrial age.

Romantic regeneration seems, then, to be an inclusive but useful term for activities shared within a group of influential thinkers and doers, ranging from farming to education, from schemes for the unemployed to saving landscapes for posterity. It was all the more romantic for being a voluntary and idealistic effort, with the attendant dangers of overenthusiasm and lack of balancing criticism.

Attitudes toward Land and Nature

Before World War I, a complex bundle of issues related to land had arisen that affected interwar attitudes and policies, creating a tension between nostalgia and ideas of the future. Underlying this was a fear of the possible consequences of dependence on imported food, especially in time of war, and therefore of the folly of allowing agriculture to stagnate. Plans for an alternative future were accompanied by an acute sense of the passing of folk culture, reflected in the object collecting and photography of Gertrude Jekyll (1843–1932) in Surrey (fig. 5) and in the well-known folk-song-collecting activities of Cecil Sharp (1859–1924), Ralph Vaughan Williams (1872–1958), and Percy Grainger (1882–1961).[20] Folklorists usually wished to integrate these relics into mainstream culture, since they seemed fresh and modern at the time, as well as carrying a quality of indigenous authenticity. The initial impulse of the Arts and Crafts movement toward a national vernacular was continued into a second generation, merging at many points with a "back to the land" impulse. Typical of this combination was activity in the Essex village of Thaxted, inspired by the Christian Socialist vicar, Conrad Noel (1869–1942), who invited Gustav Holst to settle there and encouraged Morris dancing among local workers.[21]

A similar set of forward- and backward-looking attitudes drove the culture of the garden city movement, with its solid and wholesome adaptations of country cottages for all social classes. Self-sufficient small-

5. *Cutting Heath-Turf*
Gertrude Jekyll, Old West Surrey:
Some Notes and Memories (London,
1904), 203

potkin's *Fields, Factories and Workshops*
(1898), from which he derived an anarchist
vision of cooperation in contrast to Bellamy's Fordist vision.[23] Provision of allot-
ments increased but was hampered by the
rise in land values. By the time of Kropotkin's revised edition in 1912, English land
was more productive, although he still complained about the widespread rental of land
merely for shooting. World War 1 emphasized the importance of home food production, but farming fell back into decline after
1918. Kropotkin was far from nostalgic in
the methods he advocated, putting many
examples before his readers of vegetable and
salad crops grown under glass and electric
light, as in other countries. Small-scale food
production was the underlying principle of
the distributist movement, based on Catholic
teaching, and of Guild Socialism, another
attempt to evade the grip of industrialism.[24]

At the same time, there were advances in
the study of nature. The British Ecological
Society was founded in 1913, its first president being Arthur G. Tansley, a popular
writer who was controversial in his own field
of botany. The word *ecology* and the concept
came from Germany, and the geographer
Sir Dudley Stamp dated his own awareness
of this new trend from the publication of an
English translation of A. F. W. Schimper's
Plant Ecology in 1904.[25] Jan Christian Smuts,
the South African botanist, general, and politician already mentioned, was another significant advocate of this new view of nature
based on understanding plants through their
interactions within a community rather than
as individuals. Tansley introduced the term
ecosystem in 1935 and was active in projects
such as the conservation of Wicken Fen, the
wetland reserve in Cambridgeshire. As Stamp
commented, the idea of the ecosystem played
a major part in the development "both of ecological studies and [of] nature conservation—
especially since the acceptance of man
himself as an integral part of the whole."[26]

Among a wider public the longstanding
gentry tradition of studying natural history
by observation, represented in the writings

holdings had been an ideal for land reform-
ers, influenced by the huge appeal of Henry
George's *Progress and Poverty* in the 1880s,
although the effort to settle ex-servicemen
on the land after World War 1 was largely
unsuccessful.[22] Peter Hall and Colin Ward
have explained Ebenezer Howard's formulation of the garden city as the result of his initial interest in the orderly future described in
Edward Bellamy's *Looking Backward* (1888),
modified by his reading of the articles published in 1888–1890 that became Peter Kro-

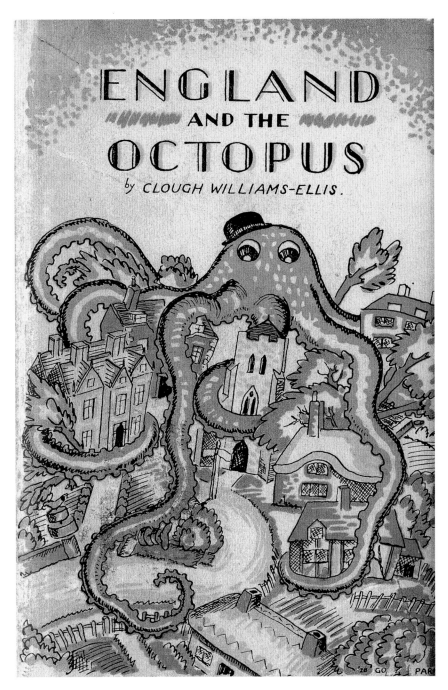

6. Sir Clough Williams-Ellis,
England and the Octopus
(London, 1928), cover

RIBA Library Photographs Collection

trend of the time, encouraged by railway companies, was to introduce a new urban working-class public to its pleasures, treating it as a source of education about attitudes to life as well as natural history—an encounter seldom without friction, but undertaken in the hope on the part of activists and commentators that ultimately the landscape would act as a restorative balance to the supposedly alienating and often demonstrably unhealthy effect of living in a town.[27]

Ideas of natural process and balance implied in ecosystems went against nineteenth-century positivism, which had asserted a linear pathway of material progress. The DIA, founded in 1915 as an outgrowth of the Arts and Crafts movement and inspired by the Deutscher Werkbund, promoted quality in design of machine-produced goods. It represented the diversity of professions and interest groups engaged in projects of recovery and improvement. The Leicester manufacturer Harry Peach, a disciple of W. R. Lethaby and one of the DIA founders concerned with the appearance of towns, began a personal campaign to publicize and oppose the growth of roadside advertising, with the aim of establishing legal controls and exhorting local authorities to take action. Inspired by Peach's work with Noel Carrington, a young publisher and design writer, the DIA yearbook for 1930 was a compilation of text and compelling images of degraded environments in town and country, assembled under the title *The Face of the Land*.[28] The foreword was written by Clough Williams-Ellis (1883–1978), who, while only rarely the designer of anything that could be described as "modern," was nonetheless committed to the improvement of the landscape and townscape by careful removal and infill.[29] As an activist he was even willing to buy important landscape features, such as the avenue at Stowe, to save them until long-term solutions could be found. His book *England and the Octopus* (1928) used wit and satire to further the aims of CPRE (fig. 6); for its successor, *Britain and the Beast* (1937), he

of the Reverend Gilbert White of Selborne (1720–1793), became a popular pastime in the late Victorian and Edwardian periods, giving reasons for escaping from the city in leisure time. These activities were linked to the rambling and cycling movements, which, along with car use, brought experience of the country into the lives of urban dwellers.

Recreational use of the country may have been resented by a few landowners, but the

7. Portmeirion, Wales, photographed in 1979

Photograph Sam Lambert; Architectural Press Archive / RIBA Library Photographs Collection

countryside with pessimism, while warning that in the next war, which many people expected, past neglect of farming would have to be reversed in order for the nation to become even partially self-sufficient. In addition agricultural land must be saved for food production from the expansion of cities, a process begun in 1938 when the Metropolitan Green Belt was enacted by parliament to halt outward expansion of London.[32] Farmers tried not only to make a living on the land but also to act as its stewards, an attitude that Street attributed to stock farmers as opposed to growers. He praised the public spirit of farmers, writing, "it should be noted that our slow old-fashioned countryfolk have farmed this island from time immemorial and can still continue to farm it, while the clever smart American farmers have ruined their land in about one hundred years."[33]

Stewardship of farmland could involve less visible aspects than trees or hedges. Organic farmers held and worked to demonstrate a fundamental belief in "the rule of return" as a means of building up and maintaining soil fertility. This idea was in contrast to the prevailing orthodoxy, supported by government-funded research, of using chemical fertilizers as a sure way of increasing crop yields, with little thought for deterioration of the soil. The organic movement attracted colorful figures, some of whom—most notably the farmer and writer Rolf Gardiner (1902–1971)—notoriously engaged with Nazi Germany in a belief that they held a common cause.[34] Explaining that organicism could support a variety of political positions, Jeremy Burchardt writes with the surprise of hindsight that only one of this group, Jorian Jenks, was imprisoned, while most of the others revised their earlier opinions of Germany in the light of the war. With the foundation of the Soil Association in 1945, they created a nonpolitical institutional structure for organic farming that, following the dominance of conventional methods in the postwar decades, had influence later on.[35]

commissioned articles from writers, planners, politicians, and other public figures toward the same end. In addition to his conservation activity, Williams-Ellis bought an estate in North Wales in 1926, as already mentioned, and turned it into a hotel in the form of a village, Portmeirion, to demonstrate sensitive development in a beautiful place (fig. 7). The mixture of vernacular and baroque in Williams-Ellis' architecture disqualifies him as a modernist by normal criteria but should not conceal his modern attitude toward society and landscape, which Lewis Mumford admired.[30]

The idea of stewardship of the soil as well as the health of consumers was one of the aims of the organic farming movement, which gained strength between the wars.[31] One of the contributors to *Britain and the Beast* was the farmer and writer A. G. Street, who viewed the future of the

That the organic movement produced many books, perhaps a number out of proportion to its influence, can be attributed in part to the personal commitment of the publisher Richard de la Mare, a director of Faber & Faber, and his colleague T. S. Eliot, who, after painting a picture of materialist despondency in *The Waste Land* (1922), became an advocate of social ideas linked to the organic movement.[36] Faber & Faber was the publisher of Eve Balfour's *The Living Soil* (1943), the book that effectively launched the Soil Association. The author, niece of the Conservative prime minister Arthur Balfour, was an organic farmer, an aviator, and a member of a jazz band. Among the organicists, she was especially dedicated to scientific research to set against the findings of the government's nonorganic

8. Rabindranath Tagore with Leonard Elmhirst, Beijing, 1924
The Dartington Hall Trust Archive

research station at Rothampstead. The nonofficial status of the Soil Association conferred an air of romantic rebellion on its members and their sometimes unconventional activities.[37]

Much of the radical thinking about agriculture and ecology was fostered by British individuals who spent time in Africa, India, or New Zealand. In these places they learned from indigenous practices, as did Sir Albert Howard in developing his Indore method of composting, or tried out new ideas in degraded environments, as Richard St Barbe Baker did in Kenya when he founded Men of the Trees, an attempt to make tree planting part of the masculine tribal culture that was immediately successful and later expanded to a worldwide affiliation.[38] The example that the healthy, long-lived Hunza tribespeople of northwest India presented to the army doctor Sir Robert McCarrison became the basis for widespread research and discussion on nutrition.

Education, Regeneration, and the Land

In one respect, the individual within the British Empire who had the most significant influence on the practice of rural regeneration was the Bengali poet Rabindranath Tagore (1861–1941), who in 1901 founded a rural school on family land at Santiniketan, providing the opportunity to learn in a natural environment (fig. 8). The Nobel Prize–winning poet was never active in England; his influence came about through a global chain of coincidence. While studying at Cornell University, Leonard Elmhirst (1893–1974), of a family of minor Yorkshire gentry, met Tagore and accepted his invitation to return to Bengal with him and set up the Institute of Rural Reconstruction. Fundraising for various projects at Cornell put Elmhirst in contact with Dorothy Straight, née Whitney (1887–1968), one of the wealthiest women in America, and they were married in 1925, united by a shared ideal of regenerating an estate in England along educational and agricultural lines inspired by

9. Dartington Hall, Totnes, South Devon, before restoration

The Dartington Hall Trust Archive

Tagore. After a search, in 1926 they discovered Dartington Hall in Devon, a beautiful historic house, partly roofless, on an estate that was typical of its kind in the 1920s in having been "let go" for several generations (fig. 9). It was an emblem of rural decline, a beautiful victim waiting to be saved in a new way.[39]

Attention has mainly been focused on the remarkable arts program at Dartington, but the primary purpose of the project was to create an exemplar by restoring the land, together with the buildings and garden, to productive use. The approach was the opposite of organic, based on the most up-to-date scientific methods, especially in poultry farming, but the underlying basis of nurturing both land and community was a balancing factor. Elmhirst's personal passion was trees, and he replanted large areas that had been deforested in the general exploitation of standing timber during and after World War I. Indeed, trees are a major theme in considering the interwar years in Britain, an index of emotional attachment to landscape, fear of its loss, and hopes for the future.[40] At Dartington, the forester Wilfred Hiley introduced an ecological sense of stable change into what had become an exploitative business, either through cutting trees for timber or through "letting go" for shooting. Experiments in keeping a balanced forest of mixed age were backed up by research and analysis.

It was arguably a modern landscape project, although as an agricultural landscape, not a work of design in the conventional sense. That aspect was reserved for the gardens of the hall, where design interventions were made by the landscape gardener Beatrix Farrand (1872–1959), who designed the courtyard in 1933–1938, and by Percy Cane (1881–1976), working after the war, both under Dorothy Elmhirst's watchful eye. The American influence represented by Farrand was also felt in the employment of Delano and Aldrich of New York as architects for new buildings for Dartington Hall School, founded in 1926, initially for the Elmhirsts' own children and those of workers on the

BLOCKS B & C: GROUND FLOOR PLAN

10. William Lescaze, dormitories at Dartington Hall, 1934

The Museum of Modern Art, New York, Modern Architecture in England *(New York, 1937), no. 38*

approach to modern architecture was typical of a number of English patrons, and after trying Lescaze for several projects on the estate, the Dartington Hall Trust reverted to less problematic, traditional designers (fig. 10).

The community on the Dartington estate offered unmatched opportunities for individual growth and development at a time when there was little state provision for adult education. This aspect of Dartington's mission was inspired in part by Tagore's school at Santiniketan. Similar projects had existed on the estates of likeminded landowners, such as the Biddulph family of Rodmarton in Gloucestershire in the 1920s, but Dartington, small though it was on a national scale, was more progressive and more influential. Run on business principles, yet supported on a cushion of financial stability unavailable to comparable enterprises, Dartington was probably the most effective and enduring example of romantic regeneration originated in the interwar period.

Educational precursors to Dartington included schools such as Abbotsholme, Derbyshire, founded in 1889, and its co-educational offshoot, Bedales, of 1893. Modern nursery education was more or less created by Margaret and Rachel Macmillan, working in the East End of London around 1900. In all these enterprises, even in the London slums, belief in the positive influence of nature in physical surroundings was paramount. In America, John Dewey implemented ideas associated with the American transcendentalists and linked to the origins of romanticism and the writings of Jean-Jacques Rousseau. These held the insights of the child as valuable, to be protected and nurtured through learning based on first-hand experience. As at Dartington, a natural setting was seen as indispensable to the free development of children and as a form of metaphor for their healthy growth. Writing in 1950, the educational administrator John Newsom gave three analogies for the education of children: the "jug and mug," the potter's wheel, and the "garden and the plant." The last, he contended, was the only possible

estate, but soon expanded to become the largest progressive school in Britain. The first headmaster, William Curry, insisted on displacing the Arts and Crafts architect Oswald P. Milne with the Swiss American modernist William Lescaze, with whom he had worked at the Oak Lane Country Day School, near Philadelphia (1929). This inconsistent

one, as it allowed for individual growth.[41] This was far from a new idea, having been pioneered by Rousseau and several famous successors, but in the mainstream, where Newsom was trying to establish it after the war, it was still contentious.

After 1920, many private schools (or public schools, as they are known in Britain) moved into or were set up to occupy redundant country houses, reinforcing the connection with landscape. Stowe, founded in 1923, had the most famous setting. Bryanston in Dorset, founded in 1928, occupied a house designed in the 1880s by Richard Norman Shaw. In accordance with the philosophy of natural growth, the traditional hierarchies and dress codes of the upper classes were relaxed, and boys wore shorts all year round. The exclusive focus on team sports was relaxed to allow alternatives in farm and estate work, an idea copied from Salem School, founded on Lake Constance in 1920, whose headmaster, Kurt Hahn, imprisoned for resisting Nazism, moved the school in 1934 to Gordonstoun in Morayshire, Scotland. While more rule-based than Dartington, these schools shared its definition of progressive ideals, which would have been inconceivable in an urban setting.

At the more extreme end of the scale of child-centered education were Homer Lane's short-lived Little Commonwealth in Dorset (1912) and Summerhill School, founded by his disciple, A. S. Neill. These progressive schools remained in the minority, but their pupils appear to have made significant contributions in many fields leading back to interpreting landscape and its uses. In a poem of 1930, W. H. Auden, who greatly admired Homer Lane and had connections with Bryanston, linked Lane with William Blake and D. H. Lawrence, describing the three as "healers in our English land."[42] Although the implication of his reference was that they were healers of the soul (1930 was the year of Lawrence's death), the rest of the poem shows the outer sickness of the land as a reflection of an inner sickness and falsity.

It would be gratifying for the art historian if all these progressive ventures had expressed their identity through modern design, but Stowe and Bryanston both employed traditional architects for their first additional buildings, and only Dartington made a major contribution to the patronage of modernism by employing Lescaze. However, a correlation between a period selection such as that of the Museum of Modern Art catalog *Modern Architecture in England* (1937), in which Lescaze's buildings are featured, and the story of regeneration and concern for rural planning, reveals several interesting links. The Pioneer Health Centre in Peckham in South London, designed in reinforced concrete in 1935 by the engineer Sir Owen Williams, was a unique medical and social experiment closely allied to the organic farming movement (fig. 11).[43] The founders, George Scott Williamson and his wife, Innes Pearse, were founding members of the Soil Association. They established an organic farm at Bromley in Kent to provide good food for the families who attended the center, finding analogies between organic farming methods and the center's own unconstrained encouragement of personal natural growth and development.

11. Sir Owen Williams, Pioneer Health Centre, Peckham, with children picking lupines
Wellcome Collection

They wrote that even in the country, the traditional centers for the community were in decline, but that there was still a need for "spaces that have met the needs of social life and the tentative adventures of ... children as they grew."[44] Later commentators have scorned the center's attachment to organic cultivation as unscientific and hence contrary to its other progressive aims.[45]

A project with the highest modernist credentials was Impington Village College in Cambridgeshire, the fourth in a series of buildings representing a new typology (fig. 12). Village colleges brought modernity to rural communities in a controlled way by putting various public functions in a building that did multiple service as a school by day and as public library and place of social recreation and assembly by night. County education officer Henry Morris, who invented the idea, wished a village college building to

express the spirit of the English countryside which it is intended to grace, something of its humaneness and modesty, something of the age-long and permanent dignity of husbandry; a building that will give the countryside a centre of reference arousing the affection and loyalty of the country child and country people, and conferring significance on their way of life.[46]

The Sawston, Bottisham, and Linton Village Colleges were designed by the county architect, S. E. Urwin, in a style developing from neo-Georgian to Dutch-inspired modernism. Impington, completed in 1939, was designed by Walter Gropius in partnership with Maxwell Fry. Impington had no specific ties to organic farming, although the land for the college was given by the fruit growers and jam manufacturers Chivers. The building was informally laid out to preserve old trees on the site and was unassertive in its forms. Photographs of children learning beekeeping there were included in a wartime pamphlet, *The Countryman's College: Britain Advances* (1943; fig. 13).

Several university academics worked through their disciplines or in other ways to shape the future of the countryside according to their ideas. The influential Cambridge literary critic F. R. Leavis, a literary modernist with strong ethical preferences, set himself against the cultural modernity of consumerism, which he saw as destroying "the organic community." In *Culture and Environment* (with Denys Thompson; 1933), Leavis contended that children had naturally good taste in visual matters until it was corrupted by "civilisation," and that the

13. Impington Village College, instruction in beekeeping

H. C. Dent, The Countryman's College: Britain Advances *(London, 1943), 28*

appreciation of buildings and places should become part of the English school curriculum.[47] Impington could be seen as a practical demonstration of the same civilizing impulse.

Another building with interesting landscape connections included in the 1937 MoMA catalog was Geoffrey Jellicoe's Caveman Restaurant at Cheddar Gorge in Somerset, a commission from Henry Thynne, Viscount Weymouth, whose family operated the property as a profitable tourist attraction (figs. 14 and 15). It was a demonstration of the values of the DIA and its commitment to public service expressed through a form of total design. The white, flat-roofed buildings stand out against the cliff face through which visitors entered the Cheddar caves. In the restaurant, a mural by Eliot Hodgkin reminded them in a jocular way of primitive life, and the furniture was all supplied by the leading middle-of-the-road modernist firm Gordon Russell Ltd., whose owner was a member of the DIA. In the second phase of building, the extended restaurant was given an imaginative glass roof, with fish swimming in a shallow pool over the heads of the customers. With its care for every detail, including art, this was total design with

English whimsy, in contrast to the roadside cafés that the DIA had started to complain about in the 1920s.

Jellicoe had already designed a variety of schemes for Gordon Russell, starting in 1929 with a flight of steps in Russell's own garden, followed in 1933 by a short planning report on the Worcestershire village of Broadway, where Russell's business was based in a model of progressive rural industry. It was typical of DIA members such as Russell to act as private individuals for the public benefit and for posterity, in this case by designating future land uses and development areas. Other local authorities and communities generally were encouraged to work in this way after the 1932 Town and Country Planning Act, although the act was in other regards an ineffectual measure for preventing the random siting of buildings. Exemplifying Geddes' motto, "survey before plan," the Broadway report represented the interpretation of modernism that adapted it to existing conditions (fig. 16). Michael Spens writes:

Jellicoe's recommendations were extremely practical. Following a full survey of historical, geological and topographical factors, he proposed a plan covering zoning, planting and special items. Within the village itself he made special recommendations covering traffic, parking and sports facilities, natural planting, and the control of building elevations and signposting. A very useful proposal related to setting up a special trust, with a professional advisory panel, for the conservation of buildings.[48]

In the turbulent years of depression in the early 1930s, the idea of planning gained in urgency. The *Week-End Review*, a weekly magazine of arts and politics, gathered a small and committed staff and published articles by Clough Williams-Ellis and other writers on the state of Britain's towns and countryside. The magazine was founded by Gerald Barry (1898–1968), who had left an editing job with the newspaper baron Lord Beaverbrook in protest against his pro-empire trade stance, which threatened, among other things, the viability of home food production.

14. Geoffrey Jellicoe, Caveman
Restaurant, Cheddar Gorge, 1934
Architectural Association

15. Geoffrey Jellicoe, Caveman
Restaurant, interior, with mural by
Eliot Hodgkin, 1934
Architectural Association

16. Geoffrey Jellicoe, Parish of
Broadway, Plan A

From Geoffrey Jellicoe, Advisory
Plan and Report for the Parish of
Broadway in Worcestershire: Pre-
pared for Residents and Traders
*(1933); courtesy Ray Leigh, The
Gordon Russell Design Museum*

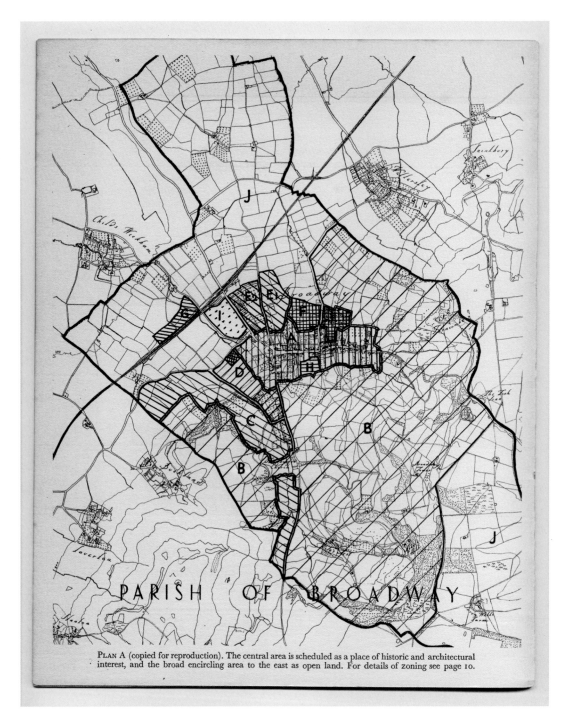

PLAN A (copied for reproduction). The central area is scheduled as a place of historic and architectural
interest, and the broad encircling area to the east as open land. For details of zoning see page 10.

In 1931 "A National Plan for Great Britain" was published anonymously as an
article in the magazine, written by Barry's
deputy editor, Max Nicholson (1904–2003),
also a noted ornithologist and a disciple
of Arthur Tansley.[49] Nicholson drew on
his knowledge of ecology in conceiving a
holistic approach to the restoration of land

and cities, together with the political and
administrative systems to guide the effort.
Within a short time, a research organization, Political and Economic Planning (PEP),
was set up by a group of advanced thinkers,
with Nicholson as secretary and Leonard
Elmhirst as a supporter and chief funder,
to seek forms of modernization in industry

and economics that would be compatible with the preservation of nature, including a proposal for the creation of national parks, also one of Tansley's campaigns.[50] PEP represented a novel form of activity and could be claimed to represent a modern approach to planning that encapsulated the idea of regeneration. The National Plan of 1931 offered a model of the kind of holistic national reorganization for which Nicholson continued to work, and which was to some extent realized under the Labour government of Clement Attlee in 1945–1951, in which Nicholson was secretary to the influential minister Herbert Morrison. As Jeremy J. D. Greenwood writes, "Morrison and his team played a key role in prioritizing the wealth of legislation that was enacted, on town and country planning, agriculture and forestry, national parks, and nature conservation, Nicholson having a deep personal interest in all of these, especially the last."[51] The nationalization of land was proposed in *Reconstruction and the Land*, by Sir Daniel Hall, in 1941; an equivalent was achieved with the restriction of development rights in the Town and Country Planning Act of 1947, which became the means by which prewar dreams of rational planning for land use, a universal form of stewardship, could begin to be realized.

Paradoxically, it could be said that the realization of many interwar hopes in this act took the romance out of regeneration by making it no longer a lonely stand against a hostile world but a bureaucratic operation dependent on the qualities of the individuals involved. Professionals who had lacked opportunities before the war worked for newly created official bodies such as new town commissions. Among them, the architect Frederick Gibberd and landscape architect Sylvia Crowe were able at Harlow New Town to create Arcadian landscapes by saving existing trees and coaxing the maximum effect in terms of formal design from the gently rolling contours of the site (fig. 17).

The Brynmawr Rubber Factory in South Wales is notable as the work of Architects Co-Operative Partnership, a young,

idealistic practice formed just before the war in collaboration with the engineer Ove Arup (fig. 18). Although funded by public money, the factory was in fact the personal vision of an industrialist peer, James Brabazon Grimston, fifth earl of Verulam (1910–1960), who conceived the idea of a new industrial plant and associated social provision while working in this notorious black spot of unemployment before the war as a volunteer.[52] The project was intended as a new model for regeneration, based on the most advanced prewar thinking, some of it nurtured at the Association of Planning and Regional Reconstruction, which Verulam founded in 1940. There the ideas of Geddes and Mumford were developed by Jaqueline Tyrwhitt, a significant if hard-to-categorize figure in postwar planning.[53]

With its valley setting and holistic approach to economics, nature, and community, the Brynmawr project has similarities, on a much reduced scale, to the Tennessee Valley Authority (TVA), which became known to British planners shortly before the war, partly through the reports of Gordon

Stephenson, a young architect-planner who had visited TVA sites in 1938. The TVA was the focus of a special issue of the *Architectural Review,* published in 1943 and later published in book form, with a text by Julian Huxley, biologist and member of PEP, giving it a sort of imprimatur by a figure who represented a link between science and a wider world of politics and action (fig. 19). (Huxley would later become the founding director general of UNESCO and founder of the World Wildlife Fund.[54]) Peder Anker notes that on two prewar visits, Huxley

became firmly convinced that the valley could serve as a model for rebuilding his own country. The analogy was apt in terms of size — the district covers an area about four-fifths the size of Britain — but what caught Huxley's attention was the potential for a synchronised plan that included geography, soil, agriculture, forestry, animal life, recreation, scenery, fishing, technical research, health, commerce, industry, architecture, housing and design.[55]

The scale of TVA and its devotion to science were modern features in its favor, but other

themes new to Britain were admired, such as community forests, a policy of racial equality, and the recreational opportunities so often lacking in the English countryside. Images from Huxley's article and book appeared in several widely circulated exhibitions and pamphlets about postwar reconstruction in Britain.

Was TVA a romantic regeneration project? If holism is seen as an essentially romantic view of the world, then its multifaceted activities, together with the idea of restoring damaged landscape and creating harmonious interactions between man and nature, fit the description. It was an example on a massive scale of a managed landscape of economic benefit combined with beauty. It also offered a political model for achieving a large-scale project within a democracy. The *Architectural Review* introduced Huxley's special issue with the expectation that

there will be so much planning on a large scale after the war that the country cannot afford to neglect the experience gained in ten years' work on the world's boldest venture in regional reconstruction.... Too many people in Britain still think of planning in terms of advisory town-planning committees without any executive power drawing up schemes for urban and district councils. There is no object lesson anywhere so convincing of the possibilities of judiciously and democratically applied regional planning as TVA.[56]

The examples selected for discussion here tell stories for which 1940, representing the beginning of World War II, was a hinge point. By that time a tradition of unconventional thinking about the role of land and landscape had accumulated. Many of the ideas of post–World War I planning had been tried out, if only on a small scale, demonstrating how to balance traditional social forms against the pressures of modernity and how to expand the role of conservation to become an active means of resolution. Scientific advances in the understanding of holism and ecology appear to have helped bring about a change of attitude, reflected in the new romanticism of the visual arts, which fed back into landscape practice, showing how to reimagine the past in the present. Many forms of practice were allied in developing and enacting visions of a future in which the nurture of people and of nature became indivisible aims.

1. See Alan Powers, "Landscape in Britain, 1940–1960," in *The Architecture of Landscape, 1940–1960,* ed. Marc Treib (Philadelphia, 2002), 56–79. In this essay, *England* is used rather than *Britain* to simplify the ramifications of an already overly complex subject by avoiding the need to cover the different circumstances of Scotland, Wales, and Northern Ireland.

2. Jellicoe's work has been widely published. See Michael Spens, *Gardens of the Mind: The Genius of Geoffrey Jellicoe* (Woodbridge, Suffolk, UK, 1992), and Michael Spens, *The Complete Landscape and Garden Designs of Geoffrey Jellicoe* (London, 1994).

3. A considerable literature is devoted to refuting various aspects of Wiener's book. For a useful summary, see Jeremy Burchardt, *Paradise Lost: Rural Idyll and Social Change since 1800* (London, 2002), chap. 12.

4. See David Matless, *Landscape and Englishness* (London, 1998), and Patrick Wright, *The Village That Died for England* (London, 1995).

5. Peter Mandler, "Against 'Englishness': English Culture and the Limits to Rural Nostalgia, 1850–1940," in *Transactions of the Royal Historical Society,* 6th series, 7 (1997): 157.

6. David H. Haney, *When Modern Was Green: Life and Work of Landscape Architect Leberecht Migge* (London, 2010).

7. Bruno Latour, *We Have Never Been Modern* (London, 1993), 76, quoted in Haney 2010, 268.

8. Neither CPRE nor DIA has a published history, but useful information about the relationship between them can be found in Pat Kirkham, *Harry Peach: Dryad and the DIA* (London, 1986).

9. See Peder Anker, *From Bauhaus to Eco-Haus: A History of Ecological Design* (Baton Rouge, 2010).

10. Richard Overy, *The Morbid Age: Britain between the Wars* (London, 2009).

11. John William Nevin Sutherland, review of *Holism and Evolution,* by Jan Christian Smuts, *Times Literary Supplement,* October 14, 1926.

12. Geddes published two major books, *City Development* (Edinburgh, 1904) and *Cities in Evolution* (London, 1915), but neither is an adequate summary of his ideas. Secondary works include Helen Meller, *Patrick Geddes, Social Evolutionist and City Planner* (London, 1990), and Volker M. Welter, *Biopolis: Patrick Geddes and the City of Life* (Cambridge, MA, 2002).

13. See Gerald Dix, "Patrick Abercombie, 1879–1957," in *Pioneers in British Planning,* ed. Gordon E. Cherry (London, 1981).

14. Patrick Abercrombie, *The Preservation of Rural England* (Liverpool, 1926).

15. Lewis Mumford, *Technics and Civilization* (New York and London, 1934), 423.

16. Mumford 1934, 371.

17. Alexandra Harris, in *Romantic Moderns* (London, 2010), offers a broad overview of many areas of activity, while framing an opposition between modernism and romanticism. For a more integrated interpretation, see Alan Powers, "The Reluctant Romantics: *Axis* Magazine, 1935–37," in *The Geographies of Englishness: Landscape and the National Past 1880–1940,* ed. David Peters Corbett, Fiona Russell, and Ysanne Holt (New Haven, 2002), 248–274, and Alan Powers, "John Summerson and Romanticism," in *Summerson and Hitchcock: Centenary Essays on Architectural Historiography,* ed. Frank Salmon (New Haven, 2006), 209–220.

18. E. M. Forster, *Howards End* (London, 1910); the theme is present in Lawrence's early novels, with a notable moment of epiphany in *The Rainbow* (London, 1915). Lawrence's late essay "Nottingham and the Mining Country," first published in *Architectural Review* 68 (August 1930): 47–50, and again in *New Adelphi,* 2nd ser., 3 (June–August 1931), appears to have been particularly influential.

19. See Andrew Causey, "English Art and the 'National Character,' 1933–34," in Corbett et al. 2002.

20. This aspect of Jekyll's work, less well known than her garden design, can be seen in her *Old West Surrey: Some Notes and Memories* (London, 1904).

21. Enthusiasm for the revival of this traditional male dance tradition originated with Cecil Sharp and spread rapidly after 1900, being also much satirized. Rolf Gardiner was an enthusiast for Morris and sword dances as vestiges of calendrical fertility rites.

22. See Burchardt 2002, 142–144.

23. Peter Hall and Colin Ward, *Sociable Cities: The Legacy of Ebenezer Howard* (New York, 1998): 11–12.

24. Distributism was a Catholic scheme for land reform and self-sufficiency, advocated by the writers Hilaire Belloc and G. K. Chesterton. Guild Socialism, based on occupational groups, was particularly associated with the architect A. J. Penty.

25. Sir Dudley Stamp, *Nature Conservation in Britain* (London, 1969), 10. See also Peder Anker, *Imperial Ecology: Environmental Order in the British Empire, 1895–1945* (Cambridge, MA, 2001).

26. Stamp 1969, 11.

27. Matless 1998, chap. 2.

28. Harry Peach and N. L. Carrington, eds., *The Face of the Land* (London, 1932).

29. Clough Williams-Ellis, *Architect Errant* (London, 1971).

30. See Clough Williams-Ellis, with an epilogue by Lewis Mumford, *Portmeirion: The Place and Its Meaning* (Penrhyndeudraeth, Wales, 1973), taken from an article in the *New Yorker*; Piers Gruffudd, "Propaganda for Seemliness: Clough Williams-Ellis and Portmeirion, 1918–1950," *Cultural Geographies* 2,

no. 4 (October 1995): 399–422, and Jan Morris et al., *Portmeirion* (Woodbridge, Suffolk, UK, 2006).

31. See Philip Conford, *The Origins of the Organic Movement* (Edinburgh, 2001).

32. Scares about food shortage were the theme of several books on organic farming, such as Gerard Vernon Wallop, Viscount Lymington, *Famine in England* (London, 1938), and H. J. Massingham and Edward Hyams, *Prophecy of Famine: A Warning and the Remedy* (London, 1953).

33. A. G. Street, "The Countryman's View," in *Britain and the Beast*, ed. Clough Williams-Ellis (London, 1937), 130.

34. Those with extreme right-wing views also included the historian Arthur Bryant, farmer Jorian Jenks, Lord Lymington, and novelist Henry Williamson. Conford discusses their positions (Conford 2001, 146–160). On Gardiner's support of National Socialism in the 1930s, see Matthew Jefferies and Mike Tyldesley, *Rolf Gardiner: Folk, Nature and Culture in Interwar Britain* (Farnham, Surrey, UK, 2011), especially the essays by Richard Griffiths and Dan Stone. The latter writes, "The fact is that [Gardiner's] rejection of Nazism [after 1934] did not go hand in hand with a rejection of any of his views. It is here that much confusion lies: to our ears much of what Gardiner had to say connects him easily with a National Socialist outlook; but his defenders are right to say that by historicizing him we can see that it was possible (perhaps still is) to believe in the need for national renewal based on the land and rejection of materialistic ideals and yet not succumb to Nazism" (160). Owing to the legacy of the prewar past, as the editors of the book write in their concluding essay, "Today's activists [in the organic movement] are reluctant to admit any connection between Gardiner's generation of organicists … and their own" (171). See also Klaus-Peter Lorenz, "Rolf Gardiner (1902–1971): Wandervogel und Ökologe," in *Naturschutz und Demokratie!?*, ed. Gert Gröning and Joachim Wolschke-Bulmahn, CGL-Studies, vol. 3 (Munich, 2006), 73–81.

35. Burchardt 2002, 137–138.

36. Conford describes these, asserting the significance of Eliot's Christianity and the forgotten role of religious belief in the organic movement, especially the difference between use and exploitation. He cites Eliot's *The Idea of a Christian Society* and *Notes Towards a Definition of Culture* as evidence (Conford 2001, 194–195).

37. For an account of the Soil Association, see Matthew Reed, *Rebels for the Soil: The Rise of the Global Organic Food and Farming Movement* (London, 2010). On Richard de la Mare, see Lawrence D. Hills and Eve Balfour, "Friend of the Soil," in *Richard de la Mare at 75* (London, 2004), 23–28.

38. Richard St Barbe Baker, *My Life — My Trees* (London, 1970). The subject is discussed in Conford 2001, chap. 3.

39. The best account of Dartington remains Michael Young, *The Elmhirsts of Dartington: The Creation of a Utopian Community* (London, 1982).

40. In addition to Elmhirst, Richard St Barbe Baker made trees his speciality, as noted above. Rolf Gardiner was particularly concerned with reforestation of his estates in Dorset. John Stewart Collis, who learned forestry with Gardiner, wrote *The Triumph of the Tree* (London, 1950). Brenda Colvin's *Land and Landscape* (London, 1950) includes emotive writing on trees.

41. John Newsom, *The Child at School* (Harmondsworth, UK, 1950), 17.

42. W. H. Auden, *Poems* (London, 1930).

43. See Innes H. Pearse and Lucy H. Crocker, *The Peckham Experiment: A Study of the Living Structure of Society* (London, 1943).

44. Pearse and Crocker 1943 and Conford 2001, 69. The organic aspect of the Pioneer Health Centre is covered in Reed 2010, 55. The two founders and the secretary of the center were among the thirteen original council members of the Soil Association.

45. As noted in Matless 1998, 320.

46. Henry Morris, *The Village College, Being a Memorandum on the Provision of Educational and Social Facilities for the Countryside, with Special Reference to Cambridgeshire* (Cambridge, 1924), quoted in Harry Rée, *Educator Extraordinary: The Life and Achievements of Henry Morris, 1889–1961* (London, 1973), 31.

47. This was evident in the writings of Margaret Bulley, such as *Art and Counterfeit* (London, 1925), cited in Leavis and Thompson 1933. See Alan Powers, "Writers and Thinkers: Margaret Bulley," *Crafts* 192 (January–February 2005): 24–25.

48. Spens 1992, 51.

49. "A National Plan for Great Britain," supplement to the *Week-End Review*, February 14, 1931, i–xvi. See also Max Nicholson, *The New Environmental Age* (Cambridge, 1987), chap. 7, "Pioneers of Conservation."

50. Overy 2009, 80–86.

51. Jeremy J. D. Greenwood, "Nicholson, (Edward) Max," *Oxford Dictionary of National Biography*, http://www.oxforddnb.com/view/article/89908?docPos=1, accessed December 2012. When responsibility for economic planning moved from Morrison's domain to the treasury, Nicholson was able to devote his time to organizing the Festival of Britain (1951), with his former colleague Gerald Barry.

52. Victoria Perry, *Built for a Better Future: The Brynmawr Rubber Factory* (Oxford, 1994).

53. See Rhodri Windsor Liscombe, "Perceptions in the Conception of the Modernist Urban Environment: Canadian Perspectives on the Spatial Theory of

Jaqueline Tyrwhitt," in *Man-Made Future: Planning, Education and Design in Mid-Twentieth-Century Britain*, ed. Iain Boyd Whyte (London, 2007), 78–98. The association and its precursor, the Architectural Association School of Planning and Research for National Development, were created by E. A. A. Rowse after his resignation as director of education at the Architectural Association in 1937.

54. *Architectural Review* 93 (June 1943). Published in book form as Julian Huxley, *TVA: Adventure in Planning* (Cheam, Surrey, 1943).

55. Anker 2001, 231.

56. Unsigned editorial note, *Architectural Review* 1943, 138.

STEVEN A. MANSBACH

Making the Past Modern: Jože Plečnik's Central European Landscapes in Prague and Ljubljana

Jože Plečnik (1872–1957) was a creative contradiction in the history of twentieth-century architecture, city planning, and especially landscape design. Celebrated variously as an expressionist, a pioneer of modern architecture, a modern classicist, a myth maker, and, during the 1980s, as the consummate postmodernist, this Slovenian-born figure might best be understood as an idiosyncratic revolutionary.[1] His modernism departed essentially from the paradigmatic model of rationalism, internationalism, and antihistoricism that remains the legacy of the idealistic pioneers of modern design and landscape architecture.[2] An investigation of Plečnik's oeuvre reveals a progressive spirit of surpassing invention, one whose ingenious invocation of history, nation, and nature defines an alternative to the conventional meaning of modernism.[3]

Almost alone among twentieth-century architects and landscape designers, Plečnik was inspired both by modern industrial aesthetics and by the appeal of antiquity; by the possibilities of new building techniques and by age-old methods of construction; by international standards of democracy and by chauvinist aspirations. His chauvinism was Slavist, and more specifically Czech and Slovenian. With an outlook so rich in antinomies, one might best approach Plečnik's work from a perspective more elastic than a conventional modernist one that prizes consistency, both stylistic and ideological. For philosophically and artistically, Plečnik was eclectic; and in his multifariousness in outlook and educational experience, he fits as comfortably with the traditions of late nineteenth-century Habsburg Mitteleuropa as he aligns with the diversity of

the twentieth-century world. This creative complexity is most manifest in his original programs for modern landscapes, especially those commissioned in post–World War I Prague by Tomáš Garrigue Masaryk (1850–1937), the principal founder and first president of Czechoslovakia (1918–1935), and even more in his work during the 1930s for his native city of Ljubljana.

The Gardens of Prague Castle

Soon after moving to Vienna in 1892, Plečnik studied with and worked for Otto Wagner (1841–1918), first in the Akademie der Bildenden Künste and later in the Austrian's cosmopolitan studio. It was there that the young architect from Ljubljana (then officially known as Laibach) developed a heightened Slavic, and distinctively Slovene, consciousness. Beginning in his student days, he thus committed himself to a lifelong task of consolidating and developing both a generalized Slavic and a particularized Slovenian culture, one that was singularly enriched by the classical strain in his formation, promoted in no small measure by his experiences in Italy in 1899 as a winner of the Prix de Rome (1898) for his diploma work at the Vienna academy.[4]

Mostly for economic reasons, Plečnik left Ljubljana in 1911 for Prague, where he secured a professorship in the city's College of Applied Arts (Uměleckoprůmyslová škola) through the intervention of a friend from his Vienna years, the architect and professor Jan Kotěra (1871–1923), whom he had probably befriended in Wagner's studio. In the multinational Bohemian metropolis, the Slovene deepened his enthusiasm for Czech art,

Prague Castle, platform, gate, and staircase leading into the Paradise Garden, c. 1921–1923
Photograph Kázmér Kovács

which he believed represented the highest form of Slavic aesthetic aspiration and spirituality, a point of view that was intended to challenge the deeply rooted Germanic claim of cultural superiority in Prague.[5] This Slavist chauvinism found resonance with Bohemia's younger generation of artists and architects, who had been emphatically and successfully rejecting German institutions, traditions, and attitudes since at least the turn of the century. In this context, Plečnik's jingoism found favor among his students, and his popularity enabled him to flourish as teacher and advocate of modern forms and traditional attitudes despite his foreign origins and close ties to Vienna. He was a study in contrasts, favoring progressive technologies and innovative design theory, interests shaped through his studies with Otto Wagner, while holding to conservative philosophical and religious leanings, solidified in the Czech metropolis. It was just this discrepant worldview that likely motivated Plečnik to enter the competition for the Paradise Garden (Rajská zahrada) for the former royal castle in Prague (the Pražský hrad).

The castle complex, which had occupied the Bohemian acropolis for most of a millennium, had housed various lines of royal administration and imperial Habsburg governance; from 1918 through 1938 it would house the presidency of republican Czechoslovakia. It was the emotional center of a new nation that could draw on a long and distinguished history in which the *hrad* had served as a European capital under the Luxemburger Charles IV (1316–1378), Holy Roman Emperor from 1347, and again in the sixteenth and seventeenth centuries under the collector-emperor Rudolf II (1552–1612). The castle was thus the incarnation of the nation's history and the emblem of both Czech subjection and independence. But by the time of the creation of the Czechoslovakian Republic in 1918, the castle and its district had fallen into considerable disrepair. Although it was a Habsburg royal and imperial seat through World War I, the royal family had seldom resided there

under the reign of Emperor (and King of Bohemia) Franz Josef I.

President Masaryk bore the challenging responsibility of honoring the castle's majestic past while adapting it to the functions of a modern republic.[6] And to accomplish this paradoxical goal for the national monument, he granted a number of commissions beginning in 1920. Significantly, among the first of these was the result of a competition for a "Paradise Garden" by which a new Eden of liberal democracy might be cultivated.[7]

As a jury member for the competition, Plečnik was not constrained from entering his own design proposal, which ultimately proved triumphant, even though the forty-eight-year-old architect had no garden design experience whatsoever.[8] His singular combination of Slavist nationalism, variations on classical architectural forms, and progressive building technologies found immediate favor with President Masaryk, who appointed him Castle Architect on November 5, 1920.[9] In this post he was responsible for what Masaryk deemed the "transformation of a castle intended for the monarchy into a democratic castle."[10]

In fact Plečnik's first task for Masaryk was not initiated in Prague; rather, it was to effect a fundamental reworking of the Palace of Lány, the Czech president's cherished country retreat, and its extensive park. Moreover, the initial focus of his castle restoration was to repave the First Courtyard and to reconstruct the decoration on the historic Matthias Gate to the castle complex. He began outlining plans for the half-kilometer-long southern gardens at the same time as his program for the First Courtyard, both datable to 1920. The Paradise Garden was the first in the southern landscape sequence (fig. 1). In his approach to this symbolic ground on which a new chapter in the Czechs' history might be laid out, Plečnik paid particular attention both to its engagement with the past and to its accessibility to a contemporary citizenry. Primary among Plečnik's objectives was the realization of an impressive

1. Prague Castle, southern gardens, Paradise Garden, 1922–1925
Photograph Kázmér Kovács

2. Prague Castle, gate to the Paradise Garden and southern gardens, completed 1925

public access to this former royal enclosure. First he designed a viewing platform at the top of the stairs to the castle district from which the citizen could gaze over the city. Turning around toward the castle, the viewer there encounters an extraordinary gate in the nineteenth-century crenellated wall (fig. 2). Erected probably as a security measure for the imperial residence following the 1848 revolution, the wall had cut off the southern gardens, then partly planted but mostly wooded, from public access.[11] With a double portal supporting a heavy architrave balanced on an engaged granite column of an invented "Doric" order, Plečnik's gate announces that the visitor is about to enter a storied environment whose architectural and political antecedents predate the Habsburg emperors who made this castle their Bohemian seat. The message is that Czech history is longer than its Habsburg period. Immediately inside the gate, one is confronted with an elongated "Mediterranean" vase atop an elaborated plinth and partially set in a soaring niche (fig. 3). The vase dramatically introduces the visitor to Plečnik's and the president's stylistic preference for simple,

3. Prague Castle, Paradise Garden, vase and plinth, marble, early 1920s

austere, and (vaguely) classicizing forms. Both felt that these carried a moral force commensurate with what they identified as the contemporary Slavic character and "native" republican virtues, newly freed from centuries of Habsburg excess and authoritarianism. Both traits become more evident as one progresses deeper into the southern gardens.[12]

From the gated platform, Plečnik ordered a broad staircase by means of which the newly independent Czech citizen might descend regally into the Paradise Garden itself (see essay frontispiece). Almost immediately after construction began, the necessary stabilization of the foundation uncovered substrata of earlier landscaping, uncultivated fields, and

a set of stairs that Archduke Ferdinand of Tyrol had had built in the 1560s; and Plečnik adapted his design program to effect a dialogue with this area's layers of history. He was also partially responsible—along with the architect and builder Karel Fiala—for overseeing an extensive archaeological excavation project through which the buried history of the castle, especially its immediately surrounding gardens and walls, might be better understood. What was revealed through excavation would help define the outlines of Plečnik's design plans both for the southern gardens and, more decisively, for the Second and Third Courtyards of the castle.[13]

The architectural discourse between present and past initiated with the staircase entrance to the Paradise Garden corresponded perfectly with Masaryk's request that Plečnik invent a design program through which to promote a "democracy of discussion."[14] Thus, instead of burying the strata of the castle garden's history, Plečnik engaged them by following the general course of the earlier staircase, reusing some of the excavated materials, and documenting the archaeological process. The long cascade of steps with low risers and wide intermediary landings along the three flights encourages a slow, deliberate descent, one that affords the visitor prolonged views of the castle, much of the southern gardens, and the city beyond the ramparts (figs. 4 and 5). This panoply of sight lines is regal in its compass and affords the citizen of the new republic the perspective once reserved for monarchs. Moreover, the nobility of viewpoint is enhanced as one walks slowly down the gently shifting axis of Plečnik's grand staircase from the gated platform at the top to the green lawn at its base. The architect's strategy was more than aesthetic, however. He shared with his patrons—President Masaryk and the president's highly intellectual daughter Alice—a belief in the role of architecture in promoting philosophical reflection and moral regeneration.[15] Plečnik conceived a grand entrance to a civic paradise. The staircase would function as a material and metaphoric passageway

4. Prague Castle, staircase leading into the Paradise Garden, c. 1921–1923

5. Prague Castle, view from the staircase into the southern gardens with bowl sculpture designed by Plečnik

6. Prague Castle, southern gardens, Rampart Garden, 1924–1925

7. Prague Castle, Rampart Garden, c. 1925, renovated 1990s(?)
Photograph Kázmér Kovács

Masaryks and Plečnik himself subscribed.[16] Moreover, it would be manifested along the rebuilt ramparts and beneath the towering walls into the further reaches of the southern gardens and into the Rampart Garden (Na valech zahrada) and the Moravian Bastion (Moravská bašta), where the architect reaffirmed his practice of creatively uniting architecture and politics, abstraction and folklore. Here, deep within the landscaped ramparts, one encounters Plečnik's inventive visual juxtapositions of classicizing vessels and historical monuments and his evocative placement of ancient geometrical forms adjacent to imaginative structures (fig. 6).[17] Here and there along the length of the southern gardens, he laid out extensive, crisply outlined strips of lawn like green carpets hedged in by walls; pathways; and terraces dotted with original forms that, compositely, were intended to prompt the visitor to gaze outward toward contemporary Prague and inward to private contemplation of beauty and faith, design and history. With similar philosophical intention, Plečnik laid out expanses of stone or sand, frequently ornamented by syncopated rows of potted plants, to impose both an aesthetic discipline and a moral rigor, thereby attempting to reconcile landscape and history (fig. 7). Not infrequently Plečnik's design yielded its love of regularity to deeply rooted nature, especially when it took the form of a mature tree around which the architect's straight path would make a semicircular detour.

The half kilometer of southern gardens was a showplace for Plečnik's creativity as both a progressive landscape designer and an architect of decisively retrospective vision, adept in using obelisks surmounting high bases with Roman-like inscriptions, as in the Slavata Monument (fig. 8), and innovative in his practice of covering pyramids with vines or filling depressions in terraces with greenery. The long stretch of gardens was a laboratory for new forms through which to educate the Czechs in the nobility of their heritage while proselytizing for a modern morality. Thus the sequence of gardens on the south side

through the architectural periods of the castle and the capital, seen to either side of the gardens, and through the moral development of the Czechs from imperial subjection to republican participation.

This ethical understanding of architectural and landscape design accorded fully with the platonic idealism (and ultimately with the Christian social morality) to which both

8. Prague Castle, southern gardens, monolith before the Slavata Monument, granite, 1925

of the castle—the Paradise and Rampart Gardens, as well as the original array of staircases, ramps, bastions, stone bowls, vases, pyramids, tables, mosaic floors, and columns that ornament and complete them—was as much an idealized as a literal landscape. It was a cultivated space in which history was encompassed and philosophy grounded. And although these extensive gardens projected a new Eden of freedom and responsibility for the Czechoslovak republic and its citizens, they were not the culmination of Plečnik's (or the Masaryks') landscape endeavors for the historic *hrad*. Through the 1920s, as work continued on the sequence of the southern gardens, Plečnik turned his focus to the Bastion Garden (Na bašta zahrada) and the Stag Moat (Jelení příkop), to the west and north of the castle complex.[18] The ideas he realized in these settings drew fundamentally on the idiosyncratic union of geometrical rigor and pure invention essayed in the southern precincts of the castle. These intellectually ambitious and physically expansive programs for the Paradise Garden and its extensions may be understood as collectively constituting the architect's first sustained foray into park

planning and landscape philosophy. Plečnik's imaginative melding of morality and garden design, history and landscape aesthetics, furnished not just the model for his other commissions at the castle but also the philosophical grounds and aesthetic strategies that he would refine and implement in his native land.

The Ljubljana Riverfront

By the mid-1930s the generalized (western) Slavist suprapatriotism to which Plečnik and his patrons in Prague had subscribed was eclipsed by a much more particularist and virulent Czechoslovak (and anti-German) nationalism. The atmosphere it established throughout Bohemia and Moravia, and in Prague specifically, discouraged Plečnik from continuing his work for Masaryk's projects. Yielding to the stridency of Czech chauvinism, Plečnik resigned as Castle Architect in 1935 and thereby surrendered control over the final designs for the Stag Moat, the tennis courts, and the Royal Garden (Královská zahrada), which he had once called "the most beautiful architectonic poem of Central Europe."[19]

Throughout his tenure as Castle Architect, Plečnik also held an appointment as professor of architecture at Ljubljana's newly constituted university.[20] Thus, he had to negotiate between the demands of Prague and those of his hometown. (During Plečnik's prolonged absences from Prague, much of the supervisory responsibility for his castle plans was entrusted to his student Otto Rothmayer [1892–1966], who from 1922 carried out Plečnik's program.) What he learned from his work for Masaryk and the Czech people, he endeavored to elaborate in Slovenia, though with one profound difference. Whereas Plečnik was charged by Masaryk with creating a symbolic seat of government worthy of a new state proud of its freedom from centuries of imperial domination, his task in Slovenia was to affirm continuities with past regimes, both actual and imagined. Whereas the commission in Prague was to adapt the past to fit the present, the challenge in

Ljubljana was to fit the present into an imagined past. In both, Plečnik would become an inventive mediator of history.[21]

Despite the different ideologies of his projects in the two Slavic centers, Plečnik drew upon his Czech experience to effect in Ljubljana a triumphal program through which the "traces of the past stand out sharply, using monuments in their capacity as urban marks of orientation and turning them into points of support for collective memory."[22] By so doing, as we shall see, Plečnik sought to transform his native city into a worthy capital for a modern Slovene nation. In short, the generalized Slavic consciousness that he evinced in Prague blossomed into a particularized Slovenian self-awareness. It was an ethnic self-consciousness that decisively determined his original engagement with both an ideated past and a projected future; it would serve, moreover, as the basis for his ingenious designs for a modern Ljubljana.

From his student days, Plečnik believed firmly in the Slavs' civilizing mission for Europe. Holding that Slavic artists were "God's elect," he went on to claim "that we are not artists [only] in order to make works of art—but that … we bring ourselves in the search for the beautiful and good—possibly close to God—to the understanding of justice, and make good people—good righteous men as perfect as possible."[23] The emphasis on the moral dimension of Slavic creativity was easily transfigured into a religious one, as Plečnik conjoined his abiding adherence to the Catholic faith with a commitment to elevating the spiritual life of his countrymen, primarily through the agency of architecture and landscape design. Plečnik's faith in the timeless relevance of the church and its teachings went hand in hand with his belief in the authority of architecture to make visible for a contemporary audience the experience of spirituality. At the most profound level, he believed in the power of modern architecture to effect salvation—for the individual, for the Slavic race, and for Slovenia. Plečnik's Catholicism must be understood as part of his national-ism; for by fulfilling his numerous commissions for the church in his homeland, he understood himself as promoting the ethnic identity of the overwhelmingly Catholic Slovenes. In the designer's mind, there was a coincidence between the universalist claims of the church and the totalizing aspirations of architecture: he perceived each as transcendent, monumental, and transformative and thereby revelatory of the highest spirit of mankind and nation. As a result, he was as committed to Catholic Slovenia (within the framework of the multiconfessional Habsburg empire and the two succeeding Yugoslavian states) as to the mostly non-Catholic republican Czechoslovakia.

Like others of his time, and especially among intellectuals throughout east-central Europe, Plečnik looked to history in order to identify an ethnic lineage upon which a modern nation-state might be constructed. Despite his recognition of affinity with and admiration for his fellow Slavs, most notably the Czechs, the architect posited a unique derivation for the Slovenes. Postulating on little concrete evidence that the original inhabitants of central Italy were likely Slavic tribes, he traced the origin of the Slovene people to Etruria. Believing uncritically in a Tuscan pedigree for his compatriots, Plečnik found it fitting to revive and adapt elemental Italian forms, such as Tuscan columns, door jambs, and tumuli, as legitimate expressions of the "national" architectural idiom. Rejecting readily accessible Slovenian decorative arts and surviving folk art as sources for a native idiom—and therefore departing from the normative practices of his contemporaries in Poland, Hungary, Romania, and elsewhere in the region—the architect turned instead to ancient Etruria as a manifestation "of unspoilt ancient Slovene national art, from which contemporary architecture should draw its inspiration."[24] An Etruscan vocabulary of forms, as well as references to Etrurian spirituality and reliance on ritual, would confer a classical monumentality commensurate with the ethnic derivation Plečnik hypothesized for his people.

Plečnik's worldview was more eclectic than systematic; he borrowed freely from a wide range (and all too frequent misreading) of religious thinkers, historians, and architectural theoreticians. Among the last, the figure who exercised the dominant influence over his architectural perspective was Gottfried Semper (1803–1879), whose arguments in favor of "variety," especially of classical forms, the Slovene would embrace as the foundation of his own design vocabulary.[25] What motivated Plečnik was likely the desire to root historically his conservative devotionalism and to justify it with an emotionally charged iconographic program. By means of such a roughly conceived ideology, he desired to counter the ever-growing reliance on the transnational "utilitarianism, typology and standardization [that] are the death of any art," not with a single style but rather with an overall architectural expression, one that might advance his vision for his Slavic brethren.[26] By drawing upon architectural history, national mythologies, and innovative technological processes, he intended to return architectural design to its originary basis and to provide his native land with a vocabulary of form proportional to his aspirations for it. To effect such an ambitious transformation, Plečnik was favored by a singular conjunction of fortuitous circumstances and natural talent.

Material and political conditions in Ljubljana were ripe for Plečnik just when he was most prepared to take full advantage of them. The end of World War I witnessed the creation of the Kingdom of the Serbs, Croats, and Slovenes as a new, modern nation of the south Slavs. Ljubljana was designated the capital city of its Slovenian component. The local elite, with the encouragement of the royal government in Belgrade, was thus finally in a position to realize the national ambition of making Ljubljana worthy of its status as a capital city. The Yugoslav kingdom passed a building law in 1931 through which the director of Ljubljana's municipal building department was granted unusually free reign to award contracts and implement

projects. Hence the engineer Matko Prelovšek (1876–1955), who served as director between 1914 and 1937, was able to vest Plečnik with public commissions of an unprecedented number and scale. Prelovšek was also a patron of Plečnik for the remodeling of his own house (1931–1933), as well as his commercial building known as the Flatiron (1933–1934).

With Director Prelovšek's encouragement, Plečnik prepared the first of several master plans for his native city between 1926 and 1928, setting out his ambitious program for a Slavic metropolis. Although the full scope was never implemented, cardinal civic and religious projects were substantially realized: public squares during the latter half of the 1920s (including the St. James/Levstikov, Congress, and French Revolution Squares); the university and the national library from 1936 to 1941; churches and monasteries from the 1920s through the 1950s; bridges, markets, and monuments during the 1930s and 1940s; cultural, commercial, and government buildings; villas and private houses; and parks, promenades, and public passageways and staircases. In contrast to most modern architects of large vision, Plečnik rarely worked on apartment buildings and was never interested in public housing projects, either in Ljubljana or in Prague. This was not because of any preference for smaller-scale buildings; indeed he sometimes worked on the grandest scale. It is likely that his reluctance to undertake multidwelling housing, especially that intended for workers, was due to his politically conservative belief in the social importance of privilege. He often proclaimed that people of noble mind should serve as an example to those less fortunate. With such a conservative outlook, it is not surprising that he viewed unsympathetically the functionalist belief in modern architecture's "social engineering."[27]

Although many of Plečnik's buildings and monuments in Ljubljana have been examined in terms of their style, history, and urban context, less scholarly attention has been focused on his landscape conceptions.[28] Yet it is in his plans for the capital's green spaces—and the landscape structures designed for them—that his unconventional modern vision can be most readily experienced. By considering Plečnik's approach to Ljubljana's Roman wall and his treatment of the banks of the Ljubljanica River, we can best perceive the outline of his ideologically charged modern landscape.

Plečnik held nature (φύσις) to be sacred. He believed that it provided an ideal model, philosophically and historically, for modern man to emulate. His faith in the contemporary value of nature was a conscious attempt to align himself with the philosophy of classical antiquity and thereby to make the past an essential part of the present. Although Plečnik's inventive variants on and innovative contextualization of the column, pyramid, and obelisk would ultimately serve as his principal architectural instruments to bring ancient forms into current usage, nature constituted his philosophical strategy: green spaces—whether geometrically organized as in Prague, or loosely orchestrated as in Ljubljana—possessed an inherent therapeutic and social value for all classes, whereas architecture alone had a more narrow social compass.[29] To revive the citizen's spirit, restore his energies, and remind him of democratic values, Plečnik had planted a variety

of trees and bushes throughout the central districts of Ljubljana. Along the capital's streets, he diverted sidewalks and pedestrian pathways to allow for the "natural" growth of the countless trees and shrubs he had planted, hoping thereby to prompt an inspiring encounter with greenery.[30] In Plečnik's theory, greenery would remind urban dwellers of their connection to nature and would soften the harshness and relentless tempo of contemporary city life. Most important, a "greened" landscape would be an effective means for the architect to orchestrate passage through space and time. And nowhere was this more ingeniously realized than in his strategy for the surviving fragment of the city's Roman wall. Here, one encounters most dramatically the twinned pillars of Plečnik's worldview: nature and history combining to shape the modern citizen.

Ljubljana had been founded by the emperor Augustus in 34 BCE as a Roman colony under the name of Emona (or Aemona). An extensive remnant of the south wall fortification (14–15 CE) had been preserved into the twentieth century as a reminder of the city's classical past.[31] Behind the wall, on the opposite side to Mirje Street, Plečnik gathered many of the stone fragments from tumbled columns, fallen archivolts, and broken ornaments into a lapidarium, which he treated as if it were one of the many burial chambers that had impressed him on his 1899 study trip to Rome and its Appian Way. But Plečnik was interested in more than the architectural record. As was the case with his work for Prague, he wished in Ljubljana to reinforce the spiritual and hereditary bonds between the present Slavic inhabitants and the distant past. In the case of the Slovenian capital, these ancestors were the original Roman settlers. To effect this linkage, he needed to do more than merely safeguard the archaeological fragments; he had to transform them into a modern demonstration of historical consequence. Between 1934 and 1937, Plečnik rebuilt the wall and studded its top with a series of pyramids (fig. 9). Surmount-

9. Roman wall, Ljubljana, segment with pyramid, 1934–1937

one of Plečnik's objectives. However, the triangular forms, occasionally with portals cut through their bases, and with interior chambers, were also intended to evoke the tumuli of Etruria. This evocation at the Roman wall of ancient Etrusco-Italic burial structures was of great significance to Plečnik, who endeavored to fabricate architecturally an imagined Etruscan genealogy for his compatriots.[32]

To give contemporary life to these exalted antique forms, the architect staggered the pyramids rhythmically both atop and alongside the wall, creating along the longitudinal axis an impressive visual syncopation that reveals itself almost cinematographically as the pedestrian proceeds along the street. Moreover, Plečnik intended the pyramidal surfaces to be covered with greenery, allowing natural grasses to vitalize the geometry. He preferred these to brightly colored flowers or exotic plants, which he reserved for private commissions and mostly avoided in public spaces. Likewise, the verges to each side of the ancient stone wall were landscaped in long bands of grass, establishing a lively contrast to the gray masonry (see

ing the wall and sometimes firmly planted on the ground (fig. 10), they emulate his use of this form for the southern gardens of Prague Castle (see fig. 6), just as they were intended to recall the Augustan Pyramid of Cestius (c. 18–12 BCE; fig. 11) and thereby reinforce the connection to Roman greatness,

fig. 10), a practice he first embraced for the southern stretches of the Paradise and Rampart Gardens of Prague's castle.[33] Further animation was given to the Emonan fortification ensemble through the planting of a row of poplar trees (no longer extant), which would create a play of shadows to enliven the wall surface and vertically reinforce the rhythmic arrangement of pyramids. Thus the citizen of modern Ljubljana, walk-

ing or driving along the street on the way home from the city center, would encounter Plečnik's historical narrative, unfolding cinematically from Etruscan, through Roman, to contemporary time.

The carefully constructed consciousness of motion through time and space, one of the defining characteristics of classical modernism, was a prominent feature of Plečnik's landscape designs.[34] Yet, when the architect creatively combined historical reference and contemporaneous movement with nature's greenery, he achieved a synthesis that had few parallels in twentieth-century art. Perhaps Plečnik's most perfect realization of this fusion of the old and the new, the man-made and the natural, can be found along the Ljubljanica River, which wends its way through the heart and history of the capital city.

The shallow Ljubljanica had often overrun its banks until, during the nineteenth and early twentieth centuries, the riverbed had been deepened and its course channeled through concrete embankments. The work on regularizing the river, long supported from the Habsburg coffers, was halted during World War I, and not until 1930 were the municipal authorities, benefiting from a special appropriation from the royal Yugoslav treasury, in a financial position to continue the project. Matko Prelovšek, in his capacity as director of the city building department, engaged the keen interest and active participation of Plečnik in a host of riparian design commissions that were realized, including bridges, storehouses, markets, sluices, and parks. It is the last two that merit attention here.

Plečnik concentrated his efforts on remaking the embankments, beginning as early as 1931 and not ending until 1945. The park project for the upper reaches of the river, in the city districts of Trnovo and Prule, dates from the beginning of the project, most likely to 1932–1933, a full decade after the architect's first efforts at landscape garden design for Prague. As one approaches this portion of the embank-

12. Gerber Staircase, Ljubljana, 1932–1933

ment, say from Plečnik's Cobbler's Bridge (1931–1932), one is first struck by the absence of the very monumentality that he had championed as both appropriate to the city's genealogy and essential to his fellow citizens' spiritual health. In lieu of the impressive cascade of steps (the Gerber Staircase; 1932–1933; fig. 12), a panoply of pyramids (as employed at the Emona wall), a complex "fan" of river spans (as at the Three Bridges, 1929–1932), a sequence of paraphrased Ionic lampposts (such as his candelabrum outside the Philharmonic Hall, 1932–1933), or an impressive colonnade (such as the one that lines the multisectioned market, 1940–1944), here one encounters a soothing succession of low, shallow terraces, which follow the gentle curve of the river (fig. 13). Whereas elsewhere along the riverbank it is Plečnik's architectural elements that thrust imposingly upward, within this parklike setting verticality is communicated solely by the stand of weeping willows, which crowns the horizontal rise of the terracing. That Plečnik assigned to nature the highest posi-

tion is noteworthy. On the one hand, it is fully congruent with his garden practice, as we have seen with his stipulation that greenery cap the Roman wall pyramids (or that it enjoy elevated status in the gardens framing the ancient Prague Castle). But in a deeper sense, Plečnik wished to bring Ljubljana's citizens into a more direct contact with nature and history; and the riverside park commission afforded him an ideal opportunity.

With gently sloping hedge-lined paths leading down from the high embankments and easily accessible from the surrounding streets (fig. 14), the terraces were particularly inviting for citizens to relax, play, or—as Plečnik presumed—launder clothes. Combining utilitarian functions with relaxation and entertainment would lend the terraces wide appeal. But Plečnik wanted to make them instructional as well. To this end, he banked up the slope to accommodate a progression of low, elongated stone benches in alignment. This landscape architecture calls to mind classical parallels congruent with Ljubljana's past, such as a shallow amphitheater or the

14. Sloped and stepped terraces on the Ljubljanica River, Ljubljana, 1932/1933–c. 1937

15. Terracing of the Ljubljanica River, Ljubljana, 1932/1933–c. 1937

flutes of a column laid on its side (fig. 15).[35] The park, then, was to be a place where one literally relaxed, played, and bathed (or laundered) in an archaeological reprise of the city's Augustan history. As the citizen sat on or walked along the stone benches of Plečnik's "Romanized" terraces, she or he presumably might glance across the regulated river to an opposite wall of soothing herbage and pathways, both camouflaging the concrete embankment, which Plečnik designed to evoke the green banks and slow windings described by Virgil in the *Georgics*.

If the architect intended his riverbank park to call to mind Latin pastoral poetry, he wanted to invoke the masculine authority of Roman engineering in his design for the sluice (1931–1935), which lay at the opposite end of Ljubljana's *flumen*. Of course, the lock was of necessity engineered to perform utilitarian functions; namely, to maintain a constant water level and to regulate the flow in the urban sections of the Ljubljanica.[36] However, Plečnik aspired to monumentalize the ideological significance of the structure and to employ it to promote a stream of historical associations among his fellow Slovenes.

Rejecting the functionalist denigration of decoration, as well as the hierarchical typology of buildings, Plečnik designed his utilitarian sluice as a major public monument, one that would function on multiple metaphoric and literal levels. At a slight distance from the walkways along the river, one can appreciate the greenery cloaking the inclined banks that the architect had planted with native shrubbery and untrimmed trees (fig. 16). This parklike framework, which hid from view the reinforced concrete that supported the embankments, is dramatically intensified when seen from the level of the river itself. The woodland-like greensward is complemented at the street level by a procession of paving and gravel that leads directly to the dressed masonry pylon gate (fig. 17). From here the pedestrian initiates a passage through history and across the water. Progressing through an Egypto-Mesopotamian-style portal, the modern citizen of Ljubljana mounts a shallow flight of stairs and then crosses a bridge supported by the three towering pylons of the sluice itself (fig. 18). But traversing the bridge entails more than motion through space. Plečnik wanted it to be a procession through time, too. Therefore, he supported the slender bridge on monumental hybrid Aeolic capitals adorned with carved heads, in place of the palmettes of ancient examples, between flaring volutes (fig. 19). This ingenious architectural composite was inspired by the

16. Sluice on the Ljubljanica River,
Ljubljana, 1933–1945

17. Masonry pylon gate to the
sluice on the Ljubljanica River
(south side), Ljubljana, 1933–1945

archaeological record at Etruscan Cerveteri, where Plečnik may have been impressed by the Aeolic pilasters from the Tomb of the Reliefs. Plečnik's "Etruscan" shafts were balanced on the other side of the lock gate by equally monumental fluted "Doric" columns, cut off a few meters above the base so that they might serve as stands for enormous antique caldrons (fig. 20), whose imposing gryphon protomes Plečnik knew from his study of Etruscan tomb art, more likely from the books he consulted than from visits to archaeological sites or museum collections. In his invention of original classicizing forms, he harkens back to the ornamental vessels he used more than a decade before in Prague's Paradise Garden. With such historical elaboration, the sluice bridge was to function as much more than a utilitarian span over the river; rather, it was to engineer a metaphoric transition through Slovenia's genealogy. By an ingenious application of historical reference to the practical task of water regulation, Plečnik unified along the Ljubljanica his nation's history and nature, its ideology and architecture.

With its ideologically charged bridge supported on imaginative architectural combinations, the lock gate marked the final phase in the architect's long engagement with redesigning Ljubljana's watercourse and its urbane mainstream. By 1945, the year of the sluice's completion, the favorable conditions under which Plečnik had worked so creatively for his native city changed decisively. Soon after the conclusion of World War II came the end of the Yugoslav monarchy, with its relative social conservatism, which Plečnik had genuinely embraced. Moreover, the end of the war also signaled the expulsion of the Germans from Czechoslovakia and the increasing influence of the Soviet Union throughout central and eastern Europe. And with the ascendancy of the Soviet system and the imposition of various forms of socialist realism, Plečnik found himself increasingly out of official favor, though he was never entirely dismissed. In short order the ingenious Slovene

18. Sluice on the Ljubljanica River with Eygpto-Mesopotamian-style portals and pylons, Ljubljana, 1933–1945

19. Bridge on the Ljubljanica River, pylon with Aeolic capital with carved head, Ljubljana, 1933–1945

20. Lock gate on the Ljubljanica River, "Doric" columns surmounted by caldrons, Ljubljana, 1933–1945

architect witnessed profoundly negative changes in the social and political character of both cities where he had enjoyed his greatest success and realized his most significant achievements. In Prague, where Plečnik's career and ideas first flourished, and in Ljubljana, where his career reached its maturity, the assumption of full authority by the Communist Party meant that the now aged architect was mostly passed over in the awarding of major commissions to build a new, classless society. Instead of encouraging the idiosyncratic modernism that Jože Plečnik personified, Soviet aesthetics proved by and large unsympathetic to forms of inventive design that departed from party principles.[37] For Plečnik and his patrons, who celebrated the past as a valued support of the present and who promoted a modern expression that affirmed singularity instead of standardization, an era of liberal creativity and optimism had functionally come to an end.

NOTES

The discussion of Plečnik's landscape program for Ljubljana derives from my article "Jože Plečnik and the Landscaping of Modern Ljubljana," *Centropa* 4, no. 2 (May 2004). Translations are mine unless otherwise indicated.

Photographs for figures 2–6, 8–10, and 12–20 are by Julia Frane.

1. On expressionism, see Peter Krečič, "Architecture in the Former Yugoslavia," in *Impossible Histories: Historical Avant-Gardes, Neo-Avant-Gardes, and Post-Avant-Gardes in Yugoslavia, 1918–1991*, ed. Dubravka Djurič and Misko Šuvakovič (Cambridge, MA, 2003), 336–338, especially note 3, in which the author attributes to Plečnik an "expressionism based on Italian mannerism." On Plečnik as a pioneer of modern architecture, see Ian Bentley, Richard Andrews, Nace Šumi, and Dunda Gržan-Butina, *Jože Plečnik, 1872–1957: Architecture and the City* (Museum of Modern Art, New York, 1983), 27. On modern classicism, see Zuzana Güllendi-Cimprochová, "Denkmalkriterium Religiosität: Zum Denkmalverständnis des Architekten Josip Plečnik (1872–1957)," *kunsttexte.de*, no. 2 (2008): 1. Pavel Janák is reported to have averred that Plečnik reoriented Prague's College of Applied Arts toward "a mature modern classicism." See Damjan Prelovšek, "The Life and Work of Jože Plečnik," in *Jože Plečnik: Architect, 1872–1957*, ed. François Burkhardt, Claude Eveno, and Boris Podrecca, trans. Carol Volk (Cambridge, MA, 1989), 49. (Original French and Slovenian editions included Prelovšek as coeditor: *Jože Plečnik, architecte* [Centre Pompidou, Paris, 1986].) On Plečnik as a mythmaker, see Anthony Alofsin, *When Buildings Speak: Architecture as Language in the Habsburg Empire and Its Aftermath, 1867–1933* (Chicago, 2007), 241–244. For mention of a host of critics who praised Plečnik's postmodernism, see Friedrich Achleitner, "A Slavic Gaudí?," in Burkhardt, Eveno, and Podrecca 1989.

2. In recent years, scholars of modern art and architectural history—in particular, those who focus on eastern Europe—have begun to challenge as too restrictive and too partial the reliance on Western European and North American modernism as a useful paradigm for comprehending twentieth-century art universally. Instead of relying predominantly on transnational styles as the most telling index of progressive art, scholars are attending increasingly to the decisive role played by local traditions, expectations, and audiences in the development and expression of modern art. Just such a contextual perspective, as provided, for example, by Damjan Prelovšek (see note 1), would disclose what he calls, rightly, "asymptomatic" aspects of Plečnik's modernism. Further, the last decade of published scholarship on the history of modern architecture reveals a searching reassessment of the meanings and purposes of modernist paradigms as originally established by Walter Gropius, J. J. P. Oud, Le Corbusier, and other fathers of functionalism. Many of the contemporary studies have appeared under the rubric of Docomomo (International Working Party for the Documentation and Conservation of Buildings, Sites and Neighbourhoods of the Modern Movement). Most are premised on the concept

of a pluralistic modernism; that is, a methodological strategy that holds that progressive architectural forms and uses defy any unitary categorical imperative. In contrast to the dominant interpretive uniformity that characterized the plurality of architectural studies from the 1930s through the 1980s, they attribute to modernism a heterogeneity of meanings and intentions. Representative of the current historiographical orientation are Hubert-Jan Hencket and Hilde Heynen, eds., *Back from Utopia* (Rotterdam, 2002); Hilde Heynen, *Architecture and Modernity: A Critique* (Cambridge, MA, 1999); and *Universality and Heterogeneity: Proceedings from the Fourth International Docomomo Conference*, September 18–21, 1996 (Bratislava, 1997). Antedating the revisionism of architectural historians was the engagement of architects. Designs from the 1960s for a postmodern architecture may rightly be understood as a critique of the theoretical claims and formal vocabulary of classical modern art and architecture.

3. Although the scholarly literature on Plečnik is vast, beginning as early as 1920 with the published appreciation by Kosta Strajnič, *Josip Plečnik* (Ljubljana?, 1920), two works remain standard for the English-reading audience: Peter Krečič, *Plečnik: The Complete Works* (New York, 1993), and, especially worthy, Damjan Prelovšek, *Jože Plečnik, 1872–1957: Architectura perennis*, trans. Eileen Martin and Patricia Crampton (New Haven and London, 1997), a revision, with an updated bibliography, of the German text (Salzburg, c. 1992). The number and variety of publications on Plečnik, many inspired or authored by Prevlošek, continue to grow, as in *Architecte Jože Plečnik (1872–1957)* (Musées royaux des Beaux-Arts de Belgique, Brussels, 2008). For a comprehensive assessment of Plečnik's activities related to Prague Castle (and Prague in general), see Zdeněk Lukeš et al., eds., *Josip Plečnik: Architekt Pražského hradu* (Prague Castle, Prague, 1996), published in an expanded English-language version, *Josip Plečnik: An Architect of Prague Castle*, various translators (Prague, 1997). See also Zdena Průchová, "Jozef Plečnik a Praha," *Umění* 20, no. 5 (1972), 442–445; and Caroline Constant, "A Landscape Fit for a Democracy: Jože Plečnik at Prague Castle (1920–1935)," in Jan Birksted, ed., *Relating Architecture to Landscape* (London, 1999), 120–146.

4. See Damjan Prelovšek, *Josef Plečnik: Wiener Arbeiten von 1896 bis 1914* (Vienna, 1979), especially 13 n. 6 for a quotation by the architect on his desire to become ever more a "Carniolan—a Slovene—in the same way as my parents" (MS 31, undated).

5. For a discussion of the cultural and political tensions between Prague's German and Czech citizenry, see S. A. Mansbach, *Modern Art in Eastern Europe: From the Baltic to the Balkans, c. 1890–1939* (Cambridge, 1999), and Peter Demetz, *Prague in Black and Gold: Scenes from the Life of a European City* (New York, 1997). On Plečnik's enthusiasm for Czech culture, see Damjan Prelovšek, "Ideological Substratum in Plečnik's Work," in Lukeš et al. 1997, 89–90.

6. On March 7, 1920, President Masaryk stated that he "observe[d] with what reverence and loving devotion people come to the castle to see the thousand years of our architectural history. So immediately after my return from abroad, I made arrangements for the necessary repairs to be carried out and for the various parts of the castle to be properly surveyed. My aim is to make the castle a worthy monument to our past." (Quoted in *Architektura ČSR* 7, no. 1 [1948]: 13, and excerpted in Prelovšek 1997, 123.)

7. Although the competition for the garden did not take place until 1920, in 1919 the new president's office had appointed the landscape gardener F. J. Thomayer as "master of gardens" for the castle complex. Thus, it is likely that Masaryk was considering a major landscaping effort soon upon assuming his political office. See Tomáš Valena, "Courtyards and Gardens: Plečnik's Interventions in the Context of Prague Castle," in Lukeš et al. 1997, 259–262.

8. According to Tomáš Valena (in Lukeš et al. 1997, 259) there were no jury members with training in landscape architecture; hence, one must conclude that Plečnik's background was less exceptional than it might appear to a contemporary audience or competition. Damjan Prelovšek makes a convincing case for Plečnik's appointment to the jury. He argues that in order to secure the architect's services for Prague following the offer of a professorship in Ljubljana (see note 20, below), the castle administration increased Plečnik's salary and named him the "official representative of Prague's College of Arts and Crafts [College of Applied Arts] on the jury for the gardens under the south wing of the Castle" (Prelovšek 1997, 122).

9. Documentation on the appointment is cited in Prelovšek 1997, 124. Although Masaryk and Plečnik came from different generations, they shared a love for antiquity and a high regard for philosophies of morals (though Plečnik's were decidedly Christian whereas Masaryk's were essentially secular). The importance of this affinity cannot be overestimated, for Masaryk could have had no architectural evidence on which to base his appointment of Plečnik to such an exalted post. As Peter Krečič has pointed out, between 1911 and 1920 Plečnik devoted his energies in Prague exclusively to teaching; he produced no significant building in Bohemia before his contact with Masaryk. See Peter Krečič, "Plečnik and the Critics," in Bentley et al. 1983, 25. Tomáš Vlček postulates that Masaryk chose Plečnik for the position because the Slovenian "had fewer personal contacts in Prague [than any local architect] and stood apart from the local cultural relations which Masaryk providently expected in Czech architects" (Tomáš Vlček, "Modernism as a Means to Achieve Democracy: T. G. Masaryk and Josip Plečnik," in Lukeš et al. 1997, 44).

10. Quoted in Prevlošek 1989, 52.

11. Tomáš Valena has written (in Lukeš et al. 1997, 262), that "whereas the courtyards [of the castle complex] had from the beginning been conceived as something like an entrance hall to the Castle, the southern gardens had remained out of bounds to the public." Thus, ensuring access was one dramatically symbolic way of reversing the loss of political rights to the Habsburg emperor, Franz Josef, who ascended as king of Bohemia in 1848 and whose death in 1916

occurred just as Czechs such as Masaryk (then in exile) were preparing for a political restoration. At roughly the same time (1920), Plečnik began working out a solution for a special entranceway to the southern gardens from the private apartment he would realize for President Masaryk (and his daughter). See Věra Malá and Damjan Prelovšek, "A Chronological Survey of Plečnik's Works at Prague Castle and Lány," in Lukeš et al. 1997, 611.

12. The generalized Mediterranean aspect of the vase may have been Plečnik's attempt to play up to Masaryk's deep love of classical Greece and Italy. The Czech president had been profoundly moved by his 1921 trip with his daughter Alice to Italy, where he had visited a number of archaeological sites and collections of antiquities. The Masaryks' respect for Mediterranean, especially ancient Roman, cultures coincided with the passion of the architect, who saw in Etruria the source of Slavic nobility in general and Slovene nationhood in particular. Plečnik's and the Masaryks' emphasis on architecture as a moral discourse, as well as a historical discussion, is evident in most of the architect's manifold commissions for the castle precinct, as well as those he carried out later in his homeland. See below.

13. For a brief discussion of the courtyard discoveries, see Prelovšek 1997, 123. For mention of Fiala, see Tamim El Haje, "Jože Plečnik: His Architecture in Prague for Freedom and a New Democracy" (MArch thesis, Texas Tech University, 2000).

14. See Vlček in Lukeš et al. 1997, 47 n. 21.

15. For a discussion of the role played by the president's daughter in the renovation of the castle, see Věra Běhalová, "Alice Masaryk, Plečnik and the Castle," in Lukeš et al. 1997, 81–87.

16. Throughout his long and productive career as a designer of sacral, commercial, governmental, educational, and recreational structures, Plečnik never wavered in accepting the Christian faith as the justification and objective of all his aesthetic endeavors. His abiding religiosity helps to explain his profound engagement with sacred architecture, church decoration, and designs for liturgical objects, all of which stimulated his inventiveness rather than leading to standardization. However, Plečnik's morality was equally important to his secular commissions. From the discussions he had with his brother Janez, a Catholic priest in Slovenia, to those conducted with Tomáš and Alice Masaryk on ethical friendship, Plečnik strove to make his architecture a moral (and historical) force in contemporary life.

Masaryk's Christianity was rather less formalized than Plečnik's. In a letter dated October 29, 1923, Alice Masaryk expressed the view she shared with her father: "[I]n Christ, I see an enhancement, not an escape.... There is no fear in the realm of the spirit, for it is governed by a divine order. But it is a very narrow path.... Beauty. How much I have thought about it ... and it has dawned on me that beauty is an expression of genuine truth and love for God and man.... [A]nd whenever God touches, there is beauty. And also where man, supported by God, touches the universe in his deeds—there is beauty." (Quoted in Běhalová in Lukeš et al. 1997, 82.)

17. As Damjan Prelovšek astutely pointed out ("Ideological Substratum," in Lukeš et al. 1997, 90), Plečnik eschewed a rigorous classicism despite his keen interest in the archaeological finds of Italy and in that nation's impressive collections of vases from ancient civilizations: Greek, Etruscan, and Roman, especially. Instead of embracing classical proportions and replicating the shapes of ancient vessels, a widespread practice among his contemporaries that he criticized as pompous, he preferred to vary classic standards and forms, though maintaining their "ideological substratum." Prelovšek in Lukeš et al. 1997, 90.

18. For an excellent brief analysis of the Bastion Garden, see Valena in Lukeš et al. 1997, 285–287.

19. See Vladimir Šlapeta, "Jože Plečnik and Prague," in Burkhardt, Eveno, and Podrecca 1989, 92 and n. 58.

20. Plečnik's appointment to the professorial chair in his native city was unexpected. Although the faculty in the division of technology at Ljubljana's university had petitioned the architect Ivan Vurnik to secure the appointment of a professor of architecture from abroad, preferably one with an international reputation, Plečnik was apparently not on the short list. Indeed, an offer was extended to Max Fabiani, who turned it down. Fortuitously, the reprinting in *Slovenski narod* (Slovenian nation) of an article originally published in the Czech journal *Styl* (6, 1920), in which the case for Plečnik's appointment as professor in Prague was made, helped persuade the Ljubljana faculty to make an offer to Plečnik, which the native son readily accepted—though without renouncing his professorial post in Prague. The Ljubljana appointment was officially made on June 16, 1920, five months before Masaryk named Plečnik Castle Architect in Prague. See Prelovšek 1997, 122. For a discussion of the initial years of the university's program of architecture under Plečnik's professorial direction, see Krečič 1993, 71–93.

21. Comparisons of Plečnik's works for Prague and Ljubljana are not uncommon in the scholarly literature. Most, however, focus primarily on his urban planning or commissions for churches. As representative of this engagement, see Andrew Herscher, "Prague and Ljubljana: Producing the Capital City," in Lukeš et al. 1997, 445–454. The connections between the architect's works in Prague and Ljubljana were first pointed out in a number of critical reviews and art-historical articles by France Stelè published in Slovenian periodicals in the late 1920s and early 1930s.

22. See Jörg Stabow and Jindřich Vybíral, "Projects for Prague," in Lukeš et al. 1997, 432.

23. Jože Plečnik to Jan Kotěra, undated, cited in Prelovšek 1997, 13.

24. See Prelovšek in Lukeš et al. 1997, 99.

25. For an analysis of the importance of Semper, in particular his *Die vier Elemente der Baukunst* (1815) and *Der Stil in den technischen and tektonischen Künste, oder, Praktische Asthetik* (1860–1863), for Plečnik's aesthetic development, see Prelovšek 1997 and Prelovšek 1979.

26. Cited in Vinko Lenarčič, "Spomini na Plečnika" [Recollections of Plečnik], manuscript, c. 1961–1963, as quoted in Prelovšek 1997, 260.

27. See Jörg Stabenow, *Jože Plečnik: Städtebau im Schatten der Moderne* (Braunschweig and Wiesbaden, 1996), 40, and Prelovšek 1997, 262–273.

28. Among recent studies of Plečnik's landscape architecture for Ljubljana should be mentioned (in addition to the comprehensive treatments of the architect's oeuvre listed in the preceding notes) Damjan Prelovšek, "Über die Ausgestaltung der Flussufer: Von der österreichischen Erneuerung bis zu Plečniks Eingriffen," in *Jože Plečnik und Ljubljana, der Architect und seine Stadt*, ed. Robert G. Dyck et al. (Stadtmuseum Graz and Arhitekturni muzej, Ljubljana, 2003; originally published as an article in *Lotus International*, 1988); and Richard M. Andrews, "Ljubljana: The River Sequence," in Bentley et al. 1983. Although it focuses primarily on Plečnik's garden designs for the Prague Castle, *I giardini del Castello di Praga* (Treviso, 2002) provides a helpful overview of the architect's strategies for garden design.

29. Although geometrically arranged gardens were preponderant in Plečnik's program for the Prague Castle, while less formalized landscape designs were common for his "greening" of Ljubljana, he employed both alternatives in each place. His extensive use of trees and orchestration of woods in the Stag Moat, the Royal Garden, and eastern parts of the southern gardens (as well as the Palace of Lány) was essential to his landscape conceptions for President Masaryk. Moreover, at the beginning of the 1930s Plečnik created in Ljubljana two extremely divergent private gardens: an elaborate one (based on geometrical flower beds, elevated parterres, and a fishpond reached by a flight of stairs) for the family villa of his principal patron, Matko Prelovšek, and a simplified, utilitarian one for his own house, in which he employed concrete tubes and stone paving (made from broken plaques) for paths and borders, and set out vegetable patches, flowering low bushes, a number of tall shade trees, and a beehive.

30. Plečnik preferred not to sculpt trees or contour bushes; rather, he advocated leaving them in the natural state and using them as "natural shapes" (for both his Bohemian and Slovenian commissions). As a result, for Ljubljana he favored trees with distinctive "profiles": birch, poplar, plane, and weeping willows, among other species. Significantly, he chose few species that carried classical references from Latin poetry. Hence there are comparatively few oaks or cypress trees, for instance, in his landscape programs.

31. Although the south wall was the most visible surviving portion of the surrounding Roman stonework, standing to a height of about three meters after its renovation by Walter Schmidt in the nineteenth century, Plečnik treated at least one additional wall fragment, where the medieval city wall intersects a segment of the original Roman wall, just in front of the National and University Library. He had the Roman portion resurfaced in local cut stone and then allowed it to be covered in greenery. This combination of herbage, local masonry, and remnants of antiquity was, as this essay claims, an ideological strategy Plečnik favored.

32. Perhaps nowhere is this more emphatically realized than in the architect's program of 1938–1940 for the city's principal cemetery of Žale (an old Slavic word for cemetery). Here, Plečnik advocated funerary monuments based on Etruscan rounded tumuli or pyramidal forms, often concealing internal chambers under a layer of earth and grass.

33. Plečnik had learned not only to exploit the color of grass (and hanging plants) but also, in working with the gardener for the Prague Castle, a man by the name of Jukliček, had mastered the use of grass as an effective cover in combination with historic buildings. See Prelovšek in Lukeš et al. 1997, 97.

34. Although thematized variously as "space-time," "vision in motion," or even "a new fourth dimension," the engagement with movement through space and time was the decisive feature for the classical avant-garde in creating a modern art (as well as science and society) during the first three decades of the twentieth century. Among the numerous classic texts on this topic, see Sigfried Giedion, *Space, Time and Architecture: The Growth of a New Tradition* (Cambridge, MA, 1941); and especially the writings of Theo van Doesburg, El Lissitzky, and László Moholy-Nagy, who, along with a host of Russian and Polish figures, may be identified as the originators of the concept as applied to modern art generally. Representative of the nature and authority attributed to space-time is Moholy-Nagy's claim for "a new dynamic and kinetic existence freed from the static, fixed framework of the past. Space-time is not only a matter of natural science or of aesthetic and emotional interest. It deeply modifies the character of social ends." László Moholy-Nagy, *Vision in Motion* (Chicago, 1947), 266.

35. Prevlošek (1997, 292) was the first to associate Plečnik's stone terraces with the flutes of a column.

36. According to Prelovšek (1997, 292), Plečnik also had the idea of using the sluice to make the river navigable and consequently planned a landing dock nearby. He also envisioned a small hydroelectric power station to be connected to the sluice. See K. Dobida, "K načrtu zatvornic na Ljubljanici" [On the plan for the lock on the River Ljubljanica], *Mladika* 1 (1935).

37. In the decade following the end of World War II, Plečnik received no major commissions in his native land or in Czechoslovakia. However, in 1952, he was allowed to receive an honorary doctorate from Ljubljana University. Moreover, in the year preceding his death in 1957, he unexpectedly received a commission from the Yugoslav party and national leader, Josip Broz Tito (1892–1980). Paradoxically, this commission permitted Plečnik to complete his career in the same way he began it, by designing a private retreat for the president of a Slavic republic: first the Palace of Lány (and the private apartment in the Prague Castle) for Czechoslovakia's Masaryk, and finally a villa on the island of Brioni for Tito, Yugoslavia's prime minister from 1945 to 1953 and president from 1953 to 1980.

FRANCO PANZINI

Pines, Palms, and Holm Oaks:
Historicist Modes in Modern Italian Cityscapes

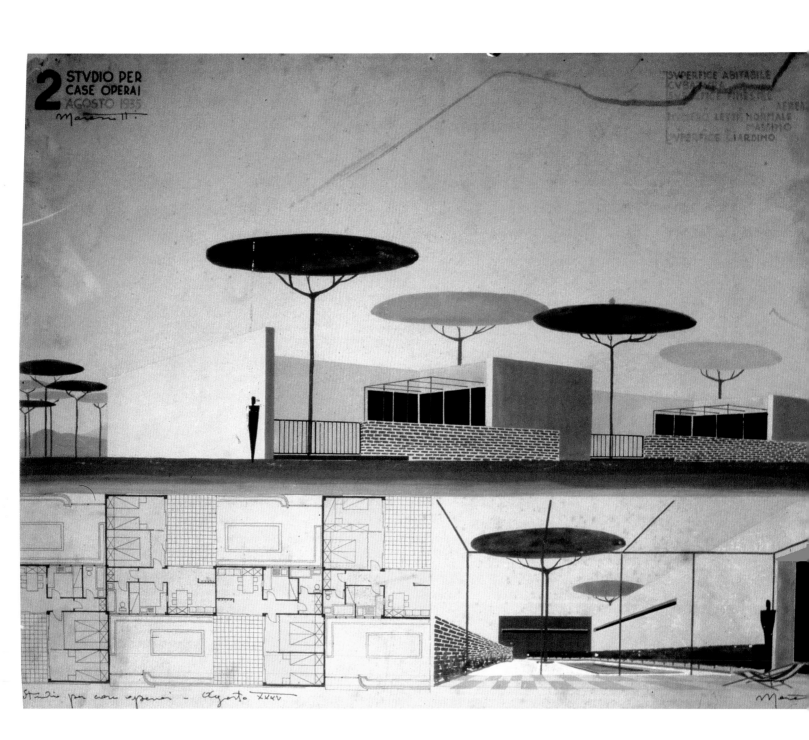

2 STUDIO PER CASE OPERAI AGOSTO 1935

SUPERFICE ABITABILE
CUBA...
...AEREA
...LETTI NORMALE
MASSIMO
SUPERFICE GIARDINO

The concept of modernity in landscape architecture during the first decades of the twentieth century has been investigated mainly in relation to the changing aesthetic of gardens, following trends in decorative and fine arts. Less scholarly attention has been given, until recently, to landscape as an essential component of modern architecture and urban planning. Modern Italian architecture and urbanism of the early twentieth century emerged in a cultural context characterized by distinct and competing regional traditions, unified primarily by reference to a shared national heritage: a legacy that combined the allure of classicism, the inspiration of the robust and unadorned features of vernacular architecture, and the symbolic potential of the landscape.[1]

The engagement of landscaping as a component of architecture fostered the modernization of Italian cityscapes, even though the vegetation involved and its figurative meaning were far from modern. Elias Canetti has observed: "Italy may serve as an example of the difficulty a nation has in visualizing itself when all its cities are haunted by greater memories and when these memories are deliberately made use of to confuse its present."[2] Italy is broadly characterized by its ambivalent relationship with history; modernization and the return to ancient roots are not seen as opposite directions. This essay highlights the role of landscape and its design in the evolution of this sort of regional modernity.

Trees and the Urban Image: An Evolving Relationship

Andrea Palladio, in the second half of the Cinquecento, vigorously reaffirmed a concept that marked Italian culture for centuries:

Now as the Streets are beautified by Buildings in Towns, so are the Ways adorned by Trees in the Country; which Trees, if planted on both Sides, not only delight our Minds by their Verdure, but highly refresh us with their Shade.[3]

Trees along streets were not a way to bring grace to a city's open spaces; these were to be naked, in keeping with the vigor of the architecture surrounding them, whereas trees were right for country roads. In dealing with spaces within a city and those outside, Renaissance treatises such as Andrea Palladio's *I quattro libri dell'architettura* (1570) or Vincenzo Scamozzi's *L'idea della architettura universale* (1615) often reiterated this distinction, even though the aim in both cases was the same: public decorum. This idea changed only in the second half of the nineteenth century, when the walls of cities were systematically demolished, making the boundary between city and country more uncertain, at a time when all Europe was impressed by the extraordinary improvements in Napoleon III's Paris, the handiwork of his prefect, Georges-Eugène Haussmann (1809–1891). This urban transformation brought great tree-lined boulevards into the very heart of the capital, which was dotted with new tree-shaded squares as well.[4]

The motivations of health, decorum, and imitation of the Parisian model were felt in Italy, and consequently the bigger city streets, especially in the new neighborhoods built outside historic centers, began to be lined by trees. In Paris boulevards and squares were decorated with a varied botanical palette reflecting not only the importance given to plantings as an ornament for residential zones but also scientific curiosity about exotic species, and even the broadening geopolitical

Franco Marescotti, design for workers' housing, 1935, ink and tempera on cardboard
Courtesy of Maristella Casciato

interests of the French empire. By contrast, the number of species planted along Italian streets was quite limited.[5] The choice of trees at that time depended not so much on a species' aesthetic qualities or its functional suitability for roadside planting as on its capacity to evoke a heroic past. This use of plants for ideological purposes preceded the advent of Fascism and was an aspect of the effort to link the nation of Italy, a new state whose independence was achieved only in the second half of the nineteenth century, with a much older history.

During the twenty-year Fascist period, those same trees, with their clear iconic power, were widely used in conjunction with the new architecture and urban planning inspired by certain principles of modernism that the regime energetically promoted.[6] That ideal greenery, linked to the memory of the ancient world, constituted a sort of romantic counterpoint to the expressive rationalism of the architecture; such plantings, juxtaposed with modern buildings, bound structures that might seem distant from tradition to their Italian environment. The geographical context of this phenomenon was broad, extending to cities throughout the peninsula and to the Italian colonies in Africa as well. But its real—and, above all, ideal—heart was Rome.

It was to the city's trees that Ottorino Respighi (1879–1936), a composer and musicologist known for his symphonic poems, dedicated one of his most famous works, *Pini di Roma*, of 1924.[7] The music describes a series of historic places at different times of day, including the catacombs, the Via Appia, and the Villa Borghese, all beautified by pines. Respighi was celebrating the city's history by linking its monuments to that specific tree.

In recent years the essence of Rome's urban landscape has been frequently and effectively brought out in films, and some sequences have become legendary, such as those in William Wyler's *Roman Holiday* (1953), in which Gregory Peck and Audrey Hepburn ride through the center of the city on a Vespa. Equally appreciated, though by a smaller audience, were the scenes in Nanni Moretti's *Dear Diary* (*Caro diario*; 1994), in which he likewise explores the city on a scooter. The earlier film displays the classical sights of monumental Rome, while the later one shows residential neighborhoods; but both have as constant protagonists of the urban scene the pines lining the city's streets and shading its gardens.

Any of the tourists swarming through Rome today would assure you that pines are integral to the city's historical setting. Yet this conviction, based on its appearance today, is not supported by the vast quantity of historical documents providing earlier descriptions of the city or its countryside.

Rome: The Metamorphoses of a Landscape

If you observe painted views of the Roman Campagna from past centuries or photographs made only a few decades before Respighi composed his music, you realize that the monuments now surrounded by trees earlier had a far different context, one in which ruins of grand, ancient structures loomed over a landscape relatively bare of trees (fig. 1). This was an area long devoted to grazing, and the unique quality of the landscape derived precisely from contrast between

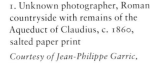

1. Unknown photographer, Roman countryside with remains of the Aqueduct of Claudius, c. 1860, salted paper print

Courtesy of Jean-Philippe Garric, Paris

the magnificence of the ancient structures and the plainness of their later environs. Many travelers on the Grand Tour described the land around the Eternal City as a place of desolation and solitude, and they expressed the disappointment they felt in crossing a territory so different from those ideal landscapes of ancient Latium depicted by painters like Nicolas Poussin or Claude Lorrain, in which a vigorous nature surrounded scenes from ancient myths. The French traveler Charles de Brosses (1709–1777), magistrate, philosopher, linguist, and politician, who traveled in Italy in 1739–1740, wrote one of the most caustic descriptions of the Roman countryside. In narrating his arrival in Rome, he did not conceal his irritation:

> You know what this famous countryside is? It is a limitless and uninterrupted quantity of sterile little hills, uncultivated, absolutely deserted, sad and horrid in the extreme. It is impossible to imagine anything uglier. Romulus must have been drunk when he got the idea of constructing a city in such an ugly territory.[8]

Some decades later, another French writer, Stendhal, though he was touched by the sight of the ruins of a world all but vanished, related:

> We crossed that deserted land and immense solitude that lies all around Rome … [where] most views are dominated by some remnant of an aqueduct or some ruined tomb, which give this Roman countryside a character of incomparable grandeur.[9]

The earliest photographs of the city itself, which showed the scenes most loved by foreigners on the Grand Tour, confirm that the landscape was relatively empty of trees. When the Via Appia was first photographed around 1850, for instance, there was no trace of the famous pines that lined it later, composing a landscape of trees and tombs that became one of the most representative images of Rome (figs. 2 and 3). Photographs from this period demonstrate that around the city, and in many areas within the walls as well, cultivated land prevailed, with

vegetable gardens, plowed fields, vineyards, and the fenced parks of villas. Ancient structures, like the baths of Caracalla and of Diocletian, towered in stark power over a bucolic scene in which the cultivated land presented none of the vigorous greenery that now shades the monumental ruins (fig. 4).

The Past as Myth

The landscape described musically by Respighi in 1924 had an ancient inspiration, but its creation dated back only a few decades, to the period following the birth of the new Italian nation and the designation of Rome as its capital. To understand this history, it is necessary to consider that in the last decades of the nineteenth century Italy was entirely new, a nation born of a union of states that were indeed contiguous but had experienced different histories with different cultures, dialects, lifestyles, and culinary traditions. The new nation's intellectuals were thus called on to create a common culture: language, architecture, history, and landscape.[10]

To construct a collective history for a nation formed of a great number of cities and territories, which, since the fall of the Roman Empire—that is, for a millennium and a half—had been in perennial competition among themselves, was an arduous task. The only shared history was ancient history. At the very basis of the political movement that led to unification was a conviction that Italy, although politically divided and partly occupied by foreign powers, had found nationhood well before other countries in Europe, including those that had perpetuated the division. Italy, it was said, had been Italy at the time of the Romans and as a nation had subjugated the world. Thus the vision of Roman Italy as prototype of the new Italy dominated the country for a century. This idea marked the heroic phase of the struggle for independence, and such propaganda gave cohesiveness and prestige to the kingdom of Italy in its claims to be a colonial

power, in World War I, and throughout the two decades of Fascism. For this reason *romanità* (Romanness) was celebrated in Italy well before Fascism's adoption of it as one of its distinctive traits. The ideal of the ancient world, and particularly of ancient Rome, became the new nation's constant point of reference.

Between the second half of the nineteenth century and the 1930s, antiquity pervaded the Italian imagination. Giosuè Carducci (1835–1907), the most popular Italian poet of this period and winner of the Nobel Prize in 1906, adopted the metrical construction of Greek and Latin poetry in his verses; women's fashion was inspired by what were presumed to be Roman originals; an orange liqueur became a fashionable drink because it was sold in a bottle shaped like ancient ones and because it bore a Latin name, Aurum.[11] The first epic films of the nascent movie industry were drawn from Roman history: *Gli ultimi giorni di Pompei* and *Marcantonio e Cleopatra,* both released in 1913. Support for the idea that the origins

of the Italian nation dated to the Roman period was found in ancient Latin literature: the works of Livy, Virgil, and Pliny the Elder gave the impression that the ancient Romans shared a sense of belonging to a common fatherland, a sense strengthened by language, religion, warlike virtues, the sense of place, and plant life. Thus even flora had its role in the determination to identify modern Italy with its ancient context. This phenomenon was further strengthened by the interest of some eminent archaeologists in the subject and by the role these men played, not only as direct investigators of material remains but also as designers able, if not to resuscitate, at least to evoke vigorously the landscape of the past.

Rodolfo Lanciani (1845–1929), the archaeologist and great topographer of ancient Rome, was famous both for his battle to protect archaeological remains from the inexorable spread of development in the new capital and for the *Forma urbis Romae,* his topographical reconstruction of the ancient city, the most detailed ever

compiled.[12] After Rome became the permanent capital of Italy in 1871, protecting
the archaeological heritage from increasing
building activity became a major cause;
historians and archaeologists pushed the
establishment of a large park incorporating
major remains of the ancient city. Lanciani
for years directed the team dedicated to
creating the first large-scale archaeological
park in the world, the Passeggiata Archeo-
logica, which links the Imperial Forums and
the Colosseum with the Baths of Caracalla
and the urban part of the ancient Via Appia.
A national law in 1887 had provided for creation of the park; it was inaugurated thirty
years later, in 1917 (figs. 5 and 6).

Giacomo Boni (1859–1925), a Venetian
archaeologist, served as director of excavations in the Roman Forum beginning
in 1898; he was one of the first to use the
stratigraphic method and was responsible
for important discoveries related to the city's
archaic period. But he was also concerned
with ancient flora and was the first to study

7. Dario Barbieri, architect and planner, Piazza Verbano, Rome, c. 1925
Author photograph

the botanical species depicted in the frescoes of Pompeii and in those of the villa of Livia, wife of Augustus, which was discovered near Rome in the 1860s. He believed that this flora should be cultivated at archaeological sites, and in 1896 he expressed his conviction in a pamphlet, *Flora dei monumenti.* This brief work was intended for the minister of public instruction, whose ministry was at that time responsible for conservation of Italy's monuments. Appropriate plantings at archaeological sites, according to Boni, were those documented in ancient times, such as "the bushes depicted with powerful realism nineteen centuries ago at Villa Livia.... Without disturbing monumental ruins with small modern gardens, inhospitable plants could be replaced by the handsome greenery preferred by the ancients."[13]

In the following years, Boni had an opportunity to put his ideas into practice. Beginning in 1907, the campaign of excavations he directed was extended to the Palatine Hill, and he was also able to re-create a portion of a sixteenth-century garden of the Farnese family, the Orti Farnesiani, which had occupied the summit of the hill. By Boni's time, this garden had all but disappeared, both because it had gradually been abandoned and because of the excavations themselves. In 1912 Boni's effort at re-creation resulted

in another booklet, *Flora Palatina*, which includes both a list of the plants used in the historical evocation and a list of the plants growing spontaneously over the ancient ruins of the Palatine Hill.[14]

The relationship between greenery and antiquity found its most fully articulated expression in the work of Antonio Muñoz (1884–1960), the art historian who held the position of director of the antiquity and fine arts administration in the offices of the governor of Rome during the Fascist period. Muñoz oversaw a great number of interventions around archaeological structures in the capital. His intention was to restore greenery to ancient structures where it had originally existed, as in the crown of trees of the Mausoleum of Augustus. But he also worked on larger-scale urban projects, where greenery was used to set the scene around grand Roman ruins as a backdrop to the celebratory needs of Fascism, as in the Via dell'Impero, the main route for parades.[15] It was thus thanks to a general interest in the ancient world and to archaeologists who recognized the role of plantings in the evocation of that world that certain arboreal species belonging to Italy's antique tradition became obligatory references in landscaping, not only at archaeological sites and in monumental areas but also in urban neighborhoods being developed: new neighborhoods with ancient plant species (fig. 7).

Trees as Symbol

In urban planning from the end of the nineteenth century through the years of Fascist rule, some plants more than others acquired a symbolic function in suggesting the authority of ancient Rome, seen in a mythic light. Of these, I propose three trees as emblematic of that transformation of urban flora: the pine, the palm, and the holm oak. These were the trees most frequently used in new neighborhoods, often in relation to the highly advanced architectural experiments of the 1930s, a seminal period in Italian architecture. Obviously, these were not the only

plants used in the greening of public places, but they seem to be the most representative in the context of re-creating or evoking the ancient landscape.

I begin this overview with the most widespread tree, the pine, especially *Pinus pinea*, the umbrella pine or stone pine. A native of the Mediterranean area, it was diffused along the coasts by cultivation in ancient times, when the Romans planted enormous pine groves to produce wood for shipbuilding. The pine was thus linked from the outset with the spread of Roman civilization. It was also used in landscaping beginning in the sixteenth century, when it was planted singly or in groups in the gardens of villas. In Rome, a famous pine grove was planted in the seventeenth century in the park of Villa Doria Pamphilj; as a highly original feature of the Roman scene, it was often photographed by early photographers who worked for cultivated foreign tourists (fig. 8). Pines were also planted as a way of marking particular points in the landscape: this was the case of the famous solitary pine of Naples, a centuries-old tree reproduced innumerable times—artfully enlarged—in paintings and postcards (fig. 9). But it was only at the beginning of the twentieth century that the use of the pine became a constant. It was the tree par excellence for any archaeological site, planted to reassure visitors that the ruins certainly were Roman, even if they were difficult to interpret.

The archaeological area of Aquileia, in Veneto, is also emblematic in its use of pines and cypresses (fig. 10). Ancient Roman Aquileia was an important port city in the imperial period and long a bulwark against barbarian invasions. When World War I broke out, there was an effort to draw on the ancient military glories of the Romans to awaken the ideals and energy, and strengthen the morale, of a nation facing an unprecedented military challenge. In a highly symbolic act, when a war cemetery was created not far from the front in 1915, the site chosen was within the archaeological area. This was called the Cimitero degli Eroi (cemetery of heroes), and many of the tomb inscriptions, in Latin, described the fallen soldiers as though they were

10. Archaeological site, Aquileia, fourth century
Author photograph

Roman legionnaires. When the cemetery was finished in the 1920s, it was shaded by cypresses, the trees of Italian funerary tradition. They girdle the cemetery and mark a path leading to a part of the archaeological site. Excavations there in the 1930s brought to light the port of the Roman city, whose ruined walls were flanked by groups of maritime pines. The juxtaposition of the rows of pines and the cypresses thus celebrated, in a botanical metaphor, the communion of those who died in the war with their predecessors, who had defended ancient civilization.

Even more significant was the use of pines in the general planting of public spaces, a function for which the pine is not entirely appropriate: its tenacious shallow roots break through road surfaces, and the tree tends to lose its lower branches naturally in the course of time, creating a danger for passersby. But its evocative value, its inherent *romanità*, was apparently considered far more relevant than the problems it created, as is shown by its widespread presence in countless Italian cities, in both middle-class and working-class neighborhoods.

The palm was the second type of tree that made its debut as an element of urban décor in these years. Many different species were

used, but the most widely planted was the genus *Phoenix*. Big palms, which do not grow spontaneously in Italy, had arrived in ancient times, having been imported from northern Africa after Egypt became a province of the empire. The palms present in Roman gardens and frequently depicted in Pompeian frescos were reminders of that exotic world and its ancient culture. But with the fall of the empire, palms had all but disappeared from the botanical panorama of gardens, to the point where there was only a single palm in the most exotic Roman garden of the sixteenth and seventeenth centuries, the Orti Farnesiani on the Palatine Hill, mentioned above, for which we possess a complete inventory of plants.[16] Palms returned to Italian gardens only in the nineteenth century, reflecting the period taste for the exotic. At the very end of the 1800s, for instance, palms were planted at Villa Torlonia in Rome to give a sort of environmental context to two Egyptian-style commemorative obelisks, which had been created a few decades earlier and had since been standing on a bare lawn (fig. 11).

The success of these plants in Italy grew with the beginning of colonization in Africa. The presence of palms as ornamental plants along roads and in public parks got a sharp boost from the Italian conquest of the coastal part of Libya, taken from the Ottoman Empire in 1911.[17] The spread of palms showed in an objective way the environmental unity of the Italian peninsula with the land of Africa, and proximity to that territory legitimized colonialist pretensions. It was not a coincidence that it was precisely palms that were planted near buildings linked to the colonial undertaking: in front of the ministry of the navy in Rome, for instance, which was built immediately after the conquest of Libya (fig. 12). As in ancient times, palms became the botanical emblem of new territories in the enlarged kingdom of Italy, and of the imperial role that history had again assigned to Rome. Palms appeared along Italian coastal roads facing the new African possessions,

11. Quintiliano Raimondi, obelisk in honor of Giovanni Torlonia, Villa Torlonia, Rome, 1842
Author photograph

12. Giulio Magni, Palazzo della Marina, Rome, 1919–1928
Author photograph

described natural and rural sites dotted with holm oaks.[18] The tree was often depicted in landscapes in Italian paintings: Piero della Francesca (1416/1417–1492), in the cycle of frescoes in Arezzo dedicated to the Legend of the True Cross, painted it many times and seemed to suggest that wood from a holm oak had been used to build the cross. This magnificent oak, also called the holly oak, with its austere dark green foliage, grows even in poor soil and can create an impressive green architecture. Arboreal rhetoric thus associated it with the Italian people, not rich but tenacious and able to realize great things.[19] The oak was present in many Renaissance gardens, constituting the so-called *selvatico,* the area of natural woods from which emerged the orderly construction of a separate area, the garden proper. At the end of the nineteenth century, even though the slowness of its growth and its austere form did not make it a particularly decorative tree for urban spaces, its use in cities increased, especially in piazzas, where it was often pruned into geometric shapes to produce dense green volumes and deep shade, contrasting with the luminosity of the surrounding architecture (see fig. 18).

Ancient Trees for New Structures

This minimal but effective vocabulary, a flora engendered by Italy's historical and political geography, assumed an even more intriguing connotation in the 1920s and 1930s, under the Fascist regime. Perhaps even more significant for the subject of this essay, this was also the period, following years of avant-garde experimentation, when a widespread call to order cooled Europe's art world. European architects renewed their attention to the classical legacy of the Greco-Roman world. Some Italian architects used that return to justify the pedantic adoption of classical styles; others, young architects united by their interest in rational architecture, saw the ancient tradition as an encouragement to seek an architectural approach that was both essential and

and they punctuated the piazzas of colonial cities as well as adding a promise of exoticism to advertising images of the newborn tourism companies.

The third tree that experienced a surge in popularity was the holm oak. If the pine represented ancient Rome and the palm evoked nearby Africa, the autochthonous holm oak, spontaneous protagonist of the peninsula's landscape, was held to represent the Italic character. Roman writers repeatedly

13. Post office, Sabaudia,
1933/1934, by Angiolo Mazzoni
Author photograph

longue durée (fig. 13). The classical and the modern, it was asserted, could coincide, and ancient trees beautifully flanking new structures bore witness to that possibility. The use of such species integrated architecture and the dimension of time. Moreover, this botanical expression, limited to a very few types of plants, corresponded with the analogous effort in rationalist architecture to reduce the choice of building materials to brick, stone, and glass.

Finally, trees in new urban areas responded, at least metaphorically, to the personal and political aversion Mussolini expressed for metropolises and urbanism; he preferred an agricultural Italy of villages and small towns. This political line of thought, termed ruralism (*ruralismo*), took shape in laws that had no effect in limiting growth of the bigger cities but did encourage both the creation of numerous new villages in the countryside and the greening of new urban quarters. These were intended to appear, at least in their plans, as both rural and modern (figs. 14 and 15). This convergence of expressive intentions in the 1920s and 1930s resulted in the integration of at least a minimal arboreal landscape with buildings that explicitly manifested a sense of modernity.

In the context of the reclamation of the Pontine Marshes south of Rome, for example, five new cities were constructed in the first part of the 1930s, with the intention of displaying an image of Fascist efficiency. The place most representative of the functionalist model of urban design then spreading throughout Europe was the new town of Sabaudia. Inaugurated in 1934, it was built in one year, following a 1933 competition won by a group of four very young architects.[20] The site chosen was an area of great natural beauty near the Tyrrhenian shore, on the edge of an area already reclaimed and transformed into agricultural land, alongside a wooded area in its original state (fig. 16).

Sabaudia's simple and effective town plan aimed at juxtaposing the sunny sharpness

expressive. Such qualities were recognized as constants in Mediterranean architecture. Italian architects who cultivated a primary language or basic rationality brought forth their vision of an essential Mediterranean style that looked back to the region's origins. They bolstered this choice by using the botanical species that in preceding decades had been taken up as a metaphor for a

14. Franco Marescotti, design for workers' housing, 1935, ink and tempera on cardboard

Courtesy of Maristella Casciato

15. Franco Marescotti, design for workers' housing at Lanificio Rossi, Schio, 1937, tempera on cardboard

Courtesy of Maristella Casciato

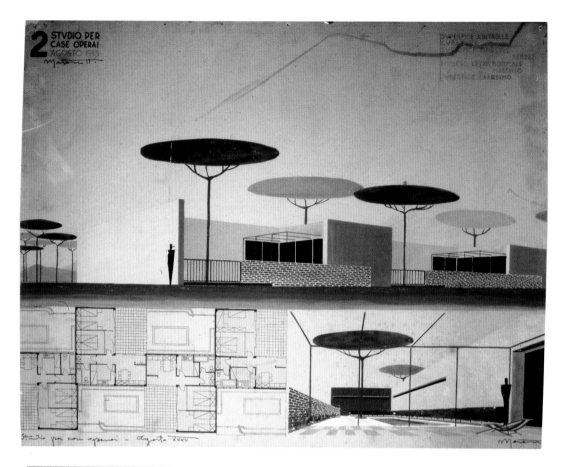

16. Gino Cancellotti, Eugenio Montuori, Luigi Piccinato, and Alfredo Scalpelli, architects, Largo Giulio Cesare, Sabaudia, with church complex in the background, 1934–1935
Author photograph

The new university campus—the Città Universitaria—inaugurated in 1935 in Rome provides another example. Marcello Piacentini (1881–1960), the powerful mediator among the different tendencies animating Italian architecture under Fascism, had prepared the general plan of the large complex. He called a series of young architects to help with the university project, choosing carefully among both rationalists and traditionalists. Despite the obvious ambiguity of this undertaking, the Città Universitaria was a collective project of great importance for Italy, and some of its buildings even now possess notable architectural interest. Piacentini framed the whole plan axially around a great piazza reminiscent of the Roman Forum. But the articulation of the volumes of the individual university buildings was freer. An example is the Physics Institute, designed by Giuseppe Pagano, one of the main protagonists of the renewal of architecture and editor from 1931 to 1943 of the well-known magazine founded as *La casa bella*. Pagano wished to achieve an architecture of rigorous formal simplicity.

Most of the trees planted within the Città Universitaria were, inevitably, pines that marked the central axis, along with thick geometrical groups of holm oaks, which composed veritable groves. The latter, with their dense shade, formed an interesting contrast with the decisively sunny geometry of the white travertine-clad buildings. But the trees also offered a metaphorical guarantee of the Italianness of the culture produced in those buildings (fig. 18).

In the colonies, an emblematic case was that of Asmara, which served as the capital of Italian Eritrea. As noted above, urban planning by Italian architects in the cities of the African colonies used palms extensively in open urban spaces. Anyone walking along the main street of Asmara is immersed in the ambiance of the 1930s: rows of palms fronting structures of that period containing apartments, shops, and cinemas (figs. 19 and 20). The appearance

of the architecture with the extraordinary natural setting that embraced and penetrated the inhabited site. Green swathes, punctuated by pines and palms planted geometrically, interrupted the built part, linking the urban landscape with its periphery, thus establishing an emotional rapport between the rational economy of the planned spaces and the exuberance of the Mediterranean surroundings (fig. 17). The effect calls to mind Le Corbusier's intentions for the contemporaneous Ville Radieuse.

17. Treescape, Via Generale
Ubaldo Gala, Sabaudia, 1935
Author photograph

18. Città Universitaria, Rome,
1935
Author photograph

19. Giuseppe Cane, Carlo Marchi, and Aldo Burzagli, Palazzo Falletta, Harnet Avenue, Asmara, 1937–1938
Author photograph

20. Shops and apartment building, Harnet Avenue, Asmara, c. 1937
Author photograph

grow spontaneously in the region; they are in fact wholly foreign to its flora. But they are a cultural sign and serve as the botanical introduction to a new city. One could say that this was a case of botanical colonialism intended to replicate an urban scene altogether analogous to what was being created in Italy, with architecture displaying a modernist aesthetic amid landscaping reminiscent of the ancient world.

The intended apotheosis of that urban scene, poised between modernism and historicism, engendered by nostalgia for an idealized Mediterranean world, with landscaping serving as a decisive element, should have been the theme of the universal exhibition planned for 1942 in Rome (known as E42). The area of the event was to have been marked by a series of monumental buildings sited geometrically, re-creating an ideal urban classicism surrounded by parks and gardens. The architect who was technical director of the exhibition, Gaetano Minnucci (1896–1980), described his intention:

In projecting this greenbelt, the character of the surrounding Roman Campagna and of the great Roman villas was not forgotten. It was a necessary setting, an indispensable harmonization with the panorama, the sky, the sun of Rome.... [P]ines, ilexes, and laurels dominate.[21]

Work began in 1937 but was suspended two years later at the beginning of the war. Construction of some of the monumental buildings had commenced, and a great number of trees had been planted so that they might mature by the opening of the E42, offering the image of a modern quarter immersed in green (fig. 21). But the unfinished porticoes and huge stone buildings were abandoned for years, like giant ancient ruins, along with the trees around them. It was the cinema, in the early 1950s, which saw their potential and used this recently constructed quarter, which looked like something out of the past, as a low-cost location for costume dramas set in the

has been perfectly maintained, which is why the city rightly aspires to be named to the World Heritage List. The presence of palms seems completely natural; we are in Africa. But immediately beyond the inhabited area, the landscape changes dramatically. The spontaneous vegetation is low and sparse, in fact more appropriate to the land the city was built on: an arid high plain twenty-three hundred meters (seventy-five hundred feet) above sea level. No palms

21. Gaetano Minnucci, Palazzo degli Uffici, designed for the universal exhibition planned for 1942 in Rome, portico and fountain, 1937/1939

Author photograph

ancient world. Thus it was the most up-to-date twentieth-century art, the cinema, that set the seal of success on the attempt to create an urban landscape that was both modern and archaic. The assimilation of the new Italian landscape with that of the ancient world was complete—at least in the imagination of moviegoers.

NOTES

1. See Michelangelo Sabatino, *Pride in Modesty: Modernist Architecture and the Vernacular Tradition in Italy* (Toronto, 2010).

2. Elias Canetti, *Crowds and Power*, trans. Carol Stewart (New York, 1962; repr. 1998), 177–178.

3. Andrea Palladio, *The Third Book of Palladio's Architecture: Translated from the Italian, and the Designs Carefully Copied by B. Cole, Engraver* (third and fourth books bound together; London, 1736), 130. The original reads: "E si come nelle Città si aggiogne bellezza alle vie con le belle fabriche; così di fuori si accresce ornamento à quelle con gli arbori, i quali, essendo piantati dall'una, e dall'altra parte loro, con la verdura allegrano gli animi nostri, e con l'ombra ne fanno commodo grandissimo." (Andrea Palladio, *I quattro libri dell'architettura* [Venice, 1570; facsimile reproduction Milan, 1968], libro 3, capo 1, 7.)

4. See Adolphe Alphand, *Les Promenades de Paris*, 2 vols. (Paris, 1867–1873; reprint Princeton, 1984). This publication, directed by an engineer of the École nationale des ponts et chaussées following the framework of the Haussmann works, represents an account of paramount importance to the history of landscape planning in the nineteenth century. It includes lists of trees and detailed plans and sections of the new boulevards.

5. See Pier Luigi Ghisleni, Marisa Maffioli, and Roberto Carità, eds., *Il verde nella città di Torino* (Turin, 1971); Elena Accati, *Torino città di loisir: Viali, parchi e giardini tra Otto e Novecento* (Turin, 1996); Benedetto Todaro, ed., *Alberate a Roma: Le*

specie vegetali nella definizione della qualità urbana (Rome, 1990); Massimo de Vico Fallani, *Storia dei giardini pubblici di Roma nell'Ottocento* (Rome, 1992); Franco Panzini, *Per i piaceri del popolo: L'evoluzione del giardino pubblico in Europa dalle origini al XX secolo* (Bologna, 1993); Leonardo Rombai, *Geografia storica dell'Italia: Ambienti, territori, paesaggi* (Florence, 2002); Aldo Castellano, Giulio Crespi, and Luisa Toeschi, eds., *Il verde a Milano: Parchi, giardini, alberate, sistemi verdi della città e del suo territorio dal Cinquecento a oggi* (Milan, 2007).

6. The National Fascist Party, headed by Benito Mussolini, ruled Italy from 1922 to 1943. On Italian architecture in this period, see Dennis P. Doordan, *Building Modern Italy: Italian Architecture, 1914–1936* (New York, 1988); Giorgio Ciucci, *Gli architetti e il fascismo: Architettura e città, 1922–1944* (Turin, 1989); Diane Ghirardo, *Building New Communities: New Deal America and Fascist Italy* (Princeton, 1989); Richard A. Etlin, *Modernism in Italian Architecture, 1890–1940* (Cambridge, MA, 1991); Paolo Nicoloso, "Urbanistica," in *Dizionario del fascismo*, ed. Victoria De Grazia and Sergio Luzzatto, vol. 2 (Turin, 2003); Giorgio Ciucci and Giorgio Muratore, eds., *Storia dell'architettura italiana: Il primo Novecento* (Milan, 2004); Paolo Nicoloso, *Mussolini architetto: Propaganda e paesaggio urbano nell'Italia fascista* (Turin, 2008).

7. *Pini di Roma* (*Pines of Rome*), *Feste Romane* (*Roman Festivals*), and *Fontane di Roma* (*Fountains of Rome*) make up Respighi's Roman Trilogy of symphonic poems.

8. The epistolary diary of de Brosses' trip through Italy was published posthumously in 1836: *L'Italie il y a cent ans, ou Lettres écrites d'Italie à quelques amis en 1739 et 1740, par Charles de Brosses, publiées pour la première fois ... par M. R. Colomb ...*, 2 vols. (Paris, 1836), 1:340; consulted in the Italian edition, Charles de Brosses, *Viaggio in Italia* (Bari, 1973), 233.

9. Stendhal (Henri Beyle), *Promenades dans Rome* (Paris, 1858), 17. The quotation refers to August 3, 1827, when the writer arrived in the Eternal City for the sixth time. Author's translation.

10. See Spiro Kostof, *The Third Rome, 1870–1950: Traffic and Glory* (Berkeley, 1973); Alberto Asor Rosa, *La cultura*, vol. 4, part 2 of *Storia d'Italia* (Turin, 1975); Lucy Riall, *The Italian Risorgimento: State, Society, and National Unification* (London, 1994); John A. Davis, ed., *Italy in the Nineteenth Century: 1796–1900* (Oxford, 2000). See also the essay by Sonja Dümpelmann in this volume, which explores the early twentieth century in Italy.

11. For example, the fashion house created in Florence in 1929 by Salvatore Ferragamo, specializing in shoes, launched a line called Pompeiana. The liqueur Aurum, a distillation of bergamot and orange, with rose essence and cane sugar, was first produced in 1914, with industrial production beginning in 1925. The name Aurum (the Latin word for gold) was coined by the poet Gabriele d'Annunzio, and the bottle (of Murano glass) was conceived by the liqueur's producer, Amedei Pomilio, who had been inspired by ancient Roman lachrymatory bottles.

12. *Forma urbis Romae* (Rome and Milan, 1893–1901) mapped ancient Rome in forty-six plates, each measuring fifty-seven by eighty-seven centimeters, showing archaeological remains and ancient monuments through the sixth century. The *Forma urbis* remains even today the fundamental work for any study of Roman topography.

13. Giacomo Boni, *Flora dei monumenti* (Rome, 1896), 2: "gli arbusti disegnati con potente suggestione realistica diciannove secoli fa a Villa Livia.... Senza infastidire i ruderi monumentali con giardinetti moderni, potrebbonsi sostituire alle piante inospitali i cespugli belli, prediletti dagli antichi." Author's translation.

14. Giacomo Boni, *Flora Palatina* (Rome, 1912).

15. Among the botanical efforts of Antonio Muñoz worthy of note were his projects for surrounding ancient ruins with greenery, as at the Temple of Venus and Rome (1935), where the stepped base and columns that had disappeared were partially simulated through plantings.

16. Tobias Aldinus, *Exactissima descriptio rariorum quarundam plantarum, qu[a]e continentur Rom[a]e in Horto Farnesiano* (Rome, 1625). The book contains a lengthy catalog of all the rare plants in the garden; the author's name is thought to be the pseudonym of Pietro Castelli, a physician and botanist who supervised the medicinal plants section in the Farnese garden on the plateau of the Palatine Hill.

17. See Brian McLaren, *Architecture and Tourism in Italian Colonial Libya: An Ambivalent Modernism* (Seattle, 2006); Mia Fuller, *Moderns Abroad: Architecture, Cities, and Italian Imperialism* (London, 2007); Giuseppe Finaldi, *Italian National Identity in the Scramble for Africa: Italy's African Wars in the Era of Nation-Building, 1870–1900* (New York, 2009).

18. *The Spring of Bandusia* (*Fons Bandusiae*), one of the *Odes* of Horace, exemplifies this attitude: "Fies nobilium tu quoque fontium, / me dicente cavis impositam ilicem / saxis, unde loquaces / lymphae desiliunt tuae." (You will become one of the noble fountains / as I sing of the holm oak hanging over / the hollow rocks from where / your waters leap with voices.) Horace, *Odes* 3.13. Author's translation.

19. References to the holm oak, symbol of strength and endurance, are also common in late nineteenth-century Italian poetry; an example from the work of Giosuè Carducci reads: "Non io son fiore a cui brev'aura è infesta, / Elce son io che a' venti indura e s'alza." (I'm not the flower to which a slight breeze is harmful / I'm the holm oak, to winds hardening and standing.) Giosuè Carducci, *Juvenilia*, libro 3, 50

(Bologna, 1880); author's translation. Even today, the emblem of Italy comprises an olive branch, representing harmony and international brotherhood, and an oak branch, embodying the strength and dignity of the Italian people.

20. Members of the design team were Gino Cancellotti, Eugenio Montuori, Luigi Piccinato, and Alfredo Scalpelli.

21. Gaetano Minnucci, "Il piano regolatore," in "L'Esposizione Universale di Roma 1942," special issue, *Architettura*, December 1938, 743. Author's translation.

SONJA DÜMPELMANN

"Per la difesa del giardino": Gardens, Parks, and Landscapes between Tradition and Modernism in Early Twentieth-Century Italy

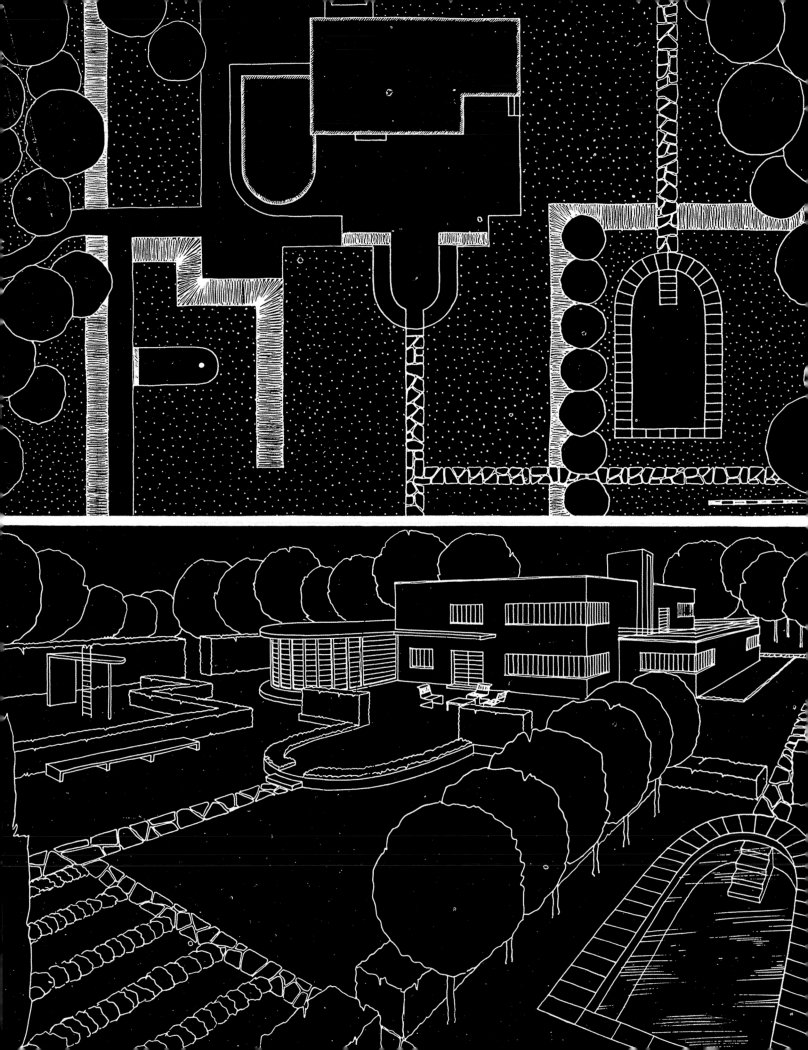

In the first decades of the twentieth century, Italian architects, landscape architects, and art critics were searching for new forms and expressions in garden art. Like their colleagues in many other countries such as the United States, Germany, France, Belgium, and Denmark, the design professionals and their critics were trying to develop what they variously called the "modern," "future," or "coming" garden (see the essay by Michael Lee in this volume).[1] Italians considered the development of garden design and culture in their country to have come to a standstill in the nineteenth century, after the adoption of the landscape garden. This garden type, with its sinuous walkways, creeks, ponds, lawns, and irregularly shaped planting masses, had replaced many geometric gardens. Garden making was seen as a neglected art form that needed to be revived.[2] Paradoxically, Italian professionals had been neglecting their heritage, while writers, architects, and landscape architects from England, the United States, and Germany, inspired by the romance of the old, overgrown Italian villa gardens, were studying them, writing about them, and using them as models for contemporary design.[3] Furthermore, members of the American and British financial aristocracy were restoring Renaissance villas such as the Villa Gamberaia and the Villa La Pietra near Florence.[4] Foreign travelers were enchanted not only by the Italian gardens they found but also by the picturesque image presented by the larger landscape, which, as the writings of Shakespeare and Goethe attested, rendered the entire Italian peninsula, or regions thereof, as a garden.[5]

The first attempts by Italians to revive their garden art were undertaken in the second decade of the twentieth century. Art critics, architects, and conservationists began creating the "giardino italiano" as both a product of the young nation's cultural legacy and international primacy and as a catalyst for its renewal. Gardens were seen as possessing the power both to represent and to transform Italian cultural production. A variety of developments from around 1910 to the 1930s played a role in this revival. Among them were the conservation movement, the strengthening of cultural nationalism and the eventual establishment of a distinctly fascist political culture, and the development of a specialized architectural press. The key events, garden writings, and designs addressed in this essay relate to and connect these developments. They demonstrate an evolution from what the cultural and intellectual elite perceived as a neglect of gardens toward a concern with them. In fact, it is perhaps the discourse that revolved around gardens in that period and its evolution, more than the designs themselves, that can be described as modern.

In laying out the discussions about gardens that occurred in the 1910s, 1920s, and 1930s, this essay shows that many architects and cultural critics, especially in the 1920s and 1930s, were caught up in debates about formal issues. The most prevalent structural paradigm that emerged in these years was that of the garden as architecture. This entailed the functional unity of house and garden, as well as of city and park—a concept that was paramount to the expression of modernity as a response to contemporary life, politics, and culture. In addition, and in particular in terms of materiality and material culture, the vernacular became a paradigm promoted

Tino Sgaravatti and Ferdinand Bredenkamp, design for a modern garden, 1932

Domus 6, no. 62 (1932): 87–89

by some garden architects and critics. Both paradigms, the garden as architecture and the vernacular garden, were products of an increasing commodification of the Italian (garden) landscape that was promoted by the growth of elite and international tourism, among other factors. Both paradigms were seen as instruments to forge and celebrate Italianness and a shared set of national values, especially once the Fascists had recognized garden art and culture as valuable instruments in their politics. During the Fascist dictatorship, cultural intellectuals and design professionals served state ideology by promoting a garden culture that built upon the past and attempted to construct spaces for the activities of a new "modern man."

Gardens as Art and Nature

The early twentieth-century debate about the protection and conservation of Italian gardens played an important role in the attempted revival of garden art and culture. Italy's preservation and nature conservation movement had, as in other European countries, begun in the second half of the nineteenth century, when increasing industrialization drew the attention of the political and cultural elite to the need to establish a legislative framework for the protection of monuments and forests. The first (albeit largely ineffective) national law for the protection of state forests had been decreed in 1877, and the first law for the conservation of monuments and art objects of high prestige and antiquity was finally passed in 1902. A number of organizations to promote the protection of nature and cultural heritage were founded around the turn of the twentieth century. In 1898, the first association for the protection of Italian mountains and forests, Pro Montibus et Silvis, was formed by Count Luigi Somani Moretti in Turin as an offshoot of the Club Alpino Italiano. Members of the recreational organization Touring Club Italiano, the Associazione per i Paesaggi e i Monumenti Pittoreschi d'Italia, the Lega Nazionale per la Protezione dei Monumenti Nazionali, and the Società

Botanica Italiana were also vocal advocates of nature conservation.[6]

Around the turn of the century, a variety of successful local protests against construction projects that were considered to harm natural heritage took place in Tivoli, in Terni, and near Ancona. However, only in 1905 did the Italian parliament broach the conservation of "natural beauties" (*bellezze naturali*). That year the first local law was decreed for the protection of the legendary pine forests along the Adriatic coast near Ravenna (fig. 1). At the time, the most important qualifying arguments for the protection and conservation of such sites were their aesthetic appeal and their relation to Italian history and culture. Ravenna's pine forests, the Pineta di San Vitale and the Pineta di Classe, were a case in point (see the essay by Franco Panzini in this volume). Planted by the ancient Romans as sources of wood and pine nuts, these forests were connected in the Italian consciousness to the memory of Lord Byron, who had lived in Ravenna in the early nineteenth century, and, more important, to Dante and Boccaccio.[7] Dante's and Boccaccio's poetry was heralded as an essential part of Italy's cultural legacy, representing a "common language" that had been invoked to bolster arguments for national unification and that after 1861 was considered a means to strengthen the political and social unity of the young Italian state.[8] Thus, it was believed that the pine forests outside Ravenna supported the creation of a unified national cultural identity.

Spurred by Ravenna's success, one of the first promoters of nature conservation in Italy, Luigi Parpagliolo, attorney and deputy director of fine arts for the Ministero della Pubblica Istruzione, argued in 1905 that the 1902 law for the protection of monuments and art objects should be extended to include natural beauties. Furthermore, he demanded that gardens should be considered monuments "because [in gardens] art has modified nature, which is like the marble or canvas in the hand of a sculptor or painter; and they

[the gardens] are therefore real and proper monuments that, apart from offering moral and intellectual entertainment, often are study material for understanding the character of their period of creation."[9] Thus, already at the beginning of the conservation movement, the claim was made that gardens were an integral part of Italian historiography and a cultural heritage worth protecting. Several attempts at realizing Parpagliolo's recommendations between 1907 and 1909 ended in failure. A decisive moment came in 1912, when threats to sell the Villa Aldobrandini in Rome to a hotel company led the Direzione delle Belle Arti to hastily amend the existing law for the protection of monuments to include "villas, parks, and gardens of historic or artistic interest" ("ville, … parchi, … giardini di interesse storico o artistico").[10] Although this amendment saved the Villa Aldobrandini, it proved largely ineffectual in the following years because of poor implementation. But despite these shortcomings, the 1912 law

signified a turning point in the treatment of garden art in Italy. Since Italian unification, liberal politics had resulted in fierce land speculation, causing the destruction of numerous villas and private gardens. The law therefore marked a shift in the perception of gardens among the Italian intellectual and cultural elite. This development also led to the first Italian twentieth-century publications on gardens, as will be shown below.

The initiatives for nature conservation slowed down as a result of World War I, but the movement gained fervor again after the war. In 1922 the first bill for "the protection of natural beauties and places of particular historic interest" (*la tutela delle bellezze naturali e degli immobili di particolare interesse storico*) was finally signed into law, and the first landscape conference was held on Capri to celebrate the occasion.[11] At the conference, gardens were considered as integral components of Capri's landscape. They were seen as contributing to the island's picturesque image, which had for centuries attracted artists and intellectuals from all over Europe and, according to the leading voices at the conference, was now, after years of neglect, threatened by mass tourism.[12]

Organized by Capri's mayor, the writer and conservationist Edwin Cerio, the conference was also an act of patriotism, an "expression of the Italianness" ("manifestazione solenne della italianità") of Capri.[13] As Cerio proudly reported in the conference proceedings, published in the following year, Capri, after years of foreign dominion under the Bourbons, the French, and the British, finally belonged to Italy.[14] To gain support for his idea of turning Capri into an Italian cultural center, Cerio assembled diverse members of the country's cultural and intellectual elite at the conference, including the futurist writer Filippo Tommaso Marinetti. As might be expected, Marinetti, despite hailing Capri's landscape as a futurist work of art with its "violent, bellicose, revolutionary … rocks" ("rocce … violente, guerresche, rivoluzionarie") and its "rhythms [made of] capricious variety, bizarreness, fantastic dynamism, and especially asymmetry" ("Questi ritmi sono la varietà capricciosissima, la bizzaria, il dinamismo fantastico e specialmente l'assimetria"), heavily criticized the restorationist tendencies of the conservationists, whom he described as attached to the past (passatisti).[15] Conservationists on the mainland had, for example, made plans to camouflage hydroelectric power plants, whereas the futurist architect Antonio Sant'Elia had proposed designs for them that would expose their technology and employ bold massing.[16] The futurists' approach to landscape and nature had also been conveyed in a manifesto by the painters Fortunato Depero and Giacomo Balla, Ricostruzione futurista dell'universo (1915), in which they had promoted the creation of an artificial landscape. Two years after the landscape conference, the artist Fedele Azari, in La flora futurista ed equivalenti plastici di odori artificiali (1924), even argued for the creation of artificial flowers with strong

colors, dynamic forms, and intense synthetic odors.[17] The "landscape" that Marinetti and his fellow futurists promoted was one that expressed speed, dynamism, and technological progress. On Capri, Marinetti commended the island's new funicular and electricity as signs of progress, thereby opposing Cerio's conservationist critique of the funicular and of the cement columns and electric lightbulbs that had become substitutes for traditional rose-covered garden pergolas. On the other hand, Marinetti—himself a regular visitor to Capri and, like Cerio, concerned about its loss of elite character to increasing mass tourism— shared Cerio's critique of neoclassical decorative objects and architecture in the island's gardens. In fact, Marinetti and the futurist architect Virgilio Marchi also joined in the conservationists' exaltation of the simple rural style of Capri's gardens and buildings.

Vernacular Gardens

In these first decades of the twentieth century, rustic vernacular architecture played an important role in the search for a new Italian architectural paradigm, and, as Richard Etlin has observed, "all architectural leaders designed vernacular architecture."[18] Influenced by the transfigured, romantic fantasy of a simple rural life, many architects were inspired by Amalfi's and Capri's rural dwellings in particular. Only one year before the landscape conference, the architects Marcello Piacentini, Gustavo Giovannoni, and Vittorio Morpurgo had shown designs for modern vernacular architecture, or "architettura rustica," at the Cinquantennale exhibition in Rome.[19] Both Piacentini and Giovannoni were interested in contextual design. In 1929 their journal, Architettura e arti decorative, published an article by Giuseppe Capponi on Edwin Cerio's house and garden, Il Rosaio, showing that outdoor spaces and gardens were considered an integral component of architettura rustica.[20]

As a parallel in landscape design but lagging behind this development in architecture,

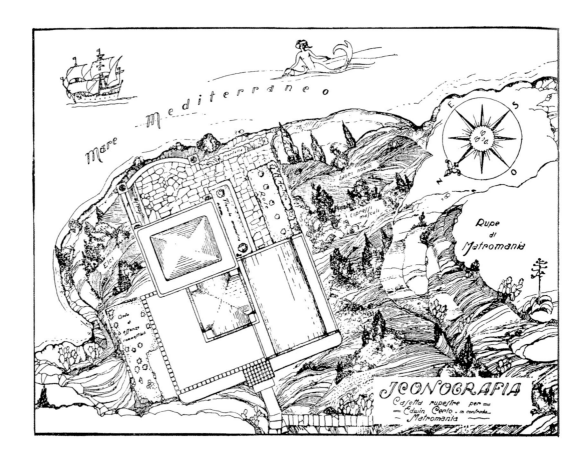

Maria Teresa Parpagliolo, Luigi Parpagliolo's daughter and one of the few Italian landscape architects of the early 1930s, hailed the vernacular gardens on Capri, their plants, and their design features, such as rose-covered pergolas, as a prototype for the modern Italian garden. In her appreciation of these picturesque gardens, Parpagliolo followed Cerio, who had argued for their conservation. Like Cerio's own garden at Il Rosaio and his design for a house and garden near the grotto of Matromania (fig. 2), Parpagliolo's "giardino rustico italiano" was meant to form a unity with the house and blend into the surrounding landscape through the use of native plants such as cypresses, laurel, arbutus, aleppo pines, and holm oaks.[21] Vernacular elements that were employed on Capri, and that also can be discerned in Cerio's designs, included rose, citrus, flower, and vegetable gardens and pergolas covered with rambling roses and vines, as well as orchards and olive groves. Parpagliolo promoted the existing ornamental features in Capri's gardens, such as stone benches, jugs, fountains, and indigenous flowering species, to enhance the gardens' picturesque aesthetic. The garden was to become a part of the larger landscape. In its various regional inflections the rustic Italian garden was considered a means to nearly disguise the house. The writer Gilbert Clavel in 1922 likened the effect to a plant that grows out of the soil and therefore conforms to the tectonic laws of the earth to which it belongs: "[S]orge di sbocco dal terreno etnico, come la pianta dalla zolla, e risponde perciò esattamente alle leggi tettoniche della terra, di cui fa parte."[22] Cerio praised the handcrafted vaulted roofs of vernacular Capri architecture not only because of their picturesqueness and local tradition but also because they could blend easily into the surrounding landscape over time. As he pointed out, their rough mortar surfaces, made from local volcanic soil and limewater, provided a fertile ground for various ruderal plant species, and the buildings thus acquired "a vegetative patina of most agreeable effect."[23]

The planting design of the rustic Italian garden would, according to Parpagliolo, build upon the species typical of the particular region. Thus, in the south and along the coast, vines, olive, pine and arbutus, myrtle, and gorse of the evergreen macchia would structure the garden. Cypress and yew trees would characterize rustic gardens in Tuscany, and poplars the gardens in the plane of the river Po.[24] Parpagliolo considered Capri's gardens modern because they provided outdoor rooms adapted to the owner's contemporary lifestyle; because they used the existing vegetation to blend the house and garden into the larger landscape; and because architectonic garden features often merged with picturesque plantings.

Parpagliolo published her advocacy of the rustic Italian garden at a time when the Fascists were promoting a "ritorno alla terra," a return to the land. They had discovered for their own purposes the architectural movement that had been developing a national modern, rural architecture since the second decade of the twentieth century. What had begun as an attempt to revive Italy's cultural production and bolster the young nation state now also served Fascist politics. Working at a time characterized politically by, among other things, Fascist ruralism and the Fascist state's interest in autarchy, some architects, such as Giuseppe Pagano and even the futurist Virgilio Marchi, were eager to invent a lineage from vernacular constructions to rationalist and futurist architecture, pointing out that flat roofs, cubic volumes, and white facades were already characteristic of Italian vernacular architecture.[25]

Although Cerio appreciated that English garden owners had "introduced horticulture and the love of flowers" to Capri, by the end of the first decades of the twentieth century many Italians had grown weary of foreigners who were appropriating their garden and landscape heritage.[26] Cultural nationalism not only lay at the heart of the first initiatives to protect and revive gardens in rural

areas such as Capri; it also furthered the promotion of gardens in the urban context and in the art world.

Gardens as Architecture

As mentioned above, the 1912 amendment to the law on the protection of monuments and art objects to include villas, parks, and gardens of historic and artistic interest meant that gardens were considered art objects that had a role in fostering a common national identity. This attitude was also apparent in several events and publications over the next two decades. In 1912 the art historian Nello Tarchiani and critics Ugo Ojetti and Luigi Dami proposed an exhibition on Italian gardens in the Palazzo Vecchio in Florence. Ojetti and Dami had developed an initial proposal immediately following an exhibition on Italian portraiture held that year in the Palazzo Vecchio.[27] While it would take almost twenty years for their plan to be realized as the Mostra del Giardino Italiano, held in 1931, in the interim a small number of texts and books on Italian gardens published in Italy attempted to establish an Italian garden tradition by reevaluating historic sites.

In 1914 Dami published an article titled "L'arte italiana dei giardini" in the monthly journal of the Touring Club Italiano in which he made three points. He claimed that garden art was essentially Italian; he made it clear that the principal character of the Italian garden was architectural (*architettonico*); and he called for the rebirth of garden art in Italy.[28] Following another article by Dami, "Il giardino toscano come opera d'arte," in 1915 the duchess Maria Pasolini Ponti published *Il giardino italiano*, the first Italian book on the Italian garden.[29] It was succeeded in 1923 and 1924 by two more volumes by Dami on the same subject.[30] Pasolini Ponti was a member of the Associazione Artistica fra i Cultori di Architettura in Roma (hereafter AACAR), which had been founded in 1890 with the intent of debating and influencing urban development in Rome, with special attention to aesthetic, archaeological, and art-historical concerns.[31] She had already edited a photographic study, *Sulla conservazione delle condizioni d'ambiente e sulle bellezze naturali della zona monumentale*, and had translated into Italian the work *Esthétique des villes*, by the mayor of Brussels, Charles Buls. As guidelines for modern city planning, the AACAR considered the principles that Buls put forward in his book together with Camillo Sitte's work, *Der Städtebau nach seinen künstlerischen Grundsätzen* (first published in 1889).

Pasolini Ponti's interest in vernacular styles and conservation became apparent in the first volumes of the series *L'architettura minore in Italia*, which she coedited for AACAR. Her book *Il giardino italiano* reflected AACAR's mission of furthering conservation, vernacular architecture, and contextual architecture and urbanism. She emphasized the important role of urban gardens, villas, and parks in promoting a harmonious city image and the citizen's well-being. In the spirit of AACAR's interest in building context (*ambientismo*) she described the Italian garden of antiquity as an "organism" (*organismo*) that maintained a harmonious relationship with its environs. Its center was the house. In this way she made a point of describing the garden as part of a larger whole, of an organic unity: "[A]ll parts were connected [with the house] through their functions[,] subordinated to the whole, and the whole was part of a general harmony with the environment." ("[T]utte le parti vi erano collegate con la loro funzione subordinate all'insieme e l'insieme faceva parte di un'armonia generale coll'ambiente.")[32] Pasolini Ponti's organic, contextual approach to the Italian garden paralleled the first attempts by Rome's director of parks and gardens Nicodemo Severi and by the architect Marcello Piacentini, in 1909 and 1915, respectively, to draw up park system plans for Rome. Renaissance and baroque villa gardens were integral parts of the projected park system and were considered a means not only to order the city and improve the living environment for citizens but also to protect the villas as part of the Roman cultural heritage. In the plans, a network of tree-lined boulevards linked gardens and parks and connected the city center with the urban periphery.[33] Despite Pasolini Ponti's seemingly idiosyncratic notion of the Italian garden as a contextual work of art, her book revealed the dominance of foreign contemporaries in the field. For example, she quoted translated passages from Edith Wharton's *Italian Villas and Their Gardens* of 1904.[34] Wharton had also stressed the close relationship between the Italian garden and its environs, and because she was a foreigner, Pasolini Ponti hailed Wharton's book as an objective account.[35]

Highlighting and supporting the architectural characteristics of the Italian garden, Pasolini Ponti and Dami not only rejected the landscape garden but also condemned eclecticism and the pluralism of styles, which until then had characterized garden design throughout the Italian peninsula.[36] For example, nineteenth-century landscape gardeners like the court gardeners Marcellino Roda and his brother Giuseppe were influenced by French garden art and publications but had continued to promote gardens that exhibited characteristics of the landscape garden, or employed the so-called mixed style (*stile misto*), which combined free-flowing and geometric forms. Instead, Pasolini Ponti and Dami supported a return to order (*ritorno all'ordine*), a general trend in the arts, architecture, and literature in the early 1920s to return to classical principles. Influenced by cultural nationalism, Pasolini Ponti and Dami condemned the style of the landscape garden as contradictory to the Italian spirit.[37] Thus, whereas Italian literati at the beginning of the nineteenth century had vehemently tried to prove an Italian origin for the landscape garden, a hundred years later its adoption in Italy was considered a faux pas in the history of Italian garden design and unworthy of scholarly consideration.[38]

With their publications, Pasolini Ponti and Dami prepared the ground for the claim by many architects in the following decades that the garden was an architectural product, to be seen as the outdoor extension of the house. A common belief among architects and art critics of the time was that the decline of garden art in Italy during the nineteenth century had been the result of gardeners taking over the design of landscape gardens from architects.[39] Reclaiming the garden terrain therefore meant designing gardens as architecture. The use of prominent architectural features associated with Italian Renaissance gardens to structure planted grounds became a favorite design principle. Though sometimes falsely attributed to Bartolomeo Ammanati, the statement by the Renaissance artist Baccio Bandinelli that "what is built must guide and be superior to what is planted" ("le cose che si murano debbono essere guide e superiori a quelle che si piantano") was quoted frequently and used to promote the revival of what was considered the Italian garden tradition.[40] Italian art critics and architects agreed that the Italian garden tradition as they understood it was to be continued and renewed by adhering to what they called Renaissance design principles while adapting to modern-day needs. Thus they called for a second renaissance of garden art in Italy.[41]

Large parts of the discussion about a new Italian garden were led by art critics and architects who considered themselves authorities on the subject. In fact, in 1931 only architects and architecture students were admitted to the design competitions, held on the occasion of the Mostra del Giardino Italiano, for a public urban park and a private urban villa garden. Botanists, agronomists, gardeners, and other professionals who were not members of a Fascist syndicate were excluded from participating, causing the garden architects Giuseppe Roda and Pietro Porcinai to protest, but in vain.[42] Since the Italian garden of the future was envisioned by most as a garden based on geometric, "architectural" forms—Dami repeatedly asserted that "the Italian garden is a work of architecture"—architects were considered the appropriate

professionals.[43] Indeed, the architecture schools (modeled on Rome's) that opened in Venice, Turin, Naples, and Florence after the creation of the Fascist architecture syndicate in 1923 instituted professorships of urbanism that in most cases also included garden art.[44] In higher education, therefore, garden art was assigned to the architects.

Not surprisingly, then, garden culture was influenced by contemporary architecture journals. *Architettura e arti decorative* had been founded in 1921. Two new and influential journals appeared in Milan in 1928: *Domus* and *La casa bella*, which provided information and outlets for the rival modern Novecento and rationalist architects respectively. Although all three journals included garden topics on a regular basis, these always remained marginal subjects. Nevertheless, during the evolution of *Domus* as one of the primary architectural journals in the 1930s, the space assigned to garden topics increased, as did their range. First addressing the bourgeois housewife with short articles offering technical gardening advice on the uses and maintenance of plants, the articles soon included Italian garden history and the presentation of small-scale garden designs in Italy and abroad. Eventually they expanded to include the discussion of public urban parks and open-space planning in an issue dedicated to the journal's so-called campaign for green (Campagna del Verde) in 1937. Although new, decorative Novecento buildings like Giovanni Muzio's Milanese Ca'Brutta in many cases destroyed gardens and open space in the dense inner cities, Novecento architect Giò Ponti, in his inaugural statement as editor of *Domus*, promoted gardens, roof gardens, porticoes, and porches that created thresholds between interior and exterior.[45] From 1937 on, gardens and public parks were seen as integral to the modern bourgeois Italian home and city. Ponti declared:

In the Italian house there is no big architectural distinction between the outside, and the inside: ... the architecture out of doors penetrates the inside.... From the inside the Italian house reaches out to the open with its porticoes and terraces, and with pergolas and porches, with loggias and balconies, roof terraces and belvederes, all very comfortable inventions for the serene Italian home, so that in every language they have been called by these names. The same architectural order therefore rules ... the facades and the inside and also regulates nature outside, with terraces, staircases, gardens — appropriately called "all'italiana" — nymphaea, and perspective vistas, kitchen gardens and courtyards, all created to give ease, and a setting to a happy dwelling.[46]

Contrasting the lighthearted, gay, and comfortable Italian habitation with "houses on the other side of the Alps," Ponti stressed the flow between dwelling and garden, a characteristic that Pasolini Ponti and Dami had attributed to Italian Renaissance gardens.

Gardens and Gender

Ponti's formulation of out-of-doors architecture penetrating the inside raises another issue of importance to the understanding of modernity: the role of gender. Luigi Dami had described the transition between the male-gendered house, or architecture, and the female-gendered garden, or nature, in 1923 as follows:

It is necessary that the house, when coming into contact with the garden, lose a bit of its pride and rigidity, lighten its oppressive masses, rarefy itself, if I may say so, give a bit more space to the openings and to the air, at the expense of its mass and its stones. On the other hand, the garden, approaching the house while courteously obeying the law of *do ut des*, should lose a bit of its disorderliness and restlessness; it should become more ordered and should behave a little more serenely and in the union should offer its most rigid forms to those brought forward by the house; and they will be the finest and most vivid the house can offer. In this way a good neighborly relationship can be established, with grace and to the advantage of both sides.[47]

In this vein Tomaso Buzzi chose to depict a female gardener to caricature the 1931

garden exhibition in Florence for *Domus*, thereby also reflecting this journal's assignment of the garden to the domestic sphere.[48] In contrast, Gherardo Bosio, in the same issue, assumed a chauvinist rhetoric. At a time when Fascist politics had already begun to promote garden art, he went as far as to argue that the Italian garden in "its male expression" was born in sixteenth-century Florence.[49] The architectural layouts popularized at this time caused the garden to be defeminized by some art critics and architects, reflecting, in the realm of garden culture, the Fascist desire to develop into a virile empire what was widely considered an effeminate, degenerate society created by centuries-long foreign rule.[50] (On gender see also the essay by Michael Lee in this volume.)

The dominance of the Italian architectural culture on the one hand, and the increasing politicization of garden art on the other, were evident in one of the few public debates on garden style between professionals in the fields of garden architecture and horticulture. In an article published in the horticultural journal *I giardini*, the garden architect Giuseppe Roda was hesitant to assert a "radical transformation" of garden design, although he agreed with the necessity to accommodate the new needs of modern life, to design gardens that were compartmentalized but maintained a unity and were part of the house. When he presented his garden for Villa La Milanina in Turin as an example of a "modern garden" ("giardino moderno"), Rome's garden director, Bruno Braschi, was appalled: it displayed design principles and forms common in late-nineteenth-century gardens, including "kidney- or oval-shaped lawns," and was in part also modeled on French examples and what Braschi called the "composite style," or the use of free-flowing and architectural forms (fig. 3).[51] It could therefore, according to Braschi, be considered neither "modern" nor "Italian," adjectives that Braschi — working within Rome's Fascist city government — considered vital for reestablishing Italy's primacy in garden art.[52]

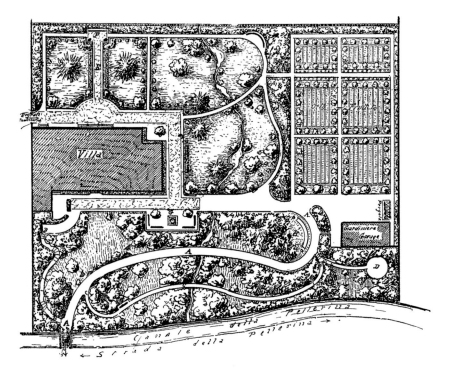

3. Giuseppe Roda, garden for Villa
La Milanina, Turin, 1933
I giardini 79, no. 4 (1933): 83

Gardens as Expressions and Agents of Political Culture

Cultural nationalism was instrumental in reviving garden art in Italy and contributed to determining that the Italian garden was to be architectural. Fascist politics continued to encourage the development of garden art and culture. After Mussolini seized power in 1922, the Roman city government had made particular efforts to invest in the design, construction, and maintenance of parks and gardens. Mussolini had realized that to follow in the footsteps of the Roman emperors Augustus, Nero, Hadrian, and Marcus Aurelius, who had created numerous gardens and parks in and outside Rome, and to establish a "third Rome," he had to integrate gardens and parks into the plans for city development.[53] Furthermore, the dictator and his followers took notice of the potential of garden culture to influence the masses.[54]

Rome's accomplishments in the field of garden art were exhibited at the Mostra del Giardino Romano of the Esposizione Nazionale Italiana in 1928. The exhibition was held at the Parco del Valentino in Turin on the occasion of the 400th birthday of the duke of Savoy Emanuele Filiberto and the

tenth anniversary of victory in World War I. The Roman presence in Turin tended toward political propaganda by drawing analogies between Emanuele Filiberto's sixteenth-century kingdom of Savoy and Mussolini's Fascist Italy, thereby stressing the Italian state's historical roots.[55] For the Roman garden exhibition, the diverse initiatives and events that had been undertaken for the promotion of garden culture in the Italian capital were displayed in and around a pavilion that, in contrast to many rationalist exposition buildings on site and to the cubist-inspired Padiglione Futurista, imitated a seventeenth-century Roman casino set in a secret garden (fig. 4). As its accompanying publication stated, the exhibition was intended to demonstrate that "the tradition of the Italian garden ... was gaining new strength" and that the first success to be witnessed in Rome was "resolutely dedicated to the work for the revival of *our* garden."[56] Charged with the design were Raffaelle de Vico and Alberto Galimberti. The former was artistic advisor to the Servizio Giardini di Roma and had designed many of the capital's new public parks and gardens from 1924 onward; the latter served as Rome's director of parks and gardens.

The designers divided the grounds into two parts. In front of the pavilion, the garden was to be "of a classical character" ("di carattere classico") with geometrical planting beds for a thousand of the city's twenty-five hundred different rose varieties. Behind the building, the garden was to resemble those of the Renaissance. There, trees were considered the architectural, "constructive" material ("materia costruttiva"). In imitation of eighteenth-century gardens, slopes on either side of the pavilion were planted in floral patterns and low, ornate hedges of myrtle and box.[57] The exhibition demonstrated Rome's reawakened potential in garden art and culture with ornaments and plants outside the pavilion, a glasshouse of tropical plants, and a display inside the pavilion of illustrations of new Roman public walks, parks, and gardens as well as the work of

4. Roman pavilion, Mostra del Giardino Romano, Esposizione Nazionale Italiana, Parco del Valentino, Turin, 1928

Governatorato di Roma, Azienda Giardini Pubblici, Mostra del giardino romano al Valentino *(Milan and Rome, 1928), 9*

5. Rose garden in front of the Roman pavilion, Mostra del Giardino Romano, Esposizione Nazionale Italiana, Turin, 1928

Governatorato di Roma, Azienda Giardini Pubblici, Mostra del giardino romano al Valentino *(Milan and Rome, 1928), 8*

the city's recently opened training school for gardeners.[58] The hemicycle planted with "thousands and thousands of roses" in Turin demonstrated one of the proud capital's horticultural accomplishments: in 1926, an experimental garden for roses had been integrated into the new public park on Colle Oppio to promote the develop-

ment of a "Mediterranean rose" adapted to the particular environmental conditions of the peninsula (fig. 5).[59] The rose—long associated with ornament, perfume, and food of the Roman Empire—symbolized *romanità,* the Roman spirit.

The Roman presence in Turin was intended to place Mussolini in a direct hereditary line to the Roman Empire by way of the house of Savoy, and a similar step was undertaken at the Mostra del Giardino Italiano in Florence in 1931. There, Mussolini could act "as a newborn Lorenzo de' Medici" under whose patronage Italian garden art, which was then considered to have reached its height in Florence during the Renaissance, would be revived.[60] Initially, the exhibition was to include the construction of a variety of show gardens in the Cascine that illustrated the phases of garden design throughout the centuries, including "giardini moderni."[61] However, various planning committee members doubted that modern Italian gardens could be created in haste if "the modern Italian garden currently does not exist" ("attualmente il giardino italiano moderno non esiste").[62] Instead, the garden exhibition was structured around ten three-dimensional, table-sized models assembled from ideas and design features that were attributed to particular regions and historical periods respectively.[63] Thus, in an attempt to establish a tradition of the Italian garden, the exhibition included idealized versions of the ancient Roman garden (fig. 6), the Tuscan garden of the fourteenth century, the Florentine garden of the fifteenth and sixteenth centuries, the Genovese and Roman gardens of the sixteenth and seventeenth centuries, the Venetian and Piedmontese gardens of the eighteenth century, the neoclassical garden in Lombardy, and the romantic garden (fig. 7). The last was added to complete the picture and to provide a contrast that would unmistakably emphasize the qualities of the Italian garden.[64] Beginning the series of miniature gardens with the ancient Roman garden established a continuity between the ancient imperial past and the present. Just how constructed this lineage was became apparent in the assemblage in each model of various design elements deemed particularly typical of one region. The exhibition of an idealized development of the Italian garden was an attempt to establish a shared culture and history.

The preoccupation with regional garden styles was visible not only in the exhibition but also in the designs that were submitted for a simultaneous competition to design a private urban villa garden.[65] In response to the competition guidelines, which, in accordance with Fascist cultural politics, asked for entries "of modern character and typically Italian" ("di carattere moderno e tipicamente italiano"), most gardens featured pergolas, arbors, cut hedges, water basins, and ornamental parterres.[66] Recalling Italian hillside gardens, some competition designs that were published in *Architettura e arti decorative*, *La casa bella*, and *Domus* were also terraced, and all were structured by a main axis that in many cases began at the front or back door of the house. The published competition entries all followed the paradigm of the garden as architecture and the *ritorno all'ordine*. Thus, the Florentine architecture student Primo Saccardi's skeletal axonometric design followed explicitly Bandinelli's much-quoted advice that "what is built must guide and be superior to what is planted" (fig. 8).

Gherardo Bosio and Mario Tinti, critics of the Florence exhibition and competition for an urban villa garden for *Domus* and *La casa bella* respectively, noted regionalist expressions and variations among the designs. Participants from Lombardy displayed pergolas, intricate garden spaces, and pathways on even ground. Several Tuscan participants submitted designs that were arranged around shallow central water basins or flat lawns. The Roman participants chose to create garden rooms with the help of terraces and high hedges. As Bosio noted, only the entries by architects from Rome and Naples included pine trees (figs. 9 and 10).[67] Like roses, pine trees (*Pinus pinea*) were considered to establish an Italian and specifically Roman identity. Although many of the legendary *pinete* along the Tyrrhenian and Adriatic coasts, such as the Pineta di San Vitale and the Pineta di Classe near Ravenna, had been

8. Primo Saccardi, competition
entry for the design of an urban
villa garden, Mostra del Giardino
Italiano, Florence, 1931

Architettura e arti decorative 11,
no. 7 (1931): 546

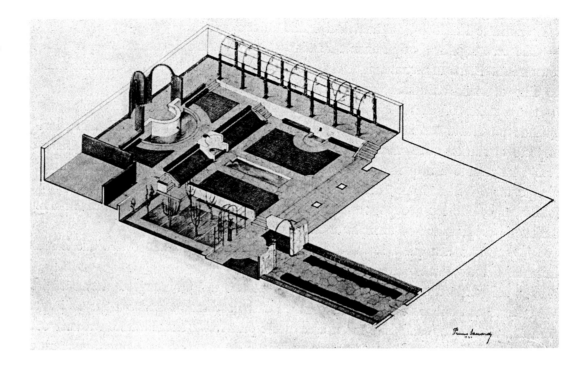

planted by the ancient Romans, the pine
forests of the Borghese, Sacchetti, and
Pamphilj villas in Rome date back only to
the seventeenth century, and pine trees had
started to appear on a larger scale in the
Roman Campagna only in the nineteenth
century.[68] Nevertheless a journalist writing
in *Capitolium* in 1934 seemed to suggest
some antique tradition: "The pine always
remains the characteristic tree of Rome; it is
impossible to imagine the Roman countryside without the Roman pine."[69] *Pinus pinea*
was considered quintessentially Italian
and Roman; its popular names included
Pino domestico, Pino italico, and *Pino
romano.*[70] The planting of coastal pine
forests had been subsidized by the state
since 1923.[71] The extensive use of *Pinus
pinea* for the ordering of the new Roman
cityscape and for the embellishment of
ruins and archaeological sites in the 1920s
and 1930s furthered the myth that it had
always belonged to the southern Italian
and Roman landscape in particular. Under
the Fascist regime, the invented tradition
of the "Roman pine," which was to connect the city with its imperial past, led to
the replacement of elm trees by pines along

Roman roadsides. In 1934, Rome's director
of parks and gardens, Bruno Braschi, could
report that *Pinus pinea* was the second most
common tree in the city after the London
plane tree.[72]

Gardens as Expressions of and Prescriptions for Modern Life

In 1928 the architect Tomaso Buzzi stated
that it was not yet possible to speak of a "true
modern garden art" ("vera arte moderna del
giardino") in Italy, and a couple of years later,
when organizing the Mostra del Giardino
Italiano, Carlo Mercatelli announced that no
vibrant garden art existed in Italy.[73] Indeed,
the competition designs for a private urban
house garden published in *Domus* and *La
casa bella* provided intricate, formal, ornamental settings for the villas, rather than comfortable, relaxed outdoor rooms for work and
play, on the one hand, or aesthetic and spatial
experiments, on the other. As we have seen,
many Italian architects and art critics in the
1920s and 1930s were caught up in inventing
and defining a national garden tradition. To
illustrate the "modern garden" in his encyclopedia entry on gardens, Luigi Piccinato, one of

9. Tullio Rossi (Rome), competition entry for the design of an urban villa garden, Mostra del Giardino Italiano, Florence, 1931

Domus 4, no. 40 (1931): 25

the tree nurseryman Ludwig Späth, and by French landscape architects André and Paul Vera and especially Jean-Claude Nicolas Forestier.[76] The work of Gabriel Guévrékian, Le Corbusier, Pierre Jeanneret, André Lurçat, and Robert Mallet-Stevens were especially prominent in articles published in *La casa bella*.[77]

In addition to this diffusion of designs from abroad aimed at sparking an interest in garden art in Italy, Italian architects and garden architects themselves followed various strategies for renewal of their art. Within the paradigm of the garden as architecture, some copied and integrated foreign motifs into their designs. They reinstated the classical Roman concept of *dulce utili*, the beautiful and useful, and in a variety of ways and forms followed Luigi Dami's advice to be "ancient and modern at the same time" ("antichi e moderni nello stesso tempo").[78]

Luigi Piccinato was fascinated by the expressionist designs of the German landscape architects Maasz and Pepinski, and by the work of the Frenchman Forestier.[79] That source of inspiration is perhaps evident in his designs of 1926 for the water basin and canal for Villa Zulema in Gardone Riviera (fig. 11). While some features, such as a symmetrical rose garden, a small forecourt with a fountain, and an orchard recalled sixteenth-century Italian gardens, others—a water basin and canal, the special use of paving stones in the western part of the garden, and a small, shaded garden room for relaxation east of the villa—made this a "modern garden." Although the combination of the beautiful and useful was an age-old trope in garden design, Piccinato considered the use of fruit trees as ornamental features a "renewal" worth mentioning.[80]

Like Piccinato, the self-taught Maria Teresa Parpagliolo was commissioned to write articles for *Domus*. In her struggle to define the new garden through her designs, she reflected on Italian history, examples abroad, and the ongoing Italian architectural debate. In a design for an imaginary twelve-thousand-square-meter garden

the first graduates of Rome's new architecture school and a former student at the Technische Universität München, referred to gardens built in Germany, the United States, France, and Spain.[74] *Architettura e arti decorative*, *Domus*, and *La casa bella* resolved this problematic situation by publishing European and American garden designs and articles by foreign landscape architects.[75] Thus Piccinato chose to present in *Architettura e arti decorative* and *Domus* numerous designs by the German landscape architects Harry Maasz, Erik Pepinski, and Otto Werner as well as

for a country house published in *Domus* in 1932, Parpagliolo was likely inspired by the garden of the seventeenth-century Villa Gamberaia in Settignano (fig. 12). Well kept and restored by the Romanian princess Jeanne Ghyka and her American friend Florence Blood, that garden played an important role in garden literature of the time.[81] Edith Wharton, for instance, praised it in 1904 as "probably the most perfect example of the art of producing a great effect on a small scale," and in 1906 Inigo H. Triggs described it as an "example of the formal garden brought to a state of perfection."[82] The Gamberaia garden had

inspired the American landscape architect Charles Adams Platt before the end of the nineteenth century, and it remained one of the most popular of Italian gardens until after World War II, cited by art critics, garden writers, and landscape architects such as Pasolini Ponti, Dami, Geoffrey Jellicoe, Pietro Porcinai, and Cecil Ross Pinsent.[83] Similar to the layout of Villa Gamberaia, Parpagliolo's design connected various geometrical garden "rooms" by a central longitudinal axis on a hilltop site and included a quadripartite citrus garden as well as a cypress exedra forming a belvedere. In addition to employing design principles

11. Luigi Piccinato, garden design
for Villa Zulema, Gardone Riviera,
1926

Domus 1, no. 4 (1928): 32–33

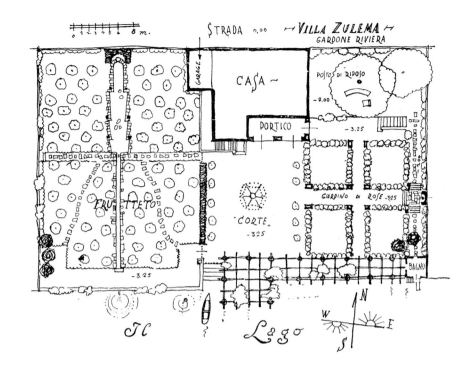

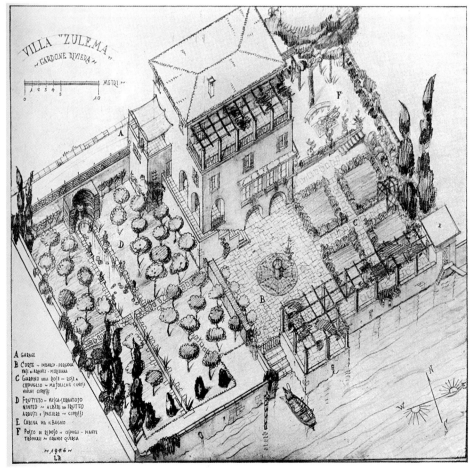

12. Maria Teresa Parpagliolo, design for a country house garden, 1932

Domus 5, no. 57 (1932): 559

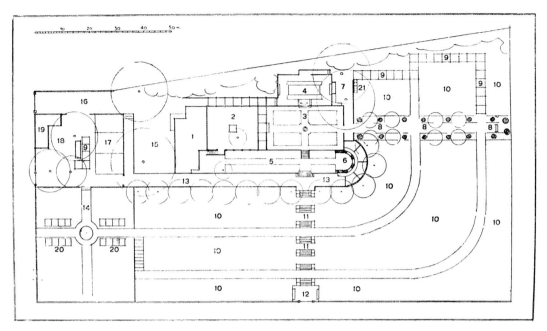

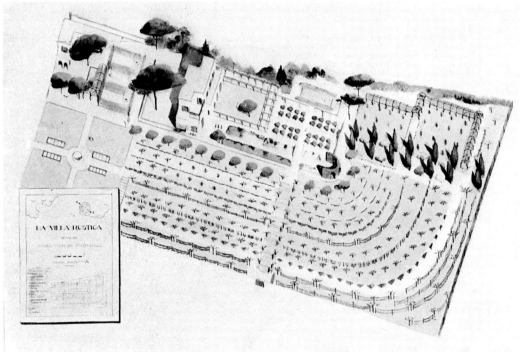

from the Italian past, such as planned vistas and the extension of the house into the garden, Parpagliolo tried to introduce what she considered modern elements from foreign garden cultures, such as mixed borders alongside the walk leading to the exedra.

In many of her writings Parpagliolo promoted floral stairways, shrubberies, herbaceous borders, and other materials and schemes that were prevalent in English cottage and country house gardens such as those designed by Gertrude Jekyll but were new to the Italian gardening world at the time. Paradoxically, the planting schemes that she recommended for contemporary Italian gardens were the very ones used to

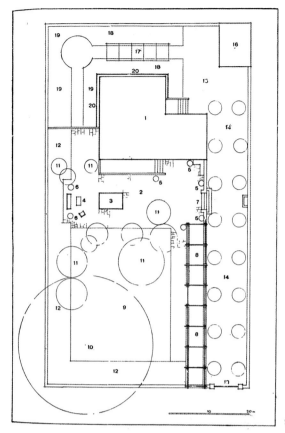

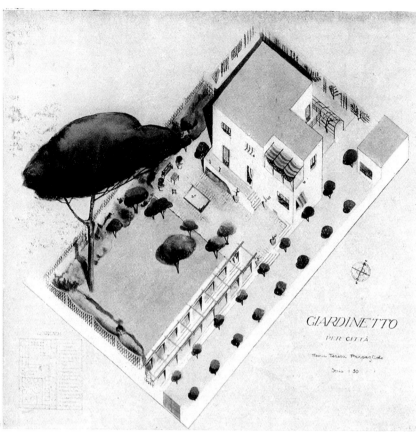

foster a sense of national identity in England, their country of origin.[84] In fact, the Roman garden director Bruno Braschi, concerned with the fulfillment of the Fascist vision of a new Roman Empire, warned of the foreign origin of "this new picturesque style" (*questo nuovo stile pittorico*), characterized by luscious and naturalistic plantings of flowering plants, herbaceous borders, floral stairways, and bedding plants between paving stones, which he considered a "defect" (*difetto*).[85]

In contrast, Parpagliolo promoted the use of these motifs and techniques in conjunction with forms inspired by the Italian garden legacy. Just after Giuseppe Pagano, architect, writer, and eventually editor of *La casa bella*, wrote about the relationship between Pompeian town houses and modern "rationalist" architecture, Parpagliolo, writing in the English periodical *Landscape and Garden*, claimed that Pompeian peristyle gardens were "the most modern Italian

gardens." She recommended the ancient plans enhanced with vibrantly colored and variously shaped plants, "if in those same layouts we should think a planting scheme more suited to our modern taste with wealth of colour and beautifully shaped varieties of shrubs, bulbs, and perennials."[86] Like many of her architect colleagues, Parpagliolo was inspired by the recent excavations undertaken by the Fascist regime in Ostia and Pompeii.[87]

In 1932 Parpagliolo designed a clear-cut, rectilinear, and seemingly white flat-roofed urban villa as the dwelling within another imaginary garden (fig. 13). The design and its graphic presentation in *Domus* resembled the entries to the 1931 competition for a private urban villa garden mentioned above. More effectively than many of the competition entries, however, Parpagliolo created outdoor garden rooms for contemporary living. Using a clearly comprehensible structure that offered diverse spaces for different

14. Maria Teresa Parpagliolo, house garden design in three phases, 1937

Domus 10, no. 109 (1937): 46–47

UN GIARDINO IN TRE TEMPI

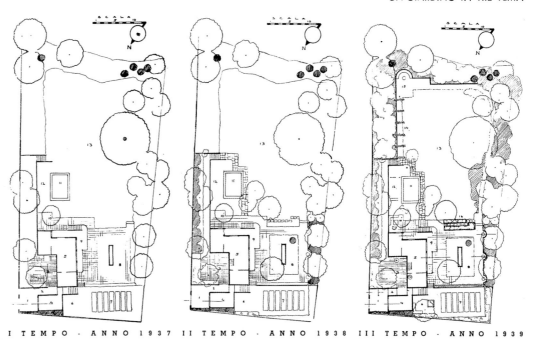

I TEMPO · ANNO 1937   II TEMPO · ANNO 1938   III TEMPO · ANNO 1939

uses, she extended the domestic sphere of her flat-roofed villa out of doors, thereby adhering to Giò Ponti's program, described earlier, which sought to define the bourgeois Italian home as modern, functional, and comfortable.[88] In her urban villa garden, a driveway flanked by red-leaved *Prunus* runs up to the garage. A kitchen garden and vine pergola are located behind the house. To the south a terrace with a water basin and a comfortable seating area provide an area of transition between the house and the open lawn, enclosed on two sides by herbaceous and shrub borders and on a third side by a pergola. A pine tree, considered characteristic of the coast and of the southern Italian countryside, towers over the south side of the garden and geographically locates it.

While architects began to consider the garden an integral component of the resi-

15. Alessandro Minali, carpet bed, IV Triennale di Monza delle Arti Decorative e Industriali Moderne, Monza, 1930

Domus 3, no. 27 (1930): 23

single-family home as a white, flat-roofed modern cube.

Despite these and other adjustments to "rational" modern life, such as the establishment of roof gardens, experiments with striking, avant-garde aesthetics or innovative spatial patterns were hard to find in Italian garden design. Only a few isolated examples appeared in *Domus* and *La casa bella*. At the IV Triennale di Monza delle Arti Decorative e Industriali Moderne in 1930, one of the leading Novecento architects, Alessandro Minali, displayed an abstract pattern as a carpet bed (fig. 15). While it clearly reflected the modernist design language fashionable in the decorative arts at the time, the technique used—bedding out—dated back to the nineteenth century. The modernist aesthetic of flowing spatial patterns, overlapping planes, and asymmetric layouts as tentatively displayed in Minali's carpet bed was fully explored in more experimental designs by the Milanese architecture students Alberto Cingria and Giulio Minoletti. For the competition for a public park held on the occasion of the Mostra del Giardino Italiano in 1931, they submitted a design based on a cubist-inspired pattern that won one of two first prizes (fig. 16).[90]

Giulio Minoletti, who throughout his architectural career produced buildings that engaged their surroundings, continued his exploration of aesthetic modernism in a small garden design published a year later in *La casa bella* (fig. 17). It was intended for a suburban house outside a big Italian city. Like the French designers Achille Duchêne and André Vera, who conceived gardens for occupational groups such as athletes and artists, Minoletti catered to a specific type of client: the well-off professional, industrialist, or merchant. The garden was enclosed on three sides by multiple rows of trees for privacy. The house opened onto a pergola-covered terrace that connected to a seating area with a rectangular pool surrounded by a low hedge. Adjacent to these intimate garden rooms, a rectangular open lawn allowed for sunbathing. The square pavers used for

dence in the same way that they began to recognize parks as parts of the city, the few professional landscape architects in practice before World War II sought to legitimize their work by adopting an architectural vocabulary, both figuratively and literally. Thus, in 1932, one year after the second exhibition of the Movimento Italiano per l'Architettura Razionale, Giuseppe Roda declared: "Today when everything is rationalized the garden, too, must be rational" ("Oggi in cui tutto si razionalizza anche il Giardino deve essere razionale"), and that "every part of it has to have a clearly defined objective" ("ogni parte di esso deve avere uno scopo ben definito").[89] Parpagliolo was thinking along rationalist and economic lines when she presented in *Domus* a house garden design that could be realized over a period of three years, or in three phases (fig. 14). Proposals for the phasing of garden layouts were common in other countries around this time, both before and after the worldwide economic crisis following the 1929 stock market crash. In this design, as in many of her small sketches in *Domus*, Parpagliolo, inspired by Neues Bauen and rationalist architecture, presented the

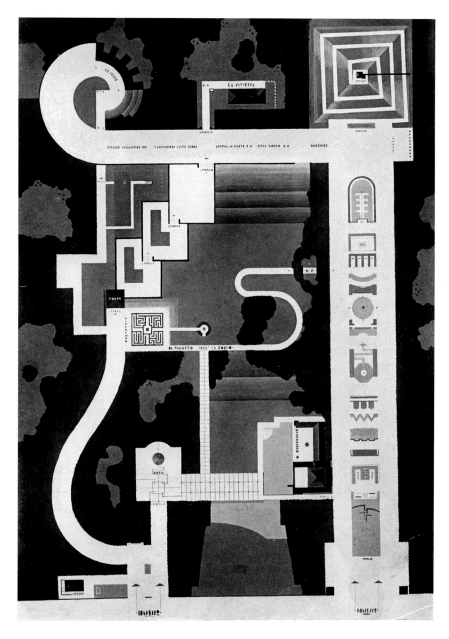

provided ample shaded areas. In the upper left corner of the plan a rectangular area was left open to accommodate the owner's desire for an orchard, a rose garden, or a kitchen garden. Minoletti's design included features that resemble 1920s garden designs by Le Corbusier as well as the Belgian landscape architect Jean Canneel-Claes' own garden in Auderghem, near Brussels, designed in 1931. Canneel-Claes had used rectangular monochromatic planting beds in a similar fashion.[91] Like many of his peers, Minoletti was no doubt inspired by developments in garden architecture abroad and copied significant design features.

In 1933 *Domus* published a garden design that was characterized to an even greater degree than Minoletti's by overlapping rectangular planes, tree lines, and hedges that formed individual garden rooms, extending the villa's interior out of doors. The architect Tino Sgaravatti, a partner in the horticultural and nursery firm Fratelli Sgaravatti, founded in Saonara near Padua in 1820, presented designs for a "modern garden" on which he had collaborated with the German landscape architect Ferdinand Bredenkamp (fig. 18).[92] Like Minoletti's design in *La casa bella,* Sgaravatti and Bredenkamp's garden designs were represented in reverse, white on black, contributing to their diagrammatic and abstract appearance on paper.

Minoletti and Sgaravatti thus provided the Italian design schemes that are absent from the Italo-Swiss architect Alberto Sartoris' chapter on gardens in *La nuova architettura* (1931), edited under the pseudonym Fillia (Luigi Enrico Colombo). Sartoris presented gardens accompanying the architecture of Frank Lloyd Wright, Ernst May, and Josef Frank, and gardens by Le Corbusier, André Lurçat, Robert Mallet-Stevens, and Gabriel Guévrékian. Italian exemplars, while numerous in parts of the book that dealt with housing, industrial buildings, churches, and public buildings, were conspicuously absent from this section.[93]

For the influence, albeit indirect, of the artistic avant-garde on garden and park

the terrace were arranged in straight pathways that delineated the lawn and divided it into two parts. The attention to detail in the ground plane was evident in rectangular planting beds for low-growing shrubs, perennials, or spring bulbs. Minoletti envisioned monochromatic beds along the straight drive and entranceway to the house as festive splashes of color that contrasted with the green lawn and foliage. Trees, densely planted at regular intervals and in lines, formed two small boschetti along the garden's southern and western edges and

17. Giulio Minoletti, design for a
modern garden, 1932
La casa bella 5, no. 54 (1932): 46–47

18. Tino Sgaravatti and Ferdinand
Bredenkamp, design for a modern
garden, 1932
Domus 6, no. 62 (1933): 87–89

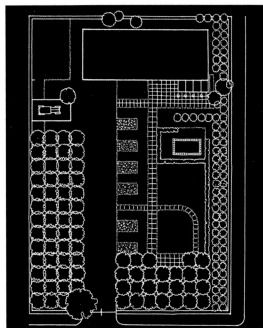

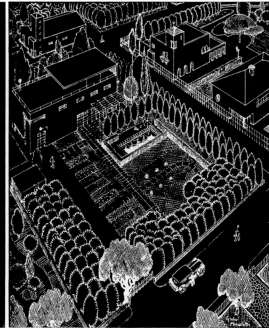

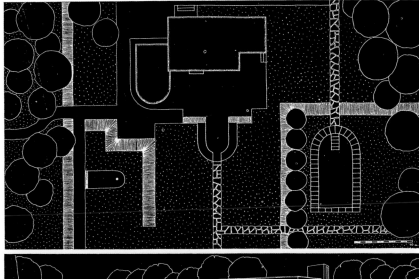

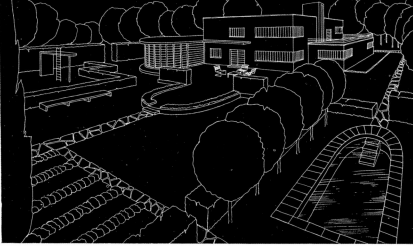

design, one has to turn to the large-scale
projects that were undertaken by the Fascist
regime in Rome. From 1925 onward, the
Fascists pursued a park building program
that also led to the redesign and reopening
to the public of many preexisting parks and
gardens. Following earlier proposals, the
1930 land-use plan for the city included a
municipal and metropolitan park system.
Demolitions in the city center to expose the
Roman monuments and enhance their visibility were accompanied by the construction of parks to stage and frame the ancient
imperial monuments. Many planning direc-
tives in the new land-use plan were, in fact,
intended to reconfigure the Italian capital
visually, making the imperial qualities to
which the Fascist regime aspired perceptible
and comprehensible to its citizens and to
Italians in general.[94] The view of this new
Rome belonged in particular to the modern
motorist. After the futurists had made the
automobile and its speed and noise the subject of paintings, sculpture, and writings, in
the 1930s parts of the Roman urban landscape were at last designed to be experienced
by the motorist.

Thus, when archaeologist Antonio Muñoz
designed the fifteen-acre Parco Traiano,

19. Antonio Muñoz, perspective sketch and design study for a scenic route connecting Via Merulana with the Colosseum, Rome

Antonio Muñoz, Il parco di Traiano *(Rome, 1936), n.p.*

opened in 1936 in the area of the Baths of Trajan adjacent to the Parco del Colle Oppio, he included a scenic route to connect Via Merulana with the Colosseum. On this *viale panoramico* (today's Viale Monte Oppio), Rome's imperial past—the ruins of Trajan's baths and the Colosseum—could be experienced while using one of the most modern means of transport: the automobile (figs. 19 and 20). The construction of the *viale panoramico* for kinesthetic experience entailed the destruction of numerous dwellings.[95] Consequently, the new green open space, fitted out with benches, fountains, a viewing terrace above the Colosseum, a path, and carriageways, testified to Mussolini's ambivalent, contradictory social politics: while he was creating parks, he was demolishing housing and thus displacing the citizens most in need of them. Muñoz paired the conservation of what were considered some of Rome's most important ancient monuments with a design that accommodated the speed, dynamism, and technological progress previously promoted especially by the futurists. For a

moment in history, it seems, the interests of "passatisti" and "futuristi" among the cultural elite met in the sweeping archaeological park realized around the ruins of the Baths of Trajan in the Italian capital.

Indeed, the struggle to accommodate both the modernization and conservation of Rome's historic city center had by then preoccupied architects, archaeologists, and urban planners alike for several decades and had led Rome to host the XII Concorso della Federazione Internazionale delle Abitazioni e dei Piani Regolatori of 1929, an international congress on housing and city planning focused on this theme.[96] As Marcello Piacentini suggested as early as 1916, international experts now deemed that parks should play a role in the conservation of historic city centers by providing buffers between the old centers and zones of urban growth.[97] Gardens and parks were finally accepted as necessary components of modern planning schemes, not only because they improved living conditions but also because, if protected, they could play a role in the

conservation of complete urban districts—and in the writing of history.

In conclusion, what made Italian gardens and parks "modern" in the first decades of the twentieth century was the discourse that developed around them and the way they were staged in that discourse. It was the recognition that gardens and parks belonged to Italy's cultural heritage, and the belief, in particular held by architects, designers, and cultural critics under Fascism, that history was malleable and could ultimately be used to create a prototypical "modern" and "Italian" garden. It was the invention and categorization of garden types undertaken by a variety of authors and architects. The paradigms of the garden as architecture and of the vernacular garden were both the products of, and the motors for, a new attention to national identity, cultural heritage, rural life, and healthy living that were promoted by cultural nationalism and Fascist politics. The fusion of the garden with the house and the city, and the garden's consequent adapta-

tion to and promotion of new lifestyles that included motoring, sports, swimming, and sunbathing was considered a response to modern times.

Despite the new concern for garden art and various attempts to revive it, Italy could provide only a few built examples. The reasons were manifold, but the lack of schools for the education of landscape architects was a factor, and one repeatedly deplored by contemporary professionals. At the Primo Convegno Nazionale del Giardino, held in Varese in 1937, the architect Enrico Ratti complained that Italy had no equivalent to the gardeners' training schools at Versailles and Kew and in Berlin, which provided advanced education including that in garden design.[98] Consequently Rome's director of parks and gardens Elvezio Ricci could argue the point with a quotation from the *Giornale d'Italia* that "garden architects in Italy have to be looked for with a searchlight" ("architetti di giardini ... in Italia sono da ricercarsi con il lumicino").[99] In the same year the landscape architect Pietro Porcinai stated that "only when in Italy, as has been the case already in Germany, England, and the United States, proper garden architects have been educated will we be able to say that our garden will proceed toward its renaissance."[100]

Thus, by the time of the Varese conference in 1937, the early twentieth-century neglect of gardens had turned into concern for gardens. Italian officials and ministerial directors came to realize that gardens belonged to a valuable cultural heritage worth protecting and that old and new gardens could be used as instruments for nation building, for fostering a common Italian identity, for improving the health of citizens, and for boosting the economy. On one hand, the conference papers revealed the comprehensive role that was finally attributed to gardens twenty-five years after the first law for their protection was passed. On the other hand, they showed how much still needed to be accomplished "per la difesa del giardino," in defense of the garden, as the title of the conference proceedings so aptly suggested.

NOTES

This essay is based on my previous publications "'La battaglia del fiore': Gardens, Parks and the City in Fascist Italy," *Studies in the History of Gardens and Designed Landscapes* 25, no. 1 (2005): 40–70; *Maria Teresa Parpagliolo Shephard (1903–1974): Ein Beitrag zur Entwicklung der Gartenkultur in Italien im 20. Jahrhundert* (Weimar, 2004); "'The Garden Is a National Amenity': Zur Gartenkultur unter faschistischer Herrschaft in Italien," in *Gegen den Strom: Gert Gröning zum 60. Geburtstag*, ed. Uwe Schneider and Joachim Wolschke-Bulmahn, Beiträge zur räumlichen Planung, Schriftenreihe des Fachbereichs Landschaftsarchitektur und Umweltentwicklung der Universität Hannover, vol. 76 (Hannover, 2004), 93–110; "Zur Gartenkultur in Italien um 1930: Entwürfe ausländischer Gartenarchitekten als Ausgangspunkt für die Suche nach dem 'giardino moderno,'" *Stadt und Grün* 49, no. 6 (2000): 404–410.

1. For the "coming garden," see, for example, Gert Gröning and Joachim Wolschke-Bulmahn, "Der kommende Garten: Zur Diskussion um die Gartenkultur in Deutschland seit 1900," *Garten + Landschaft* 98, no. 3 (1988): 47–56, and Gert Gröning, "Der kommende Garten, Anmerkungen zu einer europäischen Diskussion um Gartenkultur im ersten Drittel des 20. Jahrhunderts," *Die Gartenkunst* 7, no. 2 (1995): 268–281.

2. For a contemporary critique of the landscape garden, see, for example, Luigi Dami, "L'arte italiana dei giardini," *Rivista mensile del Touring Club italiano* 20 (1914): 553–559 (559) (cited subsequently as Dami 1914a); Luigi Dami, *Il nostro giardino* (Florence, 1923), 48; and Maria Pasolini Ponti, *Il giardino italiano* (Rome, 1915), 21, 25–26.

3. See, for example, Jacob Burckhardt, *Geschichte der Renaissance in Italien* (Stuttgart, 1912); Cornelius Gurlitt, *Geschichte des Barockstiles in Italien* (Stuttgart, 1887); W. P. Tuckermann, *Die Gartenkunst der Italienischen Renaissance-Zeit* (Berlin, 1884); Charles A. Platt, *Italian Gardens* (New York, 1894); Edith Wharton, *Italian Villas and Their Gardens* (New York, 1904); Charles Latham and E. March Philipps, *The Gardens of Italy* (London, 1905); Inigo H. Triggs, *The Art of Garden Design in Italy* (London, 1906); George S. Elgood, *Italian Gardens* (London, 1907); George Sitwell, *An Essay on the Making of Gardens* (London, 1909); Aubrey Le Blond, *The Old Gardens of Italy* (London, 1912); Julia Cartwright, *Italian Gardens of the Renaissance* (London, 1914); Georges Gromort, *Jardins d'Italie* (Paris, 1923); and Geoffrey A. Jellicoe and John C. Shepherd, *Italian Gardens of the Renaissance* (London, 1925).

4. See Vincenzo Cazzato, "The Restoration of Italian Gardens in the Early Nineteenth Century," in *Cecil Pinsent and His Gardens in Tuscany*, ed. Marcello Fantoni, Heidi Flores, and John Pfordresher (Florence, 1996), 99.

5. See Johann Wolfgang von Goethe, *Goethe's Italiänische Reise*, ed. Christian Schuchardt (Stuttgart, 1862), 248, 250; William Shakespeare, "The Taming of the Shrew: A Comedy," in *The Dramatick Works of William Shakespear* (London, 1734–1735), 6:10.

6. See James Sievert, *The Origins of Nature Conservation in Italy* (New York, 2000), 75–80, 105–137. For the Italian nature conservation movement, also see Luigi Piccioni, *Il volto amato della patria: Il primo movimento per la protezione della natura in Italia, 1880–1934* (Camerino, 1999).

7. See Luigi Piccioni 1999, 125–126; James Sievert, *The Origins of Nature Conservation in Italy* (New York, 2000), 147–148. Also see the contemporary literature that celebrated the *pineta*'s alleged cultural significance, for example, N. A. Falcone, *Il paesaggio italico* (Florence, 1914), 153–156.

8. See Benjamin George Martin, "Celebrating the Nation's Poets," in *Donatello among the Blackshirts: History and Modernity in the Visual Culture of Fascist Italy*, ed. Claudia Lazzaro and Roger J. Crum (Ithaca, 2005), 187–202 (192).

9. "… poichè in essi l'arte ha modificato la natura, che, diremmo quasi, diventa come il marmo o la tela in mano dello scultore e del pittore; e son quindi veri e propri monumenti, che spesso, oltre ad offrire godimenti morali ed intellettuali, son materia di studio per comprendere il carattere dell'epoca in cui furon creati." Luigi Parpagliolo, "La protezione del paesaggio," *Fanfulla della Domenica* 27, nos. 36–37 (1905): 13.

10. See Luigi Parpagliolo, "La protezione dei giardini in relazione alla legge delle bellezze naturali," in *Relazioni svolte al Primo Convegno Nazionale del Giardino*, ed. Istituto fascista di tecnica e propaganda agraria (Rome, 1937), 3–15.

11. See law no. 778, "for the protection of natural beauties and immobile objects of particular historic interest" ("per la tutela delle bellezze naturali e degli immobili di particolare interesse storico") decreed on June 11, 1922, published in Luigi Parpagliolo, *La difesa delle bellezze naturali d'Italia* (Rome, 1923), 201–203.

12. See Edwin Cerio, ed., *Il Convegno del paesaggio* (Capri, 1923), 5–9. For a discussion of the landscape conference on Capri, see, for example, Bruno Fiorentino, "Dal paesaggio del mito al mito del paesaggio," in *Capri: La città e la terra*, ed. Gaetana Catone, Bruno Fiorentino, and Giovanna Sarnella (Naples, 1982), 319–341 (322); Ernesto Mazzetti, "Edwin Cerio, soprintendente alla bellezza," in Edwin Cerio, *La casa, il giardino e la pergola nel paesaggio di Capri* (Naples, 1997), 7–13 (12).

13. Edwin Cerio, "Prefazione," in Cerio 1923, 1.

14. Cerio 1923, 5.

15. Filippo Tommaso Marinetti, "Il discorso di Marinetti," in Cerio 1923, 38; Filippo Tommaso Marinetti, "Lo stile pratico," in Cerio 1923, 67.

16. On the conservationists' treatment, see Parpagliolo 1923, 188–189.

17. Fedele Azari, *La flora futurista ed equivalenti plastici di odori artificiali* (Rome, 1924).

18. Richard Etlin, *Modernism in Italian Architecture, 1890–1940* (Cambridge, MA, 1991), 129–161.

19. Antonio Maraini, "L'architettura rustica alla cinquantenale romana," *Architettura e arti decorative* 1 (1921): 379–385. Various competitions for the development of a model for a rural house were organized in the 1930s. For this and the development of "a modern vernacular architecture," see Etlin 1991, 129–161, 472.

20. Giuseppe Capponi, "Architettura ed Accademia a Capri," *Architettura e arti decorative* 9 (1929): 177–188.

21. Maria Teresa Parpagliolo, "Giardini di Capri," *Domus* 3, no. 32 (1930): 58–60 (60, 81).

22. Gilbert Clavel, "L'architettura meridionale," in Cerio 1923, 71.

23. "La grana stessa della copertura è di effetto piacevole e con il tempo, quando le spore di numerose specie della flora protettiva dei ruderi e dei tetti hanno avuto il tempo di fissarsi e svilupparsi, la copertura battuta acquista una patina vegetale di piacevolissimo effetto." Edwin Cerio, "L'architettura minima nella contrada delle Sirene," *Architettura e arti decorative* 2 (December 1922): 156–176 (174). Cerio discusses the "protective flora of ruins and roofs." While influenced by the picturesque aesthetic widely known among Italian conservationists and intellectuals through John Ruskin's writings, Cerio's idea most likely is based on Giacomo Boni's concept of protecting and beautifying Roman ruins through planting of selected plant species. See Dümpelmann 2004, 167–172; Dümpelmann 2005, 49–57.

24. Maria Teresa Parpagliolo, "Il giardino di Villa Fiore," *Domus* 7, no. 75 (1934): 36.

25. See, for example, Etlin 1991, 129–161; Ruth Ben-Ghiat, *Fascist Modernities: Italy, 1922–1945* (Berkeley and Los Angeles, 2001), 136–137; Giuseppe Pagano, *Architettura rurale italiana* (Milan, 1936); Virgilio Marchi, *Architettura futurista* (Foligno, 1924).

26. Edwin Cerio, *Il giardino e la pergola nel paesaggio di Capri* (Milan, 1922), 14–17.

27. See Nello Tarchiani, "La mostra del giardino italiano in Palazzo Vecchio a Firenze," *Domus* 4, no. 38 (1931): 15–17 (15). Also see Luigi Dami's remark: "La Mostra che dell'Arte del Giardino sarà tenuta un'altro anno a Firenze, potrebbe essere un incitamento e un inizio." Dami 1914a, 553–559.

28. Dami 1914a.

29. Luigi Dami, "Il giardino toscano come opera d'arte," *Emporium* 39 (1914): 264–279 (cited subsequently as Dami 1914b); Maria Pasolini Ponti, *Il giardino italiano* (Rome, 1915).

30. Dami 1923; Luigi Dami, *Il giardino italiano* (Milan, 1924).

31. For the AACAR and its interest in conservation, vernacular architecture, and contextual design, as well as Maria Pasolini Ponti's role in this organization, see Etlin 1991, 101–161.

32. Pasolini Ponti 1915, 16–19, 27. According to Pasolini Ponti, the "organic unity" of architecture throughout the Renaissance and baroque periods derived from individual decisions of the architect based on the needs of the client, the siting of the house, the environment, sight lines, orientation, climate, and wind directions. For the role of the "organic analogy" in Italian architecture and urban design, see Etlin 1991, 109–111.

33. See Sonja Dümpelmann, "American System and Italian Beauty: Transnationale Aspekte der Parkplanung in den ersten Jahrzehnten des 20. Jahrhunderts," *Die Gartenkunst* 18, no. 1 (2006): 119–142; Sonja Dümpelmann, "Creating Order with Nature: The Emergence of Park System Planning in Twentieth-Century Washington, Chicago, Berlin and Rome," *Planning Perspectives* 24, no. 2 (2009): 143–173.

34. See Wharton 1904, 5–13, and Pasolini Ponti 1915, 10–15.

35. Pasolini Ponti 1915, 10.

36. See Dami 1924, 29.

37. See, for example, Dami 1914a, 559; Dami 1923, 48; and Pasolini Ponti 1915, 21, 25–26.

38. See, for example, Margherita Azzi Visentini, "Riflessioni sul giardino paesaggistico in Italia tra settecento e ottocento," in *Il giardino paesaggistico tra settecento e ottocento in Italia e Germania*, Kepos Quaderni 8, ed. Pier Fausto Bagatti Valsecchi and Andreas Kipar (Milan, 1996), 37–38.

39. See, for example, Pasolini Ponti 1915, 21; Luigi Piccinato, "Giardino," in *Enciclopedia Italiana* (Milan, 1933), 17:75.

40. For attributions to Ammanati, see, for example, Marie Luise Gothein, *Geschichte der Gartenkunst* (Jena, 1914), 1:264. For uses of Bandinelli's phrase, see Tomaso Buzzi, "Alcune recenti architetture da giardino costruite nel parco della Villa Bernocchi a Stresa dall'architetto Alessandro Minali," *Domus* 2, no. 21 (1929): 15–20 (15); Ugo Ojetti et al., *La Mostra del giardino italiano* (Florence, 1931), 23; Dami 1924, 13; Maria Teresa Parpagliolo and Luigi Meccoli, "Relazione sul viaggio di studio per la mostra del giardino italiano nell'Esposizione Universale di Roma effettuato dagli Architetti Parpagliolo e Meccoli del Servizio Architettura Parchi e Giardini dell'esposizione," reprinted in Massimo de Vico Fallani, *Parchi e Giardini dell'EUR* (Rome, 1988), 233–241 (235); Gherardo Bosio, "Invito alla visita delle ville medicee: A proposito della mostra fiorentina del giardino," *Domus* 4, no. 39 (1931): 56 (cited subsequently as Bosio 1931a).

41. See Dami 1923, 100, and Ermanno Biagini, "La Mostra del giardino italiano a Firenze," *Le vie d'Italia e dell'America Latina: Revista mensile del Touring Club Italiano* 11 (1931): 642–651 (645); Dami 1914a, 559; Ermanno Biagini, "La Mostra del giardino italiano a Firenze," *Le vie d'Italia e dell'America Latina: Revista mensile del Touring Club Italiano* 37 (1931), 642–651 (645); Gherardo Bosio, "Il concorso di Firenze per un giardino privato moderno all'italiana," *Domus* 4, no. 40 (1931): 22–27, 84 (24) (cited subsequently as Bosio 1931b); Pietro Porcinai, "Giardini privati," *Domus* 10, no. 118 (1937): 30–37 (31).

42. See Vincenzo Cazzato, "I giardini del desiderio: La mostra del giardino italiano (Firenze 1931)," in *Il giardino romantico*, ed. Alessandro Vezzosi (Florence, 1986), 80–88 (87, note 33); Vincenzo Cazzato, "Giardini 'regali' fra realtà e immaginazione nella mostra fiorentina del 1931," in *Giardini regali: Fascino e immagini del verde nelle grandi dinastie; Dai Medici agli Asburgo*, ed. Monica Amari (Milan, 1998), 26 n. 11.

43. Dami 1923, 55.

44. Paolo Nicoloso, *Gli architetti di Mussolini: Scuole e sindacato, architetti e massoni, professori e politici negli anni del regime* (Milan, 1999), 54, 82, 100, 103, 111; Ferdinando Reggiori, "Grandezza del giardino italiano: Il giardino italiano come espressione architettonica," *I giardini* 7, no. 83 (1937): 121–124 (122).

45. For the Novecento buildings in Milan, see Etlin 1991.

46. "Nella casa all'italiana non vi è grande distinzione di architettura fra esterno ed interno: ... da noi l'architettura di fuori penetra nell'interno.... Dall'interno la casa all'italiana riesce all'aperto con i suoi portici e le sue terrazze, con le pergole e le verande, con le loggie ed i balconi, le altane e i belvedere, invenzioni tutte confortevolissime per l'abitazione serena e tanto italiane che in ogni lingua sono chiamate con i nomi di qui. Una stessa ordinanza architettonica regge dunque ... le facciate e gli interni ed ancora regola d'attorno la natura medesima con terrazze e gradoni, con giardini, appunto detti all'italiana, ninfei e prospettive, orti e cortili, tutti creati per dare agio e scena ad una felice abitazione." Giò Ponti, "La casa all'italiana," editorial, *Domus* 1, no. 1 (1928): 7.

47. Dami 1923, 65: "Bisogna che la casa nel punto di entrare in contatto col giardino, perda un po' della sua fierezza e della sua rigidità, alleggerisca le sue masse opprimenti, si rarefaccia, se cosi posso dire, dia un po' più di luogo ai vuoti ed all'aria, a scapito dei suoi pieni e delle sue pietre. Bisognerà per converso, obbedendo con cortesia alla legge del *do ut des*, che il giardino avvicinandosi alla casa perda un po' della sua scapigliatura e della sua irrequietezza, si faccia più composto, si solidifichi un po' con serietà, e offra per il congiungimento le sue forme più irrigidite a quelle che dall'altra parte mette avanti la casa; e saranno le più assottigliate e mosse che la casa potrà. In tal modo la buona vicinanza sarà stabilita con grazia e con vantaggio comune."

48. For the caricature see *Domus* 4, no. 42 (1931): 52.

49. Bosio 1931a, 56.

50. See Claudia Lazzaro, "Politicizing a National Garden Tradition: The Italianness of the Italian Garden," in *Donatello among the Blackshirts: History and Modernity in the Visual Culture of Fascist Italy*, ed. Claudia Lazzaro and Roger J. Crum (Ithaca, 2005), 157–169 (161). For women under Fascism, see Victoria de Grazia, *How Fascism Ruled Women: Italy 1922–1945* (Berkeley, 1992).

51. Bruno Braschi, "Giardini italiani moderni," *I giardini* 11, no. 11 (1933): 237–238 (237).

52. Giuseppe Roda, "Del giardino moderno," *I giardini* 11, no. 4 (1933): 81–82; Braschi 1933, 237.

53. See Alessandro Tagliolini, *Storia del giardino italiano* (Florence, 1991), 24.

54. Dümpelmann 2004, 151–179; Dümpelmann 2005, 40–70.

55. For the Esposizione Nazionale Italiana of 1928 in Turin, see Valeria Garuzzo, *Torino 1928: L'architettura all'Esposizione Nazionale Italiana* (Rome, 2002), 18.

56. "... che si è accinta con risulatezza all'opera per la rinascita del *nostro* giardino." Governatorato di Roma, Azienda Giardini Pubblici, *Mostra del giardino romano al Valentino* (Milan and Rome, 1928), 24.

57. Governatorato di Roma 1928, 22.

58. For the gardeners' training school see Dümpelmann 2004, 319–321, and Dümpelmann 2005, 42–44.

59. For the rose beds of the Roman pavilion, see Governatorato di Roma 1928, 8, and Maria Teresa Parpagliolo, "Il roseto del colle Oppio e il premio di Roma," *Domus* 7, no. 73 (1934): 56–57.

60. Raffaella Fabiani Gianetto, *Medici Gardens: From Making to Design* (Philadelphia, 2008), 5. On exhibitions under Fascism and Mussolini "recast" in the role of Lorenzo de' Medici "as a great patron of the arts," also see D. Medina Lesansky, *The Renaissance Perfected: Architecture, Spectacle and Tourism in Fascist Italy* (University Park, PA, 2004), 73–79.

61. See Vincenzo Cazzato, "Firenze 1931: La consacrazione del 'primato italiano' nell'arte dei giardini," in *Il giardino: Idea, natura, realtà*, ed. Alessandro Tagliolini and Massimo Venturi Ferriolo (Milan, 1987), 85.

62. Carlo Mercatelli in the minutes of a preparatory meeting of the exhibition organizing committee, November 19, 1930; published in the appendix to Cazzato 1987, 103.

63. For discussion of the Mostra del Giardino Italiano, see Vincenzo Cazzato's pioneering articles (Cazzato 1986, Cazzato 1987, and Cazzato 1998). More recently, in addition to my works referenced above (2004, 2005), see Lesansky 2004, 73–79; Lazzaro 2005, 157–169 (159–166); Fabiani Gianetto 2008, 5–8; and Raffaella Fabiani Gianetto, "'Grafting the Edelweiss on Cactus Plants': The 1931 Italian Garden Exhibition and Its Legacy," in *Clio in the Italian Garden: Twenty-First-Century Studies in Historical Methods and Theoretical Perspectives*, ed. Mirka Beneš and Michael Lee (Washington, DC, 2011), 55–77.

64. See Jahn Rusconi, "La mostra del giardino italiano a Firenze," *Emporium* 73, no. 437 (1931): 259–273 (270); Cazzato 1986, 80–88 (81–82).

65. Cazzato 1987, 90.

66. Mario Tinti, "La mostra del giardino italiano," *La casa bella* 4, no. 41 (1931): 36–40, 67 (40).

67. Bosio 1931b, 22–27, 84 (25–27, 84). Bosio notes that the entries of the Roman participants could be identified on the basis of their monumental designs and their use of numerous fountains, small terraces, stairways, and pine trees. Tinti 1931, 40, 67.

68. See Giorgio Galletti, "I pini nel paesaggio di Roma," in *Oltre il giardino: Le architetture vegetali e il paesaggio*, ed. Gabriella Guerci, Laura Pelisetti, Lionella Scazzosi (Città di Castello, 2003), 271–279.

69. T. Agostini, "Alberi e fiori per il popolo di Roma," *Capitolium* 10, no. 4 (1934): 175–190.

70. Paolino Ferrari, *Alberature stradali* (Rome, 1938), 332; Bruno Braschi, "Giardini pubblici di Roma e la loro organizzazione," *Nuovi annali dell'agricoltura* 14 (1934): 443–458 (448).

71. A. Merendi, "Il pino domestico," *L'Alpe* 18, no. 6 (1931): 295–308 (297).

72. Braschi 1934, 448.

73. Tomaso Buzzi, "L'architetto di giardini," *Domus* 1, no. 4 (1928): 32–34 (32); Carlo Mercatelli in appendix to Cazzato in Tagliolini and Venturi Ferriolo 1987, 95–108 (103).

74. Piccinato 1933, 75.

75. See, for example, Jules Buyssens, "A proposito dei giardini," *Domus* 3, no. 29 (1930): 57–60; Jiro Harada, "I giardini giapponesi a paesaggio," *Domus* 2, no. 13 (1929): 26–31; Georg Bela Pniower, "Un giardino esotico nella 'Gourmenia Haus' a Berlino," *La casa bella* 3, no. 26 (1930): 34–38; Georg Bela Pniower, "Una casa d'artista nei pressi di Berlino," *La casa bella* 3, no. 32 (1930): 27–31. A number of Italian authors argued for the "rebirth" of the Italian garden: Dami 1914a, 559; Ermanno Biagini, "La Mostra del Giardino Italiani a Firenze," *Le vie d'Italia e dell'America Latina: Rivista mensile del Touring Club Italiano* 11 (1931): 642–651 (645); Bosio 1931b, 22–27 (24); Porcinai 1937, 30–37 (31).

76. Luigi Piccinato, "Giardini moderni," *Architettura e arti decorative* 6 (1926–1927): 348–373, 402–426; Luigi Piccinato, "Giardini tedeschi," *Domus* 1, no. 7 (1928): 34–37.

77. See, for example, Alberto Sartoris, "Tetti piani e giardini pensili," *La casa bella* 2, no. 12 (1929): 10–15; Maria Croci, "Un costruttore modernissimo: André Lurçat," *La casa bella* 3, no. 29 (1930): 11–15; Alberto Sartoris, "Giardini moderni," *La casa bella* 3, no. 30 (1930): 34–37.

78. Dami 1923, 100.

79. For expressionism in German garden design, see Peter Fibich and Joachim Wolschke-Bulmahn, "'Garden Expressionism': Remarks on a Historical Debate," *Garden History* 33, no. 1 (2005): 106–117.

80. Piccinato 1933, 75.

81. For the international attention given Villa Gamberaia in the early twentieth century and the influence of its design on gardens in Italy and abroad, also see Vincenzo Cazzato, "The Rediscovery of the Villa Gamberaia in Images and Projects of the Early 1900s," *Studies in the History of Gardens & Designed Landscapes* 22, no. 1 (2002): 80–98.

82. Wharton 1904, 41, and Triggs 1906, 84.

83. See Pasolini Ponti 1915, 23–24; Dami 1914, 273; Cecil Pinsent, "Giardini moderni all'italiana con i fiori che più vi si adattano," *Il giardino fiorito: Rivista della Società italiana "Amici dei Fiori"* 1 (1931): 69–73 (69); John C. Shepherd and Geoffrey A. Jellicoe, *Gardens & Design* (London, 1927); and Pietro Porcinai, "Cosa può insegnarci un vecchio giardino," *Il giardino fiorito*, no. 5 (1953), 150–151. Porcinai grew up in the gardens of Villa Gamberaia, where his father was head gardener from 1902 until 1916. His first garden design

(c. 1932), for Villa Scarselli in Sesto Fiorentino, seems to be an homage to the garden of his childhood.

84. For planting and garden design in England, see Anne Helmreich, *The English Garden and National Identity: The Competing Styles of Garden Design, 1870–1914* (New York, 2002).

85. Braschi 1933, 237–238.

86. Maria Teresa Parpagliolo, "The Lost Gardens of Pompeii," *Landscape and Garden* 1, no. 4 (1934): 24–27 (26–27). For Parpagliolo on the gardens of Pompeii, also see Maria Teresa Parpagliolo, "I giardini di Pompei," *Domus* 4, no. 41 (1931): 77–79. In associating modern "rationalist" architecture with Pompeian townhouses, Giuseppe Pagano wrote that "the modern man … discovers in this architecture of twenty or so centuries ago, underneath the decorative allegory that is no longer necessary, the ideal clarity and architectural honesty of our times." Giuseppe Pagano-Pogatschnig, "Architettura moderna di venti secoli fa," *La casa bella* 4, no. 47 (1931): 14–19 (18).

87. For the importance of the excavations see, for example, Amedeo Maiuri, *Pompei: I nuovi scavi e la villa dei Misteri* (Rome, 1931); Amedeo Maiuri, *Ercolano* (Rome, 1932); and Maiuri's address, as *soprintendente* for antiquities of the Campania and Molise to the Primo Convegno Nazionale del Giardino in Varese in 1937: Amedeo Maiuri, "Nuovi contributi allo studio del giardino romano," in *Per la difesa del giardino*, ed. Istituto Fascista di Tecnica e Propaganda Agraria (Rome, 1937), 19–25. For the ideological and nationalist implications of archaeological practice under the Italian Fascist regime and other totalitarian dictatorships see Michael L. Galaty and Charles Watkinson, eds., *Archaeology under Dictatorship* (New York, 2004), and Alessandra Muntoni, "Italo Gismondi e la lezione di Ostia antica," *Rassegna* 15, no. 55/3 (1993): 74–81. For the role of the excavations of Ostia Antica in Roman architecture in the 1920s, see Guido Calza, "Le origini latine dell'abitazione moderna," *Architettura e arti decorative* 3 (1923–1924): 3–18, 49–63.

88. See Giò Ponti, "La casa all'italiana," *Domus* 1, no. 1 (1928): 7.

89. Roda 1933, 81.

90. For a discussion of this competition see the pioneering articles by Vincenzo Cazzato (Cazzato 1986 and Cazzato 1987). On the careers of Minoletti and Cingria, see Edizioni Milano Moderna, ed., *Architetti italiani: Minoletti* (Milan, 1959), and *Albert Cingria* (Geneva, 1967).

91. Compare Christopher Tunnard, *Gardens in the Modern Landscape* (London, 1938), 64–65. See also Dorothée Imbert, *Between Garden and City: Jean Canneel-Claes and Landscape Modernism* (Pittsburgh, 2009).

92. Tino Sgaravatti, "Il giardino moderno," *Domus* 6, no. 62 (1933): 87–89.

93. Fillia (Luigi Enrico Colombo), *La nuova architettura* (Turin, 1931), 262–272. The interest of Italian rationalist architects in roof gardens and terraces and in the merging of house, garden, and landscape is apparent in the examples selected by Lugi Figini for *L'elemento verde e l'abitazione*, a collection of writings by Luigi Daneri, Figini, Gino Pollini, Mario Asnago, and Claudio Vender from the 1930s and 1940s and republished under Figini's editorship by *Domus* in 1950.

94. See Paul Baxa, "Piacentini's Window: The Modernism of the Fascist Master Plan of Rome," *Contemporary European History* 13 (2004): 1–20 (11).

95. Dwellings near the ruins of the Baths of Trajan and along the Via della Polveriera were torn down. Antonio Muñoz, *Il parco di Traiano* (Rome, 1936), 12, 14. For Muñoz's project on Colle Oppio see Sylvia Diebner, "Erholungspark versus Kulissengarten: Traditionelle Begrünung und politische Nutzung des Colle Oppio in Rom in der Zeit des Faschismus," *Die Gartenkunst* 19, no. 1 (2007): 143–162.

96. N.D.R., "Il XII Concorso della Federazione Internazionale delle Abitazioni e dei Piani Regolatori in Roma," *Architettura e arti decorative*, 9, fasc. 2 (1929): 145–146.

97. Marcello Piacentini, *Sulla conservazione della bellezza di Roma e sullo sviluppo della città moderna* (Rome, 1916).

98. Domenico Filippone, *Le zone verdi nella moderna urbanistica italiana* (Milan, 1937), 20; Enrico Ratti, "Giardini e architettura moderna," in *Per la difesa del giardino*, ed. Istituto Fascista di Tecnica e Propaganda Agraria (Rome, 1937), 39–51 (50).

99. Elvezio Ricci, "Osservazioni sulla formazione e conservazione dei giardini," in *Per la difesa del giardino*, ed. Istituto Fascista di Tecnica e Propaganda Agraria (Rome, 1937), 55–61 (61). Although the first gardeners' training schools had already been established in the late 1920s, conference participants concluded that the institution of more new gardeners' training schools and of gardening classes at departments of architecture and agriculture were necessary to educate skilled workers and garden-minded professionals.

100. "Solo quando anche in Italia, come già in Germania, Inghilterra, Stati Uniti, sorgeranno dei veri e propri Architetti giardinieri, potremo dire allora che il nostro giardino procede verso la sua rinascita." Porcinai 1937, 30–35 (31). On Porcinai's early garden designs, see most recently Kimberlee S. Stryker, "Pietro Porcinai and the Modern Italian Garden," *Studies in the History of Gardens and Designed Landscapes* 28, no. 2 (April–June 2008): 252–267. See also Gabriella Carapelli, *Pietro Porcinai e l'arte del paesaggio: Gli esordi e i lavori nella provincia aretina* (Florence, 2005); Marcella Minelli et al., *I giardini di Pietro Porcinai in Emilia Romagna e nel Veneto* (Molteno, 1999); Mariachiara Pozzana, ed., *I giardini del 20. secolo: L'opera di Pietro Porcinai* (Florence, 1998); and Milena Matteini, *Pietro Porcinai: Architetto del giardino e del paesaggio* (Milan, 1991).

JOSÉ TITO ROJO

Modernity and Regionalism in the Gardens of Spain (1850–1936): From Radical Opposition to Misunderstood Synthesis

Nationalist ideologies helped shape garden practices in many countries at the beginning of the twentieth century. In Spain this was especially true, obscuring the perception that gardens were also constructed outside such ideologies. This essay examines the evolution of Spanish gardens in this period and considers the accompanying theoretical debates between defenders of a national garden aesthetic and proponents of a modern, cosmopolitan garden that would satisfy vital and aesthetic requirements without necessarily following the dictates of a regional approach. Three periods emerge. The first corresponds approximately to the second half of the nineteenth century, before the appearance of garden nationalism; the second spans the years around the turn of the twentieth century, which witnessed the beginnings of the debate over the "jardín extranjero" (foreign garden) and the "jardín español" (Spanish garden); and the third, extending roughly from 1910 to 1936, was characterized by the domination of regionalist landscape gardening. These debates about the garden are just one manifestation of broader differences among ways of understanding Spanish society, political structures, and urban life.

The Supremacy of the *Jardín a la Inglesa*: 1850–1890

In the latter part of the nineteenth century, garden design in Spain was dominated by an eclectic practice that descended from an older landscape school called *a la inglesa* (in the English manner). This was an ambiguous term used to designate a type of garden that sought to be modern and yet was a compromise between the early nineteenth-century romantic garden and the eighteenth-century landscape garden, from which it had inherited an abhorrence of the straight line and a certain proclivity for naturalism. In Spain, the designation *a la inglesa* was used primarily for small urban gardens, in private spaces and public squares. Gardens of this type had been promoted since the final years of the reign of Isabella II of Spain (1833–1868), especially in public gardens, and thus they were also called *jardines isabelinos,* or Isabelline gardens, equivalents of Victorian gardens.[1]

Following the examples of London and Paris, the most dynamic sectors of the Spanish bourgeoisie used the garden as an instrument to sanitize Spanish cities. Liberal governments that exercised power during that period had multiple reasons to improve urban life. Cities had tortuous streets, poor housing, and bad neighborhoods, and they lacked public infrastructure. In addition, improvements promised benefits for the financial sector and construction entrepreneurs. The alienation of properties of the Catholic church, especially through laws of 1835 and 1846, was one measure that freed up urban land. Many convents and churches were demolished to create more open and healthful spaces in city centers.[2] If until then urban green zones had been limited to promenades and tree-lined streets, now systematic use was made of vegetation to offer citizens a space for healthy relaxation. Trees were planted, lawns were sown, flowers decorated the old plazas, and new open spaces were created. Consistent with the spirit of urban renewal, these planted areas followed the new Isabelline style, with berms of lawn edged with flowers and ornamented

Javier de Winthuysen, project for a garden, graphite and watercolor, n.d. (1952?)

Archivo del Real Jardín Botánico de Madrid, Fondo Winthuysen, sig. WINT DIB 63-001

1. Jean Laurent, Palacio de Indo, Madrid. c. 1870, albumen print

Ayuntamiento de Madrid, Museo de Historia de Madrid

with furnishings for comfort and cultural events, music pavilions, dance floors, benches, and visitor facilities—all following the models of Georges-Eugène Haussmann's plans for Paris in the 1860s.[3]

In 1872 *La ilustración española y americana* announced the building of new dwellings in the quarter of Madrid known as Barrio de Salamanca. The journal explained that residents, needing fresh air, valued new houses equipped with "new and pleasant gardens" ("nuevos y amenos jardines").[4] ("New" in this context could indicate either recent construction or stylistic novelty.) That text shows us how, in the stylish enlargements of Spanish cities carried out in the second half of the nineteenth century, of which the Barrio de Salamanca was the best example, the quality of private residences was associated with the presence of gardens. Amid the middle-class mansions that would occupy this elegant neighborhood, curvilinear parterres were crossed by sinuous paths, creating a microcosm of a natural landscape entirely devoid of straight lines. Photographs of the period illustrate how lawns predominate, sometimes slightly mounded to imitate a hill, and scattered with trees and masses of flowers in geometric designs imitating French *corbeilles* (flowerbeds). This was the

standard for large mansions in the Barrio de Salamanca and its vicinity, especially along the Paseo de la Castellana. The gardens have now mostly disappeared or have been thoroughly transformed, including that belonging to the same marqués de Salamanca who promoted the construction of the neighborhood that bears its name, and that of the Palacio del Indo (fig. 1). This fashion spread throughout Spain, becoming the new type of garden for large mansions in the cities' new residential growth zones (fig. 2).

Private gardening followed the example of public gardening. At the end of the nineteenth century, Spanish gardening, dominated by the style called *a la inglesa,* was soon to meet opposition with two sharply different motivations. One was functional, yet at its core ideological, and the other was aesthetic, but also ideological in its essence. The functional drawback to the prevailing style was that the transformation of public spaces in this new way, with the addition of gardens, clashed with their traditional use in cities, especially for religious purposes. An example is the *plaza mayor,* or main square, the traditional heart of the Spanish city. This was a free, unlandscaped space for military parades as well as processions, markets, fairs, bullfights, judgments, the autos-da-fé of the Inquisition, and temporary structures for religious holidays such as the feast of Corpus Christi (fig. 3). In the mid-nineteenth century, liberal governments determined that these plazas should be converted into public gardens for urban hygiene and popular pleasure (fig. 4).

In almost all cases this was a fleeting situation. In a plaza with gardens, it was not feasible to hold military parades, markets, bullfights, or grand religious festivals. The old social habits resisted the loss of privileged use, and gradually the plazas were repaved in stone, eliminating the gardens. This occurred in Madrid, Salamanca, Burgos, Valladolid, and other cities almost simultaneously because of the alternation of conservative and liberal political regimes. In other cases, the ups and downs of local politics impeded projects from ever being implemented. For example, in Granada, the garden projected

for the Plaza Bibarrambla, as far as we know, was never completely installed. A proposal was made for a fountain to be situated in the center of the public garden, but the city architect in charge warned that this location was problematic because of the siting of the altar for the feast of Corpus Christi.[5] The problems of these plaza designs arose because they implied a different use of public space, not because of an "English" aesthetic. At this point, no one argued that this style was inappropriate for a garden because it was foreign; it was simply a functional deficiency. Aesthetic opposition would take longer to evolve.

The Vision of a New Aesthetic: The Spanish Garden before Nationalism

The starting point for understanding the vision of the Spanish garden is the first known work on garden history published in Spain: *Historia de la arquitectura de jardines* (1855) by the garden author and designer Melitón Atienza y Sirvent (1827–1890). This rare volume was absent from historiographic reviews of the Spanish garden until cited by Eva J. Rodríguez Romero in 1999 and Car-

men Añón Feliú in 2005.[6] Juan Pérez-Rubín had earlier recognized the primary ambition of Atienza's oeuvre in a brief study (1856) that provides important archival documentation, although it omits mention of some of the author's publications, including his history of garden architecture.[7] We know from Pérez-Rubín that Atienza was the son of a gardener for the Real Jardín Botánico de Madrid and that he became head of agriculture in the Instituto Provincial de Málaga (1871), the city where he would be director of the Servicio Municipal de Paseos y Alamedas from 1881. His interest in gardens was lifelong. In 1856 he presented a report on the renovation of gardens in Madrid, including the creation of the Jardín Botánico de la Escuela de Horticultura y de Arquitectura de Jardines; he also designed a project for a "geographical garden" (*jardín geográfico*), a didactic landscape representing Spain's major cities, mountain ranges, rivers, and natural resources.[8] His *Historia de la arquitectura de jardines* is not only the first garden history, properly speaking, to be published in Spain but also testimony to the establishment of the study of garden architecture, a discipline that the author defined as necessary for the development of modern life.

3. Plaza Mayor, Burgos, before
the planting of gardens, c. 1905,
postcard
Private collection

4. Plaza Mayor, Burgos, with
a *jardín a la inglesa*, c. 1930,
postcard
Private collection

The full subtitle of the work gives a good idea of the author's intention: *Memoria acerca del plan de una obra de Arquitectura de jardines, utilidad de esta ciencia y consideraciones sobre la historia y las diferentes escuelas de jardinería* (Account of the plan of a work of garden architecture, the utility of this science, and considerations on the history and different schools of gardening). Although the book's subject is the utility of landscape architecture, the topic is barely mentioned. Briefly Atienza points out that this science would be useful in choosing the locations of buildings or the type of vegetation. With the exception of botanical gardens, intended for education, and crop production, intended for commerce, Atienza argues that gardens would benefit from the existence of professionals specialized in their design, that is, garden architects (*arquitectos de jardines*), who are better suited than either architects or gardeners, as they are "scientific" but share "attributes of the painter and the poet."[9] He wrote: "The function of garden architecture has become indispensable today, and only ignorance or the bigotry of a long-established attachment to ancient practices would drown out the strong voice of science."[10]

In his classification of kinds of gardens, Atienza categorized three schools of garden design: "oriental," "Greco-Roman," and "modern." The oriental is subdivided into Chinese landscape (*chino apaisado*) and Arab picturesque (*árabe pintoresco*), synonymous with Arabic-Spanish (*arábigo-español*).[11] English gardens, called *apaisado*, are, according to Atienza, oriental in origin, simply a modification of the Chinese.[12] "Greco-Roman" encompasses symmetrical gardens (*jardines simétricos*), among them the French garden, the Italian garden, and the mixed garden (*jardín mixto*); finally, "modern" includes scientific gardens (*jardines científicos*).[13] Atienza uses the term "scientific" for gardens of his period whose design was guided by the "torch of science," that is, the rules and precepts that should be followed for layout and arrangement. According to him, the old gardens were "rutinario" (unimaginative), intended only for the adornment of spaces.[14]

Atienza did not reject any type as foreign to or ideologically inappropriate for Spain. He believed that Spain had only a few examples of the English (landscape) garden because of social and economic factors (the waste of agricultural land that would result from the widespread adoption of this type, for example). Only in the case of the Chinese garden did he offer an ideological criticism, for its "lack of sentiment ("carecen de sentimiento").[15] On the basis of this reasoning, he advocated the Arabic-Spanish garden as an oriental, landscape, and scientific garden: oriental because the Arabs came from the East, landscape because the plantings did not follow the lines of the symmetrical garden, and scientific because, in his opinion, the Arabs had mastered agronomy and applied it to the construction of gardens many centuries before modern European gardens.

Thirty years later, Pedro Julián Muñoz y Rubio (?–1895), agricultural engineer, professor, and director of the Instituto Agricola de Alfonso XII, published *Tratado de jardinería y floricultura*, the best example of the preeminence of the Isabelline garden in the second half of the nineteenth century.[16] Unlike Atienza's work, this book had broad influence and a long publishing life of at least two editions after its initial publication in 1887.[17] A brief history of gardens is presented in a chapter titled "Bosquejo histórico de la arquitectura de jardines."[18] Here Muñoz laid the foundation for the volume, the aim of which was less theoretical than that of Atienza's book, which had been directed toward authorities to convince them of the benefits of establishing education in landscape gardening. Muñoz' book, in contrast, was intended for professionals in garden construction and as a manual for students of agriculture. Most of the book, dedicated to practical aspects of cultivation, was a catalog of ornamental plants with the conventional details of description as well as requirements for sowing, planting, and maintenance; flowering periods; and available varieties.

This would become a common format in Spanish gardening literature, which lacked a comprehensive history until Fernando García Mercadal's *Parques y jardines, su historia y sus trazados* (1949). In the intervening years various foreign works on gardens would become known in Spain, and some were even translated and published in Spain, such as André Lefèvre's *Les parcs et les jardins* (published in Spanish as *Parques y jardines* in 1886).[19] In the period before García Mercadal's volume, gardening and horticulture books included only chapters on Spanish garden history.[20]

In the 1887 edition of his book, Muñoz dedicated several pages to Spanish gardens, giving the Arabic-Spanish type considerable praise. As with Atienza's, Muñoz's work reveals an intent to save the Hispano-Muslim garden by clothing it in contemporary dress and transmitting the idea that it was similar to the *jardín a la inglesa*. The discussion is curious, for neither Atienza nor Muñoz rules out the Isabelline style for Spanish cities. They criticize other styles of the past, although of course not the Arabic-Spanish mode, precisely because of its similarity to the Isabelline. The keys to this similarity are specified as geographic (both were thought to be of oriental origin, that is, China or Islam); stylistic (both constitute landscape gardening and are asymmetrical); and technological (both are scientific).[21]

According to these two Spanish pioneers in the history of the garden, the Arabs had created, above all in Andalusia, a picturesque type (*género pintoreco*) based on their knowledge of natural sciences, "applying to gardens most of the [agricultural, botanical, and scientific] systems now known, and helping to propagate pleasure in and fondness for flowers."[22] The space that these two historians dedicated to the twelfth-century agricultural treatise of Ibn al-ʿAwwām (*Kitāb al-filā-ḥah*) is significant.[23] The treatise was well known from a translation of the Arabic manuscript in the library of the Escorial, published in Madrid in 1802 by the scholar José Antonio Banqueri.[24] Banqueri had been convinced of the contemporary validity of

the treatise and hoped that its publication would benefit Spanish agriculture. Picking up this idea, Atienza was certain that the treatise was relevant to current practice; he stated that "despite the time that has elapsed, it can even today benefit the science that occupies us."[25] Muñoz devoted several paragraphs to the survival of Ibn al-ʿAwwām's teachings, claiming that they "are used today by gardeners in our country."[26]

For Muñoz, the expulsion of the Muslims from Spain signaled the decline of gardening and agriculture. It also marked the return of the symmetrical garden type (*género simétrico*) inherited from the ancients ("which comes down to us from the Romans").[27] Claiming such an origin allowed the patriotic Muñoz to maintain that the formal garden was known in Spain before André Le Nôtre.[28] The subsequent fashion for the *jardín a la inglesa* indicated that modernity and an interest in returning to the Spanish roots of the Muslim Middle Ages coexisted.

After this initial chapter, the book gives instructions for construction and planting of a garden. Without entering into debates on their aesthetic value, he simply shows how to design modern gardens, which he characterizes as irregular (*irregular*), landscape (*apaisado*), or picturesque (*pintoresco*). A small section on the creation of a mixed garden is in reality a critique of the aesthetics of past gardens. Illustrated planting schemes and garden views of the recent past are subordinated to those for this type of garden, Muñoz' preferred style for modernity, a combination of the *jardín a la inglesa* with small, regularized beds next to the dwelling. Among these illustrations are two surprising plans, each for a "jardín estilo árabe" (figures 255 and 256 in the 1923 edition), which the text describes as being of great effect and elegance, and which are justified as belonging to the same order as the architecture (figs. 5 and 6).[29] These academic designs are difficult to relate to true Hispano-Muslim gardens.[30] Their geometry has slightly modernized baroque affinities. The first of these illustrations shows broderies. The second depicts a set of ponds that vaguely recall a line of wall tiles from the

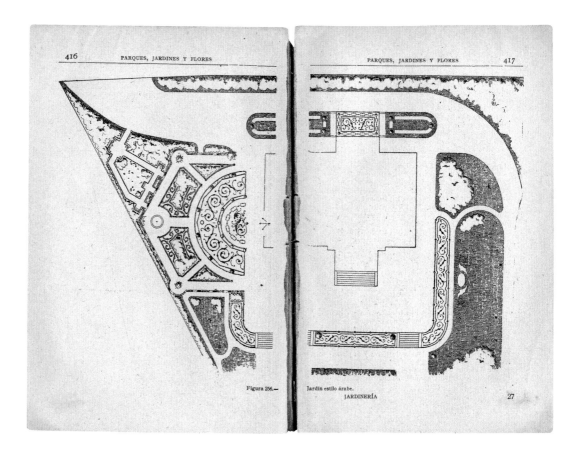

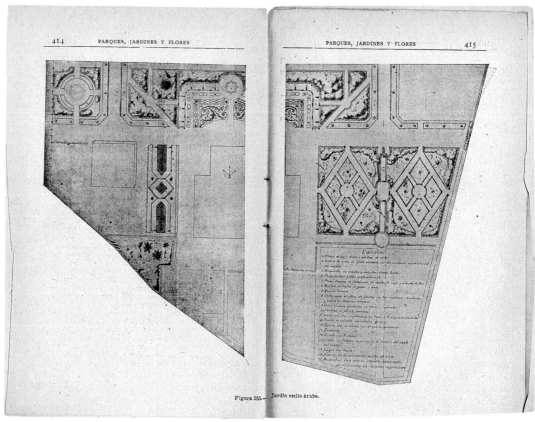

Alhambra, as well as two rhomboid-shaped parterres reminiscent of a Granada-style garden of the nineteenth century and other elements described in the text as "a star-shaped fountain of thick bricks … several cypresses planted loosely at whim … a gallery of cypress arches."[31] The tennis court is prominent, a response to values of modern life. This plan anticipates what would at the beginning of the twentieth century be the critical success of the regionalist Andalusian garden, in which mixed traditional forms are combined with the new geometrical ones that today would be generally described as art deco. The obvious difference is that this isolated example, seen in the context of the popularity of the Isabelline style, lacks the ideology of regionalism, key for assembling a national Spanish garden style, and the justification for fighting any foreign influence, especially the English.

Prologue to the Regionalist Garden: Santiago Rusiñol

At the end of the nineteenth century, nationalist elements in Spain consolidated and began to seek, in all artistic manifestations, forms that would constitute a national aesthetic. The loss of the last holdings of the Spanish empire with the granting of independence to Cuba and the Philippine Islands in 1898 stirred a strong reaction in Spanish society. In educated circles it provoked a profound questioning among what would become known as the Generación del 98. This phenomenon emerged in gardening, too, albeit with a certain lag and with notable confusion.

A new consensus sought to capture the essence of the Spanish garden, identifying features that could be differentiated from those derived from England, France, or Italy. Gardens of English derivation were henceforth considered the enemy by theoreticians of the Spanish garden. The result was that despite their preponderance in Spain, such gardens (and specifically the Isabelline more than the landscape garden) fell out of favor. The search for a monolithic "Spanish style" was complicated by the absence of a critical apparatus for Spanish garden history. If, to cite one example, the formation of the imaginary theoretical Italian garden acknowledged external factors, such as the contributions of English and American travelers,[32] this did not occur in the case of the Spanish garden.[33] The characterization of the national Spanish garden was more problematic.

The catalyst of the movement would be the work of a painter, Santiago Rusiñol (1861–1931). In 1895 he visited Granada and there discovered the garden as a theme for his paintings. His melancholic temperament and morphine addiction moved him to see old, abandoned gardens as the key to understanding life. He began to portray old formal gardens, forgotten by modern fashion. He sang the beauty of a past that had disappeared because of a society that did not value it. The gardens of Granada would form the central theme of his work for ten years. He presented his work in Granada in 1898 and in Paris the following year; these two exhibitions formed the core of his book *Jardines de España*, published in 1903. Presented as a luxurious portfolio of texts, poems, and lithographs of Rusiñol's paintings, this volume would go through many editions and reprintings in Catalan and in Spanish (fig. 7).[34] As Margarida Casacuberta points out, regionalist groups interpreted the book as "one of the most effective remedies against the ills of Spain" ("uno de los remedios más adecuados para combatir el mal de España").[35] The implication was twofold: first, an attempt must be made to prevent the old Spanish gardens from disappearing and being transformed into English gardens, and, second, new gardens must be made in the national style without threat from foreign aesthetics.

This new debate profoundly affected Spanish gardens. In the aesthetic manifestos of the beginning of the twentieth century, the garden occupied an important place. In poetry, painting, and theater it stood for elegance and beauty, social relevance and modernity. Spanish regionalist painting of the nineteenth century, in large part heir to romanticism, had focused attention on

7. *Green Architecture*, lithograph after a painting by Santiago Rusiñol

Jardins d'Espanya *(Barcelona, 1903)*

ers, but the refined and abandoned gardens of the old dominant class. The new bourgeoisie found in his paintings a type of garden with which they could identify. It was Spanish, distinct from conventional French and English gardens; it was formal, geometric, and parallel to the new fashions emerging in Europe; finally, it was endangered, so that it could be the focus of a campaign in defense of national vernacular values. It was not by chance that the territory chosen by Rusiñol to begin his paintings of old gardens was Granada. This city's distance from the centers of power and its economic poverty had produced a peculiar garden tradition in which Mediterranean elements mixed with Arab and fashionable, romantic Isabelline elements. The whole was given a local interpretation. In Granada, Rusiñol discovered what would be the leitmotif of his painting, the abandoned garden (*jardín abandonado*), a term with many meanings that he would use in one of his paintings and as the title of one of his literary works.[36] Abandonment was symbolic of the old Spanish garden, in danger of disappearing through society's neglect of the values it embodied.

Rusiñol's work was well received, and the gardens that he depicted became the paradigm of the lost and now sought-out Spanish garden. It was also the precedent for a vision that would have far-reaching implications: locating in Andalusia the most clearly genuine of what is Spanish—that is, making the Hispano-Muslim component the foundation of the national garden to be established. This was of course somewhat distortive of history, as a great part of Spain had not undergone Islamic occupation during the Middle Ages, or had for only a short time. While the field of architecture would witness a strong conflict between the neo-Andalusian, or neo-Mudéjar, and advocates of Castilian or northern elements, in nationalist garden design the triumph of Andalusian, arabizing elements was generalized.[37]

Rusiñol also made possible something that was indispensable to nationalist aesthetics: he found a way to present modern Spain as heir to an uninterrupted tradition. The book

the small, modest rural garden. This vision was becoming passé by the beginning of the twentieth century. The rising and often urban middle class required beautiful gardens to provide striking settings for parties, as places in which to be seen and photographed, and to convey the good taste and social status of their owners.

Rusiñol depicted gardens capable of upholding the tenets of the new time: not the modest, rural, and poor gardens that until then had been depicted by regionalist paint-

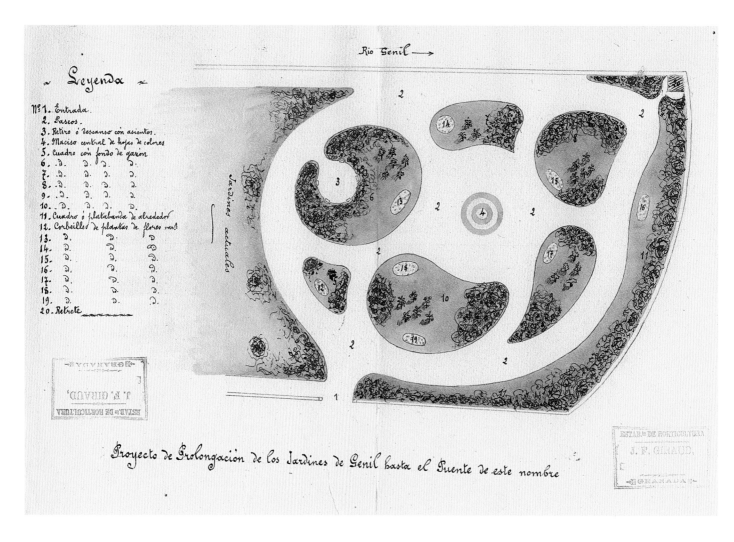

Leyenda

Nº 1. Entrada.
 2. Paseos.
 3. Retiro ó descanso con asientos.
 4. Macizo central de hojas de colores
 5. Cuadro con fondo de gazon
 6. ᵈ. ᵈ. ᵈ. ᵈ.
 7. ᵈ. ᵈ. ᵈ. ᵈ.
 8. ᵈ. ᵈ. ᵈ. ᵈ.
 9. ᵈ. ᵈ. ᵈ. ᵈ.
10. ᵈ. ᵈ. ᵈ. ᵈ.
11. Cuadro ó filatabanda de alrededor
12. Corbeilles de plantas de flores var.
13. ᵈ. ᵈ. ᵈ.
14. ᵈ. ᵈ. ᵈ.
15. ᵈ. ᵈ. ᵈ.
16. ᵈ. ᵈ. ᵈ.
17. ᵈ. ᵈ. ᵈ.
18. ᵈ. ᵈ. ᵈ.
19. ᵈ.
20. Retrete

Rio Genil →

Proyecto de Prolongacion de los Jardines de Genil hasta el Puente de este nombre

8. Juan F. Giraud, project for extending the gardens of the Genil River, 1902, graphite and watercolor

Archivo Histórico Municipal de Granada

Jardines de España certified that the Spanish garden was the legacy of a living tradition, albeit endangered and almost forgotten. Nationalistic discourse on gardens would for this reason fuse two components: the defense of old, non-English gardens, survivals of a hypothetical national value against the domination of the foreign garden, and the promotion of a modern garden now constructed deliberately in a national style, which could be presented as the credible heir to a tradition and not as an ex novo creation.

Opposition to the *Jardín a la Inglesa* in Practice

The first criticisms of the *jardín a la inglesa* in public spaces had charged that it was inappropriate for traditional uses, but they did not attack its aesthetics. The emergence of the concept of a national garden, the idea

that each country should have a typology of its own distinct from those of other countries, was accompanied by a new phenomenon in the history of gardening: the appearance of an intolerant moral and political environment.

In this new atmosphere, an owner designing a garden could opt for something more or less traditional, or *a la inglesa*, or something imitating the latest fashion in Europe. But the novelty of nationalism consisted of political judgment: to make a garden in a nonnational style was a crime against country, an attack on the values of the community. Many gardens made in Spain, especially public gardens, were criticized as being foreign, and the nationalist intelligentsia would call for a reconversion to a "Spanish" style even at the beginning of the twentieth century, when it was still not clear how to

define the style precisely. The debate as to whether or not to impose a national garden style was not limited to gardens under construction but also affected those already in existence.

To aid in understanding the extent of political debate, I shall analyze a specific case, the Jardines del Genil in Granada. The site had been a public promenade since the Arab period, presented as a gift to the city by the vizier of King Abd Allah in the eleventh century. In the sixteenth century, after the Christian reconquest of the city, the garden was a wooded area next to the Genil River on the outskirts of the city, and in the eighteenth century it was a popular promenade. It was converted into a fashionable garden and a boulevard by the French army during Napoleonic occupation from 1808 to 1812.[38] Several renovations over the course of that century preserved the tree-lined promenade and plazas graced with fountains taken from various demolished convents.[39] In 1902 a local designer, Juan F. Giraud (d. c. 1909), proposed extending the gardens with a *jardín a la inglesa*.[40] He was the owner of one of the major nurseries

in Spain, the Grandes Establecimientos Hortícolas "La Quinta," and periodically published a luxurious and extensive catalog with style recommendations: "The form of garden adopted today is the so-called landscape or English-style garden. Its capricious line allows it to be adapted to any terrain of whatever shape."[41] His project for Genil is preserved in the Archivo Municipal de Granada, with a color plan and planting details, together with a dossier concerning its installation and conservation (fig. 8).[42] Photos show the garden after completion, with a circular fountain, rustic huts, small hills of lawn in irregular forms, a few trees (especially conifers), and groups of flowers forming *corbeilles* (fig. 9).

The garden was created at a time when criticisms of the *jardín a la inglesa* were common, and the work at Genil was seen as the destruction of a Spanish garden in order to install a foreign one. It is not surprising that these gardens were criticized by local intellectuals who were political and cultural regionalists and declared themselves admirers of Santiago Rusiñol. In 1919 Antonio Gallego Burín wrote:

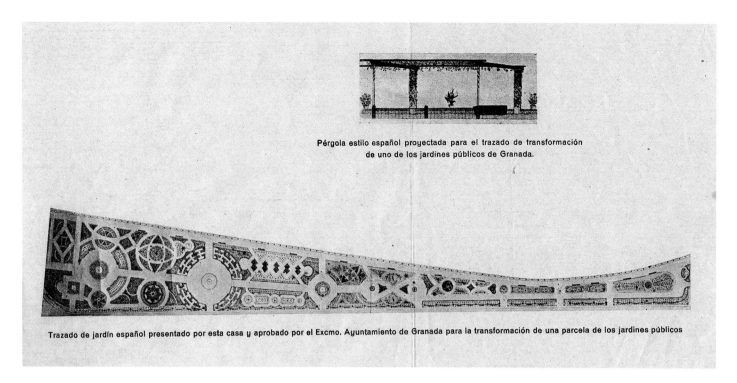

Pérgola estilo español proyectada para el trazado de transformación
de uno de los jardines públicos de Granada.

Trazado de jardín español presentado por esta casa y aprobado por el Excmo. Ayuntamiento de Granada para la transformación de una parcela de los jardines públicos

10. Juan Leyva, *Design for a Spanish Garden, Jardines del Genil, 1924–1927*
Catálogo de los Establecimientos Hortícolas "La Quinta," *no. 2 (Granada, n.d.); private collection*

The old gardens of La Bomba [the Genil River] had all this enchantment; but it disappeared when a period of English fervor left them with no hidden nook in which to pray. The Granadan gardens, with their vaults of greenery, their melancholy fountains, their passageways of myrtle [*arrayán*], have gone forever.... These, our gardens, are vanishing ... our garden is being lost. Only [the gardens of] the Alhambra are left to us. Will they too be converted into an English garden? We Granadans need our gardens. We need more gardens.[43]

In 1924 Francisco de Paula Valladar, another Granadan intellectual, urged the restoration of old gardens. He wrote,

These attempts at gardens ... are not Granadan; [nor are] the English masses that are put in place to destroy our own gardens.... Nobody assumes that the intent is to leave the Genil gardens ... in the state that they are in.... Some will still remember how those poetic gardens were.[44]

It was not by chance that Valladar and Gallego Burín, in their political outlook, defended conservative Andalusian regionalism.[45] Valladar died in 1924, but Gallego Burín developed fascist affiliations and became the first mayor of Granada after the fall of the city to nation-

alist forces in 1936. The *jardín a la inglesa* that Giraud had laid out in 1902 became the symbol of the garden that had to be banished. It was attacked in local newspapers, where demands were made for its elimination and replacement with new gardens in a style that could be called Spanish.

An important testament to nationalistic fervor is found in the catalog of the garden designer Juan Leyva, who acquired the horticultural establishment of Giraud, in which Leyva criticized the "style that is called English" for being amorphous and stated his preference:[46]

In Spain, there was a period (not long ago) that is still remembered, in which most public and private gardens were transformed by an indefinite style that is called English, without its having anything absolutely English about it.... [W]hat today we call the Spanish garden is the Arab garden modernized. For all the reasons given, we should always favor constructing this garden with preference over any other.[47]

Leyva presented the city government with a plan to destroy the *jardín a la inglesa* of Giraud and replace it with a Spanish garden (fig. 10). As in the case of the Arab garden of

11. *Section, Pergola along the Genil River,* Jardines del Genil, Granada

Helen Morgenthau Fox, Patio Gardens *(New York, 1929)*

12. *Concrete Pergola, Parque de María Luisa, Seville*

Helen Morgenthau Fox, Patio Gardens *(New York, 1929)*

Pedro Julián Muñoz, the proposed designs were Spanish only because they did not look French or English. The important aspect of their newly proposed style was not its aesthetics but the lack of foreign stylistic elements, such as grass surfaces or serpentine paths. The plan was approved; thus the *jardín a la inglesa* of Giraud lasted only a few years. Although it has not been possible to locate any information in the Archivo Histórico Municipal on this project, the plan is known to scholars because it was published in one of Leyva's catalogs.[48] We know that the Spanish garden had not been constructed in 1924, when Valladar was writing, but was by 1927. An interview with Leyva that year affirmed that his plan had been finished, although greatly simplified in its layout.[49] Two years later, a drawing of the pergola of this garden was published by Helen Morgenthau Fox in her book *Patio Gardens* (fig. 11), produced in 1929 as a guide to transplanting Spanish gardens to other places, following the models of Jean-Claude Nicolas Forestier in the parks of Montjuïc in Barcelona and María Luisa in Seville (fig. 12).[50] This example is significant because it comprises all the elements of the debate on garden design in Spain at the beginning of the twentieth century: a nineteenth-century promenade, its modernization *a la inglesa* (1902), its condemnation as foreign (1919–1924), its subsequent elimination, and the creation of a new garden in an undefined style and a discourse evincing the need of the regionalists to create a national style (1925–1927).

The Construction of a New Style: Forestier and the Spanish Garden

When Juan Leyva made his proposal for the Genil River, the catalog of elements that could be used to characterize the Spanish garden had not been consolidated. The new garden style that regionalists considered imperative was undefined. Therefore, older gardens served as models for the regionalist

garden. The key role in establishing the new aesthetic would belong, paradoxically, to a foreigner: Jean-Claude Nicolas Forestier (1851–1930).[51] He arrived from France in 1911, called to Seville by the duke of Montpensier to transform the landscape gardens of the Palacio de San Telmo,[52] dating from the mid-nineteenth century and donated by the duke to the city with the name Parque de María Luisa (fig. 13).[53] At that time, Seville was the center of a regional architectural style, the *neo-sevillano*, and the arrival of a foreigner to renovate the gardens was not well received. Sevillans agreed that the Parque de María Luisa should be restored in a way that "dispensed with any foreign stamp" and maintained the "character of Andalusian gardens."[54] Although he was a foreigner, Forestier chose to design gardens of regional inspiration, leaning especially toward designs inspired by the Alhambra and the Generalife, reinterpreting spaces such as the Patio de la Acequia, the Patio de la Sultana, and the Patio de los Leones, whose geometry incorporates changing scale, and including flora adapted to the warmer climate of Seville and materials such as traditional Sevillan ceramics. The results favorably surprised all his opponents, constituting the paradigm for a new national garden style (fig. 14).

The work of Forestier had profound repercussions within and outside Spanish territory. His designs and books served as reference works for the regionalists' new style in two complementary aspects, layout and constructive elements. The layouts employed parterres of clean geometry, rectangles, and straight lines, partitioned into terraces of slightly differing heights, and fountains and pools, also of simple geometric shapes and in many cases linked by small channels of water. The constructive elements were taken both from the Islamic period and from later monuments, including the Alhambra, the Generalife, the Alcázar of Seville, and the Alcázar of Córdoba. These elements, more than anything else, served to characterize the style. Tile benches, pebble-decorated pathways, and terracotta brick headed a long list summarized in Fox's *Patio Gardens*. She wrote,

To-day in Spain there is a renaissance in gardening, which is largely due to a Frenchman, Monsieur J. C. N. Forestier.... His creations have made the whole world aware of the delights of the Spanish garden, so that now in Paris, Westchester County (New York), the Côte d'Azur, California, and South Africa, tiled channels for water, ceramic benches, and pavements, glorietas, and pots are becoming a familiar part of garden scenery.[55]

Fox's book responded to an increasing demand for garden literature and attention to fashion. She declared, "When we adapt the Spanish garden, we, too, will make a chic modern version to fit in with our present way of thinking and living."[56] Architects and landscapers who sought "modernity" included the Spanish style among their possibilities. And the Andalusian style was the synecdoche of Spanish, the part substituting for the whole and occluding the existence of other territories, of other garden elements. The foreigner looking at Spain saw Andalusia: "The typical Spanish gardens were built in Andalusia," wrote Fox.[57]

In this propitious atmosphere Forestier was decisive in the formalization of the national Spanish style. Rusiñol, the Andalusian gardens, and Forestier would become its pillars. The French contributed designs, especially for the parks of Montjuïc and María Luisa, that became the mirror in which the new Spanish gardens could be visualized, and it would be the master Forestier who, directly or indirectly, would train

the most influential landscape gardeners of Spain in the first half of the century (fig. 15). According to his teachings, modernity and regionalism would be the components of all the gardens to be built; the tension between the two contrary forces would be resolved in different ways by the authors and works of this period. There would be landscape gardeners who leaned decidedly toward the regionalist model and others who looked to international models of modernity, the complex set of experiences that occurred in the rest of Europe.[58] Some incorporated components of both, although this did not blur a clear separation line.

It was not only Forestier who contributed to sources for the Spanish garden. Designers went directly to the Hispano-Muslim (Spanish and Andalusian) monuments for inspiration for the new formal geometry imposed in gardens worldwide. It was not a paradox but a sign of the times that the French illustrator and lover of gardens Ferdinand Bac introduced the Mexican Luis Barragán (1902–1988), one of the greatest architects

IBERICA

EL PROGRESO DE LAS CIENCIAS Y DE SUS APLICACIONES

REVISTA SEMANAL

Dirección y Administración Observatorio del Ebro

AÑO VII. TOMO 2.º   23 OCTUBRE 1920   VOL. XIV N.º 349

LOS JARDINES

DE

MONTJUICH

Los grabados de esta portada y los que ilustran el artículo de la pág. 248... reproducen los proyectos que para el Parque de Montjuich ha trazado el afamado arquitecto de paisajes Mr. J. C. N. Forestier

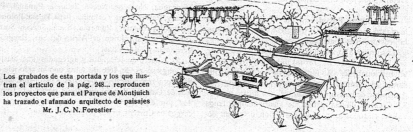

of the twentieth century, to the Alhambra.[59]
There, Barragán recalled, "having walked
through a dark and narrow tunnel of the
Alhambra, I suddenly emerged into the
serene, silent and solitary Patio de los Mirtos [de los Arrayanes] hidden in the entrails
of that ancient palace. Somehow I had the
feeling that it enclosed what a perfect garden
no matter its size should enclose: nothing
less than the entire Universe."[60] The Alhambra and its gardens served as inspiration
for the regionalists as well as the moderns.
The former saw its decorative elements, its
fountains, ceramics, and paths; the latter, its
purity of line, essentiality, space. The Patio
de los Arrayanes, memorable for Barragán,
is a nearly intact medieval Arabic garden,
but at the same time it seems to anticipate a
minimalist landscape of today.

In the final period under study (c. 1910–
1936), there was, paradoxically, no recognized profession of landscape gardening.
Designers of gardens were predominantly
regionalists whose designs were devoid of
aesthetic pretensions. The garden occupied
a prominent place in Spanish society of the
period, not only appearing in poems, novels,
and paintings, but also being of consummate interest to architects. The journal
Arquitectura, the official publication of the
Colegio de Arquitectos de Madrid, published in 1922 an issue dedicated to gardens
of Spain. It included articles by Rusiñol,
Forestier, the painter Javier de Winthuysen,
and the young Leopoldo Torres Balbás, just
before he became one of the directors of
the Alhambra. But it was in the illustrated
magazines, which multiplied during these
years, that the garden would find its best
vehicle of transmission. Photographs and
color drawings in society pages, articles,
and advertisements showed readers houses
and gardens that were the height of elegant
living and a showcase of potential designs
(fig. 16). The only landscape gardeners (then
termed *jardineros*, *arquitectos de jardines*,
or *arquitectos-paisajistas*) that we can truly
consider as such were one regionalist, the
painter Winthuysen, and one modernist,

the architect Nicolau Maria Rubió i Tudurí.
Both undertook diverse projects, many of
which were documented in archives; those
of Winthuysen are on deposit at the Real
Jardín Botánico de Madrid, those of Rubió
in the Colegio de Arquitectos de Cataluña.
Certainly, in this period many gardens were
made, but mostly by nurserymen, horticulturists, and artisans, not by professionals
dedicated to garden construction. There
were also gardens made by architects to
complement their buildings, such as those by
the regionalists Aníbal González and Juan
Talavera, or, closer to the international modern movement, Fernando García Mercadal
and José Luis Sert.

Last were designs by artists who used
the garden as a vehicle of aesthetic expression. This category included painters such
as Winthuysen, Joaquín Sorolla, and José
María Rodríguez-Acosta, and writers
such as Vicente Blasco Ibáñez and Joaquín
Romero Murube. This was a diverse group,
one including amateurs who created few
gardens and who perhaps belong to a different category: owners who designed the

gardens of their private houses. With sensitivity and determination they created an atmosphere that reflected their taste and aesthetic choices. Many excellent private and anonymous gardens were the result of collaboration, in most cases between owners and nurserymen, yet this is often forgotten by the historian.

In the following sections of this essay, the choice to group the complex reality of gardening before the Spanish Civil War into two blocks, regionalist and modern, results in reductionist terms that should be understood as a simplification. The former did have features of modernity, such as geometry not copied directly from ancient examples, and the second responded to influences from regionalist as well as from traditional gardens.

The Aesthetic Domination of Regionalist Landscape Gardening (1910 - 1936)

Forestier's success paralleled that of neo-Sevillan architecture. He designed the renovation of Parque de María Luisa at the same time that architects in Seville were making other regionalist gardens for private houses and in public parks. Juan Talavera (1880–1960) and Aníbal González (1876–1929) would become the most influential in this genre, although their work was limited to designing layouts, while planting was under the supervision of technicians, agriculturists, and horticulturists. Thus, González' Plaza de España includes an Andalusian garden, and Talavera redesigned the Jardines de Murillo in Seville with the collaboration of the municipal engineer Francisco Doblado.

Similar to the history of the Jardines del Genil in Granada, the Seville gardens were transformed in style from English to Spanish. The Alcázar of Seville exemplifies the swiftness with which the Sevillan style solidified. In 1910, one year before the arrival of Forestier and the first plans for the Parque de María Luisa, a garden was built in the old Huerta de la Alcoba of the Alcázar, in the English style, which

was at that point the norm in sophisticated Spanish gardening.[61] A year later, in 1911, another renovation was undertaken in another garden of the Alcázar, that of the Retiro, behind the Galería de Grutescos of the Alcázar. At the king's initiative, a naturalistic wooded area was designed as a mixed garden with a small formal garden. It was begun by the architect José Gómez, who had worked on the Huerta de la Alcoba, but the few months that had elapsed since the start of the project had coincided with a critical point in Sevillan garden design, and a key personality had intervened: the marqués de la Vega-Inclán, director of the Alcázar. Benigno de la Vega-Inclán (1858–1942) was cultured, a great lover of gardening, and director of the royal office of tourism, and had introduced into Spain modern criteria for the restoration of monuments. He had already worked on El Greco's house in Toledo, where he had made a domestic garden in the traditional Spanish fashion.[62] The intervention of Vega-Inclán at the Alcázar delayed the installation of the garden and introduced changes that moved it gradually toward a new, fashionable aesthetic that was Sevillan and Forestierian.[63] Whereas the Huerta de la Alcoba was begun in 1910 and finished in 1911 as a *jardín a la inglesa*, the Huerta del Retiro was begun in 1911 as a *jardín a la inglesa* and finished in 1916, but in the Sevillan style, as a Spanish garden (fig. 17).

This evolution ended with a third work at the Alcázar, the Jardín de los Poetas, designed later (1956–1958) by Joaquín Romero Murube (1904–1969), a poet and director of the Alcázar from 1934 until his death. Romero Murube had distinguished himself in various writings as a defender of the Sevillan garden, although, like Winthuysen, he had always criticized the excesses of its superficial, ornamental, neo-Sevillan imitations. This third garden, which was, from its beginning, regionalist, met with no objection from Sevillan society.[64]

17. Unknown photographer,
Huerta del Retiro, Alcázar, Seville,
c. 1930
Private collection

that Joaquín Sorolla (1863–1923) made
for his house in Madrid (fig. 18). The triumph of Andalusian fashion in gardening is
underscored by the fact that this artist from
Valencia (eastern Spain) would, in Madrid
(central Spain), make a garden in the style
of Andalusia (southern Spain).[65] He began it
in 1910, just after a trip to Andalusia, where
he repeatedly visited and painted landscapes
and gardens. The neo-Andalusian style
could assimilate diverse spaces for his house,
inspired specifically by the Alcázar of Seville
and the Generalife of Granada.[66] Although
it seems certain that Sorolla's garden preceded the influence of Forestier, Sorolla
knew the French designer's work firsthand
and admired it; later he stated: "The Sevillan people today have a garden, the Parque
de María Luisa, which causes all foreign
parks to pale by comparison."[67] Sorolla's
intention of making an Andalusian garden
included even the materials used. The wall
tiles, for example, were manufactured by the
Mensaque ceramics workshop in Seville, and
some elements provide a truly poetic symbolism, as with the planting of myrtles from the
Patio de los Arrayanes of the Alhambra itself,
sent to Sorolla by Modesto Cendoya, director
of the Alhambra, in 1917.[68] Sorolla's garden
was constructed as a place of repose, but it
also served as a subject for his paintings and
would be the main motif of the works of his
final period.

Among Sorolla's followers, the painter
and garden designer Javier de Winthuysen
(1874–1956) was undoubtedly the most
important. Carmen Añón has accurately
observed of Winthuysen's aesthetics: "His
gardens, in a period of clear decadence in
Spanish gardening, … correspond to an eternal classicism which he neither wished to nor
could dispense with, and in those gardens
he reflects what at that moment of his life he
was incapable of reflecting in his painting"
(fig. 19).[69] Winthuysen abandoned painting
for more than fifteen years. He wrote:

The absurdities of the multiple modern trends with their
pretended originality beyond all aesthetic reason

The success of this recently invented
type of garden was not limited to Seville.
Whether imitating the designs of Forestier
or copying the more emphatic aspects of the
neo-Sevillan style, or simply incorporating
appropriate miscellaneous elements, gardens
in the Spanish style multiplied. Perhaps the
most striking work early on was the garden

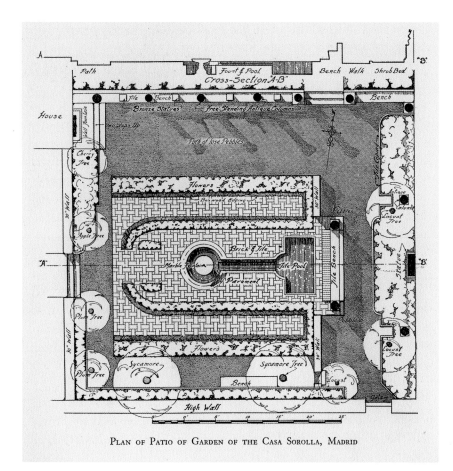

PLAN OF PATIO OF GARDEN OF THE CASA SOROLLA, MADRID

weighed upon me in the sense that I worried whether I was antiquated and incapable of evolving, and as I did not accept painting as more than dabbling, I did not merely refuse to accept all of that, but I was repulsed by it and I took absolute refuge in my gardens.[70]

He did not warn that the garden was giving rise to a similar phenomenon.

Regionalism in Spanish painting appeared at the end of the nineteenth century and was already outdated at the beginning of the twentieth, when the modern movement in art had conquered nationalism. Regionalism in Spanish garden design was slower to materialize but then ultimately dominated modernist landscape, in contrast to other European countries, where regionalism and modernism coexisted. Winthuysen abandoned painting because he did not understand contemporary artistic movements. Yet he did not feel that he was behind the times in taking refuge in classical gardening. He was either ignorant of or unconcerned with avant-garde trends in garden design.

18. *Plan of Patio of Garden of the Casa Sorolla, Madrid*

Helen Morgenthau Fox, Patio Gardens *(New York, 1929)*

19. Javier de Winthuysen, project for a garden, graphite and watercolor, n.d. (1952?)

Archivo del Real Jardín Botánico de Madrid, Fondo Winthuysen, sig. WINT DIB 63-001

20. Exposición Hispano-Americana, Seville, photograph by Abelardo Linares, c. 1930
Private collection

One might say that when Winthuysen began as a gardener, he was within Forestier's orbit, but his formal apprenticeship was independent, he was self-taught, and his sensibility and good taste enabled him to avoid falling into the most tawdry trends of the neo-Sevillans. He criticized gardens that were considered neo-Sevillan simply because of the use of colored tiles or yellow sand paths, signs of an imitative regionalism. He was more refined and less obvious than the architects of the Exposición Hispano-Americana of 1929 in Seville (fig. 20). In opposing the new fashion, he wrote: "The current resurgence [of the Sevillan garden] with its industrialization has been prostituted, offering itself to the masses with trinkets and gaudiness, sometimes forming, more than gardens, a collection of ceramic samples."[71] His gardens were always, in the words of Carmen Añón, "dignified, sensitive, and far superior to the gardening that at this time was developing in Spain."[72] Winthuysen's work combined the values of the vernacular garden with the wisdom of the classical European garden.

The debt that Spanish gardening owes to Winthuysen is not limited to his designs. He also struggled indefatigably to defend the historical gardens of Spain by documenting them, by appealing to the government for their protection, and through publications, lectures, and raising awareness of their value along the intelligentsia, many of whom were his close friends. His book *Jardines clásicos de España* (Madrid, 1930) is notable as the first scholarly research on gardens in Spain, although only the first part, on the gardens of Castile, was published. His moving memoirs, the title of which ironically describes him as "un señorito sevillano" (a Sevillan rich kid), show intimate aspects of this work, even in the difficult circumstances of the Spanish Civil War, including using his meager personal resources to supplement inadequate funds from the government for study trips and research expenses.[73] For Winthuysen, the effort was part of his lifelong passion for gardens.

Modernist Landscape Gardening and the Domination of the Regionalist Aesthetic

Against the ideological triumph of the regionalist garden, there were several shows of resistance from those who sought to make gardens from a different perspective. While the regionalists forged radical opposition to the modern garden, the nonregionalists seemed to accept the battle as impossible to win and chose one of two options: ignoring regionalism by simply designing personal gardens that were ahistorical in their relationship to contemporary life, or seeking a synthesis between the modernist garden and those of the past, including in their contemporary designs elements typical of traditional gardens.

The difficulty of introducing parameters of modernity into gardens of a period dominated by regionalism can be understood in the work of one of the architects who brought the modern movement to Spain. In 1926–1928 Fernando García Mercadal (1896–1985) designed and built what was considered the first modernist architectural work in Spain, the Rincón de Goya in Saragossa, an architectural complex with a main building commemorating the centennial of the death of Francisco de Goya.[74] He had

traveled in Europe and maintained friendships with the most advanced architects of the modern movement: Walter Gropius, Ludwig Mies van der Rohe, and especially Le Corbusier.[75] From the beginning he showed interest in gardens; the Rincón de Goya itself had one, although it remained unfinished during his life. In 1949 he published his book *Parques y jardines*, mentioned earlier as the first systematic history of Spanish gardens. Despite his opposition to the theory and practice of regionalist architecture, his buildings and gardens also show elements of tradition, a kind of search for modernity within traditional forms, based on a widespread concept of the Spanish vanguard in that period, *mediterraneidad* (Mediterraneanness).[76] Some aspects of Mercadal's designs are close to regionalist gardens in that they express the influence of European modernist design more in terms of volume and in the use of architectonic topiary than in geometry or in layout (fig. 21).

The clearest theoretical and practical design position that ignored nationalist regionalism was represented by Nicolau Maria Rubió i Tudurí (1891–1981). He did not enter the debate because his objective

22. Jardines de Santa Clotilde,
entry court
Author photograph, 1991

23. Jardines de Santa Clotilde,
stairs
Author photograph, 1991

was to make a regional garden based on ecological systems rather than on national characteristics; as he wrote later in his career:

The task of gardening that some of us have developed in
the east of Spain, and in the Balearic Islands, has the aim
of serving the art of the Latin garden. This is not a question of local objectives, but of cultivating broad formulas
and applying them to an entire climate zone and spirit
similar to ours.[77]

In his book *El jardín meridional* (1934),
Rubió championed a style that was in practice a nonstyle, a garden of southern Europe
and the Mediterranean, determined by climate and by history. It was eclectic and had
many possible variants.[78] In his allusion to
climate, we can detect a trace of Forestier,
who had defined Spanish gardens as being
of the "climate of the orange tree," although
the term *meridional* for Rubió was broader
and, in any case, nonnationalist. He searched
for a personal style that would assume a
vague form derived from the site and from
historical styles offering a repertoire of
possibilities.[79]

The first and best of his gardens, Santa
Clotilde, near Blanes (Spain), thus offers a
mixture of resources of classical landscape
gardening and formal solutions (fig. 22). It
is a strange work in which the hand of the
designer combines with that of the owner,
Raúl Roviralta Astoul, marqués de Roviralta
de Santa Clotilde. As with many Spanish
gardens of this period, little is known about
the extent of the intervention of each participant: owner, landscape designer, gardener,
artist. The formal treatment of space is clear,
mixing the geometry of straight paths with
natural landscape in the rest of the terrain.
The steps and walks take classical forms
with low hedges, sculpture created expressly
for the site, and allées of cypresses. The
combination of these elements recalls the
inspirational Tuscan landscape that Rubió
had visited during the garden's design stage
(fig. 23).[80]

It is clear that the concerns of Rubió,
both as a theorist and as a landscape
designer, were far from the articulation
of a national Spanish garden. Although
it would be simplistic to suggest that this
distance was due to his Catalonian nationalist politics, it should be noted that for
a Catalonian nationalist at the beginning
of the century, it was difficult to assume
principles of regionalist Spanish gardening
that looked to the Arab heritage of southern Spain, with Andalusia as the reference
point and a view to Seville and Granada as
sources of inspiration. Nevertheless politics
was probably not the chief reason Rubió

turned away from regionalism; rather, it seems that his closeness to the new architectural trends, his modernity, and his cosmopolitan character outweighed regionalist influences.

Garden design in Catalonia had an antecedent of the highest level, the work of Antoni Gaudí. In many of his projects, he laid out the spaces around his buildings and, in a few important cases, he designed gardens and their embellishments (pergolas, sun shelters, loggias, bridges, benches, fountains).[81] In Catalonian art nouveau, the modern garden was produced not by recovering straight-line geometry, but by assuming the curved lines of the *jardín a la inglesa* and incorporating diverse elements into a highly personal aesthetic. Gaudí was not the only Catalan architect to explore these new directions. The most radical experiences of modernity in the gardens of Spain would be produced between 1928 and 1936, when the architects of the modern movement in Catalonia who had formed the Grupo de Artistas y Técnicos Españoles para el Progreso de la Arquitectura Contemporánea (GATEPAC) began to give importance to the garden in their projects. Of special interest is the collaboration between the architect José Luis Sert and the gardener Arturo Rigol, an ephemeral partnership because Rigol died in an accident at the age of thirty-six in 1935, and Sert went into exile as a result of the civil war (fig. 24).[82]

An alternative approach in this third period was the search for a synthesis of modernism with the aesthetics of the past, exemplified in the work of José María Rodríguez-Acosta (1878–1941). Like Sorolla and Winthuysen, he was a painter. And, like Winthuysen, he was a regionalist painter who, disconcerted by the direction of contemporary art, stopped painting and took refuge in the garden. However, his personal background and the options he pursued were quite different. Rodríguez-Acosta was a cultivated and cosmopolitan millionaire who traveled throughout Europe and Asia studying contemporary art.

After he put painting aside, from 1914 to 1928 he dedicated his time to designing his garden and his house and studio in Granada, close to the Alhambra (fig. 25). For him, a garden design was an alchemical exercise that transformed the maker. He began construction in a subtle form of regionalism, refined and elegant, without the crude details of some regionalist varieties: no tiles, no frogs in the fountains, no rustic pergolas. Gradually, his garden aesthetics moved farther and farther away from the regional elements toward different sources: classical models, local Granadan gardens, and modern architecture — a mixture that we might compare to the postmodern aesthetic at the end of the twentieth century.[83] The garden was constructed on bold terraces and divided into small enclaves that for Rodríguez-Acosta held symbolic meaning, representing the sum of dualities: one patio embodying the feminine, with a central pool and a statue of Venus; another, the masculine, with a cypress labyrinth and a statue of Apollo.[84] Life is evoked by water and death by a mannerist tomb, dated to 1603, of a Castilian nun; a statue of Psyche with a spout alludes to the mind and to sex. But above all, it is a garden of elegant geometry, full of gestures of mathematical perfection, with subtle and highly studied symmetries. It is formally strange, extraordinary, and singular (fig. 26).

This garden began in a tone of regionalism and ended in a key of modernism. And when the work on it ended, its designer returned to painting. But his painting was now different; the process of garden design had transformed the painter's gaze, and his new work was modern and personal. The garden was extraordinarily well received in some circles; even before it was finished, it had been treated enthusiastically in books published outside Spain, where it was seen as an indicator of the rebirth of the garden in Spain.[85] Later it met with misunderstanding and mistreatment in negative reactions of defenders of regionalism. For

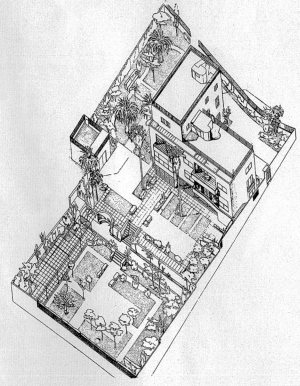

CASA GALOBART - Barcelona - Perspectiva axonométrica.

CASA GALOBART - Arquitecto: J. Luis Sert. - Diferentes aspectos de los jardines realizados con la cooperación de Artur Rigol, jardinero.

20 —

24. José Luis Sert and Artur Rigol,
Casa Galobart, Barcelona, 1932
AC, *no. 8 (1935), author collection*

25. José María Rodríguez-Acosta, sketch of a garden for his house and studio in Granada, 1916, graphite

Archivo de la Fundación Rodríguez-Acosta

to Italy, where this type of garden is more common."[87]

Even though these regionalist critics acknowledged the beauty of the work, they thought that it should not have been constructed in Granada. Precisely the opposite is true: the design fully respects the values of the urban landscape. The geometry of the white house, with divided volumes, creates a dialogue with allées of cypresses while expressing the spirit of modernity, not the naïve invention of a neo-Arab style. A neo-Sevillan hotel built nearby in the same period provides an instructive contrast to Rodríguez-Acosta's garden: the hotel's enormous, heavy mass, in a doubtful Arab style and painted red, violates the values of a hillside dotted with small white houses surrounded by gardens of cypresses. But this sort of analysis of the landscape was impossible for the regionalists, whose first and foremost demand on the garden was the primacy of components of unquestionable local affiliation. In the 1920s Rodríguez-Acosta repeated his experiment at the home of his brother in the Albayzín, the medieval quarter of Granada. This garden also combined local influence and traces of the modern European garden, with unusual geometries based on rhomboids and triangles (fig. 27).

The architect Leopoldo Torres Balbás (1888–1960) developed similar solutions for a new garden at the Alhambra of Granada: a dialogue between the historical tradition and the modern one, resulting in a new and personal work that eschewed the most typical elements of regionalism.[88] Torres Balbás' garden at the Alhambra (1923–1936), begun with a reading of Rusiñol and Forestier, was reinterpreted in a personal key. He did not imitate the new Andalusian gardens, but rather created a modern work with elements from tradition. His approach was not understood, and the garden was considered, surprisingly enough, French.[89] Its lack of elements imitating a fantasy Arab garden was not forgiven (fig. 28).

These works were carried out in the 1920s and early 1930s, and political events that

example, Francisco Prieto Moreno, in his book *Los Jardines de Granada*, states three times within a brief space that Rodríguez-Acosta's garden was outside the typical Granadan style because only the climate and the changes in level gave it a local flavor.[86] More explicit still is the criticism of Teresa Ozores y Saavedra, marquesa de Casa Valdés, in *Jardines de España*: "It is a garden that is not in its environment.... What a pity that although it has many traditional Granadan elements, to create a garden of sheer beauty the owner should turn

26. Garden by José María Rodríguez-Acosta for his house and studio, Granada, 1914–1928, central axis

Photograph Francisco Fernández, 1999; private collection

27. Garden by José María Rodríguez-Acosta for his brother's house, Albayzín quarter, Granada, 1920s

Photograph Hervé Brunon, 2006

followed soon afterward prevent us from knowing what would have happened if the evolution in garden design had continued. In 1936 General Francisco Franco launched his military campaign against the Republican government, and the victory of fascism in Spain meant the triumph of cultural nationalism. In their synthesis of tradition, climate, history, and modernity, García Mercadal, Rubió i Tudurí, Sert, Rigol, Rodríguez-Acosta, and Torres Balbás would have no heirs. Their works were misunderstood and pushed aside by nationalists. The criticism originated in a conservative mindset that invoked a code of national values. Santa Clotilde was labeled as fundamentally a garden of Tuscan influence; the work of Torres Balbás in the Alhambra as French; and the garden of Rodríguez-Acosta as Roman or Italian. Indeed, the three architects who designed nonregionalist gardens (Sert, Rubió i Tudurí, and García Mercadal) were castigated as unsympathetic to the new regime and were disqualified from exercising their profession, either temporarily or permanently.[90]

The subtlety of the works of these artists was misconstrued, even unintelligible, in the new cultural climate. The succeeding generation did not comprehend the modernists' respect for tradition, which represented a delicate balance between personal discourse and reflection on their own time. The oversight would seriously impair the future of Spanish gardening. It took years—until the 1950s and 1960s—for gardens of interest to be produced, and these are few and little known. The art of gardening is currently being reborn in Spain, but that story would take us beyond this brief overview of the debate concerning the modern garden in Spain during the opening decades of the twentieth century. As we have seen, those decades offered rare and notable gardens of surpassing beauty, on a par with the best works of European gardening of that time.

NOTES

1. The most up-to-date history of the Spanish garden is Ana Luengo Añón and Coro Millares Escobio, eds., *Parámetros del jardín español* (Madrid, 2007). The period under consideration here corresponds to the third volume, especially the contribution by Ana Luengo, "El modernismo vernáculo," 107–128.

2. See Clementina Díez de Baldeón, *Arquitectura y clases sociales en el Madrid del siglo XIX* (Madrid, 1986).

3. See Francisco Javier Monclús and José Luis Oyón, eds., *Atlas histórico de ciudades europeas*, vol. 1, *Península ibérica* (Barcelona, 1994). The bibliography on the transformations of Paris is extensive; see especially Jean des Cars and Pierre Pinon, *Paris: Haussmann* (Paris, 1991).

4. "Nuevas construcciones en el barrio de Salamanca," *La ilustración española y americana*, April 16, 1872, 231–234.

5. "[El jardín] tenía el inconveniente de no poderse situar en el centro de la plaza el altar para las celebraciones de las grandes fiestas [religiosas] del Corpus." Report of the municipal architect, quoted by Ángel Isac Martínez de Carvajal, in "La ciudad de Granada y el palacete de los Mártires a mediados del siglo XIX," *Cuadernos de arte Universidad de Granada*, no. 24 (1993): 215–241. On the history of this plaza in the nineteenth century, see Fernando Acale Sánchez, *Plazas y paseos de Granada, de la remodelación cristiana de los espacios musulmanes a los proyectos de jardines en el ochocientos* (Granada, 2005), 286–322.

6. Eva J. Rodríguez Romero, "Jardines de papel: La teoría y la tratadística del jardín en España durante el siglo XIX," *Asclepio*, no. 51 (1999): 129–158; Carmen Añón Feliú, "Sentimiento y construcción del jardín español," in *Histories of Garden Conservation*, ed. Michel Conan, José Tito Rojo, and Luigi Zangheri (Florence, 2005), 362. Thanks to Carmen Añón for providing a copy of Atienza's book.

7. Juan Pérez-Rubín, "Melitón Atienza (1827–1890) y sus proyectos de jardín 'geográfica' (Madrid, 1856) y jardín 'botánico-zoológico de aclimatación' (Málaga, 1878–1882)," *Acta botanica malacitana* 27 (2002): 232–234.

8. Pérez-Rubín 2002, 233 and n. 3. He could not locate Atienza's report, but I located the printed report and plans: Melitón Atienza y Sirvent, *Extracto del estudio de anteproyecto de un jardín geográfico* (Madrid, 1863).

9. Melitón Atienza y Sirvent, *Historia de la arquitectura de jardines* (Madrid, 1855), 8.

10. "La utilidad de la arquitectura de jardines se ha hecho hoy indispensable, y solo la ignorancia ó el fanatismo de un rancio apego hácia las prácticas antiguas, seria el único que tratase de ahogar la enérgica voz de la ciencia." Atienza y Sirvent 1855, 8.

11. Atienza y Sirvent 1855, 51.

12. The term for "English garden" in nineteenth-century Castilian was not *jardín paisajista* (landscape garden) but rather *jardín apaisado* (literally, garden in the form of a landscape). (Castilian Spanish today still uses the term *apaisado*, but to refer to horizontal orientation, as of a sheet of paper.) Miguel Colmeiro, director of the Real Jardín Botánico de Madrid, wrote: "Los jardines chinos se imitaron en Inglaterra, y después en el resto de Europa, tomando la denominación jardines a la inglesa o ingleses, que son los de moda en el día, y los que en efecto merecen la preferencia … conviniéndoles perfectamente la calificación de jardines apaisados, que es ya lo común nombrarlos." (Chinese gardens were imitated in England, and afterward in the rest of Europe, taking the name of gardens in the English style or English gardens, which are fashionable today, and which in fact deserve preference … perfectly qualifying as landscape gardens, as they are now commonly called.) Miguel Colmeiro, *Manual completo de jardinería arreglado conforme a las más modernas publicaciones* [Madrid, 1859], 410. Colmeiro's text makes it clear that, in nineteenth-century Spain, the terms *jardín inglés*, *jardín apaisado*, *jardín a la inglesa*, and *jardín chino* were often used interchangeably for any type of garden not designed in straight lines.

13. Atienza y Sirvent 1855, 50–52.

14. Atienza y Sirvent 1855, 55.

15. Atienza y Sirvent 1855, 52.

16. Pedro Julián Muñoz y Rubio, *Tratado de jardinería y floricultura: Historia de la jardinería; creaciones antiguas y modernas de la arquitectura de jardines…* (Madrid, 1887).

17. One in 1902, "corrected and augmented," and another in 1923, the "third greatly augmented edition." A "third much augmented edition" was issued in 1928. Several discrepancies in date are due to the existence of a good number of reprint editions. In any case, the editions of 1902, 1923, and 1928 are posthumous, as the author died in 1895. His obituary was published in *La ilustración española y americana*, January 8, 1895.

18. Muñoz y Rubio 1923, 12–28.

19. Andrés [André] Lefèvre, *Parques y jardines* (Barcelona, 1886), slightly abridged version of *Les parcs et les jardins* (Paris, 1882).

20. Works preceding that of García Mercadal's *Parques y jardines, su historia y sus trazados* (Madrid, 1949) limit historical review to brief chapters. In general they focus on garden construction or miscellaneous themes, sometimes notable, presented as a catalog of examples of historical gardens arranged geographically or chronologically.

21. "[Los árabes] conocedores de las ciencias naturales, crearon el género arábigo-español" ([Arabs] knowledgeable about natural sciences, created the Arabic-Spanish type). Muñoz y Rubio 1923, 22. "En las creaciones modernas de los parques y jardines se percibe claramente la intervención de la ciencia" (Intervention of science may be clearly perceived in modern creation of parks and gardens). Muñoz y Rubio 1923, 27.

22. "… aplicando a los jardines la mayoría de los sistemas conocidos en la actualidad, y contribuyeron a propagar el gusto y la afición por las flores." Muñoz y Rubio 1923, 22.

23. Atienza y Sirvent 1855, 43–44; Muñoz y Rubio 1923, 22–24.

24. José Antonio Banqueri, *Libro de agricultura del doctor excelente Abu Zacaría Yahia Abén Mohamed Ben Ahmed Ebn el Awan* (Madrid, 1802).

25. "[A] pesar del tiempo transcurrido puede en el día consultarse con ventaja hasta para la ciencia que nos ocupa." Atienza y Sirvent 1855, 43.

26. "… se usan hoy por los jardineros en nuestro país." Muñoz y Rubio 1923, 23.

27. "El género simétrico que nos legaron los romanos." Muñoz y Rubio 1923, 24.

28. Muñoz y Rubio 1923, 25.

29. "Dos planos, figuras 255 y 256, de jardín, estilo árabe, de gran efecto y elegancia, sobre todo cuando las construcciones en él son del mismo orden." Muñoz y Rubio 1923, 413.

30. These plans are absent from the first (1887) edition of Muñoz's book. I cite them from the "third greatly augmented edition" of 1923.

31. "Fuente en estrella de ladrillos gruesos," "Varios cipreses sueltos plantados a capricho," "Galería de ciprés recortado" (Muñoz y Rubio 1923, fig. 255). On the typical character of topiary cypresses in Granadan gardens, see José Tito Rojo and Manuel Casares Porcel, "La bailarina del Generalife y las topiarias arquitectónicas de ciprés en los jardines granadinos del siglo XIX," *Cuadernos de la Alhambra*, no. 35 (1999): 57–92, and José Tito Rojo and Manuel Casares Porcel, "L'arte topiaria nei giardini spagnoli di tradizione araba," in *L'arte topiaria*, ed. Margherita Azzi Vicentini (Treviso, 2004), 22–32.

32. On Italian gardens see Leonardo Parachini and Carlo Alessandro Pisoni, eds., *Storia e storie di giardini* (Verbania, 2003), especially the contributions by Domenico Luciani ("Ritrovare e reinventare i 'giardini italiani': L'aporìa del restauro," 35–43) and Margherita Azzi Visentini ("Storia dei giardini: Osservazioni in margini al recente sviluppo di questa disciplina in Italia," 45–86).

33. The first foreign books on the Spanish garden appeared far later than those on Italy and do not collectively shape a clear vision of the Spanish garden. They are, furthermore, very diverse in their positions on the reality that they describe. Most, but not all, are of Anglo-American origin: Rose Standish Nichols,

Spanish and Portuguese Gardens (Boston, 1924); Mildred Stapley Byne and Arthur Byne, *Spanish Gardens and Patios* (New York, 1924); Constance Mary Villiers-Stuart, *Spanish Gardens* (London, 1929); Helen Morgenthau Fox, *Patio Gardens* (New York, 1929); Georges Gromord, *Jardins d'Espagne* (Paris, 1926). There are also more general books that provide valuable information on gardens, notably Henry Inigo Triggs, *Garden Craft in Europe* (London, 1913), and Austin Whittlesey, *The Minor Ecclesiastical, Domestic and Garden Architecture of southern Spain* (New York, 1917). Hispano-Muslim gardens first received attention from Jean-Claude Nicolas Forestier and in brief references in garden history books published outside Spain; see José Tito Rojo, "La construcción teórica de un estilo: El jardín hispanomusulmán," in *Histories of Garden Conservation*, ed. Michel Conan, José Tito Rojo, and Luigi Zangheri (Florence, 2005), 321–358.

34. Two editions in 1903 were followed by another two in 1914, also in portfolios, but of lesser quality, and various others in the form of notebooks, books, or series of postcards. Each of the editions had idiosyncrasies, and they did not all reproduce the same selection of paintings. The publishing history of Rusiñol's *Jardines de España* remains to be studied. Even the most complete bibliographic reviews do not recognize some of the versions that I have seen in libraries and private collections. The question is beyond the scope of this essay, and I touch on it only to indicate the long-lived influence of this work. The first reference edition was published in 1903 in Catalan: Santiago Rusiñol, *Jardins d'Espanya* (Barcelona, 1903).

35. Margarida Casacuberta, "Los jardines del alma de Santiago Rusiñol," in *Els jardins de l'anima de Santiago Rusiñol* (Girona, 1999), 208.

36. See Santiago Rusiñol, *El Jardín abandonado: Cuadro poemático en un acto* (Barcelona, 1902), and a work representing the Jardín del Cúzco in the town of Víznar, near Granada (oil on canvas, 1895; published in Rusiñol 1903).

37. Because of the country's great diversity, nationalism in Spain had regionalist variants. In fact nationalism did not necessarily support the idea of a unified Spain; in this period, movements for regional independence were germinating with greater or lesser strength, not only in the Basque country and in Catalonia, but also in other territories. The scant cultural weight of gardening at this time precluded, except in the case of Andalusia, serious attempts to produce regional styles that would have influence throughout Spain, and debates as to the existence of other typologies of regional gardens were almost always confined to a local sphere.

38. We know of these transformations from travelers' accounts, but we lack information regarding their real depth. Constant changes during this period prevent attributing specific elements to intervention by the French army.

39. The transformations of this boulevard before 1902 are mentioned in Isac Martínez de Carvajal 1993 and Acale Sánchez 2005, particularly those of the period 1840–1900.

40. Juan (Jean) Giraud was a French horticulturist living in Granada and the author of various garden projects. After his death his work was continued by his son Pedro.

41. "La forma de jardín hoy adoptada es la llamada apaisada o a la Inglesa. Su trazado a capricho permite adaptarse a todo terreno, cualquiera que sea su forma." Pedro Giraud, *Manual de horticultura: Catálogo descriptivo; grandes Establecimientos Hortícolas "La Quinta"* (Granada, [c. 1910]). This corresponds to no. 3 of the period of Pedro Giraud's ownership of La Quinta.

42. *Jardines del Genil, Expediente para la prolongación de los jardines del Genil desde los actuales hasta el puente del mismo nombre*, 1902, Negociado de Fomento, Archivo Histórico Municipal de Granada, sig. 2175.

43. "Los viejos jardinillos de la Bomba tenían todo ese encanto; pero desapareció cuando una época de furor inglés los dejó sin un rincón escondido donde poder orar. Los jardines granadinos, con sus bóvedas de verdura, sus fuentes melancólicas, sus calles de arrayán, se fueron para siempre ... estos, nuestros jardines, se van perdiendo. Sólo [los jardines de] la Alhambra nos quedan. ¿Se convertirán también en un jardín inglés? Los granadinos necesitamos nuestros jardines. Necesitamos más jardines." Antonio Gallego Burín, "Los jardines," *El sol*, July 21, 1919.

44. "Estos intentos de jardines ... no son granadinos; como [tampoco lo son] los macizos ingleses que se colocaron destruyendo nuestros jardines propios.... No supone nadie que se intente dejar los jardines del Genil ... en el estado en que están.... Algunos recordarán todavía como eran aquellos poéticos jardines." V. [Francisco de Paula Valladar], "Los jardines de Granada," *La Alhambra*, no. extra 50 (1924): 5–7.

45. See José Antonio González Alcantud, "El andalucismo de dos notables granadinos: Valladar y Burín," in *Granada la andaluza*, ed. José Antonio González Alcantud and Rafael G. Peinado Santaella (Granada, 2008), 183–211.

46. Juan Leyva was a businessman and a member of Granada's city council. When he acquired the La Quinta nursery from Giraud around 1920, he carried on publishing the catalog, which his son also continued until about 1975. The quality of the catalog was declining; in the period of Pedro Giraud it ran to more than a hundred pages in a hardcover binding, whereas in the final years of Leyva's ownership, it was a stapled pamphlet of fewer than twenty pages. The La Quinta catalogs from the time of the Girauds and of Juan Leyva are not in any library or public archives; most are preserved in the collection of Manuel Casares Porcel and José Tito Rojo.

47. "En España ha habido una época (no muy lejana) de la cual aún quedan reminiscencias, en que se han transformado la mayoría de los jardines públicos y particulares, por un estilo indefinido que se ha llamado inglés, sin que de inglés tenga absolutamente nada…. [L]o que hoy llamamos jardín español es el árabe modernizado. Por todas las razones expuestas, debemos siempre tender a construir este jardín con preferencia a ningún otro." Juan Leyva, *Catálogo de los Establecimientos Hortícolas "La Quinta,"* no. 3 (Granada, c. 1930), 75.

48. Juan Leyva, *Catálogo de los Grandes Establecimientos Hortícolas "La Quinta,"* no. 2 (Granada, n.d.).

49. "Granadinos de valía. Excmo. Sr. D. Juan Leyva: Entrevista a pleno Sol," *Granada comercial*, unnumbered issue (1927). The anonymous interviewer praises Leyva for the project and for donating to the city the plants to make the garden: "A very accomplished horticulturist; this is demonstrated by his great project, specifications and plan for public gardens and a park for Granada, which have begun to be executed brilliantly; and by his making a donation of all types of plants from his private gardens and replanting them, when he left the city government, which then did not conform to the approved plan."

50. Fox 1929, 125. The pergola is very similar to one shown in a drawing by Jean-Claude Nicolas Forestier in his *Jardíns: Carnet de plans et de dessins* (Paris, 1920), which Leyva surely imitated.

51. Forestier was in charge of the gardens of Paris and built parks and gardens in other French cities, Morocco, Spain, and Latin America. He had great theoretical influence on the development of landscape gardening in Spain in the early twentieth century. He is the subject of a large bibliography; an indispensable reference is Benedicte Leclerc, ed., *Jean Claude Nicolas Forestier, 1851–1930: Du jardin au paysage urbain* (Paris, 1994). Regarding Forestier's influence outside his own country see also the essay by Sonia Berjman in this volume.

52. Concerning Forestier's work in Seville, see Sonsoles Nieto Caldeiro, *El jardín sevillano de 1900 a 1929* (Seville, 1995), and Antonio Tejedor Cabrera, "Jardines históricos de Andalucía" (doctoral diss., Universidad de Sevilla 1998).]

53. See Cristina Domínguez Peláez, *El Parque de María Luisa, esencia histórica de Sevilla* (Seville, 1995), and Vicente Lleó Cañal, *La Sevilla de los Montpensier* (Seville, 1997).

54. Accords of the Comité de la Exposición de Sevilla (1911), in Nieto Caldeiro 1995, 72.

55. Fox 1929, 12.

56. Fox 1929, 12.

57. Fox 1929, 11.

58. See Dorothée Imbert, *The Modernist Garden in France* (New Haven, 1993), and Jane Brown, Sofia Brignone, and Alan Ward, *The Modern Garden* (London, 2000).

59. "… and it is to him [Ferdinand Bac] that I am indebted for my longing to create a perfect garden." Luis Barragán, ceremony acceptance speech, Chicago, 1980, The Pritzker Architecture Prize, *http://www .pritzkerprize.com/1980/ceremony_speech1*, consulted December 8, 2012. In the original Spanish: "Y fue Bac quien despertó en mí el anhelo de la arquitectura de jardín." Luis Barragán, "Discurso de aceptación del Premio Pritzker, redactado y firmado en México, D.F. entre los meses de abril y mayo; presentado en Dumbarton Oaks, E.U.A., 3 de junio," in Antonio Riggen, ed., *Luis Barragán: Escritos y conversaciones* (Madrid, 2000), 58–61, 59.

60. Barragán 1980. In the original Spanish: "… caminando por un estrecho y oscuro tunel de la Alhambra, se me entregó, sereno, callado y solitario, el hermoso patio de los Mirtos de ese antiguo palacio. De alguna manera tuve el sentimiento de que contenía lo que debe contener un jardín bien logrado: nada menos que el universo entero." Riggen 2000, 60.

61. The gardener Juan Gras had supervisory and financial responsibility for the work; the project was perhaps by the architect José Gómez. It is difficult to attribute works that were carried out by the management, undoubtedly with intervention in the layout, and for which Gras and Gómez worked as employees of the institution and not as contractors. On this garden, see María Reyes Baena Sánchez, *Los jardines del Alcázar de Sevilla entre los siglos XVIII y XX* (Seville, 2003), 129–134.

62. See Vicente Traver Tomás, *El marqués de Vega-Inclán* (Castellón, 1965).

63. Baena Sánchez 2003, 137–142. On the intervention of Vega-Inclán, see Nieto Caldeiro 1995, 143–147.

64. On Romero Murube's vision of gardening, see José Tito Rojo and Manuel Casares Porcel, "From the Andalusí Garden to the Andalusian Garden: Continuities and Re-inventions," in *Middle East Garden Traditions: Unity and Diversity*, ed. Michel Conan (Washington, DC, 2007), 287–305. See also the biography by Joaquín Arbide, *La leyenda de Joaquín Romero Murube* (Sevilla, 2003), and a special issue dedicated to Romero Murube's work: *Minervae Baeticae: Boletín de la Real Academia Sevillana de Buenas Letras*, no. 23 (segunda época, 1995). On his stint at the Alcázar, see Eduardo Ybarra Hidalgo, "Joaquín Romero Murube," in *Los conservadores municipales del Real Alcázar* (Seville, 2003), 65–82.

65. He would not be the only one; somewhat later, in 1918, another artist from Valencia, the writer Blasco Ibáñez, would build an Andalusian garden (Fontana Rosa) on the Côte d'Azur of France.

66. See Florencio de Santa-Ana y Álvarez-Ossorio, "Sorolla y el jardín de su casa madrileña," in *Jardines de España* (Fundación Mafre, Madrid, 2000), 71–89; and Pilar de Miguel Egea, "Los estudios de jardines de Sorolla," in *Sargent/Sorolla* (Museo Thyssen-Bornemisza, Madrid, 2007), 253–261.

67. "El pueblo sevillano tiene hoy en el Parque de María Luisa un jardín que hace palidecer a todos los Parques extranjeros." Quoted by Felipe Cortines Murube in "Un momento de Sevilla: La apertura del Parque," *Bética,* April 20, 1914, n.p.

68. Santa-Ana 2000, 84.

69. "Sus jardines en una época de evidente decadencia en la jardinería española, … corresponden a un clasicismo eternodel que ni puede ni quiere desprenderse y refleja en los jardines aquello que en este momento de su vida no se encuentra capaz de reflejar con su pintura." Carmen Añón, "Javier de Winthuysen," in *Javier de Winthuysen, jardinero* (Real Jardín Botánico de Madrid, 1986), 24.

70. "Los absurdos de las múltiples tendencias modernas con sus pretendidas originalidades ajenas a toda razón estética, pesaron sobre mí en el sentido de preocuparme si yo era un anticuado incapaz de evolucionar; y como yo no aceptaba la pintura sino como un *dilettanti* aquello no solamente no lo aceptaba sino que me repelía y me refugié en absoluto en mis jardines." Javier de Winthuysen, *Memorias de un señorito sevillano,* ed. Winthuysen Foundation Inc. (n.p., 2005), 192.

71. Javier de Winthuysen, "Influencias del estilo neo-sevillano," *La voz,* July 5, 1929.

72. Añón 1986, 24.

73. Winthuysen 2005. The term *señorito,* "son of a *señor*" (gentleman), or "rich kid," is used in a derogatory sense in Andalusia.

74. Sigfried Giedion, "L'architecture contemporaine en Espagne," *Cahiers d'art,* no. 3 (1931): 157–164, 158.

75. *Fernando García Mercadal* (Colegio Oficial de Arquitectos de Aragón, Saragossa, 1985).

76. Delfín Rodríguez, "Fernando García Mercadal: La arquitectura y el mar," in *Roma y la tradición de lo nuevo* (Academia de España, Rome, 2004), 132–143.

77. "La labor de Jardinería que algunos desarrollamos en el Levante Hispánico, y en las Baleares, tiene precisamente por objeto servir al arte del jardín latino. No se trata de alcanzar objetivos localistas, sino de cultivar fórmulas amplias y aplicables a toda una zona de clima y espíritu parecidos al nuestro." Nicolás María Rubió y Tudurí, *Del paraíso al jardín latino* (Barcelona, 1981), 149–150.

78. Nicolau Maria Rubió i Tudurí, *El jardín meridional* (Barcelona, 1934).

79. It is paradoxical that Javier de Winthuysen was a follower of Forestier, though there was no strong personal relationship between the two men, while Rubió was not a follower but nevertheless had been Forestier's student, having begun his practice collaborating with Forestier in Barcelona.

80. The authorship of the garden of Santa Clotilde has been disputed. At the time of the publication of Manuel Ribas i Piera and Miquel Vidal Pla's *Jardins de Catalunya* (Barcelona, 1991), I attributed the project to Rubió. In later years the wife of the owner, Odile Creus Roviralta, wrote newspaper articles claiming authorship for her husband with the help of the painter Domènec Carles. See "Jardín de Santa Clotilde," *ABC,* March 30, 1992, 16, and "La verdad sobre los jardines de Santa Clotilde," *La vanguardia,* March 21, 1992, 20. This authorship was also reflected in the period of the creation of the garden, when it was described as "[l]'èxit conjunt del seu creador artístic, el pintor Domènec Carles, i del seu propietari Raül Roviralta" (the joint achievement of its artistic creator, the painter Domènec Carles, and its owner[,] Raül Roviralta): "Una casa vora el mar: Santa Clotilde," *D'aci i d'alla,* no. 176 (1934): n.p. In the same year, however, Rubió i Tudurí claimed authorship in captioning the last illustration of his book *El jardín meridional* "proyecto N. Mª Rubio. Decoración D. Carles."

81. Juan Bassegoda Nonell, *Los jardines de Gaudí* (Barcelona, 2001).

82. Arturo Rigol's gardens await a detailed study. At the time of his death AC magazine published a complimentary article signed by the architects' collective GATEPAC, which was the editor of the journal: "Arturo Rigol, jardinero," *AC,* no. 16 (1935): 21–23.

83. See Rafael Moneo and Francisco Fernández, *El carmen: Rodríguez-Acosta* (Granada, 2001).

84. It is a Roman statue of Bacchus, but it was traditionally interpreted as Apollo.

85. Nichols 1924, 191–192; Byne and Byne 1924, 177–178; Gromord 1926, pls. 106–109; Villiers-Stuart 1929, 133–134.

86. Francisco Prieto Moreno, *Los jardines de Granada* (Madrid, 1952), 173.

87. "Es un jardín que no está en su ambiente…. Es lástima que teniendo tantos elementos tradicionales granadinos, para crear un jardín de suma belleza, se volviese su dueño hacia Italia, donde esta clase de jardines son muy corrientes." Teresa Ozores y Saavedra, marquesa de Casa Valdés, *Jardines de España* (Madrid, 1973), 50.

88. José Tito Rojo, "Leopoldo Torres Balbás, jardinero," *El fingidor* 21 (2004): 5–7.

89. See Carlos Vílchez Vílchez, *El palacio del Partal Alto en la Alhambra* (Granada, 2001), 146: "Pensamos que el jardín que traza Leopoldo Torres Balbás no responde a la idea del huerto-jardín hispano musulmán granadino que encontramos en el Generalife, sino al jardín de estilo francés impuesto a partir del siglo XVIII en todas las cortes europeas." (We think that the garden designed by Leopoldo Torres Balbás responds not to the idea of the Granadan Hispanic Muslim vegetable garden that we find in the Generalife, but to

the French-style garden imposed from the eighteenth century in all the European courts).

90. Sert, permanently disqualified, was exiled to the United States; Rubió i Tudurí, also permanently disqualified, was exiled to France; and García Mercadal was temporarily disqualified. See Juan Ignacio del Cueto, "Depuración político-social de arquitectos en la España de posguerra," *Bitácora*, no. 13 (2005): 24–27. Torres Balbás was dismissed as architect-conservator of the Alhambra and suffered three proceedings and "public censure" by the Colegio de Arquitectos de Madrid. See Alfonso Muñoz Cosme, *Vida y obra de Leopoldo Torres Balbás* (Seville, 2005).

ANITA BERRIZBEITIA AND KAREN M'CLOSKEY

Critical Practices in Modernism:
Origins in Nineteenth-Century American
Landscape Architecture

Modernism in landscape architecture has traditionally been associated with the invention of new spatial configurations that prioritize program and function over form and ecological criteria over abstract aesthetic expression. These shifts parallel those that occurred in other fields of art and design, such as the shift from figuration to abstraction in painting and sculpture, from narrative to tonal assemblages in music, and from compositions based on aesthetics of hierarchies, balance, and symmetry to those based on function, program, and technology in architecture. In this essay we explore a less known facet of modernism in landscape architecture: its vocation as a critical practice in the formative years of the profession. During the last decades of the nineteenth century new methods of work and new types of landscapes were invented to address social and environmental challenges wrought by rapidly industrializing and expanding urban environments. The critical is thus lodged less in the formal than in the methodological, and it had as its consequences the reshaping of practice and the creation of new categories of public landscapes as well as of the legal frameworks and institutions that would manage and protect them.

In the English language the predominant sense of the word *critical* is that of fault-finding.[1] *Critical*, *criticism*, and *critique* have roots in the Greek word *kritikos*, meaning judgment or discernment. Similarly in design fields, critical practices constitute some form of judgment that results in resistance to or rejection of the status quo. Resistance and rejection arise when established modes of practice no longer adequately address emerging environmental, social, economic, or political conditions. Critical practices explore and propose strategies that make manifest those resistances. More important, they critique—they find fault with—past practices with the intention of provoking change and, in the best cases, succeed in creating new standards of practice.

The term *critical practice* did not come into use until after its companion term *critical theory* emerged in the 1930s in the humanities, specifically with the Frankfurt School. Especially useful is Max Horkheimer's assertion that critical theory is explanatory, practical, and normative, all at the same time. That is, it must explain what is wrong with current modes of practice, identify applicable ways to change them, and provide practical goals for transformation and clear norms for evaluation. This first generation of critical theorists looked to create a comprehensive social theory, one that would bring together various spheres of knowledge including economics, history, sociology, and philosophy. This approach was a means to counteract the characteristics of capitalism's expansion, which evolved through specialization, rationalization, and standardization and had its roots in Enlightenment thought, though it would not reach full force until industrialization. Thus the social function of critical theory was to direct capitalism toward democratic ends.[2] Horkheimer's framework is especially useful for defining a critical landscape architecture in the United States during the country's rapid growth in the nineteenth century, when liberal capitalism enabled unregulated use of land and natural resources, cities did not have adequate provision for public open spaces, and policy was not in place to guide development.

How Do We Detect the Critical in a Project?

In contrast to traditional design theories, which form the knowledge base that guides and, to a certain extent, defines design practice, critical design theory and practice motivate a change in orientation, establishing differences from previous practices and generating new methods of work. The alliance between avant-gardism and criticality in art and architecture is well recognized.[3] Though landscape architecture has yet to be identified with the critical discourse that originated in art and architecture in the first decades of the twentieth century, recent literature describes an avant-garde in landscape in the early to mid-twentieth century, in which visual and formal ruptures and responses to technological advances are clearly visible.[4] Both the 1920s exposition gardens in France, which transferred artistic principles to landscape, and the work of Garrett Eckbo, Dan Kiley, and James Rose in the United States in the 1930s and 1940s, which transferred architectural principles to landscape, are cited as representative of modern landscape architecture.[5] Because these shifts were immediately recognizable as formal, material, and programmatic innovations, and some, like Gabriel Guévrékian's garden at the Villa de Noailles in Hyères, were linked to surrealist aesthetics, they have been associated with the avant-garde. Yet the broader definition of criticality (following Horkheimer, Peter Bürger, and others[6]) is that those formal, material, and programmatic ruptures are the result of ideological challenges to the institutional or political frameworks within which work is produced. In other words, changes in formal languages and techniques alone are not sufficient to define a critical landscape architecture; they must be accompanied by a widening of the sphere of influence of practice, the creation of new methods of work that later are folded into standards of practice, and new forms of social practice. Critical practices in landscape architecture have historically challenged modes of land tenure, land use, and resource utilization. The critical engages social and environmental variables through the working out of innovative techniques and material configurations.

Origins in American Landscape Architecture, 1850 – 1900

The cultural conditions that prompted the emergence of critical practices in the United States during the last three decades of the nineteenth century were laissez-faire capitalism, broadly institutionalized since colonial times; accelerated urbanization; and, as a result of these, an environmental crisis not unlike the one we face today. The population of the United States more than tripled during the second half of the nineteenth century. New York's population increased more than sixfold, while Boston's quadrupled.[7] In addition, westward expansion enabled by building railroads promoted land speculation and resource exploitation. In 1840 three thousand miles of railroad were built. This figure tripled by 1850; by 1900 the network of railroads in the United States had grown to almost two hundred thousand miles.[8] Between 1850 and 1900, according to one summary, "land settlement reached vast proportions" as the nation's farms increased from 1,449,000 to 5,737,000.[9]

The exhaustion of natural resources was a widely discussed topic by the turn of the twentieth century, as it is today. The prediction was that the nation's coal, oil, and forests would soon be depleted. Americans feared an increase in the price of energy from high-cost mining and lumbering and dependence on imports from abroad.[10] At the same time, the United States was rapidly increasing its production of energy to support the expansion of manufacturing. The production of coal almost doubled during the first decade of the twentieth century.[11] It was the world's leading producer of coal by

1905, with an output more than 50 percent greater than that of Great Britain, the second largest producer.

The probable consequence of such rapid growth had been comprehensively laid out in George Perkins Marsh's *Man and Nature; or, Physical Geography as Modified by Human Action,* published in 1864. This was the first text that specifically linked societal collapse to environmental degradation. More than one-third of the book is devoted to forests, in particular the effects of deforestation on flooding, soil erosion, and climate change. Marsh wrote that because private interests were not motivated to sustain forests, and laws that impinged on such interests were difficult to enforce, forests that were cut for fuel or timber should be taxed. He lamented that there was little respect for public property in the United States and that federal control of American forests was not feasible.[12] Marsh's descriptions of decimated forests were vividly reflected in maps produced in 1880 for the tenth US census. Although the United States had been mapped extensively during the nineteenth century by both the government and land speculators, the 1880 census stood out as the first comprehensive accounting of the country's natural resources. The increase in production of iron, steel, coal, copper, and cotton was especially rapid in the decades following the Civil War, and the need for data to guide legislation in a country on the cusp of industrialization was urgent. The census included physiogeographical descriptions and reports on agriculture, mining, oil deposits and products, and waterpower as well as the first report on the forests of the nation, directed by Charles Sprague Sargent, then director of the Arnold Arboretum of Harvard University. For his census report, Sargent mapped the forests at many scales, producing national, state, and regional maps that gave a clear picture not only of the extent of the forests, the types of species, and their spatial patterning, but also of their rate of disappearance (figs. 1 and 2).

The profession of landscape architecture, as distinct from landscape gardening, arose in the United States as a reaction against these conditions. The extraordinary accomplishments of several of its founders—H. W. S. Cleveland (1814–1900), Frederick Law Olmsted Sr. (1822–1903), Charles Eliot (1859–1897), and Warren Manning (1860–1938)—are extensively documented and often discussed in relationship to aspects of American culture such as the love of wilderness, the transcendentalism of Emerson and Thoreau, and romanticism.[13] Here, however, we focus on a fundamentally critical aspect of their work: their challenge to, and ultimately successful intervention in, federal land policies that formed the basis of the Public Land Survey System of the United States. For Cleveland, Olmsted, Eliot, and Manning, growth per se was not the problem. Rather, it was the wholesale privatization of property, by both corporations and individuals, which led to the exploitation of resources and lack of provision for future generations. Thus two types of critical practices emerged in the United States at this time: those that rejected or resisted colonial and postindependence modes of land tenure, and those that explored the intersection of capitalist and environmental values, that is, the conjoining of seemingly opposite goals of maximization of profit and conservation or preservation of resources.

Projects That Rejected or Resisted Colonial and Postindependence Modes of Land Tenure

The privatization of lands in the American territory had been ongoing since the beginning of colonization (through royal charters given by the British Crown), as had the extraction of profits from their exploitation through agriculture, mining, harnessing of hydrological power, and lumbering. The basic premise of the national land system created in the years immediately following independence extended this mode of land tenure through the creation of the public domain. The term *public domain* describes lands that were owned by

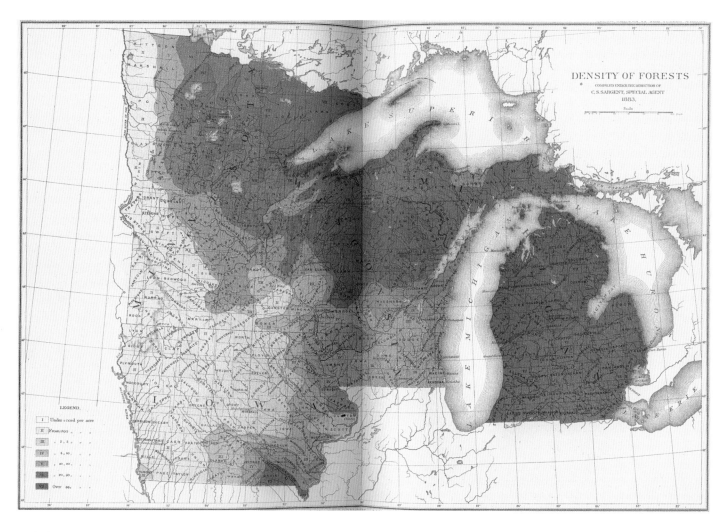

DENSITY OF FORESTS
COMPILED UNDER THE DIRECTION OF
C. S. SARGENT, SPECIAL AGENT
1883.

LEGEND.
I   Under 1 cord per acre
II   From 1 to 2   "
III " 2, 5 "   "
IV   " 5, 10 "   "
V   " 10, 20 "   "
VI   " 20, 50 "   "
VII Over 50 "   "

1. Charles Sprague Sargent, *Map of the United States Showing the Relative Average Density of Existing Forests*, depicting decrease in the density of the forest in the Great Lakes Region from more than fifty cords per acre to under one cord per acre

Tenth US Census, Report on the Forests of North America (Exclusive of Mexico) (*Washington, DC, 1883*)

the federal government and made available to individuals or corporations for purchase as private property.[14] The first public domain comprised those territories west of the Appalachians, east of the Mississippi, and north of the Ohio River that had been claimed by seven of the original colonies through grants given by the British Crown but, at the time of the formation of the union, had to be turned over to the nation as land held by all. As the United States acquired more lands through direct purchase or treaty, the national territory expanded to the west, eventually reaching 1.8 billion acres. The method for measuring and describing lands that were to be transferred through grants, settlements, or sales to individual ownership became institutionalized through the Land Ordinance of 1785, which created an unprecedented process of system-

atically gridding the entire territory *before* it was settled.

Financially the public domain was a resource for compensating those who had fought in the Revolutionary War, paying national and foreign creditors that had funded the war, and raising cash. Ideologically, and especially for Thomas Jefferson, the ordinance represented an equitable way of distributing land to all Americans, who would make their living by cultivating it. The grid and the process of subdivision into sections were the epitome of Enlightenment rationality—universalizing, singular, objective—and represented the aspirations of the fledgling republic. The grid connoted equality, personal liberty, individualism, self-reliance. While the intent of the ordinance grid was to assure equity through precise

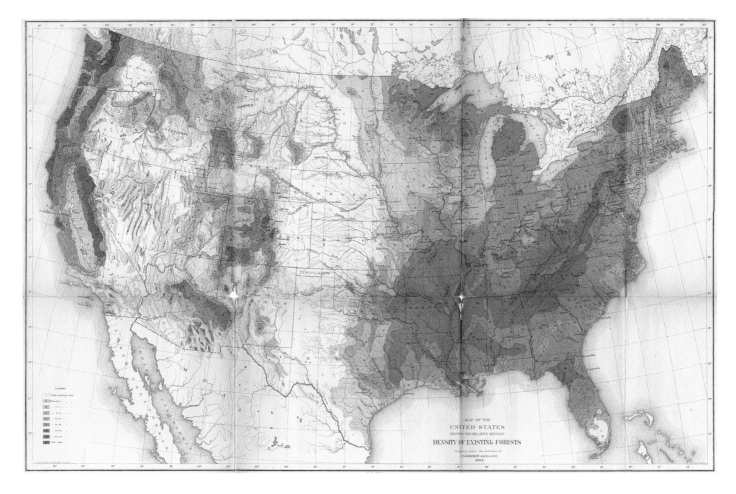

2. Charles Sprague Sargent, *Map of the United States Showing the Relative Average Density of Existing Forests*, depicting decrease in the density of the forest for the entire United States from more than two hundred cords per acre to under one cord per acre

Tenth US Census, Report on the Forests of North America (Exclusive of Mexico) *(Washington, DC, 1883)*

measure, it also involved laissez-faire government policies that offered opportunity unhindered by federal restrictions. All lands, regardless of their natural features or what they contained in mineral or forest resources, were available for purchase by anyone, for any purpose. Even the waterways came under private ownership, and no lands were set aside for public infrastructure. The result was that the ordinance promoted monopolies and land speculation but did not anticipate necessary variations in use as it did not register environmental differences among regions of the United States, some of which were simply not suitable for agriculture.

The United States had in effect devised a national land system that had only one category of ownership: private. The enormous significance of the protection of the Yosemite Valley in 1864 and of Yellowstone in 1872 is that for the first time enlightened citizens concerned about the indiscriminate exploitation of resources succeeded in withdrawing lands from the public domain and preserving them in perpetuity from development. These constitute the first instances of a critical landscape practice in the United States. From this point onward, the national land system began to expand its categories, primarily as a result of the action of citizens. The preservation and conservation of these remote lands entailed convincing Congress to create the legislation and pass the acts, a lengthy and controversial process that nevertheless eventually succeeded in the introduction and creation of laws and government organizations to protect lands from private economic interests. Today the US national land system represents a broad range of categories, including parks, forests, national wildlife refuges, the wilderness preservation system, the wild and scenic river system, and others.[15]

H. W. S. Cleveland and the Management of Westward Expansion

At an urban scale, the text that explicitly demonstrates landscape architecture's ability to challenge and control the effects of the Land Ordinance of 1785 is *Landscape Architecture as Applied to the Wants of the West*, by H. W. S. Cleveland, published in 1873.[16] This is arguably the first American manifesto on landscape architecture, and it is distinct from those related to the avant-garde work of later modernists in that it did not concern itself with questions of design per se.[17] Rather, Cleveland undertook the task of explaining the profession for a general audience unaware of the extent and pace of land-use transformation. He was fundamentally concerned with the relationship between settlement and resource management. He argued for two necessities: making provisions for westward growth (expansion) through forest management and planning of towns based on natural features rather than the ordinance grid, and providing for the increasing densification of urban populations through an interconnected system of parks. In both cases, he positioned landscape, and not the grid, as the framework to direct development while simultaneously creating long-term economic and social advantages. In other words, the inherent structure of the landscape would provide the most resilient system through which to direct profitable development. He wrote:

We have our choice of sites in a virgin region, comprising every variety of soil, climate, and topographic character ... and the question is certainly worthy of consideration, whether a judiciously prepared design, adapted to the natural features of a situation ... might not in itself constitute a very powerful attraction.[18]

Cleveland was less concerned with disrupting formal and aesthetic protocols than he was focused on the nature of public space via accessibility and connectivity. He argued for creating public areas along rivers and ravines to bring air into the city, coupled with parks and broad avenues to make a system acces-sible to all residents.[19] Using Central Park in New York as an example, he cited the limitations of single large parks, which are not easily accessible to those who lack the means or the time to get to them.[20] The publication of *Landscape Architecture as Applied to the Wants of the West* followed closely on Cleveland's first lecture regarding what would become his most important commissioned work: the Minneapolis Park System. In two addresses to the Chamber of Commerce in St. Paul (1872 and 1885) and one to the Minneapolis Parks Commission (1888), Cleveland argued for preserving land because he saw the growth of the two cities into one larger conglomeration as inevitable. But as a challenge to the haphazard development that had already occurred, he did not distinguish among urban, suburban, and rural settlements, but rather called for an approach to development that would take advantage of the natural features of any given site, irrespective of location.[21] His book is a plea for various levels of government to preserve lands both for public use and as a resource for future use. As he stated, these matters would not regulate themselves but would need to be established through government action and policy.[22] His purpose was to demonstrate as a landscape architect how conservation would project on the land and the effects it would have on a nascent public realm (fig. 3).

Charles Eliot and the Metropolitan Park System, Boston

When Charles Eliot and Sylvester Baxter began to elicit public and private support for the creation of a system of parks around Boston in 1890–1891, others already existed: in Boston (the so-called Emerald Necklace, designed by Frederick Law Olmsted, 1878–1881), Buffalo (also by Olmsted, begun in 1868), Minneapolis (H. W. S. Cleveland, 1883), London, and Paris, among others.[23] However, the scale of the park system Eliot and Baxter proposed, encircling the city at a ten-mile radius from the center, entailed the creation of new institutions and new

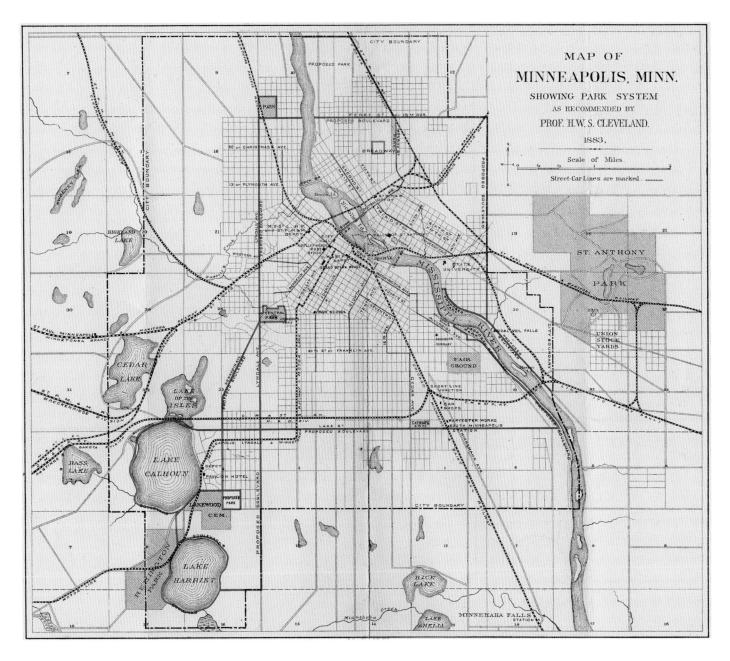

3. H. W. S. Cleveland, plan for the Minneapolis Park System showing the juxtaposition of the ordinance grid against his proposed landscape structure

H. W. S. Cleveland, Suggestions for a System of Parks and Parkways *(Minneapolis, 1883)*

methods of work. Criticality lies not so much in the proposal itself as in its execution.

In the late nineteenth century, most if not all of the lands that formed the original thirteen colonies, especially those in and around cities and towns, were privately owned and developed or on the verge of development. Setting aside land in private hands in and around urban areas was a totally different problem from withdrawing lands in remote places not yet occupied. According to Eliot, those landscapes of

uncommon beauty "characteristic of the primitive wilderness of New England" were already fragments scattered around Boston. In addition, lands in the park system Eliot envisioned would extend across counties and towns, each with its own regulations and sets of political interests. At that time there were twenty-seven separate political units surrounding Boston's historic center, all of which needed to be brought to a consensus, and the difficulties of reconciling conflicting interests and desires were Eliot's biggest challenge.[24] Eliot had to invent the institutions, both public and private, that would support the formation and protection of the system in perpetuity. Recognizing the economic, ecological, and aesthetic importance of removing land from speculation, Eliot founded The Trustees of Public Reservations, a private, nonprofit corporation whose purpose was to create a regional land trust within the Commonwealth of Massachusetts to preserve sites of scenic and historic value. This scheme was based on the experience of similar institutions in the commonwealth, such as Boston's Museum of Fine Arts. Eliot reasoned that, just as the museum was under the care of a board of trustees who received works of art and funds as donations, a corporation under the tutelage of a board made up of citizens from various areas would be in charge of receiving land donations with money to support their maintenance. Because preservation has a financial impact on counties by sheltering from taxation lands placed under preservation status, the formation of the corporation had to be established by law. Eliot, after enlisting the support of the Appalachian Mountain Club and other institutions and citizens and collecting petition signatures from each county in the state, introduced a bill in the General Court of Massachusetts, which passed in May 1891.[25] The Trustees of Public Reservations began accepting land donations immediately after its founding, and at present, as The Trustees of Reservations, it manages twenty-five thousand acres of ecological and historical importance.[26] As secretary of the corporation, Eliot led a process that took inventory of existing public lands and of the laws that supported their acquisition and maintenance. This resulted in a petition to the General Court for an inquiry into the actions necessary to protect scenery for public enjoyment. The outcome was the provisional creation of the Metropolitan Park Commission in June 1892. During that fall, Baxter, as secretary of the Board of Boston Parks Commissioners, and Eliot, as landscape architect of the board, produced their full reports for the General Court.[27] The combined report included a recommendation that the state pass a bill establishing the Metropolitan Park Commission to oversee the creation of the country's first regional park system.[28] The model was the Metropolitan Drainage Commission, a state agency with the power to plan and build a sewer system that, like Eliot's park system, also spanned many political units. The commission had the power to acquire the lands necessary to build a continuous system and to manage it independently of the political will of the municipalities through which it passed. The Metropolitan Park Commission was finally approved by the governor of Massachusetts in 1898. On the basis of his extensive field work, Eliot identified areas within a ten-mile radius of Boston that the commission should acquire through private donations or purchases. Thus even before the sites were chosen, Eliot and Baxter engaged a legislative framework to create the land-use category that would underwrite their protection.

Eliot had to imagine, conceptualize, disseminate, and implement his plan using techniques of representation that were new in the practice of landscape architecture. To provide a better structure for development, he used cartographic techniques to determine which lands should form the system, and he used the same techniques to convey his intentions to the public. To break with established norms of practice, a critical practice must, by necessity, assume alternative frameworks of conceptualization. In this case, Eliot broke from an aesthetic framework as a basis for decision making and instead used what today we call the overlay method to guide his process. His 1893 plan for the Metropolitan Park System (see fig. 4) was originally produced by drawing different types of information on separate sheets of tracing cloth and then layering them to make a composite map by sun printing, which could then be reproduced by photolithography. One layer mapped topography; a second, hydrological systems; and a third, vegetation. In his biography of his son, Charles W. Eliot describes the process:

Gray sun prints obtained from the three sheets superimposed in the printing frame, when mounted on cloth, served very well for all purposes of study. Photolithographed in three colors, namely black, blue, and brown, the same sheets will serve as guide maps for the use of the public and the illustration of reports.[29]

The rationale for site selection was elegant in its logic and its economy. Describing the city as a territory that lay between a ring of hills to the west and the sea to the east, in his contribution to the report to the legislature Eliot established the following goals: first, protect the three rivers that were the main drainage ways of the metropolitan area (the Charles, the Neponset, and the Mystic) to provide for flood control; second, protect the seashore to assure public accessibility; third, protect the tops of the highest hills for public accessibility and maintenance of view sheds; fourth, provide for even distribution of large reserves in a ringlike shape within ten miles of the center as the anchors that would guide the expansion of the city; fifth, and contrasting in scale, maintain a constellation of small municipal playgrounds and parks. Later on parkways and boulevards would be added for connectivity, forming the last layer of a complex system of extraordinary (to use a word from current design vocabulary) "performativity," in which landscape, from a regional to a neighborhood scale, served as the structuring element for future urban expansion.[30]

Although use of overlays for site selection is generally attributed to Ian McHarg, who disseminated the method in 1969 with the publication of *Design with Nature*, the Metropolitan Park System of 1893 appears to have been the first application of such a process, and it represented a radical break from previous approaches to design. How did Eliot make the conceptual leap from a plan-driven design methodology to a systemic notion of landscape, one in which the structure of the landscape is given not by

spaces, axes, or views but by geology, hydrology, and vegetation patterns? Further, how did he think of interpreting the landscape as a system of superimposed phenomena that have different material origins but are interrelated? It is difficult to ascertain with precision the origins of this method, but we can speculate on at least two disciplines that had been gaining visibility in Eliot's professional circle. Cartography and geology had developed rapidly and simultaneously in the United States in the decades after the Civil War. As mentioned earlier, the nation's lands had been extensively mapped during the nineteenth century by private developers and speculators, by the government, and also by small interest groups such as the Appalachian Mountain Club, a Boston-based outing group in which Eliot participated.

However, what seems important here are two advances in mapping technique made by the United States Geological Survey (USGS), founded in 1879, in the decade before Eliot began his work. The first was the introduction of the contour line to describe topography. Unlike hachures, used until then in topographical maps, contour lines afforded a precision that allowed landform patterns to be read as differentiated yet continuous surfaces, making more potently visible the relationship among topography, hydrology, and geological processes. The second was the introduction of color in USGS topographic maps and the Geologic Atlas of the United States. This entailed what was essentially an overlay method. A color was assigned to each type of information; for example, blue was used for hydrologic features, brown for contours, and black for trails, railroads, boundaries, and buildings. For each data set, a copper plate was engraved and the information transferred to a lithographic stone inked with the appropriate color. Each map was the result of printing the sheet of paper from as many stones as there were colors in the map. In this case, each sheet of paper received impressions from three different lithographic stones. For the process to be accurate, each impression

4. Charles Eliot, *Map of the Metropolitan District of Boston Massachusetts Showing the Existing Public Reservations and Such New Open Spaces as Are Proposed by Charles Eliot Landscape Architect in his Report to the Metropolitan Park Commission,* January 2, 1893, depicting existing public open spaces in green and proposed open spaces in orange

Charles Eliot, *"Report of the Landscape Architect,"* Report of the Board of Metropolitan Park Commissioners *(General Court of Massachusetts, House 150) (Boston, 1893),* inset map

had to register exactly with all the others in the group.[31]

If the technique seems to have been informed by those of the USGS, the conceptual shift would have originated in Eliot's understanding of the geology of the Boston Basin as a series of layers that accumulated over time and determined the visible characteristics of the region. His geology classes at Harvard included field trips to places such as the Blue Hills, which later became one of

the reservations of the Boston Metropolitan Park System. There Eliot would have learned the practice of fieldwork for observation and data collection, a significant part of his methodology.

The mapping technique allowed Eliot to present a completely new reality to the public and the legislature, one no longer based on political boundaries or on land as real estate, which instead allowed him to focus on the landscape as structure, through

5. Charles Eliot, *Map of the Metropolitan District of Boston Showing the Public Reservations and Holdings of the Metropolitan Park Commission,* December 1, 1901, depicting metropolitan reservations and parkways in darker green with local parks and reservations in lighter green

Charles W. Eliot, Charles Eliot, Landscape Architect *(Boston and New York, 1903)*

the interrelatedness of its parts and the continuity of its systems (figs. 4 and 5). In opposition to the political system, which fragmented the landscape, the park system unified it. The significance of data gathering and analysis for the burgeoning field of landscape architecture was that it provided new criteria and methods for selecting land that were independent of its value as capital. In addition, the technique legitimized planning recommendations by making the intent and the decision-making process legible to the public.

In a later endeavor, using the same overlay technique as Eliot, Warren H. Manning (1860–1938) went on to use spatial analysis at an unprecedented scale and level of complexity. In 1915–1916, while serving on the National Parks Committee of the Department of the Interior, Manning undertook his National Plan, a mapping project of the entire United States.[32]

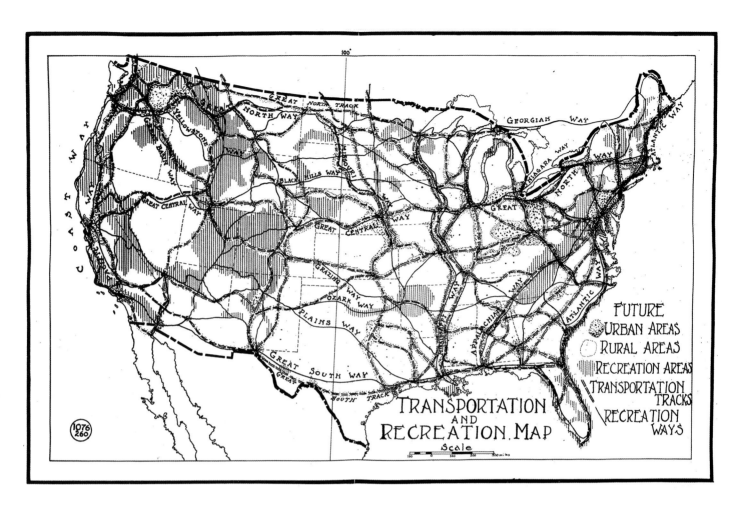

FUTURE
URBAN AREAS
RURAL AREAS
RECREATION AREAS
TRANSPORTATION TRACKS
RECREATION WAYS

TRANSPORTATION
AND
RECREATION. MAP
Scale

6. Warren H. Manning, *Transportation and Recreation Map*, showing a connected system of roadways and parkways from Manning's National Plan, c. 1915–1916

Image courtesy of the Warren H. Manning Papers, Iowa State University Library, Special Collections Department, Map 191a

Without client or funding, he produced more than one hundred maps documenting resources for exploitation—such as forest cover, arable soil, and oil deposits—coupled with suggestions for commercial and recreational corridors. He also proposed a national reservation system, which would include scenic and recreational lands combined with reservations for forest reserves and wildlife, all connected by national "recreation ways" (fig. 6). His goal was to create what we would today call a database at a national scale, to assure the most appropriate use of land in anticipation of future needs and prevent wasteful resource consumption.

Though aesthetics and scenery were important to Manning and Eliot, the aspect of their planning that became replicable and standardized was not a design style but a process of working that accounted

for both the need for development and the need for conservation. Their approach was fundamentally modern in that it was economically and socially progressive, not nostalgic, because it sought to create the structure for long-term growth of a region while providing for the preservation of land that they believed had greater social and ecological than direct exchange value. Both The Trustees of Public Reservations and the Metropolitan Park Commission were the first entities of their kind, and their creation resulted in new forms of public land ownership and management at the regional level. Frederick Law Olmsted Sr., Cleveland, and Eliot were instrumental in introducing and implementing the concept of a new category of land use to counter the effects of revenue-dominated land policy. Working to withdraw lands from the public domain or from private ownership in key areas, in the face of long-established national land policies, constituted a critical practice. The type of modern public landscape they advocated is an American invention, one that was subsequently adopted by countries throughout the world and continued to spread in the United States. According to a recent study, "fully one-third of the U.S. land base is owned by all citizens and managed in trust for the American people."[33]

Projects That Mediated between Maximization of Profit and Preservation of Nature

Cleveland's arguments were always framed in economic terms: how to balance immediate with long-term profit. A frequent contributor to A. J. Downing's *Horticulturalist* magazine and Charles Sprague Sargent's *Garden and Forest*, Cleveland also wrote two long essays on forest management. The last third of *Landscape Architecture as Applied to the Wants of the West* is an essay titled "Forest Planting on the Great Plains." He viewed forest planting as necessary for habitation, to provide a continuous, managed supply of wood for railroads and settlers and to increase the viability of agriculture by protecting crops from wind.[34] His essay was intended for a broad audience, and he compiled many sources that supported his argument for forest cultivation and management, including agricultural associations and rail companies. He also cited Marsh's *Man and Nature* regarding desertification. Though Cleveland was skeptical about the cause-and-effect relationship between forests and rainfall, he argued that, in their immediate vicinity, forests indisputably retain humidity.[35]

In addition to advocating for forests to control local climate and protect crops, Cleveland was also concerned about deforestation. Projecting the needs of the rapidly expanding railroad system, he calculated the amount of timber needed just to supply railroad ties—a not insignificant amount of lumber given the extent of the network—and argued for planting man-

aged forests systematically alongside the rail lines. He recommended that forests be planted as groves, not in continuous lines, and on the summits and north sides of slopes, leaving the southern exposure for cultivation.[36] The Kansas Pacific Railway had successfully tried experimental nurseries to demonstrate that trees could grow on plains without irrigation, but Cleveland noted its lack of commitment to follow through with forest planting even after these efforts proved viable.[37]

In 1882 Cleveland wrote *The Culture and Management of Our Native Forests for Development as Timber or Ornamental Wood*. In this work also, he pointed to the problem of privatization of land that had led to destruction of forests. Once again, while he accepted privatization as necessary, he proposed a way for cities and states to direct private land use more fruitfully. Echoing Marsh, Cleveland noted:

Much has been said, it is true, about the preservation of those [forests] that remain; but the words seem meaningless, in view of the fact that private property is beyond the control of the Government, and Congress declines even to grant means to prevent the destruction of that which still pertains to the public domain.[38]

Though he stated that it was important to plant new forests, he acknowledged the difficulty of persuading individuals to invest in them and maintain them. He concluded that management of existing forest on private lands was necessary, but that there was no demand for such oversight because no one was aware that it was possible or necessary. He wrote that demand must be created by demonstration so that individuals (that is, farmers) would begin to manage their woodlots for production. He further argued that the city or state must, through legislation, cordon off existing forest and develop the land in one of three ways: leave it in its unimproved condition, maintain it as an open area with specimens, or develop it as managed forest to enable clear comparison of the results of different management

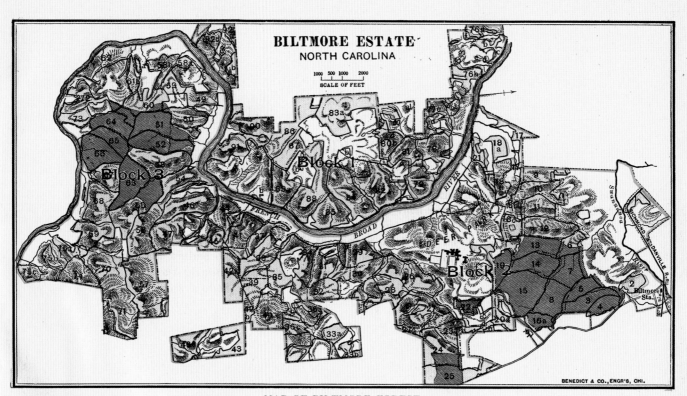

MAP OF BILTMORE FOREST.

Blocks Bounded by Red Lines; Compartments Numbered from 1 to 92; Forest Lands, Green; Improvement Cuttings, Dark Green.

7. Map of Biltmore Forest

Gifford Pinchot, Biltmore Forest, the Property of Mr. George W. Vanderbilt: An Account of Its Treatment, and the Results of the First Year's Work (Chicago, 1893)

Frances Loeb Library, Harvard Graduate School of Design

regimes. This "illustrative forest" should be within the city so as to be accessible to as many people as possible.[39] Though Cleveland was not able to demonstrate his theory, it became a reality a decade later when Olmsted and Gifford Pinchot began their experimental forest at Biltmore.

Frederick Law Olmsted and Experimental Forestry at Biltmore

Olmsted and Pinchot's Biltmore forest, begun in 1888 near Asheville, North Carolina, for George Washington Vanderbilt, was to be a major component of the revitalization of thousands of acres on the Biltmore estate (fig. 7).[40] As was common practice, before Vanderbilt purchased the property the land had been farmed until the soil could no longer support agriculture, and was then abandoned.

To break with still prevalent colonial notions of the landscape as a site for exploitation, the seven-thousand-acre timberland was constructed using techniques of forestry developed in Germany and France, coupled with economic strategies commonly used by American merchants and financiers for the accumulation and reproduction of wealth. The forest management program, geared to produce a sustained yield of different-sized lumber, was combined with an economic program to secure profit and the most efficient use of financial resources. Especially important were the gradual acquisition of land around the estate, eventually totaling more than one hundred thousand acres, and the conceptualization of the forest as a work of infrastructure for the distribution of its goods. To support his forest operations, Vanderbilt built a public road from Asheville to Biltmore, 18 miles of additional roads, two bridges, several dams along the creeks to deliver logs, 150 miles of forest roads that are still in use today by logging contractors, and a village complete with housing, schools, and churches.

The financial profitability of the land, Vanderbilt's main interest in the project, was also in alignment with Olmsted and Pinchot's agendas, although not for the same reasons. For both Pinchot and Olmsted, the Biltmore forest was first and foremost an opportunity to demonstrate to the country that it was possible to cut trees for lumber and retain the physical integrity of the forest—a radical idea at the turn of the century. Olmsted was keenly aware of the strategic potential of this work: "This is to be a private work of very rare public interest in many ways. Of much greater public interest—utility, industry, political, educational, and otherwise, very possibly, than we can define to ourselves."[41] Still, the value of the project had to be demonstrated and, to succeed, it had to be verified in terms of profit. Pinchot's mentor, German forester Sir Dietrich Brandis, had advised him that the only way forestry could be initiated in America was by demonstrating its uses to the public at large within the context of a private estate.[42] Part of Pinchot's contract was that Vanderbilt, in addition to paying him a salary of twenty-five hundred dollars per year, would finance an additional two thousand dollars for a timber exhibit at the World's Columbian Exposition in Chicago in 1893. For this occasion Pinchot distributed three thousand copies of his manual *Biltmore Forest: An Account of Its Treatment, and the Results of the First Year's Work.* The manual is an exhaustive account of the work involved in establishing a productive program for a forest, from the analysis of site conditions to the compartmentalizing of the site into sections to setting up a card catalog of details; techniques of planting, managing, and planning; staffing; the working plan and production program; lists of expenses and receipts; methods of quantification; and division of labor for every aspect of lumber production. The manual also included photographic documentation of the different types of forestry operations at Biltmore. Because the intention was that the forest be financially self-sustaining, close attention was given to the costs involved in all aspects of its operations; this intention guided all decision making.

The experimental nature of Pinchot's work at Biltmore is well documented, both by him and his successor at Biltmore, German forester Carl Alwin Schenck.[43] According to Schenck, the infantile maladies of American forestry were due to a widespread public misconception, which did not exist in Europe, that differentiated between forestry and lumbering. Pinchot's task was largely that of calibrating the two in order to forge a new practice of forestry, one specifically suited to American culture. The challenge was how to apply a tradition of forestry that had developed in Europe as a revenue-generating measure for the state, where even the smallest branch, in Pinchot's words, "down to the size of a pencil," had the potential to produce revenue, to conditions in the United States, where there was no perceived need for such a tax.[44] Furthermore, although government timber could be given away or sold with the land, it was illegal to sell it apart from the land.[45] This restriction eliminated any incentive for landowners to conserve the resource for profit. In addition, general opinion held that timber was inexhaustible, and it was often given away.[46] Olmsted and Pinchot had to recast forestry as an issue of habitation on the land, not of quantification for taxation. Their challenge was how to convey that the forest yielded its crop of lumber, firewood, and other products, as well as a series of equally important by-products, such as erosion control, climate control, and regulation of stream flow.

Eventually the techniques developed at Biltmore for producing a profitable forest, one that could be harvested without destroying it, demonstrated a strategy for using land to address national issues of resource conservation. As with Eliot and the Boston park system, it was in the implementation of the project that the critical showed itself most precisely. Furthermore, the experience at Biltmore produced knowledge that could be applied elsewhere. The Biltmore Forest School, the first in the country, graduated more than three hundred foresters before it closed in 1913. The success of its management practices unleashed numerous efforts to regulate consumption of natural resources in the country. Pinchot himself, after leaving Biltmore in 1895, developed his practice as a consulting forester and began the Yale School of Forestry. Most important, he initiated a massive campaign to change public opinion toward adopting a more balanced use of natural resources. He was appointed chief forester for Theodore Roosevelt's administration and in 1905 founded the US Forest Service.[47]

Conclusion

Critical practices do not simply resist; they resist through concrete action by proposing alternative models of practice that yield new methodologies and results. Olmsted and Pinchot's Biltmore Forest, Cleveland's writings and his Minneapolis Park System, and Eliot's Boston Metropolitan Park System were explanatory, practical, and normative. We know from the various records and diaries left by these landscape architects that all of these projects dealt with challenging, real-world conditions. They expressed what was wrong with prevalent modes of land ownership that fostered the wasteful consumption of resources, constituted alternatives, and demonstrated possibilities for implementation and norms for evaluation, satisfying the goals of both capitalism and environmentalism. They did not recoil from the realities of capitalism; on the contrary, these designers used the same arguments (financial value, profit, and economics) and the same techniques of representation (the mapping of resources that enabled the efficiencies called for under capitalism) as did those who were instrumental to the rise of America's economic power. And while most of the billable work in their offices at this time came from project-scale, traditional design (such as gardens, estates, and parks), they were simultaneously leading a national conversation on issues of resource utilization and conservation. Theirs was not an abstract, utopian alternative to capitalism, but one that accepted its values and worked within its frameworks. Critically calibrating the free-market, wasteful capitalism of postindependence America to the new, more cautious liberalism of the late nineteenth century, the work of Cleveland, Eliot, Olmsted, and Pinchot provided a new form of practice that reflected the evolution of American democracy from individualism to collectivism.[48]

To conclude, we can say that a modern work of landscape architecture is lodged in the congruence of the physical and the worldly. The physical comprises the biological and ecological requisites of the materials of nature as well as the performative characteristics that the material acquires once it has been reconfigured into designed landscapes. The worldly comprises institutions, such as the law, and economic systems, such as capitalism, that give structure to the world as we know it. The work arises out of a critical position that is activated in specific ways to provoke, define, and structure change within the bounds imposed by the material and the institutional. Because it reflects and acts upon the institutional, the critical is by necessity historically determined: that which was critical in late nineteenth-century America is not necessarily critical in mid-twentieth-century or early twenty-first-century America. The critical shifts its grounds for action as well as its methods of operation. It is experimental and new, yet it is grounded in the cultural and political realities of its time; it uses new technologies and techniques that originate in other fields; it results in projects that have great public utility; it invents and establishes new standards of practice; and it is ideological in the ways in which it creates bridges between the physical and the worldly. Modern landscape architecture began as a critical practice that questioned the methods and boundaries of landscape design, and in doing so it established new terms of engagement with rapidly industrializing and urbanizing environments.

1. Raymond Williams, *Keywords* (New York, 1983 [1976]), 85.

2. Paraphrased from *Stanford Encyclopedia of Philosophy*, s.v. "Critical Theory," accessed May 29, 2008, http://plato.stanford.edu/entries/critical-theory/.

3. For avant-gardism and criticality in art, see Peter Bürger, *Theory of the Avant-Garde* (Minneapolis, 1999 [1984]); for architecture see K. Michael Hays, "Critical Architecture: Between Culture and Form," *Perspecta* 21 (1984): 14–29, and Robert E. Somol, ed., *Autonomy and Ideology: Positioning an Avant-Garde in America* (New York, 1997).

4. See Patrick M. Condon and Lance Neckar, eds., "The Avant-Garde and Landscape: Can They Be Reconciled?" special issue, *Landscape Journal* 10, no. 1 (spring 1991): vii–viii.

5. See in particular James C. Rose, "Freedom in the Garden" and "Plants Dictate Garden Forms," both published in *Pencil Points* in 1938, and "Articulate Form in Landscape Design," published in *Pencil Points* in 1939. These essays are reprinted in *Modern Landscape Architecture: A Critical Review*, ed. Marc Treib (Cambridge, MA, 1993), 68–75.

6. See notes 2 and 3.

7. In 1850 the US population was 23,191,876, New York City's was 515,547, and Boston's was 136,881. By 1900 the US population was 76,212,168, New York City's was 3,437,202, and Boston's was 560,892. US Bureau of the Census, "Population of the 100 Largest Urban Places: 1900," June 15, 1998, accessed February 6, 2009, http://www.census.gov/population/.

8. It peaked in 1916 at 254,000 miles (as compared to today's interstate highway system of 50,000 miles). The federal government discontinued its Railroad Land Grant policy in 1871; however, between 1850 and 1870, it had ceded over 129 million acres (7 percent of the continental United States) to eighty railroad companies. *Land and Freedom*, "Railroad Land Grants," accessed March 13, 2009, http://www.landandfreedom.org/ushistory/us13.htm.

9. Vernon Carstensen, ed., *The Public Lands: Studies in the History of the Public Domain* (Madison, WI, 1963), xvi.

10. Paul W. Gates, *The Jeffersonian Dream: Studies in the History of American Land Policy and Development*, ed. Allan G. Bogue and Margaret Beattie Bogue (Albuquerque, 1996), 15.

11. Emory R. Johnson et al., *History of Domestic and Foreign Commerce of the United States* (Washington, DC, 1922), 316.

12. George Perkins Marsh, *Man and Nature; or, Physical Geography as Modified by Human Action* (New York, 1864). "Few of the new provinces which the last three centuries have brought under the control of the European race, would tolerate any interference by the law-making power with what they regard as the most sacred of civil rights—the right, namely, of every man to do what he will with his own" (232–233). Even in France "law has been found impotent to prevent the destruction, or wasteful economy, of private forests." His footnote cites others who "agree that the preservation of the forests in France is practicable only by their transfer to the state, which alone can protect them.... It is much to be feared that even this measure would be inadequate to save the forests of the American Union. There is little respect for public property in America, and the Federal Government, certainly, would not be the proper agent of the nation for this purpose" (233).

13. These seminal figures were pioneers on the topic of urban expansion, as evident in projects such as Boston's Emerald Necklace, Buffalo's park system, and the Minneapolis Park System. H. W. S. Cleveland (1814–1900) was cofounder of the Boston-based landscape architecture firm Cleveland and Copeland, established in 1854 and in practice until the Civil War, before which time he worked as a scientific farmer on land he had purchased in New Jersey. Cleveland worked briefly with Olmsted and Calvert Vaux on Prospect Park in Brooklyn before re-forming his own practice in Chicago in 1869. His time spent on a coffee plantation in Cuba in the 1820s, his subsequent education as a civil engineer, employment as a surveyor for railroads, and later work on his farm contributed to his knowledge of landscape management and concern about deforestation and improper land use with westward expansion. Cleveland designed a wide range of projects—residences, cemeteries, subdivisions, and parks—though the Minneapolis Park System is considered his most significant achievement. Frederick Law Olmsted Sr. (1822–1903) had an exceptionally diverse background. His work as a journalist, which involved extensive travels across the United States, Europe, and China, along with earlier studies that included scientific farming, surveying, and engineering, provided the basis for his designation of the profession of landscape architecture. In addition to carrying out hundreds of design projects, he was also part of the burgeoning conservation movement and was instrumental in the founding of the first national parks. Charles Eliot (1859–1897) earned his undergraduate degree from Harvard in 1882. He became an apprentice in Frederick Law Olmsted Sr.'s firm in 1883 prior to opening his own office in 1886. In 1893, Eliot partnered with Olmsted Sr. and his stepson, John Charles Olmsted (1852–1920), forming the firm Olmsted, Olmsted and Eliot, which remained in practice until Eliot's death. Warren H. Manning (1860–1938) worked for Olmsted Sr. from 1888 to 1896, initially as a horticulturist because of his extensive knowledge of plants, gained while working at his father's nursery in Massachusetts. While employed by Olmsted, he worked on the Biltmore Estate and the World's Columbian Exposition in Chicago. Manning opened his own office in Boston in 1896 and was a founding member of the American Society of Landscape Architects. Throughout his career he worked on projects ranging from estates and subdivisions to campus plans to parks systems. His approach to planning was driven by a resource-based methodology, as evidenced in his most ambitious work: the National Plan (1912–1913).

14. The history of the public domain is extensive. For this essay useful resources were Carstensen 1963; Thomas Donaldson, *The Public Domain: Its History* (Washington, DC, 1884); Roy M. Robbins, *Our Landed Heritage: The Public Domain, 1776–1936*

(Lincoln, NB, 1942); Vernon Carstensen, "Patterns on the American Land," *Land and Liberty in American Society: The Land Ordinance of 1785 and the Northwest Ordinance of 1787,* special issue of *Publius* 18, no. 4 (autumn, 1988): 31–39; and Gates 1996.

15. See the following websites: for the National Park Service: http://www.nps.gov/index.htm; the US Forest Service: http://www.fs.fed.us; the National Wildlife Refuge System: http://www.fws.gov/refuges; the National Wilderness Preservation System: http://www.wilderness.net/index.cfm?fuse=NWPS&sec=fastfacts; and National Wild and Scenic Rivers System: http://www.rivers.gov, all accessed July 14, 2010.

16. H. W. S. Cleveland, *Landscape Architecture as Applied to the Wants of the West; with an Essay on Forest Planting on the Great Plains* (Chicago, 1873).

17. See note 5 as well as Garrett Eckbo, Daniel U. Kiley, and James C. Rose, "Landscape Design in the Urban Environment," "Landscape Design in the Rural Environment," and "Landscape Design in the Primeval Environment," published in 1939 and 1940 in *Pencil Points* and reprinted in Treib 1993, 78–91.

18. Cleveland 1873, 82–83.

19. Cleveland 1873, 63.

20. Cleveland 1873, 44–45.

21. "In making my examination and selection of lands I have endeavored so far as possible to remain in ignorance of ownerships, in order that my decisions might be governed solely by a regard to the public good." Cleveland 1883, 14.

22. Cleveland 1873, 80.

23. In conceiving of a park system at a metropolitan scale, Eliot collaborated with journalist Sylvester Baxter, who had been studying European precedents for park systems and municipal administration. See Sylvester Baxter, *Greater Boston: A Study for a Federalized Metropolis Comprising the City of Boston and Surrounding Cities and Towns* (Boston, 1891).

24. Baxter 1891, 10–11.

25. Charles W. Eliot, *Charles Eliot, Landscape Architect* (Boston and New York, 1903 [1902]), 325–335.

26. See http://www.the trustees.org.

27. Charles Francis Adams, Philip A. Chase, William B. De Las Casas, Sylvester Baxter, and Charles Eliot, *Report of the Board of Metropolitan Park Commissioners* (General Court of Massachusetts, House 150), January 1893; Cynthia Zaitzevsky, *Frederick Law Olmsted and the Boston Park System* (Cambridge, MA, 1982), 123.

28. The Metropolitan Park Commission was renamed the Metropolitan District Commission in 1919. It recently merged with the Department of Environmental Management to form the Department of Conservation and Recreation. Though it began as a regional system, it is now state operated.

29. Eliot 1903 [1902]), 496.

30. Charles Eliot 1893, 89–92.

31. Bailey Willis, "The Development of the Geologic Atlas of the United States," *Journal of the American Geographical Society of New York* 27, no. 4 (1895): 350–351.

32. Manning served on the National Parks Committee from 1915 to 1919. The National Parks Service Act was established in 1916. Manning's unpublished plan was more than nine hundred pages; a shortened version was published in 1923 in *Landscape Architecture Quarterly* (now *Landscape Architecture Magazine*), thereby reaching a large professional audience.

33. Michael P. Dombeck, Christopher A. Wood, and Jack E. Williams, *From Conquest to Conservation: Our Public Lands Legacy* (Washington, DC, 2003), xi.

34. "The first step toward the settlement of the country, therefore, should be the planting of tracts of forest wherever it is practicable along the line of railroad, or elsewhere." Cleveland 1873, 112.

35. Cleveland 1873, 104.

36. Cleveland 1873, 145.

37. Cleveland 1873, 131–132.

38. H. W. S. Cleveland, *The Culture and Management of Our Native Forests for Development as Timber or Ornamental Wood: An Essay Read by Invitation to a Committee of the Massachusetts Legislature, and to the National Forestry Congress at Cincinnati* (Springfield, IL, 1882), iv.

39. "Let any State or city select a tract of woodland at some easily accessible point, and put it under a proper course of management, as an experimental forest, and it would very soon excite an interest which could not fail to increase." Cleveland 1882, xvi.

40. Vanderbilt initially hired Olmsted to design a landscape of parklike scenery with open, pastoral meadows and groves. Finding the site unsuitable for such a use, Olmsted persuaded Vanderbilt to hire Gifford Pinchot (1865–1946), a formally trained forester, to oversee the planting and management of the forest.

41. Quoted in Charles Beveridge and Paul Rocheleau, *Frederick Law Olmsted: Designing the American Landscape,* ed. David Larkin (New York, 1995), 225.

42. Gifford Pinchot, *Breaking New Ground* (New York, 1947), 15.

43. Carl A. Schenck, *The Biltmore Story: Recollections of the Beginning of Forestry in the United States* (St. Paul, MN, 1955), 6.

44. Pinchot 1947, 13.

45. Pinchot 1947, 24.

46. Pinchot 1947, 24.

47. The Division of Forestry was started in 1886, but with Pinchot's appointment in 1905 the US Forest Service was placed within the Department of Agriculture. Pinchot had pushed for categorizing trees as crops because they are planted for the purpose of harvesting.

48. Gates 1996, 98.

SONIA BERJMAN

*Benito Javier Carrasco (1877–1958)
and the Redefinition of Landscape
Architecture in Argentina*

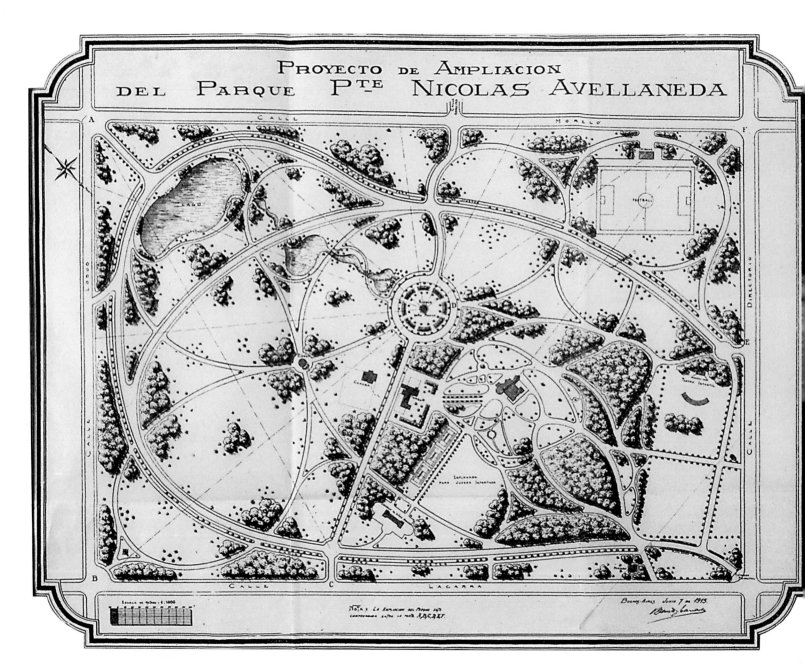

While the Western world was at war in 1914–1918, a revolution in landscape design was taking place in the public promenades of Buenos Aires, led by Benito Javier Carrasco, the city's director of promenades, whose new ideas of social and professional change are the subject of this essay. Argentineans, of whom a majority were European immigrants and their descendants, followed the news from the front. In the streets and cafés people argued passionately about the war reports. Nevertheless, daily life continued, and the inhabitants of Buenos Aires worked, studied, and amused themselves. Among the most popular venues for outdoor amusement and recreational activities were the parks and squares of the city.

South American public promenades derive from French sources, especially the Service des promenades et des plantations de Paris, founded in 1855 by Adolphe Alphand and continued by Édouard André, whose projects, publications, and even collaborators were readily accessible in the region from the mid-nineteenth century. Charles Thays (1849–1934), André's principal collaborator and one of the great French landscapers, created most of the public parks and private gardens in Argentina, as well as some in neighboring countries, over twenty-five years around the turn of the twentieth century.

In spite of Thays' prominence, his disciple, the Argentinean Benito Javier Carrasco, was poised to change some of the features for which his work was most famous. These included the use of a combination of picturesque English and geometrical French styles, which André had established in European public gardens, and water features, sculptures, buildings, lawns, and mixed groves.[1] Those parks were designed as attractive environments where people could enjoy varied scenery, appreciate nature, and understand landscape as art. In a social context, the activities pursued in such environments were supposed to emulate Parisian models, such as flower parades, cycling, strolling, conversation, and taking tea in elaborate teahouses.

Carrasco understood that the design of contemporary public space, as a basic component of urbanism, was both science and art, a conception that he promulgated in the region. During the first half of the twentieth century, Carrasco developed his skills in multiple ways: as a designer, builder, publisher, lecturer, professor, city planner, and public official. His actions showed his clear political ideology, influenced by the socialist ideal of a better life for the less privileged. His numerous writings (see the appendix) offer us an integrated landscape theory that represented a commitment to improving the physical environment for the citizenry.[2] In 1918 he wrote:

Just as sewers, safe water, and other improvements are needed for our comfort and hygiene, just as schools and libraries are needed for education and progress, so are public parks and promenades essential in crowded cities for the improvement of daily life, for better morals and health, and for progress insofar as that refers to the city's embellishment and ornamentation.[3]

Thus, the revolution in landscape design can be seen in innovations that responded to new city life and a growing and increasingly worldly urban population. Carrasco's park projects included state-of-the-art sports

Benito Javier Carrasco, Parque Avellaneda, Buenos Aires, enlarged 1915, plan
Archivo del Jardín Botánico de Buenos Aires

1. Benito Javier Carrasco in his early thirties
Caras y caretas, *February 22, 1908*

Plata), Carrasco graduated in 1900 as an *ingeniero agrónomo*. His thesis subject, under the direction of Charles Thays, was the phytography of trees in the municipal botanic garden of Buenos Aires.[6] In that first piece of academic writing, Carrasco emphasized that phytography (the botanical description of plants) was then rarely studied. Like Thays, he was a supporter of using indigenous plants together with imported ones. He wrote that his teacher "will not rest until he has gathered in our parks and promenades all the countless and beautiful Argentinean flora."[7] Carrasco himself continued this task throughout his life. The relationship between the two men lasted until the elder's death in 1934. Carrasco in turn directed the thesis of Carlos León Thays (Charles' son), on the preservation concerns of Thays the elder and the organization of Argentina's national parks.[8]

Upon his graduation in 1900 Carrasco went to work on the staff of the Dirección General de Paseos Publicos, the agency in charge of the public parks and gardens of Buenos Aires. At the beginning of 1908 he returned from a long journey abroad (including Europe and the United States) that was devoted to the study of his discipline. It was then that he published his first article, on the city of the future, which appeared in a popular magazine, *Caras y caretas*. This was the first demonstration of the interest in an updated approach to urbanism that would mark the rest of Carrasco's career. He argued that the city of the future should no longer be like the Buenos Aires of those days, centered only on a downtown; instead, attention should be directed to the open areas where new development was still possible (far from the city limits at the time). Carrasco considered these areas ideal for the construction of "the true city, the magnificent city of the near future, the city that can become the pride of America and of our people" ("la verdadera ciudad, la grandiosa ciudad del futuro no lejano, la ciudad que llenará de orgullo a América y a la raza").[9] Considering the city as a whole, Carrasco

facilities, children's cultural attractions, productive agricultural activities on state-owned lands, and a botanical museum and library, herbal collections, and seed nurseries. Carrasco also organized Argentina's first university chair in garden art and landscape, in 1918.

In spite of Carrasco's profound impact on the theory and practice of landscape design in Argentina, his name has been lost to history. This essay aims to recover his contribution to the evolution of Buenos Aires, a contribution that is still evident today.

Early Career

Carrasco was born and died in Buenos Aires (fig. 1).[4] It was precisely to his mother city that he dedicated his work in every area that might improve its urban qualities or make its parks and gardens more beautiful or amenable. He saw those parks and gardens both as an indispensable respite for the populace and as pleasure grounds that are necessary in such a large city.[5]

As a student at the former Facultad de Agronomía y Veterinaria of the Provincia de Buenos Aires (today Universidad de La

planned four large-scale parks spread across its width with a network of avenues following the existing main streets. He proposed that the municipality purchase large tracts of undeveloped land as green space reserves. With this approach, Carrasco showed respect for the topography of the still unspoiled areas as well as concern for workers' housing by designing park neighborhoods as model projects.

Carrasco's first article offers practical, economical, and basic ideas, opposed, as he stated, to the "vain and expensive as well as unattainable solutions" ("fantasmagorías tan costosas como irrealizables") so commonly chosen by the city authorities.[10] He exploited all possible forums to publicize his views, including academia, professional publications and meetings, and popular newspapers and magazines. We cannot be sure if the timing of this early article was coincidental or was determined by the visit of a French expert, Joseph Bouvard, director of the Service d'architecture, des promenades et plantations of Paris, who had been hired by the mayor in 1907, evidence of Argentina's prevailing taste for French culture. A "preference for French architects and the superiority that we recognize in them without envy" was criticized in a contemporary article in *Caras y caretas* in which it was argued that the government should hire from the large pool of well-trained local experts.[11]

Director de Paseos

Carrasco was promoted to director of the Parque 3 de Febrero (popularly known as Parque de Palermo or Bosques de Palermo) and finally to *director de paseos*, a post that he filled from 1914 to 1918, at which point he was forced to resign under political pressure.[12] His work as director of this agency is extensively explained in a report published in 1917, *Memoria de los trabajos realizados en los parques y paseos públicos de la Ciudad de Buenos Aires: Años 1914–1915–1916*.[13] Although it covers only a portion of Carras-

co's period of service, it is important because it was the agency's first attempt to publish such a document. (A second report was published by Carlos León Thays in 1933, and none has been published since.) Carrasco's report includes a background review of Buenos Aires' promenades and a general section outlining his most important ideas about public parks. It describes the current state of the city's promenades, reviews in detail what had been done under his direction, and provides a series of invaluable drawings and photographs. The report begins by stating, "To know a city's level of progress it is necessary only to study its public promenades" and emphasizes "the value and the importance that open spaces have for the aesthetics and most especially for the healthfulness of a city."[14] Inevitably, Carrasco compares Buenos Aires to other cities he had studied, not only in Europe but also in the United States: Paris; Vienna; Berlin; Boston; Washington, DC; and Minneapolis. (Unfortunately he does not go into detail about what he may have seen in those cities.) The resources invested in green spaces should not be estimated in monetary terms, he states, but in the "innumerable and invaluable benefits that public promenades offer to the population" ("los innumerables y valiosos beneficios que los paseos públicos reportan al pueblo").[15]

One of Carrasco's most lasting contributions is set forth in a chapter with the suggestive title "Breves consideraciones sobre algunos temas de carácter social y moral que se han implementando por la actual Dirección de Paseos" (Summary of considerations regarding some social and moral goals implemented by the current Dirección de Paseos). He writes, "This Directorate knows that its task is not limited to the creation of parks and gardens but that it also has a social mission to accomplish"; that is why, he explains, it built first-class sports facilities in the public promenades for young people's, workers', and students' competitions.[16] Soccer fields, tennis courts, handball grounds, and other sports facilities were constructed in several public parks

2. Parque Chacabuco (opened 1903), Buenos Aires, tennis courts, 1917

Municipalidad de la Capital, Dirección General de Paseos Públicos, Memoria de los trabajos realizados en los parques y paseos públicos de la Ciudad de Buenos Aires, años 1914–1915–1916 (Buenos Aires, 1917)

3. Parque Avellaneda (opened 1914), Buenos Aires, playground, 1915

Municipalidad de la Capital, Dirección General de Paseos Públicos, Memoria …, 1917

period, in the Parque de Palermo alone, sixty-four athletic championship events took place, and, in addition to sports, musical programs such as choral concerts were performed in public parks.

Children and modern conceptions of childhood occupied a central role in Carrasco's thinking and formed an important aspect of his initiatives. New practices were being promoted that made playing in the open air "a cultural project, to draw children away from bad habits and forbidden games." Many children, he wrote, "hardly knew … the benefits and joys of healthy practices."[18] Sports facilities for low-income residents were built in numerous parks: Palermo, Chacabuco (fig. 2), Los Andes, Avellaneda, San Martín, Herrera, and Independencia. In the Parque Centenario a special gymnasium provided a place for more than forty-five hundred children to practice games each Sunday. In the Parque Avellaneda, a Spalding gymnasium was built, following a model imported from the United States that was designed for all sports played with a ball: baseball, basketball, soccer, softball, volleyball. The concept is named for Albert Spalding of Chicago, who in 1876 founded a sporting goods company that produced different types of balls. Children's playgrounds with swings, toboggans, trapezes, and sandboxes became common features in neighborhood squares (fig. 3). But the most successful facility for children was the *teatro infantil* (children's theater). The stage moved from promenade to promenade every weekend, with performances by a children's theatrical company (fig. 4).

Carrasco also promoted productive uses of state-owned land in accordance with the ideas of Clemente Onelli, the director of the Buenos Aires zoo. Dairies and kitchen gardens were established; olive oil, honey, wool, cow's milk, and goat milk were produced and sold to the public and distributed to welfare institutions. In Parque Avellaneda an artisan's school was organized where women could learn to make indigenous folk textiles.

(Palermo, Chacabuco, Avellaneda, Centenario). Following the precept *mens sana in corpora sano*, Carrasco thought that public promenades ought to "provide the elements that will strengthen the physical and moral characteristics of our youth, the citizens of tomorrow—elements that will invigorate their spirits and make them strong."[17] The success of these facilities was immediate: in 1915 and 1916, almost two thousand permits were granted to use the grounds and more than thirty thousand young people took part in sports events. During the same

4. Children's theater, c. 1914–1918
Municipalidad de la Capital, Dirección General de Paseos Públicos, Memoria ..., 1917

5. Instruction at the gardener's school, Jardín Botánico, Buenos Aires
Municipalidad de la Capital, Dirección General de Paseos Públicos, Memoria ..., 1917

today named for the naturalist Cristóbal M. Hicken, was created in 1914 "with the goal of training professional gardeners for the government services who have sufficient theoretical and practical knowledge" (fig. 5).[19] The botanical museum, which showcased native Argentinean flora, provided an important public service; its learned staff served both professional and amateur audiences.[20] The library became the most important botanical library in the city. Eventually it served as a basis for the municipal botanical institute created in Parque Avellaneda.[21]

From the 1917 report we can also learn about Carrasco's scientific work in the creation of the Rosedal, a rose garden in the Parque de Palermo, as well as his establishment of a gardeners' school, a botanical museum, a library, a photography workshop, herbal collections, and seed nurseries in the Jardín Botánico. The gardener's school,

Style and Design Philosophy

For Carrasco, garden art consisted of the intelligent disposition and cultivation of a piece of land for use, enjoyment, and/or ornamentation. Carrasco's design work at the directorate was personal and was distinctive in the region at a time when French garden tradition was still influencing public promenades.

Carrasco's *Parques y jardines*, published in 1923, is the centerpiece of his written

work and his best-known text. It is still the most important publication on this subject in the Argentinean landscape bibliography. The book is organized along the lines of the French classical garden art treatises published in the nineteenth century.[22] It begins with "Breves consideraciones históricas sobre el arte de los jardines," an inaccurate title, as the "considerations" are, in truth, not brief and are very well researched, recounting the history from Greece to André Le Nôtre. Carrasco thought that Le Nôtre's landscape work was in many respects unsurpassed.

Carrasco's text defines contemporary gardens according to three parameters: size, purpose (private, public, or scientific, such as a botanical garden or zoo), and style. According to his classification, previous garden designs embraced the following styles:

The classical or symmetrical (in his terminology, *jardín francés*), in which nature is subordinated to geometric composition

The romantic or picturesque (*jardín inglés*), in which nature is copied or idealized

The combined style, a balanced combination of the two.[23]

Carrasco characterized his "new style" as a "modern conception of the classical style" (*concepción moderna del estilo clásico*).[24] We can infer that for Carrasco, the term "modern" was synonymous with "contemporary," that is, built in his own time. He employed it mainly with regard to small gardens and rose gardens, with beds made up of one type of flower; playgrounds; open-air "salas verdes"; walls and columns covered with climbing vegetation; monumental trellises; and pergolas, benches, statues, and vases. Carrasco wrote that this style achieved its peak in the United States at the time he was writing, but gives no examples, crediting the teaching of landscape architecture for its success.

Carrasco's stylistic vocabulary reflects his wish to show himself as a contemporary professional and to distance himself as far as possible from the French landscape designer Jean-Claude Nicolas Forestier (1861–1930), a highly influential designer who worked on an international scale and in a style more closely attached to the Beaux-Arts tradition. In fact they shared an interest in going beyond the idea of the park as luxury artwork by introducing social welfare components and treating it as integral to urbanism.[25] Forestier was known for public parks not only in Paris but also in Spain, Cuba, Mexico, Morocco, and Argentina. He designed in a new or "modern" French style that was well represented in the Exposition internationale des arts décoratifs et industriels modernes in Paris in 1925. If one compares examples of Carrasco's "concepción moderna del estilo clásico" with Forestier's work, they are somewhat similar. But Carrasco would not acknowledge any debt to his professional archrival.

On the basis of visual characteristics and social ideas, however, we might ask if we should understand Carrasco's style as similar to the contemporaneous style developed by the group of French urbanists led by Forestier, and if Carrasco's social ideas could have come from the French Musée social movement, which influenced Forestier.[26] The Musée social, despite its name, was founded in Paris in 1894 as a welfare foundation for research in fields including urban hygiene, and was an important participant in the birth of urban studies. The Musée introduced Ebenezer Howard's garden city concept in France, and its members were also founders of the Société française des urbanistes. The Argentinean chapter was founded in Buenos Aires in 1911.

Forestier's book *Jardins: Carnet de plans et de dessins* was published in 1920; he visited Buenos Aires in 1923, the year of publication of Carrasco's *Parques y jardines*, which could hardly have been a coincidence.[27] Whereas Forestier's book is based on examples of his own work, Carrasco's is more theoretical, with only a few citations of his professional achievements. Forestier

6. Parque de Palermo, Buenos Aires, Rosedal (opened 1914), aerial view, 1920

Archivo General de la Nación, Argentina

had been engaged by the local government to design a park system for Buenos Aires, under the auspices of the Comisión de Estética Edilicia (commission on building aesthetics). The commission was organized in 1923 by Carlos Noel, mayor of Buenos Aires, with his brother, the architect Martín Noel, as president and Forestier as the team's landscaper. Carrasco and his colleagues were furious at the hiring of a foreign professional and tried in every possible way to forestall Forestier's visit, but without success.[28]

Principal Public Works in Landscape

The year 1914 was productive for Carrasco. The Rosedal (rose garden) in Parque de Palermo was one of his most important projects because of its location, novelty, function, complexity, and longevity. Its location was Argentina's first public park, opened in 1875, and still its most important and visited one. The Rosedal is among the best-known rose gardens of the period, along with the Roseraie de L'Häy (1899) near Paris, designed by Edouard André and owned by Jules Gravereaux. Not many years later Buenos Aires acquired its own example. The similarity of the Rosedal to the gardens of Vizcaya in Miami is striking. Designed for the Florida home of James Deering, which was completed in 1916 and designed by the New York painter Paul Chalfin and the Colombian landscaper Diego Suárez, the Vizcaya gardens took some years to develop, so it is difficult to say who influenced whom.[29]

Carrasco's Rosedal covered thirty-four thousand square meters. The first planting was of 15,000 rosebushes corresponding to 1,189 inventoried cultivars (fig. 6). The roses were arranged in a harmonious contrast to the green lawns, which served to enhance their colors. Construction was completed in just six months, and the garden was inaugurated on November 22, 1914. As complementary works, Carrasco built a 130-meter-long pergola, a pavilion, a so-called Hellenic bridge, and other ornamental structures (figs. 7, 8, and 9). As time passed, new constructions were added nearby: the Patio Andaluz; the Jardín de los Poetas,

7. Parque de Palermo, Buenos Aires, Rosedal, "Hellenic" bridge
Municipalidad de la Capital, Dirección General de Paseos Públicos, Memoria…, 1917

8. Parque de Palermo, Buenos Aires, Rosedal, pergola and rosebushes
Municipalidad de la Capital, Dirección General de Paseos Públicos, Memoria…, 1917

today containing twenty-five poets' busts; a music stage on the lake; an aviary; and restrooms.

Carrasco's 1917 report proudly noted that the Buenos Aires rose garden had an almost unique advantage: it offered free entrance to the public at any time, whereas rose gardens in all other cities except Montevideo

were surrounded by iron fencing and could be visited only during certain hours.[30] This magnificent setting quickly became one of the city's fashionable destinations, and even today the rose garden is one of its most popular and beloved promenades (fig. 10), although most of its visitors know nothing of its author.[31]

In 1914 Carrasco also designed the Plaza Seeber. It was one of only a few gardens in the city with a *parterre de broderie à bas niveau*, a sunken parterre modeled on French baroque gardens. The parterre, which measured eighty-four by thirty-one meters, had a central sculpture and balustrades at both ends. The Plaza Seeber has a distinctive fan-shaped plan and was designed also with *boulingrins* (bowling greens) along the two straight sides. Unfortunately these unusual garden features have not been maintained in good condition. A pavilion in the French neoclassical style of the Louis XVI period stands on a 2.5-meter-high elevation (fig. 11). Today, this magnificent public park is spoiled by an enormous and ugly statue of the dictator Juan Manuel

9. Parque de Palermo, Buenos Aires, Rosedal, pond and pergola

Municipalidad de la Capital, Dirección General de Paseos Públicos, Memoria ..., 1917

10. Parque de Palermo, Buenos Aires, the Rosedal at the time of its opening, 1914

Municipalidad de la Capital, Dirección General de Paseos Públicos, Memoria ..., 1917

11. Benito Javier Carrasco, Plaza
Seeber, Buenos Aires, opened 1916,
plan
*Archivo del Jardín Botánico de
Buenos Aires*

12. Benito Javier Carrasco, Parque
de Palermo, Buenos Aires, Jardines
de Invierno, opened 1914, plan
*Archivo del Jardín Botánico de Bue-
nos Aires*

13. Parque de Palermo, Buenos
Aires, Jardines de Invierno, par-
terres and sculpture
*Municipalidad de la Capital, Direc-
ción General de Paseos Públicos,
Memoria …, 1917*

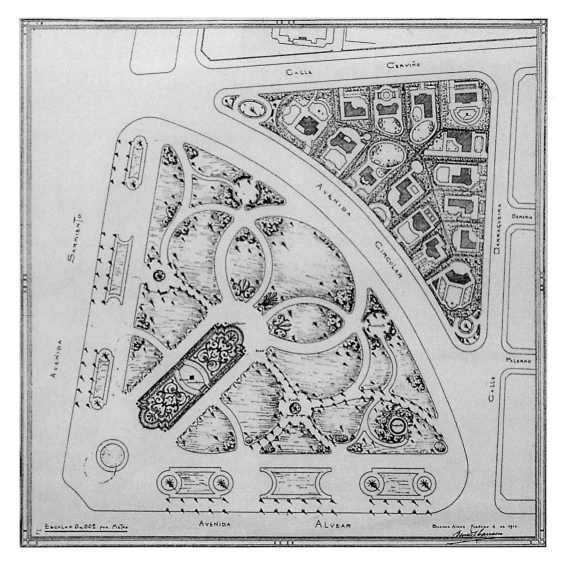

de Rosas in the middle of the parterre and a dog-walking area on one side.

Carrasco's Jardines de Invierno (winter gardens) at the Parque de Palermo were opened in 1914 (figs. 12 and 13). The reason for their name is unclear, as they have no particular relation to the season. Covering twelve hectares, these gardens, marked by symmetry and semicircular motifs, had two distinctive elements, a six-meter-tall trellis with climbing plants (fig. 14) and a music stage twelve meters in diameter, surrounded by small semicircular pools. Underneath the stage was a space filled with water, which served as a sound box. Open-air music performances on the stage became a Buenos Aires tradition (fig. 15). Carrasco built a somewhat similar perfor-

mance area in the same year at the Parque Lezama with seating for two thousand people, in the form of a Roman amphitheater to take advantage of a natural slope (fig. 16).

One of Carrasco's constant concerns was the landscape treatment of the long riverfront of Buenos Aires. It extends for seventeen kilometers from the northern part of the city to the northern areas along the Río de la Plata. After detailed study he published a report to the minister of public works of the Provincia de Buenos Aires on the embellishment of the waterfront along an area that included Vicente López, San Fernando, San Isidro, and Las Conchas counties.[32] He had been commissioned to plan and build a promenade joining the city

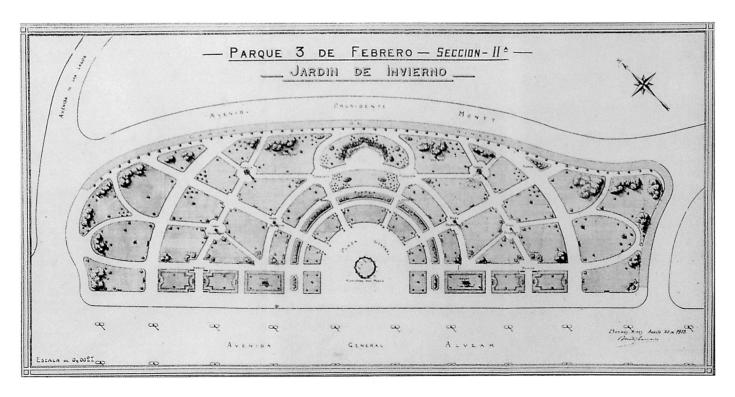

proper to the Tigre settlement, a weekend and tourist destination in the northern zone of the Río de la Plata delta. Its suburban waterfront was to have been connected to the city waterfront. The intent was that it would "follow the most picturesque zone of the riverside and foster ... the birth of new settlements, which will contribute to financing the construction."[33] Carrasco's dream was never fully realized in spite of

his efforts. What did materialize was a longtime desire of Buenos Aires residents: a southern riverside drive, the Costanera Sur. The first drawing for it is dated 1912, but the built work was not inaugurated until 1918, a short time after Carrasco's resignation (fig. 17). It comprised a long stretch of riverfront in the southern part of the city, taking the form of a garden avenue for pedestrians and vehicles overlooking the river, with buildings for recreational activities, rest areas, soccer fields, tennis courts, and other amenities. This riverside avenue was screened from unsightly port facilities by a poplar grove. In this design Carrasco followed a classical, symmetrical style. A great axis was formed by a pier connecting to a small artificial island (with a pool, bathing resort, restaurant, and cafeteria), a *rond-point* with flowerbeds (with another pool), and a central semicircular terrace. On both sides of this monumental axis Carrasco designed rustic, romantic gardens containing gazebos and terraces. Today, this promenade—formerly one of the most important and popular of the city—is greatly changed, especially in its relationship to the river. The bank has been filled

14. Parque de Palermo, Buenos Aires, Jardines de Invierno, benches and trellis

Municipalidad de la Capital, Dirección General de Paseos Públicos, Memoria ..., 1917

15. Parque de Palermo, Buenos Aires, Jardines de Invierno, open-air concert

Caras y caretas, April 25, 1914

in, so the water is no longer near what was intended to be the waterfront.

For enlargements of Parque Patricios (1914) and Parque Avellaneda (1915) Carrasco moved away from the classicizing regularity of previous works, using unrestrained curves, although the sports fields proper were strictly geometrical, and the entrance axis was always present, marked by gardens, gateways, or buildings (figs. 18 and 19). Carrasco's plazas and squares generally followed the French classical garden model, although they were decidedly modern in their function as places for all social classes.

Carrasco and City Planning

As we have seen, Carrasco was interested in what was known in Argentina as the new science of urbanism (*la nueva ciencia del urbanismo*). This idea was clear in his first article, published in 1908. There is no doubt that he had been impressed by American and European achievements in city planning during his trip to those regions. Subsequently he produced numerous city plans, both real and ideal.

His foremost intellectual creation was the *proyecto de ciudad moderna* (modern city plan) included in his book *Parques y jardines*. There he proposed a modern city grid that was a composite of orthogonal, concentric, and radial plans combined with picturesque landscape gardens. It was zoned for a commercial center, an industrial zone, a garden neighborhood, and a

16. Parque Lezama (opened 1896), Buenos Aires, open-air auditorium, opened 1914

Municipalidad de la Capital, Dirección General de Paseos Públicos, Memoria …, 1917

17. Costanera Sur, Buenos Aires, at its inauguration, 1918

Archivo General de la Nación, Argentina

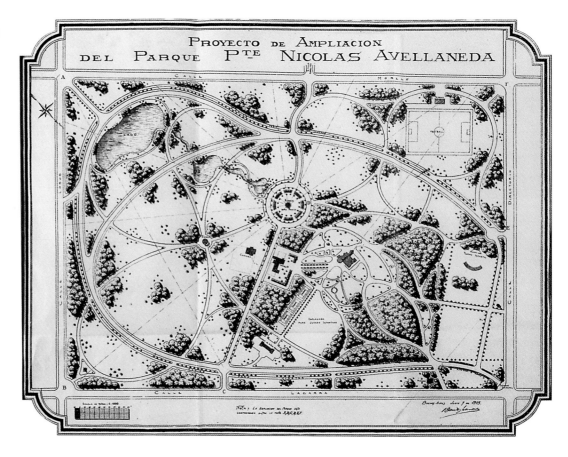

sports area. The park system, the street
system, and the climate were all taken
into account.

Among plans for specific Argentinean
cities are those for Mendoza, Córdoba,
Concordia, and La Calera (working alone);
for Salta, Rosario, and Tucumán (working with Angel Guido); and for Mar del
Plata (working with Angel Guido and Della
Paolera). Carrasco's evolving ideas during
this period culminated in a paper entitled
"Conveniencia de estudiar técnicamente
la transformación de nuestras ciudades"
(1921).[34] Among his key ideas were that zoning should be introduced into city planning
and that citizens should be concerned about
the disposition of public land and granting
of permits to divide large properties. With
regard to Buenos Aires, he proposed that
the city's green space should be increased
from 5 to 20 percent of its total area and
that the ring road (the Avenida General
Paz) should be the greenbelt for the city as

a whole. In addition, he argued that preliminary legal and financial studies were needed to achieve any plan.

That same year, several city council members proposed a law that all future land acquisition designated for public promenades should follow Carrasco's ideas.[35] But the project was never discussed or approved. Almost twenty years later, Carrasco continued to write about this failure:

A misunderstanding of the subject and political confusion led to the failure of this technically astute initiative. If it had received the attention it deserved, our city would have the system of open spaces that it lacks.[36]

Carrasco's discussion of workers' neighborhoods shows the influence of socialist and Musée social ideas and expresses his commitment to improving living and working conditions:

The construction of neighborhoods near factories or workshops, with healthful, beautiful, and economical houses, is a universal aspiration to enhance the physical environment where the inhabitants are precisely those people who contribute with their work to the country's progress and growth.[37]

In 1939 he returned to this subject when he presented a paper on urbanism and workers' housing to the Primer Congreso Panamericano de Vivienda Obrera:

Housing for the people comprises not only workers' neighborhoods, but also those inhabited by the middle class.... So as families move to the periphery, whether through individual initiative, or through large-scale private initiative, or through direct governmental action, housing must (from the urbanist's point of view) be subject to the following parameters: a) Zoning ... b) land division ... c) orientation ... d) green space ... e) road system ... f) hygienic conditions ... g) environment.[38]

The congress, impelled by Carrasco's paper, drew up a manifesto concluding that every workers' housing project should be part of a larger urban or regional planning scheme; that the seven considerations Carrasco named were fundamental; and that there was need for a workers' housing institute in every Latin American country. Participants at the congress included, in addition to Carrasco, Baptista de Olivera (engineer from Brazil), Eugenio Barofio (architect from Uruguay), and Walter Hilton Scott (engineer from Argentina).

Then, in 1935, during the Primer Congreso Argentino de Urbanismo, Carrasco proposed the foundation of an urban and municipal studies institute independent of any university or other agency. It was based on the model of the Institut d'urbanisme in Paris and, had it been realized, would have been oriented toward graduate study.

In an article on urban planning, "¿Qué es un plan regulador de urbanismo?" (1940), Carrasco wrote:

If one studies social change in major nations worldwide, one can see that the multiple efforts that have been carried out are due to the victory of democratic rights and to the modification of the principles governing political institutions, whose aim is to make the physical environment in which citizens live more satisfactory. In summary, one can say that the study of those two key subjects guides the science and art of urbanism, which, in our time, is essentially a socioeconomic question.[39]

These eloquent words summarized his position on the role of urbanism among both experts and ordinary citizens in modern life. Today, Buenos Aires is quickly losing its European heritage in architecture and landscape because of lack of well-conceived protective legislation and business development, and because of the failure of city officials to solve problems such as urban hygiene and transportation safety. Carrasco's concerns are still relevant, but his goals have yet to materialize. As he wrote as late as 1957,

Cities cannot go on becoming isolated stone or brick deserts. They must have habitable conditions that fulfill the needs of hygiene, comfort, beauty, space, recreation, and organic arrangement of its active centers. In a word: they must adjust themselves to the rules of urban planning.[40]

Landscape Teaching

In his academic work, Carrasco started a debate over where and how the subject of park and garden planning and design should be taught as a component of urbanism. He started landscape instruction in 1918 as chair at the Facultad de Agronomía y Veterinaria of the Universidad de Buenos Aires, but it was an elective, not a mandatory subject. He published two pamphlets on this subject, one with Emilio Coni in 1920 and one as sole author in 1938. The first of these was devoted to the reorganization of the Facultad de Agronomía of the Universidad de La Plata. It established the foundation for a new curriculum based on examples from abroad:

Opinion is unanimous that one ought to follow the modern tendency, which is oriented toward practical ends. The United States of America is the culmination of this approach. It has been followed all over the world and began in France, the intellectual mother of our country, whose curricula have always been the rule.[41]

Carrasco named American universities where landscape studies were established: Harvard and the universities of Pennsylvania, Illinois, Iowa, and Michigan. His new curriculum included an innovation in the fourth and last year: the subject of parks and gardens. These were to be studied not only from the point of view of advantages that would accrue to agriculture, but also as they pertained to the aesthetics of towns and cities.[42]

In spite of its brevity (seven pages), the second pamphlet, on parks and gardens as a component of urbanism, is of utmost interest, as it was written in 1938, twenty years after Carrasco had created the new chair of parks and gardens at the Universidad de Buenos Aires, and it synthesizes his ideas and confirms his longstanding commitment to the subject. To Carrasco, the designer and builder of parks and gardens is neither the gardener nor the horticulturist who prepares the vegetation, nor even the architect (who works with inert materials and tries to create an enduring work). To teach the design of parks and gardens one has to unite technical aspects (agronomy) with artistic sense. That is why he introduced this curriculum in the school of agronomy of the Universidad de La Plata even though a group of distinguished students had asked the university authorities to establish the chair in the school of architecture. Carrasco's argument was that relevant subjects, among them botany, topography, drawing, silviculture, and meteorology, were taught only in the school of agronomy. In fact, he expected that a new and specialized school would be created, offering landscape studies, comprising "so-called urban studies under the title of city planning or regional planning."[43] He invoked European landscape design as a model:

When organizing and preparing the curriculum, I took special care in giving it the university level it should have, raising it to aspire to the outstanding work by the great European masters such as Le Nôtre, William Chambers, Kent, Barillet-Deschamps, André, Vacherot, and many others.[44]

His aim was to unite "the agricultural fine arts" (*las bellas artes de la agricultura*), which would go so far as to include regional and national planning, urban and suburban forests, groves of roadside trees, the conservation of natural beauty, and the planning of garden cities: "All should be discussed in consultation with agronomic engineers who have studied them and who must have artistic and even moral standards that qualify them as honest and trained specialists."[45]

Late Career

After Carrasco resigned his position as *director de paseos*, he founded a landscape firm with his former municipal collaborators, named Oficina Técnica de Parques y Jardines. To publicize it, he published a pamphlet describing his personal background, including a brief theoretical and historical description of the subject. This 1921 publication touched on the same topics as the 1917 report but in more summary fashion.

The topic to which Carrasco devoted the greatest effort during his postdirectorate career was the protection of Buenos Aires, understood as a scientific and social action based on modern principles of urbanism. His approach to this ideal included the foundation in June 1925 of Los Amigos de la Ciudad, a nongovernmental organization, by a group of multidisciplinary professionals who fought to achieve a better Buenos Aires. Carrasco was a member of the organization's first board of directors, which included architects, geographers, painters, politicians, historians, and outstanding citizens from various fields.[46] In 1927 Los Amigos de la Ciudad published a book of collected articles by Carrasco originally published from 1923 to 1926 in the newspaper *La Nación.* The selection included studies on public health, housing, traffic, monuments, and street and avenue design, among other topics. Six of the pieces discussed how to develop a plan for urban transformation.

CARICATURAS CONTEMPORÁNEAS
Ingeniero BENITO CARRASCO, por CAO

Conclusion

Carrasco's best-known works are still in existence today: the Rosedal, Plaza Seeber, the Costanera Sur, and the enlargement of Lezama and Avellaneda parks. Many of his important initiatives remained unfinished when he was forced to resign as *director de paseos.* It is impossible to establish how many of his projects were carried out, both because of a lack of documentation and, most of all, because gardens are ephemeral works of art made of biological material that changes and dies over time.

A careful reading of Carrasco's career leads us to admire his pioneering work in overarching and critical issues that matter to the city and to its inhabitants. He identified perennial problems of his day. His proposals were always based on the principles he had established for himself as a citizen and a professional. He faced indifference to his proposals, but he did not give up; he

defended them tirelessly. He surpassed his mentor Charles Thays in being not only a great park builder but also a theoretician of green spaces and urbanism; the promenades in Buenos Aires put into material form his convictions about social equality (fig. 20).

Argentina's long cultural dependency on European centers meant that local theories and professionals were not honored with the reputations they deserved; Carrasco was not respected by Buenos Aires' governmental authorities, who assumed that locals could not compare with Europeans. They preferred to hire French landscapers such as Bouvard or Forestier. This was a paradox, as Carrasco himself was among those who had introduced design principles from Europe and the United States. But that achievement did not satisfy politicians who made decisions and imported designers esteemed and accepted as arbiters of taste. Carrasco's work, however, proves them wrong.

Chronological List of Publications by Benito Javier Carrasco

Fitografía de varios árboles indígenas cultivados en el Jardín Botánico Municipal. Buenos Aires, 1900.

"La ciudad del porvenir." *Caras y caretas* 490 (February 22, 1908).

"Sistema de parques en las ciudades." Paper presented to the Congreso Científico Internacional Americano, Buenos Aires, July 1910.

"Parques Nacionales en los Estados Unidos: Necesidad de imitarlos." *La Nación,* May 7, 1912.

Plano y memoria descriptiva de las obras de embellecimiento de la costa (Elevada al Señor Ministro de Obras Públicas de la Provincia de Buenos Aires por la Comisión nombrada por Decreto de fecha abril 22 de 1912). Buenos Aires, 1914.

Anfiteatro para música en el Parque Lezama. Buenos Aires, 1915.

"Studies of Landscape Engineering." Paper presented to the Panama-Pacific International Exposition, 1915.

Municipalidad de la Capital, Dirección General de Paseos Públicos. *Memoria de los trabajos realizados en los parques y paseos públicos de la Ciudad de Buenos Aires, Años 1914–1915–1916.* Buenos Aires, 1917.

"Anteproyecto de ensanche y modificación del Paseo del Puerto." *La Nación,* March 21, 1920.

Coni, Emilio A., and Carrasco, Benito J. *Enseñanza superior agronómica.* Buenos Aires, 1920.

"Conveniencia de estudiar técnicamente la transformación de nuestras ciudades." In *Segundo Congreso Nacional de Ingeniería,* 160. Buenos Aires, 1921.

Oficina técnica de Parques y Jardines. Buenos Aires, 1921.

"Avenida Costanera de la Capital Federal al Tigre." In *Memoria general del Primer Congreso Nacional de Vialidad (mayo 1922),* 205. Buenos Aires, 1923.

Letters to *La Nación* concerning visit of Jean-Claude Nicolas Forestier to Buenos Aires, October 4 and October 7, 1923.

Parques y jardines. Buenos Aires, 1923.

Paper presented to the Primer Congreso de Municipalidades, Buenos Aires, 1926.

Algunas consideraciones sobre la urbanización de ciudades. Buenos Aires, 1927.

"Diversos aspectos urbanos de París." *La Nación,* July 1, 1928.

"El plan de urbanización de la ciudad de Córdoba." *La Nación,* January 29, 1928, and *La Prensa,* February 5, 1928.

"Es inadecuada la ubicación que se piensa dar a un monumento." *La Nación,* April 10, 1929.

Observaciones generales sobre el problema del tráfico. Buenos Aires, 1929.

¿Sabe usted lo que significa un plan regulador? Buenos Aires, 1929.

Paper presented to the Segundo Congreso de Municipalidades, Córdoba, 1929.

"Toda comuna debe tener su plan regulador y de extensión." *Revista Parlamentaria,* March 1933.

"Creación del Instituto de Altos Estudios Urbanos." In *Primer Congreso Argentino de Urbanismo,* 626. Buenos Aires, 1937.

Como se estudia el zoning en Estados Unidos. Buenos Aires, 1938.

Conceptos técnicos y artísticos que deben tenerse en cuenta para arbolar debidamente las carreteras. Buenos Aires, 1938.

Letters to *El Diario* concerning tree pruning, April 13 and June 14, 1938.

Importancia de la enseñanza de Parques y Jardines en la Facultad de Agronomía de la Universidad de Buenos Aires. Buenos Aires, 1938.

"Los árboles en el urbanismo." *Boletín de Los Amigos de la Ciudad,* July–September 1938, 27.

El urbanismo y la vivienda popular. Buenos Aires, 1939.

Parques y jardines. Buenos Aires, 1940.

"¿Qué es un plan regulador de urbanismo?" *Boletín del H. Concejo Deliberante de la Ciudad de Buenos Aires* 19 (November–December 1940): 81.

"Parques y jardines." Manuscript, 1941–1942. Biblioteca Nacional de Lima (Lima, Perú, National Library). Sección Manuscritos. E-940.

"Evolución de los espacios verdes." *Boletín del H. Concejo Deliberante de la Ciudad de Buenos Aires* 33/34 (1942): 25.

"Cuidar la estética urbana." *La Prensa,* September 11, 1956.

Palabras pronunciadas con motivo de reanudar los cursos al ser reincorporado en junio de 1945, renunciando después, en 1946 junto con 1200 profesores al ser avasallada la autonomía universitaria. Buenos Aires, 1956.

"El urbanismo de las grandes ciudades." *La Prensa,* February 5, 1957.

NOTES

1. Sonia Berjman, *Plazas y parques de Buenos Aires: La obra de los paisajistas franceses* (Buenos Aires, 1998); Sonia Berjman, *Carlos Thays: Un jardinero francés en Buenos Aires* (Buenos Aires, 2009).

2. Sonia Berjman, ed., *Benito Javier Carrasco: Sus textos* (Buenos Aires, 1997).

3. "Así como las obras sanitarias, las canalizaciones de aguas y demás mejoras se imponen para nuestro confort e higiene; así como la fundación de escuelas y bibliotecas son necesarias para la educación y progreso del pueblo, los parques y paseos públicos son indispensables en las ciudades populosas para el mejoramiento de la vida, el acrecentamiento de la moralidad y de la salud, y el progreso urbano en cuanto se refiere a embellecimiento y ornato." Municipalidad de la Capital, Dirección General de Paseos Públicos, *Memoria de los trabajos realizados en los parques y paseos públicos de la Ciudad de Buenos Aires, Años 1914–1915–1916* (Buenos Aires, 1917), 5.

4. On December 3, 1877, and October 15, 1958.

5. "Y fue precisamente a su ciudad natal que consagrara su dedicación a todo lo que pudiera representar el mejoramiento del urbanismo y la más bella o propicia conformación de sus parques y jardines, en los que veía desahogos indispensables de la población y a la vez cuadros amables y necesarios en toda ciudad de la magnitud de la nuestra." "Benito J. Carrasco: Su fallecimiento," *La Nación*, October 17, 1958.

6. Benito J. Carrasco, *Fitografía de varios árboles indígenas cultivados en el Jardín Botánico Municipal* (Buenos Aires, 1900).

7. "No descansará hasta reunir en los parques y paseos, toda la inmensa y hermosa flora Argentina." Carrasco 1900, 13.

8. Carlos León Thays served as *director de paseos* from 1922 to 1946.

9. Benito J. Carrasco, "La ciudad del porvenir," *Caras y caretas* 490 (February 22, 1908).

10. Carrasco 1908.

11. "Predilección por los arquitectos franceses y la superioridad que sin envidia alguna les reconocemos." "M. Bouvard en Buenos Aires," *Caras y caretas* 447 (April 27, 1907).

12. He was replaced by his brother Eugenio Carrasco, who had been educated in Belgium as an agronomic engineer. This event caused such animosity between the two brothers that they never spoke again.

13. Dirección General de Paseos Públicos 1917 (as cited in note 3).

14. "Para conocer el grado de adelanto de una Ciudad basta estudiar sus paseos públicos.... El valor y la importancia que los espacios libres tienen para la estética y, especialmente para la salubridad de una población." Dirección General de Paseos Públicos 1917, 5, 6.

15. Dirección General de Paseos Públicos 1917, 6.

16. "Compenetrada la Dirección de que su tarea no debe limitarse a la creación de parques y jardines, de que tiene también una misión social que llenar." Dirección General de Paseos Públicos 1917.

17. "Se ha preocupado de contribuir a esos fines, aportando los elementos necesarios para el acrecentamiento de los rasgos físicos y morales que templan y vigorizan el espíritu de la juventud y que hacen fuertes y conscientes a los hombres del mañana." Dirección General de Paseos Públicos 1917, 33.

18. "Una obra de cultura, alejando y sustrayendo de los malos hábitos, de los juegos prohibidos, a infinidad de niños que hasta hace poco tiempo no conocían los beneficios ni las alegría de las sanas prácticas." Dirección General de Paseos Públicos 1917, 35.

19. "Como una medida de previsión para el futuro y con el fin de formar jardineros idóneos para los servicios municipales y con suficientes conocimientos teórico-prácticos." Dirección General de Paseos Públicos 1917, 36. Candidates had to be at least fourteen years old and of Argentinean citizenship, and had to have passed the fourth grade. All the matriculants were given scholarships and required to attend for eight hours daily (two hours of theoretical studies plus six of practice) over the course of three years.

20. Dirección General de Paseos Públicos 1917, 18–19. After almost a century of service, the museum was dismantled in the early 1990s.

21. Although the institute no longer exists, the library was reopened in the Jardín Botánico some years ago after a long period of inactivity.

22. Alfred Auguste Ernouf and Adolphe Alphand, *L'art des jardins* (Paris, 1886); Edouard André, *L'art des jardins: Traité général de la composition des parcs et jardins* (Paris, 1879).

23. Benito Javier Carrasco, *Parques y jardines* (Buenos Aires, 1923), 60.

24. Carrasco 1923, 60.

25. Berjman 1998, 228. Regarding Forestier's influence, see also the essay by José Tito Rojo in this volume.

26. Bénédicte Leclerc, ed., *Jean Claude Nicolas Forestier 1861–1930: Du jardin au paysage urbain* (Paris, 1990).

27. Jean-Claude Nicolas Forestier, *Jardins: Carnet de plans et de dessins* (Paris, 1920).

28. See Berjman 1988, 215.

29. See www.vizcayamuseum.org.

30. "La roseraie porteña ... tiene sobre sus similiares extranjeras la ventaja de ofrecer libre acceso al público en cualquier momento, mientras que las otras, con excepción de la de Montevideo, están circundadas por verjas y sólo pueden ser visitadas en ciertas horas del día." Dirección General de Paseos Públicos 1917, 15.

31. Because of lack of maintenance, the rose garden began to die little by little. In 2008 a multidisciplinary

technicians' team, which I advised, undertook the enormous task of its restoration. The result has been spectacular and today the garden seems to be four years old instead of almost a century. Unfortunately it has been necessary to enclose it with a tall fence to protect it from increasing vandalism. Entry is limited to winter and summer hours—the opposite of the unlimited access for which the garden had been lauded in the past. At its 2012 convention in South Africa the World Federation of Rose Societies gave the Rosedal its Award of Garden Excellence and the book *El Rosedal de Palermo de Buenos Aires, 1914–2009 95° Anniversario*, by Sonia Berjman and Roxana Di Bello, its literary award.

32. Benito J. Carrasco, *Plano y memoria descriptiva de las obras de embellecimiento de la costa elevada al Señor Ministro de Obras Públicas de la Provincia de Buenos Aires por la Comisión nombrada por Decreto de fecha abril 22 de 1912* (Buenos Aires, 1914).

33. "Recorriendo de esta suerte la parte más pintoresca de la costa y propendiendo … al surgimiento de nuevos núcleos de población que, por otra parte, habrán de facilitar la financiación de la obra." Carrasco 1914.

34. Benito J. Carrasco, "Conveniencia de estudiar técnicamente la transformación de nuestras ciudades," paper presented at Segundo Congreso Nacional de Ingenieros, Buenos Aires, November 1921.

35. Municipalidad de la Ciudad de Buenos Aires, Versiones taquigráficas, December 20, 1921.

36. "Este trabajo tuvo el honor de ser patrocinado por tres concejales de entonces, los doctores Juan José Díaz Arana, Virgilio Tedín Uriburu y Carlos Alberto Acevedo. La incomprensión del problema, y la ofuscación política malograron esta iniciativa técnicamente estudiada. De habérsele prestado la atención que ella merecía, nuestra capital tendría el sistema de espacios libres de que hoy carece." Benito J. Carrasco, "Evolución de los espacios verdes," *Boletín del H. Concejo Deliberante de la Ciudad de Buenos Aires* 33/34 (1942): 25.

37. "La construcción de barrios cerca de las fábricas o usinas, en casas económicas, higiénicas y bellas, como una aspiración universal de mejorar el medio físico donde se desenvuelve la vida de los que contribuyen con su trabajo al progreso y engrandecimiento del país." Carrasco 1923, 67.

38. "Vivienda popular no es, pues, únicamente el barrio obrero sino también aquellos en que radica una buena parte de la clase media…. De modo que, siendo por iniciativa individual al producirse la migración de las familias hacia la periferia, o por iniciativa privada en grande escala o por la acción directa del Estado, la vivienda popular desde el punto de vista del urbanismo debe estar supeditada a las siguientes normas: a) Zonización … b) parcelamiento … c) orientación … d) espacios verdes … e) vialidad … f) condiciones de higiene … g) ambiente." Benito Javier Carrasco, *El urbanismo y la vivienda popular* (Buenos Aires, 1939).

39. "A poco que se estudie la reforma que del régimen de la vida social se ha venido operando en las principales naciones del mundo, se observa que los múltiples esfuerzos realizados obedecen a la conquista de los derechos democráticos y que reclama la modificación de los principios que rigen a las instituciones políticas, y la que tiene por objeto hacer más satisfactorio el medio físico donde se desenvuelve la existencia de los ciudadanos. En síntesis, puede decirse que el estudio de estos dos grandes capítulos orienta la ciencia y el arte del urbanismo que, en el momento contemporáneo, es una cuestión de carácter esencialmente económico social." Benito J. Carrasco, "¿Qué es un plan regulador de urbanismo?" *Boletín del H. Concejo Deliberante de la Ciudad de Buenos Aires* 19 (November–December 1940): 81.

40. Benito Javier Carrasco, "El urbanismo en las grandes ciudades," *La Prensa*, February 5, 1957.

41. "La opinión unánime incita a seguir la tendencia moderna, y pide que la orientación sea dirigida hacia fines prácticos. A este respecto, los Estados Unidos de Norte América dan la nota culminante. Esa corriente se sigue en todo el mundo, empezando por Francia, que ha sido la madre intelectual de nuestro país y cuyos planes han servido siempre de norma." Emilio Coni and Benito Javier Carrasco, *Enseñanza superior agronómica* (Buenos Aires, 1920), 5.

42. "Los parques desde el punto de vista de las ventajas que reporta la ganadería, como reparo para las haciendas, etc., sino también como estética de los pueblos y ciudades cuyo desenvolvimiento se hace actualmente sin plan ni programa." Coni and Carrasco 1920, 19.

43. "Los estudios llamados de Urbanismo con el título de city plan, regional planning." Benito J. Carrasco, *Importancia de la enseñanza de Parques y Jardines en la Facultad de Agronomía de la Universidad de Buenos Aires* (Buenos Aires, 1938), 5.

44. "Al organizar y preparar el programa que debía regir, tuve especial cuidado en darle a la asignatura el rango universitario que le correspondía, elevándola al nivel que acusa el destacado contenido de los trabajos realizados por los grandes maestros de Europa como Le Nôtre, Williams Chambers, Kent, Barillet-Deschamps, André, Vacherot y muchos otros." Carrasco 1938, 4.

45. "Todo esto tendrá que ser entregado y consultado a los ingenieros agrónomos que se hayan dedicado a estudiar esta materia y tengan condiciones de artista y también morales que los habilite como capacitados y honestos especialistas." Carrasco 1938, 6.

46. Together with Pedro Luro, Arturo Prins, Tedín Uriburu, Besio Moreno, Julio Dormal, Ernesto de la Cárcova, Alejandro Bustillo, Luis Agote, Cupertino del Campo, Miguel Cané, and many others.

LANCE HUMPHRIES

*Baltimore and the City Beautiful: Carrère &
Hastings Reshapes an American City*

On April 6, 1917, the United States declared war on Germany and entered World War I. Several weeks later a French war mission arrived in Washington to meet with President Woodrow Wilson and other government officials to solicit American assistance. At the beginning of May, Baltimore's mayor, James H. Preston (1860–1938), upon learning that the commissioners were returning to Washington, invited them to stop over in Baltimore so that citizens could demonstrate "the feeling of affection which the city holds for them." Preston cited Baltimore and Maryland's deep historical attachment to the marquis de Lafayette (1757–1834), the Frenchman who fought alongside George Washington during the Revolutionary War. Lafayette had camped near Baltimore during the war, he and his male heirs had been made citizens of Maryland by the state legislature, and he had been famously received in Baltimore during his 1824 farewell tour. Preston worked feverishly to secure this visit to his city, lobbying the US Department of State, which was handling the already full schedule of the delegation. A week into his campaign Preston struck on the idea that made the stop irresistible to the French party: while in Baltimore the delegation would break ground for a monument dedicated to Lafayette's memory. Preston believed this memorial would be a fitting addition to the legacy of the "Monumental City," a name John Quincy Adams was said to have given the city during a visit in 1827.[1]

The groundbreaking for the Lafayette statue turned out to be a galvanizing moment in the city's design and planning history, enabling a number of large-scale city

plans to coalesce into reality—ideas that for more than a decade had been only aspirations. These plans would transform several significant areas of the city. Although the involvement of the Olmsteds in Baltimore park and civic planning is well known, the central role that the New York firm of Carrère & Hastings played in the development of the city in the first quarter of the twentieth century is little discussed.[2] This essay will survey the planning history of the city in this period, focusing on three sites—Mount Vernon Place, St. Paul Street, and the Civic Center—in order to demonstrate the breadth of Preston's ambition and to document the extensive role of Carrère & Hastings in Baltimore, all in an effort to reassert the city's important position in the history of American city planning at its inception as a professional discipline. Finally, it seeks a better understanding of what was meant by "modern" by planners, the public, and politicians in this dynamic moment of American urban design.

During his two administrations (1911–1919), Preston ambitiously pushed Baltimore toward grand-scale civic celebrations and improvements. In 1914 the city and country marked the one hundredth anniversary of the American victory at Fort McHenry during the Battle of Baltimore in the War of 1812. Preston effectively lobbied the federal government to have the use (but not ownership) of Fort McHenry turned over to the city of Baltimore, adding this prized parkland with historic associations to the city's holdings. Further, for this site he obtained a $75,000 congressional appropriation for a monumental sculpture honoring Francis Scott Key, who had been inspired by the events of the battle to write "The Star-Spangled Banner." During Preston's administration a number of other public monuments were erected celebrating the War of 1812.[3]

Two major anniversaries followed that of the Battle of Baltimore. July 4, 1915, was the one hundredth anniversary of the laying of the cornerstone of Baltimore's Washington Monument, designed by Robert Mills (1781–1855) as the first public monument to Washington in the United States. September 1915 marked the centennial of the laying of the cornerstone of the Battle Monument, designed by Maximilian Godefroy (1765–c. 1840), which honored the city's fallen in the Battle of Baltimore. Notably, both monuments were centerpieces of urban spaces that were designed along very different lines: the Washington Monument sited in the middle of a park-like setting, the Battle Monument the focal point of a paved plaza (today's Monument Square).

When the United States entered World War I two years later, Baltimoreans, under Preston's dynamic leadership, were eager to display publicly their commitment to the ideals of freedom and democracy. In the few short weeks he had to plan the momentous groundbreaking, Preston cast about for a place to locate the new Lafayette memorial. Initial ideas were the Homewood area, near the Johns Hopkins University campus, and a site at the corner of St. Paul and Centre Streets, at the northern extreme of a planned improvement on St. Paul Street. Both locations were rejected for one in Mount Vernon Place, the setting around the Washington Monument. Many statues were already erected here, and one last location had recently been committed for a statue of Baltimore's famous nineteenth-century author Edgar Allen Poe (1809–1849).[4]

The Historic Development of Mount Vernon Place

Mount Vernon Place was hallowed ground. Robert Mills' Washington Monument was the result of several years of advocacy on the part of the city to fund a public work by a state-enabled lottery. In 1814 Mills won a competition with a design for a multitiered column topped by a statue of Washington in a quadriga that was intended for the city's former Court House Square (now Monument Square). However, residents' fear that Mills' towering design might topple on their houses in the event of some natural disaster was the impetus to move it north of the city to land donated by Revolutionary War hero John Eager Howard (1752–1827) from his large estate, Belvidere. On this 200-square-foot parcel of wooded land the column was begun in 1815, at the head of one of the city's future main thoroughfares, Charles Street. The statue of Washington, by Henrico Causici (1790–1833), was raised to the top in 1829, and other details of the column, less elaborate than the design submitted, were gradually completed.[5]

Howard's heirs, working with designs developed by Mills, donated additional land around the monument for a plan that benefited not only themselves but the public. The intersection of two streets was widened into a Greek cross, forming broad "places" (Mount Vernon Place to the east and west and Washington Place to the north and south), which offered impressive views of the monument from the cardinal directions and

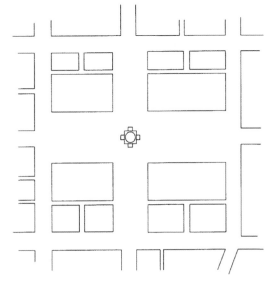

1. Mount Vernon Place, plan, 1831, as redrawn by the Historic American Landscapes Survey

Library of Congress, Prints and Photographs Division, HALS MD-1

provided numerous building lots that could be sold for development (fig. 1). Between the early 1830s and 1850, the "squares," as the arms of the cross were more often called, were gradually enclosed with first wooden and then wrought iron fences, and uniform perimeter trees were planted.[6] (For purposes of discussion here, "Mount Vernon Place" refers to the central site of the monument and all four squares.)

In 1875–1876, in preparation for the centennial of American independence, the city decided the squares looked old-fashioned and not in keeping with the emerging elegance of the houses and mansions by then surrounding them. Frederick Law Olmsted Sr. (1822–1903) with Thomas Wisedell (1846–1884), representing the leading landscape design firm in the nation, was commissioned to redesign the south and north squares. In 1877 the fences were removed, and low, rough-hewn stone walls and other details were installed at the ends of each square, as well as concrete paths,

all in multiple colors, considered in keeping with the style now called High Victorian Gothic. In the south square a straight path formed a strong central axis leading to the Washington Monument from the entrance at Centre Street, while in the north square curvilinear pathways cut across the square (figs. 2 and 3). The east and west squares would subsequently be treated by the city in a manner similar to the north square, and in these three squares the tradition of uniform perimeter trees was retained. Fountains were installed in all but the north square as well as gaslight fixtures and, by the early years of the twentieth century, a number of bronze statues of allegorical and historic figures.[7]

It was to this location, rich in historical associations, that on May 14, 1917, the French war commissioners were escorted to the cheers of the thousands gathered along the route. After a brief dedication speech at the base of the Washington Monument, Preston and commissioners René Viviani,

3. Mount Vernon Place, plan showing existing conditions of the Olmsted-era design, c. 1916, as redrawn by the Historic American Landscapes Survey and revised by author

Library of Congress, Prints and Photographs Division, HALS MD-1

the French vice premier and minister of justice; the marquis Pierre de Chambrun (1865–1954), a great-grandson of Lafayette; and Marshal Joseph Joffre, a French war hero, walked down the hill to the east end of the east square. There, all three Frenchmen, beginning with Viviani, broke ground for the statue in the middle of an existing bed of pansies in full bloom (fig. 4). A participant placed a pansy in each of the commissioners' buttonholes, and they were quickly whisked off to the train station after a brief hour in Baltimore. As the crowd dispersed, those seeking souvenirs of the portentous event stripped the flower bed, taking the flowers as a keepsake of the hallowed ground.[8] As neither plans nor funds were immediately at hand for the Lafayette statue, Preston was adroit in seizing the opportunity to have the French commissioners break ground for the statue. Within several weeks of the ceremony, the Lafayette Memorial Committee was assembled, garnering support from

Baltimore's Municipal Art Commission, the Municipal Art Society, and several patriotic societies.[9]

Needs for Renewal and Improvement

In the weeks before the groundbreaking for the statue, Preston had been informed by Baltimore City's Board of Park Commissioners of plans to repair the broken concrete sidewalks in Mount Vernon Place. Preston shortly thereafter observed that it had been "rapidly deteriorating in appearance and in value" and was "in danger of becoming a lodging-house and business neighborhood." He argued that by "beautifying and renewing the City's portion of this beautiful section, that the property on the square can be renewed and raised, at all events prevented from degeneration." At this very moment he also had other large-scale plans that had long been in development, including an improvement project for St. Paul Street and one for a civic center, both of which embraced extensive land acquisition, demolition, and redesign as public parks. The impending 1918 Annexation Act, which would triple Baltimore's size, would require significant investment in infrastructure improvements to connect this new land with the existing city.[10]

The park commissioners assured the mayor that a concrete repair plan could be developed by Frederick Law Olmsted Jr. (1870–1957), whose family firm in Boston had been involved with various local projects for a number of years. In 1912–1913, the younger Olmsted had been hired by the Johns Hopkins University to plan the university's entrance on Charles Street and develop ideas for resolving nearby street approaches. In a private memo, Preston informed each park commissioner that because of his experience since he had been in office, he did not "think especially highly" of Olmsted: "I have found him vacillating, uncertain and unsatisfactory.... I would suggest that if you are going to have a landscape or city planning man, that you make a change. Mr. Hastings, of Carrirre [sic] & Hastings ... who sits

4. Marshal Joseph Joffre breaking ground for the Lafayette memorial while Baltimore Mayor James H. Preston gestures in appreciation, 1917
Maryland Historical Society

century to meet the demands of modern transportation systems, new technologies of lighting and communications, and shifting demographics. Hastings eagerly replied that he would come to Baltimore, as he was "most interested in anything that has to do with the civic development of your beautiful city."[12]

After the groundbreaking Preston had briefly considered the sculptor Daniel Chester French (1850–1931) for the creation of the Lafayette memorial statue. Preston decided on Hastings after consulting with influential Baltimore architect William M. Ellicott (1863–1944), who endorsed engaging Hastings as opposed to a sculptor because "the problem is so largely architectural in its balance between the [Washington] Monument, and the parkings etc., surrounding it."[13] In addition to the firm's general architectural reputation it was well known that Hastings had designed the pedestal and architectural setting in the court of the Louvre for an equestrian statue of Lafayette designed by Paul Wayland Bartlett (1865–1925), who was also considered as sculptor of the Baltimore memorial. At an early stage in the design Bartlett's participation seemed so likely that in one of his drawings Hastings used the silhouette of the Paris sculpture to suggest the appearance of the Baltimore memorial (see fig. 12). The design history of the sculpture itself is not recounted here; ultimately the commission was given to another American sculptor, Andrew O'Connor (1874–1941), who had worked with Carrère & Hastings on bas-reliefs for the Memorial Amphitheater in Arlington National Cemetery.

on the National Fine Arts Commission in Washington and comes through Baltimore quite frequently, is a very exceptional man in this line, or Mr. Ernest Graham, of Burnham & Graham, would be available."[11]

In the end Preston took matters into his own hands and invited Thomas Hastings (1860–1929), of the New York firm of Carrère & Hastings, to Baltimore to discuss "one or two civic problems," taking the opportunity to include the Lafayette memorial. The two had met in Washington, when Preston appeared in front of the Commission of Fine Arts, on which both Hastings and Olmsted Jr. served, in conjunction with Preston's advocacy of the memorial to Francis Scott Key for Fort McHenry. The Baltimore mayor and the New York architect apparently found themselves to be kindred spirits in ideas about city planning, and both were passionate about promoting City Beautiful principles. This movement defined a new modernism that stressed artistic public design as good for the health and prosperity of a community. It would dramatically reshape many American cities for the new

Carrère & Hastings

Hastings was, by 1917, the surviving member of the architectural practice that he had begun in 1885 with John Merven Carrère (1858–1911). As a team they were responsible for one of the most outstanding civic accomplishments of their age, the New York

Public Library (1897). This commission catapulted them to fame in the early twentieth century, garnering numerous public and private commissions. In their architectural practice the team had become recognized as masters of carefully thought-out plans and for their emphasis on designing buildings from the inside out and on ordering the components of a structure according to the importance of their functions. The ordering dictated not only the elevation of a structure but also its ornamentation.[14] This design approach, which was characteristic of the partners' training at the École des Beaux-Arts in Paris, drew on a wide range of historic precedents.

The partners also displayed a particular interest in harmonizing a building with its site. Regarding their recently completed First Church of Christ, Scientist, in Philadelphia, one architecture critic observed in 1911: "The public seems to be awakening to the fact that the architect can improve his building, and to an extent worth payment in the treatment of the setting, and Messers. Carrere and Hastings have, perhaps more than any other architects practicing in the country, accomplished this result."[15] Their exceptional sensitivity to site design allowed the firm to become leaders in the emerging field of city planning, which gained enormous momentum in the early twentieth century during the City Beautiful movement. The architectural, landscape, and city planning history of the firm was largely neglected after the rise of international modernism, but its contributions in these fields are now recognized as among the most important of the late nineteenth and early twentieth centuries. However, the firm's long engagement with the major urban center of Baltimore has not received full consideration in recent studies.[16]

Both Carrère and Hastings had professional and personal connections to Baltimore well before Preston took office in 1911. The architectural pair met in Baltimore while both were in the employ of the firm of McKim, Mead & White, which in the 1880s

had designed the Ross Winans house (1883) on St. Paul Street in the Mount Vernon area and the Robert Garrett mansion on Mount Vernon Place (1884). As both the Winans and Garrett fortunes had been made in the railroad industry, it is not surprising that while working on these projects the duo found their first major individual patron in the Florida railroad tycoon Henry Flagler.

While Carrère and Hastings may have formed their professional alliance working together in Baltimore, Carrère's connections to the city went much deeper. His great-grandfather John Carrère (1759–1841) had immigrated to Baltimore from France in the 1790s and immediately found a place among the city's rich mercantile class. Several generations of Carrères grew up in Baltimore, including the architect's father, John Merven Carrère. By the turn of the twentieth century Carrère was related to some of the oldest and most distinguished families in the city.[17]

Carrère's connections to Baltimore, his position as a rising star in American architectural circles because of his work as a civic planner, and his role as chief architect and head of the board of architects responsible for designing the Pan-American Exposition in Buffalo (1901) inspired an invitation to him from the Arundell Club in Baltimore to speak on "park extension and municipal architecture." The Municipal Art Society joined in sponsoring this lecture at its annual meeting in January 1902, on the subject of the extension of park systems and their relation to city planning. Carrère's lecture was one of several given at the meeting, the other principal talk being on the city of the future.[18] The Arundell Club was a women's club formed in 1894 to support efficient government management. The Municipal Art Society was founded in 1899 by Baltimore citizens interested in promoting park development and civic planning. It did so by sponsoring lectures and exhibitions on art and architecture and by encouraging civic leaders to integrate the arts into planning decisions. In its early years the society viewed adequate parks and the orderly

5. Mount Vernon Place looking
west, c. 1903
*Library of Congress, Prints and
Photographs Division*

development of the city proper to be the
two most important issues facing the city.
The founding of this nongovernmental organization followed the formation of the city's
Art Commission, organized in 1895 and
composed of the mayor and seven appoin-
tees from cultural organizations. Since the
Municipal Art Society was not affiliated
with the city, it had greater freedom to promote its agenda, and during this period its
opinion clearly mattered to those in city hall,
as its membership grew quickly. At the close
of its first year, in December 1899, it sponsored the first national municipal art conference, bringing in authorities on art and civic
planning from around the country.[19]

In his Baltimore lecture, Carrère spoke to
the promotional interests of the society in
one of his earliest public pronouncements,
if not his first, of his park and city planning philosophies — ideas that would guide
his and the firm's design choices through
the next several decades. In discussing his
philosophy for parks within and outside a
city, Carrère explained that in "the city the
treatment would be mostly formal. In some
instances, as in the case of public squares, it
would be almost entirely architectural." He

noted, in fact, that the Pan-American Exposition had introduced "a phase of landscape
work which until lately has not been popular
in this country — the extremely formal development of landscapes, — but it is becoming
better appreciated." Carrère noted that the
exposition might "lead to some interesting
development in the same way that the object
lesson of monumental architecture did in the
case of the Chicago Exposition."[20]

While a city might have a highly formal center, Carrère argued, radiating out
from this would be streets planned with
good views of architectural or sculptural
points of interest along the way; farther
out, parkways would emerge, and "nature
would gradually assert herself" in the form
of parks encircling the city. Carrère cited
Paris as the outstanding example of this
formal-to-natural progression, beginning
at "the very heart" of the city, the Place de
la Concorde. He observed that a similar
treatment could be realized in Baltimore,
perhaps beginning at Mount Vernon Place,
which "naturally occurs to one as the central point of the city." Noting that it was
"dignified and full of character," he also
observed that it was unfortunate that some
of its approaches from the cardinal directions were "not beautiful avenues with trees
of such a character as to be easily kept low
or at a height as would lengthen the perspective leading up to the monument and give
it a dignified approach which it now lacks,
without hiding it." Speaking to a current
concern of the Municipal Art Society, Carrère noted that "abnormally high buildings"
were appearing on Mount Vernon Place, a
reference to the building in the mid-1890s
of two multiunit high rises, the Hotel Staf-
ford and The Severn apartments, both of
which introduced changes in scale and use
(fig. 5). The society's concern about these
buildings, which to its members signaled an
unacceptable transformation of the physical
and economic character of Mount Vernon
Place, led to the passage of a 1904 Maryland
law restricting the height of the surrounding buildings, the first building height law

enacted in the state. As a corrective, Carrère suggested trees as a framing device to create uniformity around the squares, while hiding any irregularities around its perimeter.[21]

Above all, Carrère stressed that Baltimoreans must develop a long-range plan for the growth of the city, developed by a commission of experts "so competent and so distinguished that their opinion will be accepted as authoritative." Even if this scheme was not followed to the letter, the master plan would deter the haphazard development that had plagued American cities, including Baltimore, since the nineteenth century. Few American cities, he noted, had such a distinguished beginning as nearby Washington, where Pierre Charles L'Enfant had set out an impressive plan, one that, regrettably, had not always been followed.[22] Baltimore in particular grew quickly in the late eighteenth century and early years of the nineteenth. An 1812 account of the city noted that it had numerous well-built public buildings and houses but that none of them were situated in public view on the city's main thoroughfare, Baltimore Street. By the time of Carrère's speech a modest cluster of public buildings had emerged around Monument Square, but little had been accomplished in the central part of the city to position public buildings in distinguished settings.[23]

Carrère's speech not only encouraged but emboldened the Municipal Art Society to continue to push for park expansion. On April 20, 1903, the society invited Frederick Law Olmsted Jr., then working on a new park project in Baltimore (Wyman Park), to speak to the group on his work on the Senate Park Commission in Washington. That project, embodied in what is often called the McMillan Plan, attempted to recapture the intent of L'Enfant's original design for Washington, which, Olmsted informed the group, was "stimulating" where it had been realized, but "disappointing" where it had been abandoned. Within two weeks of the lecture, the society commissioned Olmsted's firm to develop a master plan for the extension of parks throughout the city, fronting

the money for the project on the assumption that the city would see its value upon completion and reimburse the organization. The report was presented to the society in November 1903, the Board of Park Commissioners adopted its resolution and payment, and society president Theodore Marburg (1862–1946) presented the final document to the city on February 5, 1904.[24]

Just days later, the Great Baltimore Fire destroyed nearly all of the city's central business district. Much of the rebuilding that followed was devoted to immediate reconstruction of office buildings so that the city could return to business. In this catastrophic environment, city and park planning took a back seat, and the Municipal Art Society's promotion of the master plan for the center of the city was postponed. Although the Burnt District Commission, which was responsible for planning reconstruction, did take the opportunity to widen some streets, Sherlock Swann, the commission chairman, would later report to Mayor Preston that there had been "decided antipathy to the acquirement of any property within the Burnt District lines for park purposes."[25]

The 1909 City Plan

Once the emergency had passed, the Municipal Art Society once again pushed for the development of a city plan and in 1906 invited Carrère and another New York architect, Arnold W. Brunner (1857–1925), to serve on an advisory commission to investigate a new plan. They were logical choices, as the pair, in association with Daniel H. Burnham (1846–1912), had developed Cleveland's 1903 Group Plan, a highly publicized city plan, and Carrère with partner Hastings was designing new Senate and House office buildings for Washington and a planned extension to the Capitol. The project was launched with the goal of making Baltimore "the most beautiful city in America," and Olmsted Jr., then still working on the McMillan Plan for Washington, was subsequently asked to assist.[26]

In November 1909 Carrère and Brunner, without Olmsted, presented their findings to Mayor J. Barry Mahool (1870–1935), the city council, and representatives of important business interests.[27] Brunner made the point that their work was not to be viewed as the "City Beautiful," but as the "City Sensible," suggesting that if wise choices were made the results would be beautiful. As they had advocated in Cleveland, Carrère and Brunner recommended grouping public buildings around a large open space, suggesting that even mediocre buildings could have dignity if placed in a planned scheme. Acknowledging that there were two ways to design cities, the pair noted: "We have chosen the formal method of design rather than the picturesque. We are not insensible to the charm of many of the Old World cities but this charm is largely the result of time and tradition and the picturesque is not to be deliberately constructed." Suggesting a significant change in taste from nineteenth-century landscape design, they observed that the picturesque was "mere affectation. Our minds do not work that way; an orderly arrangement is the most natural for us."[28] Thus, they argued for a contemporary approach that was in the design language of a formal, or geometrically symmetrical style.

The 1909 plan largely addressed creating a civic center around Baltimore City Hall, which by this period was surrounded by a jumble of buildings in various stages of decay (fig. 6). Baltimore's city hall (1867–1875) had been designed in the Second Empire style by local architect George W. Frederick (1842–1924). Erected at the northwest corner of Holliday Street and Fayette Street, the building replaced a number of early nineteenth-century mansions. By the time it was built, however, the elites had abandoned this street, as well as areas directly east on Gay Street, and their houses had either been demolished for commercial structures or altered into factories, tenements, and saloons. The placement of City Hall here may have been the impetus for establishing an east–west axis that

had emerged by the time of the 1909 plan, marked by buildings that included a US post office on the east side of Monument Square (on Calvert Street) to the west and a new courthouse on the west side of the square.

The 1909 plan called for the acquisition of all of the property east of City Hall, the demolition of all these earlier structures, and the rebuilding of the area into a cohesive complex including formal open space and a concentration of public buildings (figs. 7 and 8). This civic center included a large annex directly to the east of City Hall, behind which an open space would lead to the Jones Falls, a stream that entered the city from the north. The approach was several blocks long, framed by formal lines of pleached trees and entered through a monumental gateway on the east. Around this core of buildings and park, other public buildings required by the city, state, or federal government could be placed in the future. Referring to Georges-Eugène Haussmann's Paris and the Ringstrasse in Vienna, Brunner and Carrère proposed several new monumental approaches to the center, including one designed by city civil engineer Calvin W. Hendrick, which buried the Jones Falls. Although the stream had provided much of the city's early water power for milling operations, it also frequently flooded its banks and by the early twentieth century was often dirty and stagnant. Containing it was forward thinking not only for public safety and hygiene, but because it created a tree-lined boulevard leading to the Civic Center. At its northern end the boulevard would merge with Mount Royal Avenue and by extension link to one of the city's large early parks, Druid Hill Park, and to the larger network of parks envisioned in the 1904 Olmsted park plan. Farther west, the committee proposed that Howard Street could be extended and artfully connected with Mount Royal Avenue, thereby forming a belt around the city. The assembled parties endorsed the plan, and in 1910 Mayor Mahool legally constituted the Commission on City Plan to further its objectives.[29]

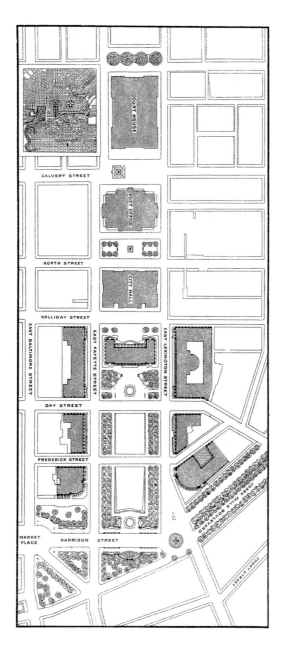

In May 1911 James Preston came into office with a mandate and a blueprint to promote large-scale change in the civic landscape. The *Baltimore American* quoted his statement that he was determined "to bring about a city beautiful, as exemplified by a modern system of ornamental street lamps." He advocated a "Great White Way" installation (using lighting with very bright luminous arc bulbs covered by decorative globes, then being promoted by George A. Miller of New York) in time for the Demo-

cratic National Convention, to be held in the city in June 1912. Baltimore had been using a combination of gas and electric fixtures since the early 1880s and was the first American city to be lit with gas streetlights. The new system, which replaced some of the older lighting, encompassed sixty blocks and was stated to be the largest installation of its kind in the country, making Baltimore "the most beautifully lighted city on the American Continent."[30]

Hastings' Commission

Preston's Mount Vernon Place project was a new initiative of his second term, but solutions to his other "civic problems," the St. Paul Street Improvement and Civic Center projects, had moved at a glacial pace for several years. The Civic Center idea had been proposed in 1909 by Carrère and others and was reenergized by a 1915 ordinance approving property acquisition. The St. Paul Street project responded to a recommendation in the 1909 plan for improved streets heading north out of the central business district and connected the proposed civic center via a tree-lined boulevard to Mount Vernon Place. The mayor authorized an ordinance to realize the project in March 1915, enabling the acquisition and demolition of properties. City engineer Hendrick, who in Preston's first term had successfully buried the Jones Falls—although not as the artistic tree-lined boulevard mapped out in the 1909 plan—provided plans recommending that the St. Paul Street area, with little alteration to the existing steep grade, be turned into a park with a central walkway for pedestrians (fig. 9).[31]

After deciding on Hastings to address this trio of projects, over the course of two years Preston exchanged hundreds of letters with his chosen architect and met with members of the firm in New York and Baltimore on numerous occasions. The mayor's selection of Hastings to realize the Lafayette statue and tackle contemporary urban problems was heartily endorsed by the Baltimore

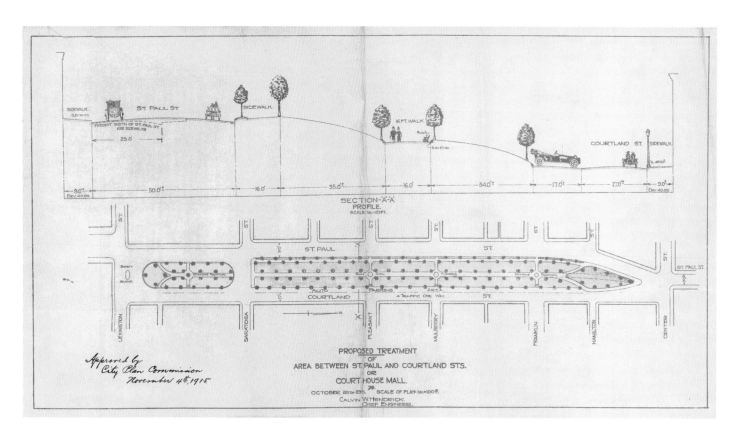

9. Calvin Hendrick, plan for
St. Paul Street, 1915
Baltimore City Archives

architectural community as well as its civic
planning leaders, who were invited in June
1917 to meet Hastings on his visit to Baltimore to discuss the mayor's plans. Within a
month after Hastings was selected to provide
designs for the three projects, Hendrick's
plan for St. Paul Street was abandoned, and
he resigned from office—the engineer apparently not having provided Preston with solutions capable of realizing his City Beautiful
ideals. Architect William M. Ellicott, an
active member of the Municipal Art Society, later described this plan as an "artistic
failure ... without either quality or dignity."[32]

At the heavily attended June 1917 meeting of stakeholders, Hastings observed that
the projects were "to be treated as one great
municipal project, so that one will fit in with
the other," and that with such an approach a
"uniformity of architectural beauty could be
assured." He further observed that, although
city plans of this magnitude had been proposed elsewhere in the United States, few
had been accomplished, and Hastings was
impressed that the city was already acquiring

properties and pulling them down, indicating
that it meant to realize a plan.[33]

Preston subsequently announced that the
city was in good hands to carry out "entirely
the splendid plans that will put Baltimore
in the forefront of cities with more than
utilitarian tendencies," observing that these
emerging plans would have both "economy
and art." As the work developed Preston
said that Baltimore must remain competitive
in the region: "Washington, at our doors,
is destined to be the most beautiful city in
the world. She is building for beauty and
we must not overlook beauty also.... We
must, therefore, reconstruct and renew the
old. Rebuild modern and beautiful lines,
and while planning for a great commercial Baltimore let us lay plans for a more
beautiful, more artistic and more cultivated
Baltimore."[34]

At a meeting in September 1917, the
mayor, the Commission on City Plan, the
Municipal Art Commission, and the Board
of Park Commissioners as well as the
Municipal Art Society endorsed Hastings'

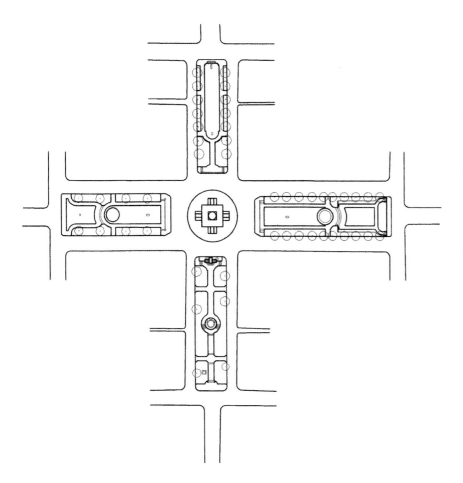

10. Carrère & Hastings, early
designs for Mount Vernon Place,
1917, as published in *American
Architect*, redrawn by the Historic
American Landscapes Survey, and
revised by author

*Library of Congress, Prints and
Photographs Division,* HALS MD-1

However, throughout his remaining
time in office he pushed for the realization
of these plans under either his own or his
successor's auspices.

Mount Vernon Place

Despite the initial wave of enthusiasm for
the Lafayette statue, this memorial and the
Mount Vernon Place project proved the
most challenging to accomplish. Unlike St.
Paul Street or the Civic Center area, Mount
Vernon Place was thought to be sacrosanct,
and in contrast to the other locations, whose
wealthy residents were long gone, it was
home to some of the city's most influential
citizens. After much debate regarding the
site for the Lafayette statue, a location at the
top of the south square was selected, where,
Preston observed to President Woodrow Wilson, "these two great leaders will be historically and artistically grouped together with
fitting dignity."[36]

Hastings was given the latitude to redesign completely the hardscape of all four
squares, although he was encouraged to
retain the round fountain basins in the east
and west squares.[37] The hardscape work
for Mount Vernon Place was mapped out
in a series of plans, including the surviving
drawings for proposed concrete sidewalks,
granite steps, marble retaining walls, balustrades, and fountains. Hastings' first plans
for the squares displayed an intimate scale
inherently suited to the design of small
formal gardens that were conceived as outdoor rooms (fig. 10). Simplified lawn panels
became a principal design element, made
possible by the reduction in the complexity of the pathway shapes: the Olmstedian
curvilinear circulation was largely replaced
by fewer, more regular geometric shapes and
straight lines, in keeping with the classical
simplicity of the monument (see fig. 3). The
south square in this initial scheme was little
altered in plan, but it and the other squares
were altered in section. In the south square
the central pathway, which had formerly
been a rather steeply pitched ramp with one
major terrace at the point of the fountain,

initial recommendations for the three projects. It is clear that the designs for Mount
Vernon Place and St. Paul Street were the
mayor's priority, and these two projects
were to be treated as one construction
project, with the Civic Center to follow.
Accounts of Hastings' presentation observed
that the plans were so comprehensive and
convincing, both "technically and artistically," that "not a single alteration, addition or subtraction was suggested," a signal
achievement in view of the knowledgeable
and engaged audience.[35]

The projects each evolved in a different
way: federal government policies relating
to wartime work and public sentiment during war as well as procedural and financial
hurdles altered their courses of development. The three projects would prove too
ambitious to be fully accomplished during
Preston's second term in office, and he lost
his bid for reelection to a third term in early

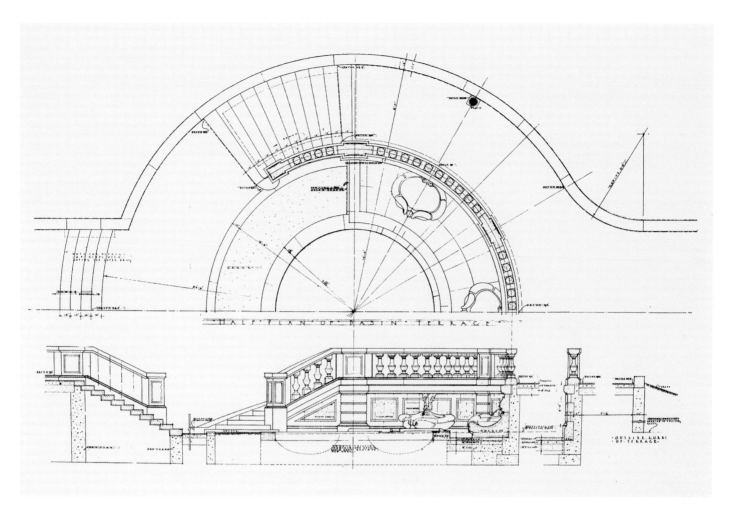

11. Carrère & Hastings, Mount Vernon Place, south square, plan and section of fountain, 1917

American Architect, *January 16, 1918*

was significantly regraded into several broader terraces, including a reconfigured terrace for a new fountain (fig. 11) and a large one at the northern edge, which was to serve as the platform for the Lafayette sculpture. Hastings made several renderings of the Lafayette statue, including a distant view showing it dramatically silhouetted against the Washington Monument and carefully framed by foliage (figs. 12 and 13; compare fig. 14). This new grading and breaks in perspective caused by the various balustrades, foliage framing, and juxtaposition of the dark shadowy mass of the statue against the white marble of the monument were developed to emphasize the Washington Monument as the "architectural climax" of the entire composition. In the three other squares regrading for all of the park ends closest to the monument, where the ends of

the squares were lengthened and squared off, created the space for new surrounding balustrades. Also, as the mounding constructed during the Olmsted era in the centers of these three squares was to be leveled, most of the sculptures were lowered in grade. The stone walls enclosing the squares were to be replaced with new marble balustrades and retaining walls.[38]

As the design progressed, it was monitored in the popular and the professional press. Questions were raised in the *Baltimore Sun* about the proposed balustrades. Hastings responded in a letter to architect Josias Pennington, president of the Commission on City Plan, which was published in the *Baltimore American*, arguing that the same question could be asked of the "most famous square in the world," the Place de la Concorde:

THE · LAFAYETTE · MEMORIAL · MONUMENT ·

FOR · THE · CITY · OF · BALTIMORE

SCALE '⅛' = 1'-0"

12. Carrère & Hastings, Mount Vernon Place, south square, Lafayette statue and Washington Monument, 1917

American Architect, January 16, 1918

One of the most important principles of good planning when designing a public square is to always bear in mind that the square should be lower in the center than on the sides. A very unfortunate situation has always obtained in these four arms to Mt. Vernon Square. The ground with the grass on it was higher than the side roads. The only possible way to lower them was to meet their intersection with the roadbed around the monument by way of a low terrace to make the transition. Given this terrace, the only thing was to put the balus-

trade on it, — a balustrade which one associates with the human scale gives real scale to the monument and makes it look its real size. It also gives the Square platform for the monument to stand upon instead of a circular one which was badly related to the four corners of the buildings around the monument.[39]

Hastings' observations suggest how functionality and design were intertwined in the firm's design decisions here as they would be elsewhere.

Carrère and Hastings believed that sculpture should be integral to an architectural program. As the sculptures had been placed on or around pathways that were being moved, their former positions no longer made sense, especially because, according to Hastings, the statues, including the allegorical bronzes of War, Peace, Order, and Force, by Antoine-Louis Barye (1796–1875), had been "thrown down anywhere, unrelated to anything and not properly appreciated."[40] In an attempt to make some of the sculptures integral to the architectural framework of the squares, Hastings moved the four Barye allegories from their positions in the center of the west square, placing them on the corner plinths of the new balustrades of both the west and east squares, facing the monument, an arrangement he believed would be especially evocative after the placement of the new Lafayette bronze in the south square.[41] The addition of the Lafayette statue and the repositioning of the allegories transformed the sculptures from a collection of art objects, some with local significance, to a program with national and symbolic meaning linked to the American Revolution and to democracy.

A lighting plan and the question of whether the parks should be electrified concerned William Mohr, superintendent of lamps and lighting, who reported that the "gas lighting systems now installed in these [Mount Vernon Place] Squares is inadequate and antiquated, and it seems to me a more modern type of lighting and fixture should be considered to harmonize with the new conditions." Hastings, in the interest of

13. Carrère & Hastings, Mount Vernon Place, south square, Lafayette statue and Washington Monument, 1917

American Architect, January 16, 1918

at the time presented a canopy of uniform size and height within each square. In 1915 eight "beautiful and symmetrical" matched pin oaks had been transplanted to the west square in celebration of the Washington Monument centennial, while the east square had an older canopy of silver maples. The north square as well had an older canopy of uniform trees, European lindens (see, for example, fig. 2). While the north square had a few shrubs at its entrances, the east and west squares had none, their only ornamentation being planting beds with annuals. The south square presented an appearance different from that of the others, as it was fully planted with a mixture of largely deciduous shrubbery, with only some perimeter trees remaining from an earlier planting campaign. Dating from the Olmsted period, this landscaping was a solution to the problem created by the small size and steep grade of this square, which did not lend itself to a grass plat.[43] Hastings' first stage of work kept the existing trees and shrubbery until the hardscape had been installed, after which necessary planting adjustments could be made (see figs. 12 and 14).[44] The firm also presented the city with a detailed groundplane planting plan for the west, north, and east squares. Hastings encouraged the use of evergreens at points where they might be seen near the white marble balustrades, a striking contrast he thought "would appeal to the general public" year round. Hastings noted that these evergreens could be boxwood or holly plants, in keeping with the "Colonial" character of the monument and reenvisioned squares.[45]

In a letter to the trustees of the Peabody Institute, Hastings described his firm as the "architects commissioned to restore certain features of the Mt. Vernon Square so as to harmonize with the splendid old Washington statue, designed by Mills, and which is Colonial in character; and at the same time we have been asked to design the architectural features of the Lafayette memorial to compose and harmonize with their surroundings." That a monu-

economy, first suggested that the "ornamental post and globe" used in some of the city's squares would be sufficient. Although he was subsequently asked to design a unique light fixture, it is unclear whether a new design was presented. The lights first installed, consisting of a round ball globe on a decorative pole (fig. 15), were different from those used on the contemporaneous project on St. Paul Street.[42]

For the initial campaign Hastings encouraged the retention of the existing trees in the west, east, and north squares, which

14. Mount Vernon Place, south
square, 1946
Maryland Historical Society

fied features surrounding the Washington Monument should be of the same, or as nearly as possible the same, material as the monument itself."[47] To accomplish this, the marble for the new work came from the Beaver Dam quarries near Cockeysville, Maryland, north of Baltimore—the quarry area that had supplied the marble for the monument.[48] The architect made multiple references to his search for "Colonial" (that is, "American") inspirations and suitable hard- and softscape materials. Clearly he wanted to make the Washington Monument the "dominating feature" of Mount Vernon Place, as was reported of "this dignified city development" in *The American Architect*.[49]

As plans for the project were under development, critics brought up the wartime restraint on new building projects. Other newspaper articles and letters to Preston from representatives of civic organizations voiced concerns about wartime spending, particularly in Mount Vernon Place. They also complained that the changes might alter Mount Vernon Place's "original" condition. Pennington insisted that nothing being altered was part of the "old original condition" of the squares, but merely the work "carried out some forty years ago," deflecting any charge that the current plans were impinging on the authenticity of the Mills-era design. Criticizing the Olmsted design from the 1870s, Pennington observed that the "present arrangement of the squares was carried out in a style of work which has been so frequently referred to as not in any way harmonizing with the architectural style of the monument." Hastings went so far as to say that these "so-called Gothic Victorian accessories made out of polished granite around the old colonial monument" were an act of architectural "vandalism" on the part of someone who could not have understood the monument (see fig. 2). "Our own work in the case of Mount Vernon Square is one of devout submission to the character and temperament of the men who designed the monument in every detail."[50]

ment from 1815 was viewed as "Colonial" was typical of the American Colonial Revival, which drew loosely from classically inspired antebellum design sources.[46] In designing these new surroundings, for instance, Hastings traveled to Charlottesville, Virginia, to examine Thomas Jefferson's University of Virginia, which he informed Preston embraced "much interesting Colonial architecture." He also studied architecture books published in the United States around the time Mills designed the column, claiming that he drew the balustrade and molding profiles from an 1815 pattern book. Hastings also insisted that it was "important that the newer modi-

Opposition was expressed not only in concern for retaining the "original" character of Mount Vernon Place but also in reception of the new design. Despite Hastings' insistence that the new work was in fact retrieving a lost original harmony of design, criticism of the project was couched in terms of concerns about "modern" change. One letter to the editor observed that the squares of Mount Vernon Place were among "the most charming in America. They have what no modern planning can give them, atmosphere, color, charm. What might be the finest scheme of civic planning for a new town in the Middle West, is the poorest taste in an eastern city whose character has been stamped upon it by the passing years." The writer proposed: "Suppose the new plan should be more truly classical, more letter perfect?" It might not even so be an improvement: "Are we not in danger of being deceived by high sounding phrases, and cleverly rendered architectu[r]al drawings?" As the rhetoric and worry about

this change escalated in the late spring of 1918, the editors of the *Baltimore Sun* published their own thoughts on the matter: "There is no doubt of what we have; there is a great deal of doubt as to what the Mayor proposes to give us in its place. Marble magnificence, the artificial pomp and circumstance of the modern landscape artist's staged effects, may impress the minds of veneering and fashion-plate types, but there is danger that in this modernness we shall lose a spiritual asset which can never be replaced."[51]

Despite concerns, Preston and the Board of Park Commissioners were in full agreement that the work should go forward. However, responding to pressures, some of them financial, Preston pulled back on the implementation of plans at Mount Vernon Place, commencing work on all the south square modifications but only the installation of the balustrades in the three other squares. The day armistice was declared, on

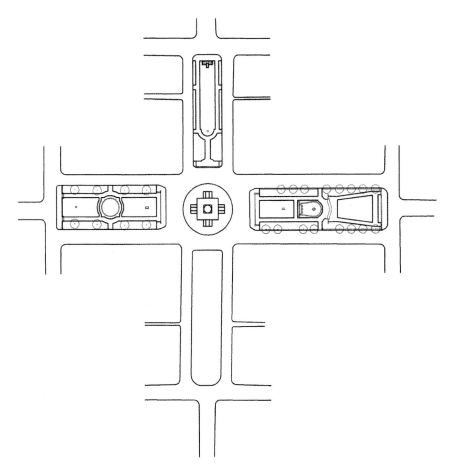

16. Carrère & Hastings, new designs for Mount Vernon Place, 1919, redrawn by the Historic American Landscapes Survey from blueprints in the collection of the Maryland Historical Society and revised by author

Library of Congress, Prints and Photographs Division, HALS MD-1

November 11, 1918, Hastings wrote to the park commissioners encouraging them to complete the parks according to the original plans. Reiterating his strong interest and his vision for the squares as a whole, he repeated: "I do hope your Board will find its way clear to secure the money to perfect this Square and make it entirely in character with the splendid old Washington Monument."[52]

With the war over, Hastings was brought back to town at the commencement of 1919 and encouraged to rethink, without reservation, his designs for the three partially completed squares. In February 1919 the firm submitted additional plans for the completion of the east, west, and north squares. Each carefully delineated where new work was already in place and what yet needed to be accomplished (fig. 16). The east square fountain was redesigned as an elaborate cascade responding to the steep

grade, and the sidewalk pattern altered in response. In the west square, a new circular fountain was composed of circular and square shapes. In the north square an exedra was designed for the Howard statue, and in all the squares any vestiges of the Olmsted-era steps and walls were scheduled to be removed.[53] While Preston launched his unsuccessful attempt at a third term, he placed this new work on hold, but the south square work was completed, the plantings were augmented, and the new lighting was installed throughout.[54]

St. Paul Street

Hastings' plan for St. Paul Street moved forward to completion under Preston's administration with very few complications or changes to its original design.[55] The conditions of this site, which was being cleared when the architect was brought in, included an extreme change of grade on its very narrow east–west axis between St. Paul Street on the west and Courtland Street on the east. The planned improvement had to reconcile this shift, which left the first floors of the buildings on the east side of Courtland easily two stories below the entrances to the buildings on the west side of St. Paul.

The architect approached this project as a "sunken garden," the term most often used to describe the proposed work at the time. Notably, Hastings observed that, in contrast to his work at Mount Vernon Place, "there was no historic monument with which our design had to conform" and therefore "greater freedom of design." Thus his "object [was] primarily a practical study … to improve the circulation and to connect the Municipal Center with Mt. Vernon Square, [and] at the same time improve the general character of the neighborhood, which though so near to City center had become stagnant and out of touch with its vicinity."[56]

On St. Paul Street, the central area of the street improvement was treated as a divided boulevard, with a long retaining wall, extending for several city blocks between Saratoga and Franklin Streets, cutting away

17. Carrère & Hastings, St. Paul Street Improvement, elevation, 1917

Baltimore Municipal Journal, *October 5, 1917; Enoch Pratt Free Library*

18. Carrère & Hastings, St. Paul Street Improvement, plan of central area, 1917

American Architect, *January 16, 1918*

the hillside and adding drama and monumentality. This feature, originally intended to be built of stone, with the stairs in either marble or granite, and the walls of Indiana limestone with inset panels of brick, was carried out in concrete and brick (fig. 17). The plan (fig. 18) called for a series of alternating cascading stairways, the more elaborate ornamented with a fountain, likened by the press to an "old Italian type," or more specifically, by Hastings, to the Spanish Steps in Rome. New uniform electric street lighting, the "Ornamental Luminous Arc Lamp" the city had adopted several years

before as the Baltimore standard, replaced an admixture of earlier electric and gas fixtures on both St. Paul and Courtland Streets.[57]

Allées of pleached trees on St. Paul Street were to be pruned into crisp cubic forms, acting as a unifying device to hide the many irregular building shapes behind them (see fig. 17). On the lower level on the park side of Courtland Street, a row of evenly matched trees flanked the sidewalk. In the central park area, "grouped shrubbery and floral arrangements" were planned at various intersections of the curvilinear pathways. While

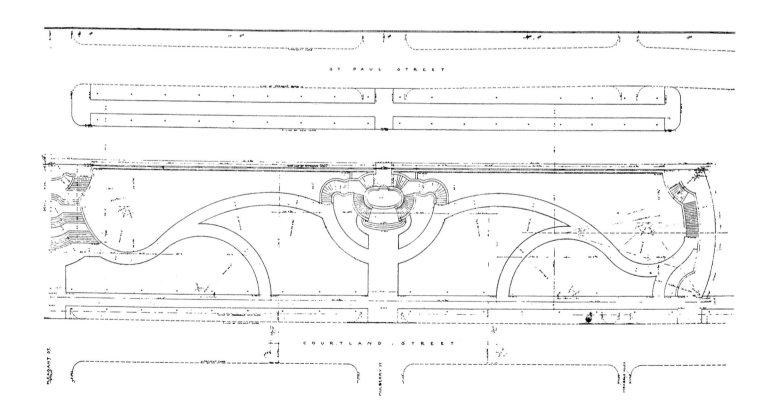

19. St. Paul Street Improvement,
1919
Baltimore Sun, *1919, author
collection*

20. St. Paul Street Improvement,
c. 1920s

*Library of Congress, Prints and
Photographs Division*

outside portion of which massed shrubbery framed the large centerpiece of masonry work. With plans approved and the existing buildings demolished, a year-long building and planting campaign commenced in April 1918 (figs. 19 and 20).[58]

Civic Center

As mentioned, Preston's priorities immediately after hiring Hastings were clearly focused on Mount Vernon Place and St. Paul Street, but Hastings had created the original drawings for the 1909 city plan (see figs. 7 and 8).[59] At the time Hastings was brought in, in June 1917, the Municipal Art Society had recently reaffirmed its wish for a city hall annex, behind which would be a park area, followed by a convention, music, and exhibition hall at the realized Fallsway, the street that covered the Jones Falls, which had been completed in 1915. The convention center was frequently discussed, as is any large-scale civic undertaking, as an economic development tool, apparently in response to the 1912 Democratic National Convention, which had recently been held in the city.[60]

the southern and northern terminuses of the improvement were of different shapes and uses (a sunken car park on the south and a park at the north), the transition to both of these areas was a curved street, on the

21. Carrère & Hastings, Civic Center, plan, 1918

Baltimore Municipal Journal, *November 22, 1918; Enoch Pratt Free Library*

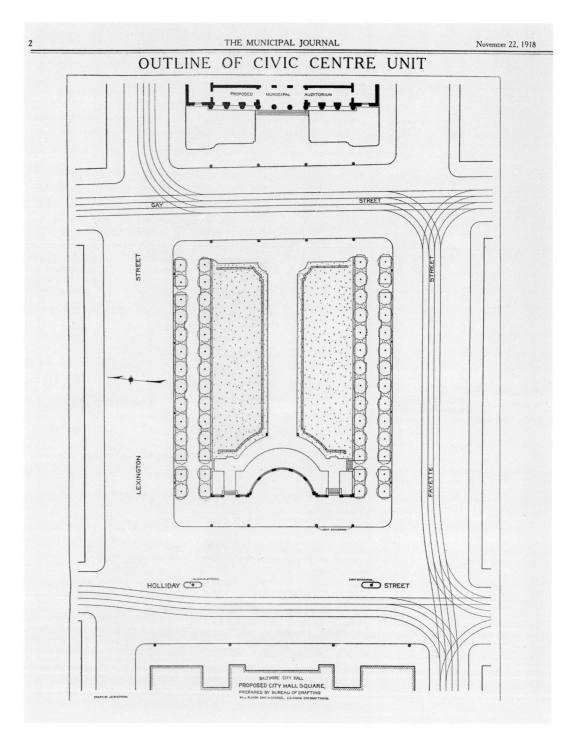

In the winter of 1917–1918, while the other two projects were moving forward, Hastings continued to work on ideas for the Civic Center, and by March 1918 Preston had reviewed well-developed plans for this project. In April Hastings was authorized to make working plans that could be carried out by the next administration, especially the proposed park design, which had been moved from the east of the annex, as suggested in the 1909 plan, to directly in front of City Hall (fig. 21). As the grade of the property between Holliday and Gay streets was not flat, Hastings opted, as elsewhere, to treat the green space as a "sunken garden," accommodating the grade change with four small flights of stairs on the west, leading up to a balustrade, which topped the short retaining wall. The entire composition was made to provide an axially symmetrical framed view of City Hall to the west, as well as to provide similar framed views of the planned new building to the east. The lawn panels on the west gained interest by following the curve of the central area of the balustrading, and on a smaller scale, similar incurvate corners ornamented the Gay Street entrance. The shape of these panels was to be emphasized by a hedge mimicking the layout of the concrete pathways. Rows of Norway maples were planned for the north and south sides of the park.[61] As this project evolved, however, the idea of a paved square like the Place Vendôme emerged, with Hastings' endorsement, some arguing that an "ornamental park without the possibility of utility" would serve no civic function here, unlike a paved space where masses of people could congregate, especially important if, as was also suggested, the new public space might serve a memorial symbolic purpose. Even after Preston lost his bid for a third term, he pushed for the development of Civic Center, and in the final days of his term Hastings sent down a plaster model of the project.[62]

The Legacy of Preston and Carrère & Hastings

In early May 1919 Preston received from Carrère & Hastings the firm's "Report of the City Plan Committee of the City of Baltimore" regarding the development of the newly annexed territories, a document he had commissioned the previous fall. This planning document embraced numerous recommendations regarding the future development of the city, including parkways, transit hubs and nodes with park designs at their intersections, bridges, a combined railroad and rapid transit station, and developments to the harbor, among other improvements.[63]

In the final week of Preston's administration, at a ceremony on May 15, the St. Paul Street project was officially turned over to the Board of Park Commissioners, which took the opportunity to rename the improvement Preston Terrace. (It is now called Preston Gardens.) Preston invited Hastings, in town for the dedication, to a meeting with the incoming mayor, William F. Broening (1870–1953). As part of his dedicatory speech Hastings noted that "any civic problem well solved to adapt itself to the practical needs of a people and to its spiritual uplift must express itself in beauty of plan and construction." In speaking of Preston, Hastings observed that in all of his experience with federal and municipal work, he had never known of an elected official "who has had so wise and comprehensive an understanding of the physical and social conditions of a city and who has had a vision as particular and clear of the future opportunities and possibilities in the development of a growing community." These qualities had resulted not only in what was realized but also in what he had initiated for his successors in Baltimore: "truly [we] may say the City which has the promise of becoming The City Beautiful of these United States of America."[64]

Although perhaps seen by the public during Preston's administration as "court architect," Hastings stayed on after Mayor Broening took office. Broening, with Hastings' Civic Center model at hand, continued to like the idea of a paved plaza for the Civic Center. However, as the project materialized it became a competition for a combined city and state war memorial project. Most of the architects invited in 1921 to participate were from Baltimore, but several nationally recognized firms were invited, including Carrère & Hastings. Baltimore architect Laurence Hall Fowler (1876–1971) submitted the winning design. His plan for the park area in front of City Hall was a not a fully paved plaza but a sunken paved plaza flanked by trees on the north and south, as Hastings had suggested. Hastings' international

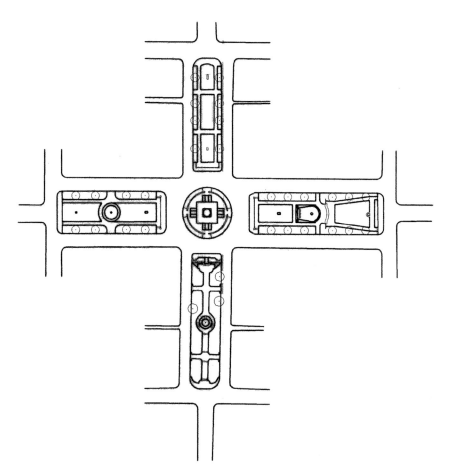

22. Carrère & Hastings, designs
for Mount Vernon Place as realized (1920) and replanted
(1922–1928), redrawn by the Historic American Landscapes Survey
from early photographs and
revised by author

*Library of Congress, Prints and
Photographs Division,* HALS MD-1

achievements continued to be touted as
assurance that Baltimore had put the projects at Preston Terrace and Mount Vernon
Place and the city expansion plan in the best
hands. An article in the city's own journal that hailed Hastings as "Architect and
Prophet" quoted his statement: "Our monuments of to-day should adequately record
the splendid achievements of our contemporaneous life, the spirit of modern justice
and liberty, the progress of modern science,
and the genius of modern invention and dis-
covery, [and] the elevated character of our
institutions." Arguing that "to express our
present age we should neither break with the
past nor select from it arbitrarily," the architect argued for "the style of our own time."[65]

At Mount Vernon Place in the fall of
1919, the park board and Broening took up
Hastings' plans from February. After further meetings Hastings was asked to retain
the west square fountain and simplify the

walkway pattern in the north square. He
provided final plans for these requirements
at the end of the year (fig. 22).[66] This hardscape work was completed by the end of
August 1920, and grass was planted in the
just-completed north, west, and east wings.
With the masonry work completed, the
parks department became interested in the
views to and from Mount Vernon Place and
in addressing the existing tree canopy. Hastings was brought in to examine the state of
the work and recommended the replanting of
oaks in the west square, which had not fared
well since their planting in 1915, with either
oriental planes or European lindens. At this
time he also suggested that "small elms" be
planted on the sides of the south square to
replace the larger framing trees on the sides
as they died. He also agreed with the park
commissioners that the view out of Mount
Vernon Place should be addressed by planting trees on Monument Street to mitigate
the view in that direction, which was largely
industrial in nature.[67] Hastings' observations
encouraged the parks department in early
1922 to announce that the trees in Mount
Vernon Place would be replanted, the city
forester observing that the oaks in the west
square were dying and that the silver maples
in the east square were "all past maturity
and past any tree surgery on the part of
foresters. In such a formal environment it
would not do to remove dead and half dead
trees and leave the few living ones where
they are." The forester recommended that
the oaks and silver maples be replaced with
American elms, a course of action that was
put into place in the late fall (fig. 23; see also
fig. 15). Several years later, as the lindens
in the north square began to fail, the entire
square was replanted in elms, maintaining
the tradition in these three squares of uniform trees, an important element of Carrère
& Hastings' design philosophy.[68]

As the principal work was completed on
the squares, controversy arose once again
regarding the siting of the Lafayette monument. Architects like William M. Ellicott
defended the location, stating it was the

crowning glory of the entire conception, as
it was a "great symbol of the relation of two
nations in the cause of human liberty."[69] The
sculpture arrived in the early fall of 1924,
and with President Calvin Coolidge, Governor of Maryland Albert C. Ritchie, Mayor
Howard W. Jackson, and other notables in
attendance, the Lafayette statue was dedicated on the Frenchman's birthday, September 6, in front of a crowd said to number
twenty thousand. Coolidge implored the
audience to take the opportunity to "re-
dedicate ourselves to the inspiring memory
of a true son of world freedom … in the
shadow of the stately monument reared to
his great friend, Washington."[70]

Thus Preston's campaign for improving
the city of Baltimore, begun seven years
before in a bed of pansies, finally achieved
its objective. Its legacy survives to this day
in Baltimore's built environment in two
realized projects by Carrère and Hastings,
perhaps rare survivals of City Beautiful
landscape design and recognized as "among
the most successful and fully realized of the
firm's urban designs."[71] Further, Carrère &
Hastings' long work in establishing a civic
center lives on in the project realized by
Fowler. Preston seized every opportunity he
could to promote the beautification of his
city. The projects demonstrate the tenacity
required to reshape the urban landscape,
as was true of other City Beautiful dreams,
many of which were never realized.

An early version of this essay was written for the Historic American Landscapes Survey, National Park Service, largely focusing on Carrère & Hastings' work at Mount Vernon Place, Baltimore. This report has been expanded to include a broader discussion of their work in the city. I thank J. Laurie Ossman for early assistance with the work of Carrère & Hastings. I also thank Nicol Regan for graphic design assistance in revising several Historic American Landscapes Survey drawings for inclusion in this essay.

1. See "French Commission Will Ask for Army," and "The Visitors from France," *Washington Post*, April 25 and 26, 1917. See "French Invited to City," *Baltimore Sun*, May 2, 1917, and the change of purpose for the visit in "Plans Monument to Gen. Lafayette," *Baltimore American*, May 7, 1917.

2. See, for example, David Holden, "1904 Olmsted Bros. Report: The Advancement of City Planning in Baltimore," *Olmstedian* 15, no. 2 (fall 2004), and Duncan Stuart with research assistance from Eric Holcomb, "Baltimore City Planning: The Critical Role of the Olmsted Firm," *Olmstedian* 17, no. 2 (spring 2008).

3. On this moment in the fort's history see Mark Davison and Eliot Foulds, *Cultural Landscape Report for Fort McHenry* (Brookline, MA, 2004), 81–86, which also discusses the Key monument. On the 1812-related monuments, see the unpublished report by Kathleen G. Kotarba and Walter Edward Leon, "The Monumental City: Famous Baltimore City Public Monuments," Commission for Historical and Architectural Preservation, Baltimore, 2002, nos. 16, 28, 53, 56, 57, and 78.

4. On the location change see "Joffre May Visit City on Return from West," *Baltimore Sun*, May 8, 1917, and "Enthusiasm for Lafayette Statue," *Baltimore American*, May 16, 1917.

5. For the monument within Mills' larger career, see John M. Bryan, *Robert Mills: America's First Architect* (New York, 2001), 105–119.

6. Several variations on the final scheme survive in the collection of the Maryland Historical Society (hereafter MdHS). See Mary Ellen Hayward and Frank R. Shivers Jr., eds., *The Architecture of Baltimore: An Illustrated History* (Baltimore, 2004), 118, and an unexecuted example illustrated on 119. See the laws regarding Mount Vernon Place in "Appendix B: Historical Data Relating to Parks and Squares," in *46th and 47th Annual Reports of the Board of Park Commissioners to the Mayor and City Council of Baltimore for the Fiscal Years Ending December 31, 1905, 1906* (Baltimore, 1907), 80–81. Not mentioned in these reports is the iron fence; on it see "Improvement of Washington Place" and "Improving Mt. Vernon Place," *Baltimore Sun*, April 13 and 17, 1850.

7. Work began in March 1875 as noted in "Appendix B" 1907, 81. Those involved and details of the plans for the north and south squares are discussed in "Washington Monument Surroundings," *Baltimore Sun*, June 8, 1877. See also M. Edward Shull, "Mount Vernon Place," *Olmstedian* 15, no. 1 (fall 2003).

8. See "Baltimore Bows to Joffre and Viviani," *Baltimore American*, May 15, 1917, and "Baltimore Acclaims Joffre; French Mission Is Lionized During Hour's Visit to City," *Baltimore Sun*, May 15, 1917.

9. See Lafayette Memorial Committee, membership list, and other documents, all file 118, Baltimore City Archives (hereafter BCA preceded by file number). The papers of Mayor James H. Preston (hereafter Preston) at the BCA are extensive.

10. See J. V. Kelly, Secretary, Board of Park Commissioners, to Preston, April 13, 1917, enclosing Olmsted Brothers to J. V. Kelly, April 11, 1917; both 3a, BCA. Preston voiced this concern in "The Mayor's General Message to the City Council," *Baltimore Municipal Journal*, October 18, 1918, 3. Preston's papers and the *Baltimore Municipal Journal* all reveal the convergence of these civic challenges.

11. The park commissioners' communication to the mayor: Kelly to Preston, April 13, 1917. On Olmsted's involvement see "Big Plan for Parkway," April 18, 1912; "Oval Facing Homewood," October 24, 1913; and "Hopkins Oval Work Starts," November 16, 1913; all *Baltimore Sun*. On Hastings see Preston to George Washington Williams, April 19, 1917, 3a, BCA. Preston's frustrations with Olmsted may have been the result of Olmsted's involvement with the mayor's Fort McHenry and Key memorial projects, for which he had been hired by the city to assist in plans but in his role as a member of the Federal Commission of Fine Arts was also passing judgment on them. This dilemma is outlined in Davison and Foulds 2004, 81–83.

12. Preston, Hastings, and Olmsted are placed in the same meeting of the Federal Commission of Fine Arts in "To Help Key Memorial," *Baltimore Sun*, October 10, 1914. See Preston to Thomas Hastings, Hastings & Carriere [*sic*], May 31, 1917, 118, BCA, and Hastings to Preston, June 5, 1917, 118, BCA. On the City Beautiful see William H. Wilson, *The City Beautiful Movement* (Baltimore, 1989). Although both Carrère and Baltimore are mentioned in this volume, their contributions to the larger movement receive little elaboration. On this period in Baltimore's development see Sherry H. Olson, *Baltimore: The Building of an American City* (1980; revised and expanded edition, Baltimore, 1997), in particular the chapter "The Art of Urban Landscape, 1900–1918," 245–301.

13. William M. Ellicott to Theodore Marburg, June 11, 1917, 118, BCA.

14. The work of the firm has recently been cataloged in Mark Alan Hewitt et al., *Carrère & Hastings Architects*, 2 vols. (New York, 2006). See also Laurie Ossman and Heather Ewing, *Carrère & Hastings: The Masterworks* (New York, 2011).

15. On the church and its site see "Architectural Criticism," *Architecture*, April 15, 1911, 49–50.

16. This essay adds another dimension to Hastings' public work, which, according to Hewitt et al. 2006 (1:253–254), was of less interest to him than to Carrère.

17. On the Carrère genealogy see Thomas Barbour, "Some Notes on the Backgrounds of the Carrere, Buchanan, and Related Families," [c. 1888], filing case A, MdHS, and "Buchanan Family Reminiscences," *Maryland Historical Magazine* 35, no. 3 (September 1940): 262–269, which discusses the Carrère connections.

18. See "Mr. Carrere to Lecture," *Baltimore Sun*, December 15, 1901, which lists these credentials, and "Illustrated Lecture, Delivered by John M. Carrere," *Architects and Builders Journal* 3, no. 7 (February 1902): 8–9, 11–14. See also *The City of the Future by Albert Kelsey; The Municipal Art Society, Its Activities, Aims and Hopes by Theodore Marburg. Addresses Delivered at the Annual Meeting of The Municipal Art Society of Baltimore, Johns Hopkins University, January 8, 1902* ([Baltimore], 1902). This publication did not include Carrère's speech, noting that it had just been published. See the report of this meeting, "To Beautify the City," *Baltimore Sun*, January 9, 1902.

19. See Charles H. Caffin, "Baltimore Municipal Art Conference," *Harper's Weekly*, December 23, 1899, 1332.

20. "Illustrated Lecture," 8, 11, 13. Hewitt et al. 2006, 1:253–254, note the seminal nature of this lecture and subsequent reworkings included for delivery in Harford in 1910.

21. "Illustrated Lecture," 8, 11–12; see the firm's visual realization of this ideal in Hewitt et al. 2006, 1:252. See Garrett Power, "High Society: The Building Height Limitation on Baltimore's Mt. Vernon Place," *Maryland Historical Magazine* 79, no. 3 (fall 1984): 197–219, which discusses the 1904 law, among other preservation actions.

22. "Illustrated Lecture," 8.

23. See "The City of Baltimore," *Niles' Weekly Register*, September 19, 1812, 46. This article is one of many that discuss the rapid growth of the city.

24. On Olmsted's speech and his employment at Wyman Park, see "To Beautify Washington," *Baltimore Sun*, April 20, 1902. See Olmsted Brothers, *Report upon the Development of Public Grounds for Greater Baltimore* (Baltimore, 1904), including Marburg's presentation letter of February 5, 1904, to the park board president outlining the genesis of this project (8–9). On the McMillan Plan within the context of the City Beautiful and early city planning efforts see Richard Longstreth, ed., with a new introduction by Therese O'Malley, *The Mall in Washington, 1791–1991*, National Gallery of Art, Studies in the History of Art, vol. 30 (Washington, DC, 2002), in particular the essays by Thomas S. Hines and Jon A. Peterson.

25. Sherlock Swann to Preston, March 14, 1917, 78a, BCA.

26. See "For an Ideal Baltimore," January 16, 1906, and "Mr. Olmsted to Co-operate," January 31, 1906, both *Baltimore Sun*.

27. See the report on the presentation "To Beautify the City," *Baltimore Sun*, November 20, 1909, which notes that Olmsted could not attend. Given Olmsted's joining the team after it was formed and Carrère's 1908 comment that he was doing all the work (quoted in Hewitt et al. 2006, 1:259), his role may have been limited.

28. See Municipal Art Society, *Partial Report on "City Plan"* (Baltimore, 1910), 4, 5, 7, 14. The report contains a transcript of the hearing, a preface outlining the plan's history, and supporting documents in appendixes.

29. Municipal Art Society 1910, 19, 20–21, 23, 40 (and plan opposite), 47. See also "To Beautify the City."

30. "Soon to Be a City of Lights," *Baltimore American*, January 16, 1912. See Stuart Stevens Scott, "Baltimore's Great White Way," *Municipal Journal* [New York], August 8, 1912, 184, which illustrates a street scene with an example of the new pole. See John Allen Corcoran, "The City Light and Beautiful," *American City* 7, no. 1 (July 1912): 46, 48–49 (example illustrated on 48). Preston is quoted on Baltimore's recent extensive installation of these lamps, noted to be produced by the General Electric Company of Schenectady, New York, and to use a pole design patented by the city. See two advertisements, the first by the General Electric Company, the manufacturer of the bulb, and the second by the Lundin Electric and Machine Co., Boston, the manufacturer of the pole (design no. 4024, illustrated), the latter of which notes Baltimore's place in national lighting: *Public Service* 13, no. 3 (September 1912): 131 and 136. The 1900 findings of Baltimore's Municipal Lighting Commission were reported in various civic periodicals. See, for instance, Allen Ripley Foote's review "Electric Lighting in Baltimore," *Municipal Affairs; A Quarterly Magazine Devoted to Consideration of City Problems from the Standpoint of the Taxpayer and Citizen* 4, no. 1 (March 1900): 232–235. The first electric arc lamps were installed in 1882.

31. Hendrick's plan is sketched out in "St. Elizabeth Bought," *Baltimore Sun*, November 2, 1915.

32. The abandonment of Hendrick's plan is noted in "Lafayette Memorial Site South of Monument Urged," August 10, 1917, and his resignation in "Hendrick to Talk Soon," August 22, 1917; both *Baltimore Sun*. See Ellicott's letter to the editor, "The Mount Vernon Place Improvements," *Baltimore Sun*, October 27, 1918. The outcome of Hendrick's St. Paul Street plan exemplifies the move of urban design from the hands of engineers to "artists" (architects) during this period.

33. Hewitt et al. 2006, 1:259–262, catalog the Mount Vernon Place project, in which the St. Paul Street work is mentioned. Hastings' newer work at the Civic Center is not discussed. The quotations are from, respectively, "Takes Up Civic Plans," *Baltimore Sun*, June 23, 1917, and "Points Way to City Beautiful," *Baltimore American*, June 23, 1917.

34. Preston's goals are noted in "Memorial Site for Lafayette," *Baltimore American*, August 10, 1917; on his regional competition see "Greater Baltimore—A

City Beautiful and Useful," *Baltimore Municipal Journal*, November 22, 1918, 1.

35. See the city's own account of the meeting, "Plans Approved for Beautification of City," *Baltimore Municipal Journal*, September 14, 1917, 6.

36. The change in location is noted in "Hastings Plans His Work: Architect Approves of Site Chosen for Lafayette Memorial," June 29, 1917, and "Lafayette Memorial Site South of Monument Urged," August 10, 1917, both *Baltimore Sun*. Preston made his observation to Wilson in a letter of November 9, 1918, 118, BCA, in which he asked the president to write an inscription for the base.

37. The retention of the fountains is evident in the earliest plans submitted and in later discussion about a new design for them when an additional design phase commenced.

38. The south square design intent is discussed in "Plans Approved for Beautification of City," 6. In these earliest existing plans, the steps and wall at the east end of the east square and some coping at the north end of the north square were to be retained in addition to the two circular fountains.

39. Hastings to Josias Pennington, December 23, 1918, 80, BCA. The letter appeared as "Hastings Defends Use of Balustrades," *Baltimore American*, December 28, 1918.

40. Hastings to Pennington, December 23, 1918. Pennington noted in other correspondence that the placement of the statues had been determined by available space in the old arrangement (Josias Pennington, Commission on City Plan, to J. Cookman Boyd, March 17, 1919, 80, BCA).

41. For an appreciation of the new locations of these bronzes see J. Carrell Lucas to Preston, November 14, 1918, 80, BCA. Preston, as elsewhere, noted that he left these kinds of artistic decisions up to Hastings: Preston to J. Carrell Lucas, November 15, 1918, 80, BCA.

42. See William Mohr to George Weems Williams, President, Board of Park Commissioners, January 14, 1918, 121, BCA, and his other letters from this period. J. V. Kelly, secretary of the Board of Park Commissioners, writing to Carrère & Hastings, suggested the need of a lighting study (January 16, 1918, 121, BCA). Upon receipt Hastings replied to Preston on January 19, 1918 (121, BCA), regarding "economy" but saying that he would investigate a design. "Parking Estimates Ready," *Baltimore Sun*, March 14, 1918, noted that "artistic electric lamps" would be used, but the installation was deferred, as reported in "City to Put Up Statue," *Baltimore Sun*, April 6, 1918.

43. The existing trees in the squares are documented in "Big Oaks Nearly Ready," *Baltimore Sun*, March 17, 1915 (west square), and "Mount Vernon Place to Have Fine New Trees," *Baltimore Sun*, May 7, 1922 (east square); the species for the north square is suggested in a letter to the editor, *Baltimore Sun*, March 26, 1918. See also McHenry Howard, "The Washington Monument and Squares," *Maryland Historical Magazine* 13, no. 2 (June 1918), which outlines the history of the squares, noting (181) that in the late nineteenth century the trees were ash (south), European linden (north), and maples (east and west). He implies (182) that the Olmsted firm installed the south square shrubbery to good effect, noting that if left as grass the square would have appeared "mean" and "uninteresting."

44. See "Plans Approved for Beautification of City," 6, which had noted that no changes would be made to the softscape. Hastings, subsequently writing of the south square, noted that after construction was finished he would do "some elimination and some planting." See Hastings to Preston, January 17, 1919, 80, BCA. When it was inaccurately stated that the shrubbery would be removed, a debate ensued in the *Baltimore Sun*; see "Old Shrubbery to Go," January 15, 1919, and "Old Shrubbery to Stay," February 5, 1919.

45. Hastings to Preston, November 16, 1918, 118, BCA, notes sending the plans and evergreens. The specific "Colonial" plantings are mentioned in "Mt. Vernon Place in Movies," *Baltimore Sun*, March 15, 1919, which names other possible plant varieties.

46. Hastings to the Board of Trustees, Peabody Institute, July 19, 1918, 118, BCA. On the Colonial Revival see Alan Axelrod, ed., *The Colonial Revival in America* (New York, 1985). Hastings is discussed throughout Mardges Bacon's essay, "Toward a National Style of Architecture: The Beaux-Arts Interpretation of the Colonial Revival," 91–121.

47. See Hastings to Preston, October 27, 1917, 118, BCA, regarding Charlottesville; "Hastings Defends Big Improvement," *Baltimore American*, November 24, 1918, on the pattern book reference; Hastings to Preston, November 13, 1917, 121, BCA, on his interest in similar materials. Hastings does not mention his 1815 source, but it could have been an issue of one of Asher Benjamin's publications, such as his *Rudiments of Architecture* (Boston, 1814), which includes plates (23, 24), showing similar balusters and pedestals.

48. See Preston to Hastings, October 25, 1917, 121, BCA, introducing the Beaver Dam Marble Company to the architect. The mayor's office to Addison H. Clarke, April 26, 1918, 118, BCA, refutes a claim that it was Indiana limestone, confirming that it was Beaver Dam marble. In "Defends Improvements," *Baltimore Sun*, May 8, 1918, Hastings stated that Indiana stone was never considered.

49. "Washington Monument, Baltimore, Md.," *American Architect*, July 6, 1921, 12.

50. As quoted in "Hastings Defends Use of Balustrades" and "Hastings Defends Big Improvement."

51. "E. E. G.," letter to the editor, March 26, 1918, and "Come, Mr. Mayor, Let Us Reason Together," editorial, May 9, 1918, both *Baltimore Sun*.

52. See Hastings to J. V. Kelly, November 11, 1918, 3a, BCA.

53. These blueprints survive in the collection of the MdHS. An additional version of the plan for the west square is in the collection of the Baltimore City

Department of Recreation and Parks. The firm was not consistent in the surviving 1917 and 1919 plans regarding showing existing or planned new trees.

54. "South Wing of Squares Open," *Baltimore Sun*, March 6, 1919, and Preston to Hastings, April 19, 1919, 80, BCA, regarding the lights.

55. The surviving plans submitted in September 1917 and published in January 1918 in *American Architect* appear to be those used for the project. Subsequent alterations have obscured the fact that the project was built as proposed; namely, the Orleans (or Bath) Street viaduct was cut across the garden; Courtland Street was widened, eliminating some pathways in the garden; and the upper tree-lined boulevard was abandoned.

56. See Hastings as quoted in "Greater Baltimore—A City Beautiful and Useful," 3, and the brief description in "St. Paul Street to Be Important Adjunct to Civic Center," *Baltimore Municipal Journal*, October 5, 1917, 4, and the accompanying rendering (a reprint of a version of that in *American Architect*). The text notes that the lower-level shrubbery was not included in order to show the details of the retaining wall and steps. For an interpretation of this early urban renewal project from the perspective of racial segregation, see Antero Pietila, *Not in My Neighborhood: How Bigotry Shaped a Great American City* (Chicago, 2010), 50–52. The author is in error that this neighborhood was called Gallows Hill; that area was on the east side of the Jones Falls.

57. "Shows City Beautiful," *Baltimore Sun*, September 14, 1917, mentions materials originally suggested for walls; for "old Italian type," see "Plans for Civic Center Approved," *Baltimore American*, September 12, 1917. Hastings notes the similarity to the Spanish Steps in "Greater Baltimore—A City Beautiful and Useful," 3. The arc lamps are discussed in correspondence about the St. Paul project, where they are described as more powerful than smaller incandescent lights. The latter required more poles and were therefore more expensive. See William Mohr to Hastings, February 2, 1918; Mohr to Hastings, February 20, 1918; and Preston to Hastings, March 1, 1918; all 121, BCA. The light poles evident in the earliest photographs of the project appear to be the model so named and discussed in note 30 above.

58. The beginning of work is noted in "A Question of Principle," *Baltimore Sun*, April 25, 1918. See "City Improvements Will Be Pushed," *Baltimore American*, November 22, 1918, for the planting of the trees on St. Paul Street, and Preston to Hastings, April 19, 1919, 80, BCA, regarding trees, topsoil, and grass, apparently for the lower level. Preston to Board of Park Commissioners, February 6, 1919, 3a, BCA, notes that Hastings had developed a planting plan for this project. It remains unlocated, but early photographs suggest that the trees and shrubbery were planted in accordance with Hastings' plan published in *American Architect* (see fig. 19). The species of these plants is not detailed, but photographs suggest that the trees planted on the lower level may have been maples, as was proposed for the Civic Center.

59. According to a newspaper report of a meeting in which Preston discussed the 1909 plan, he credited Hastings with the drawings. As Hastings was in attendance, this attribution seems likely, although it is not mentioned in the 1909 plan. See "First Action on Memorial Project," *Baltimore American*, January 4, 1919.

60. See "Wants City Hall Annex," March 9, 1917, and "Lafayette Memorial Site South of Monument Urged," August 10, 1917, both *Baltimore Sun*.

61. See "Mayor at City Hall," *Baltimore American*, March 10, 1918, and "City to Put Up Statue," *Baltimore Sun*, April 6, 1918. The earliest datable plan (shown here as figure 21) is illustrated as "Outline of Civic Centre Unit," part of the article "Greater Baltimore—A City Beautiful and Useful," 2. The caption describes the details mentioned here.

62. At the conclusion of the war many ideas regarding the Civic Center circulated in the newspapers; see, for instance, "For Great Paved Square," *Baltimore Sun*, December 7, 1918, for the plan promoted by civic leader Sherlock Swann. On the utility of a paved space, see Swann to Preston, November 26, 1918, 80, BCA. Inviting a number of individuals to see the model, Preston recapitulated the history of the project and reiterated the similarity to the Place Vendôme; see Preston to Philip Cook (and copies to others), May 19, 1919, 80, BCA.

63. This report is mentioned in "Will Plan for Annex," *Baltimore Sun*, August 8, 1918. A copy of the report of May 1, 1919, with photographic illustrations of numerous plans, is in 80, BCA.

64. Hastings as quoted in "Sunken Gardens Are Dedicated," *Baltimore American*, May 16, 1919. Copies of the full speeches are in 80, BCA: see "Mr. Hastings [*sic*] Speech," [1919]. Preston's speech was more pragmatic, thanking the appropriate parties; see "Mayor Preston's Speech," [1919].

65. See "Model of Civic Center," *Baltimore American*, April 26, 1919; "Mayor for Paved Plaza," *Baltimore Sun*, January 15, 1920. The history of this project is discussed in Karl Singewald, "The War Memorial, in Baltimore," *Baltimore Municipal Journal*, May 11, 1923, 2–3. See "Thomas Hastings, Architect and Prophet," *Baltimore Municipal Journal*, August 25, 1922, 6, which discusses his recent receipt of a gold medal from the Royal Institute of British Architects.

66. See "To 'Balance' Square," October 8, 1919, and "New Plans for Square," December 4, 1919, both *Baltimore Sun*; and "Mt. Vernon Squares Plans Explained," *Baltimore American*, December 4, 1919.

67. See "Mount Vernon Square Work Ends Tomorrow," *Baltimore Sun*, August 29, 1920, and "Mt. Vernon Square Is Now Completed," *Baltimore American*, August 29, 1920. See "Hastings Would Close Monument Street Hill," *Baltimore Sun*, September 10, 1920, discussing the need for screening, which he voiced later in "Trees Urged as Aid in Monument Vista," *Baltimore Sun*, December 27, 1923. Photographs dated to around this time in the collection of the MdHS

document the parks as of this moment of work, showing the west square replanted and the east square
immediately before it was replanted; see photographs
PP11.422–424.

68. "Mount Vernon Place to Have Fine New Trees,"
May 7, 1922, and "Residents Mourn as Workmen Fell
Mt. Vernon Trees," November 16, 1922, both *Baltimore Sun*. The failing linden trees are documented in a
letter to the editor, *Baltimore Sun*, May 7, 1927. Their
replacement is documented in a photograph from 1928:
Keystone-Mast Collection, UCR / California Museum
of Photography, University of California, Riverside,
image 1996.0009.KU88935. In discussing subsequent
shrubbery plantings the new species is mentioned in
"Square North of the Monument Now to Get Improvements," *Baltimore Sun*, January 9, 1932.

69. Agitation emerged in 1921–1923 regarding the
site of the statue, including a public hearing in 1923.
Ellicott is quoted in "City-Wide Congress Backs G.O.P.
Fight," *Baltimore American*, October 29, 1921.

70. See "President Coolidge Speaks at Unveiling," *Baltimore Municipal Journal,* September 10, 1924, 2–3,
which provides a hindsight history of the Lafayette
statue, and "City to Unveil Statue Today to Lafayette,"
Baltimore Sun, September 6, 1924.

71. Hewitt et al. 2006, 1:259.

MARDGES BACON

*Rockefeller Center: Modernist Paradigm
for the Urban Core*

REINHARD & HOFMEISTER
CORBETT, HARRISON & MAC MURRAY
HOOD & FOUILHOUX
ARCHITECTS

With the completion of its initial phase of development, New York's Rockefeller Center (1927–1940) introduced the first rationally planned and coordinated group of skyscrapers (fig. 1). In recent decades Rockefeller Center has been the subject of much historical analysis, but largely from an American point of view.[1] My objective is to consider the history and criticism of the project from a transatlantic perspective. On two levels—that of design inception and that of reception—this cross-cultural examination will help inform our understanding of American modernism as involving a dynamic exchange with its European counterpart.

Initially conceived during the late 1920s as a site for a new opera house and adjoining plaza, the Rockefeller project drew on a tradition of hierarchical planning by virtue of its architects' training in Beaux-Arts design principles. When the project evolved into a commercial complex, a new design team refocused its ensemble planning with a central office tower and the grouping of other skyscrapers around a privately owned public space.[2] At first the object of polarized critical commentary at home, Rockefeller Center met with a different reception abroad. European modernists were the first to recognize that it could serve as a vital social nucleus for the urban core and a paradigm for European postwar reconstruction. My strategy, then, is to trace briefly the evolution of its ambitions, both architectural and urban, as native expressions of pragmatic and visionary traditions at the intersection of received ideas from Europe. More specifically, I examine the project from the standpoints of authorship, the deployment

of proficient planning and modern building techniques, the transnational exploration of visionary ideas, the design of open and green spaces, and the modernist understanding of the city in three dimensions. Together these help define the elements that distinguish Rockefeller Center as an enduring model of enlightened city making.

From Opera to Commerce

At the start Rockefeller Center was a collaborative venture based on ideas that matured within an international context. By January 1928 a cultural project to provide the city with a new opera house took shape as a real estate proposition between John D. Rockefeller Jr. and Columbia University, subsequently with the Metropolitan Life Insurance Company, which owned the mortgage. One of the largest real estate developments of the period, it was unusual among large-scale projects of the time in receiving no government financing.[3] As Winston Weisman determined more than a half century ago, Benjamin Wistar Morris, an American architect trained at the École des Beaux-Arts in Paris, designed a revenue-producing scheme of May 1928 on three blocks extending from Fifth to Sixth Avenue and from 48th to 51st Street (fig. 2).[4] In effect, the enterprise, now called Metropolitan Square, was conceived as an aggregated block, or superblock, an emerging idea in New York City real estate development that would bring a new urban scale to the heart of Manhattan.

Morris' plan situated the opera house to the west of the plaza with three thirty-five-story commercial buildings at the other compass points. It reflected the hierarchy and

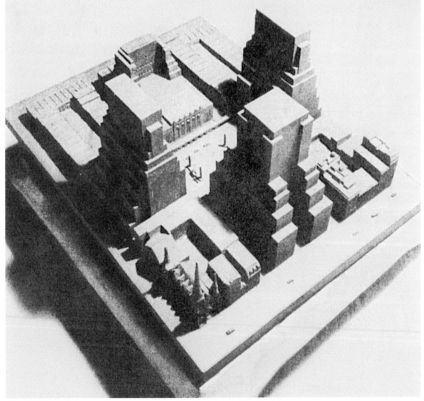

symmetry of Beaux-Arts planning.[5] A raised terrace not only bridged the street grid but also linked the components and provided pedestrian access to revenue-producing shops.[6] Rockefeller subsequently consulted with the New York commercial developer John R. Todd, who in turn called upon two architects, L. Andrew Reinhard and Henry Hofmeister, to draw up plans. Like Morris, both were trained in Beaux-Arts design principles. Their study of September 1928 introduced a four-story shopping arcade with a central promenade that led to a plaza.[7]

The following spring, as a result of a limited competition organized by the Metropolitan Square Corporation advisory board, Harvey Wiley Corbett, another Beaux-Arts-trained architect who had worked with Morris on the opera house, developed a formal landscape for the plaza extending west from the grade of Fifth Avenue to a second-story terrace in front of the opera house (fig. 3). The raised plaza allowed vehicular traffic to

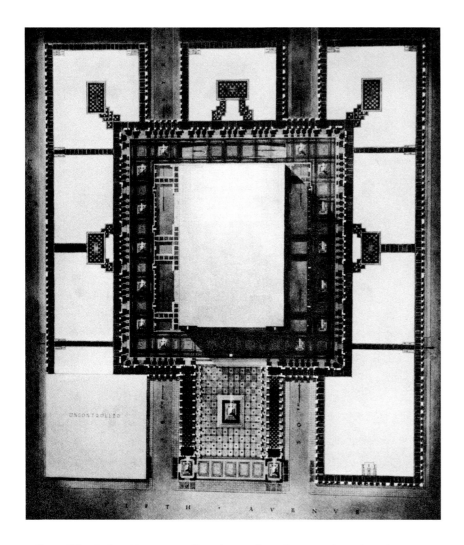

3. Harvey Wiley Corbett, Metropolitan Square, landscape plaza, May 1929

Drawings Collection, Avery Architectural and Fine Arts Library, Columbia University

flow beneath it along 49th and 50th streets. Whereas the fountains and parterres of Corbett's scheme recalled the ordered landscapes of Beaux-Arts *projets*, his multilevel solution for Metropolitan Square drew on his own civic proposals, in conjunction with the Regional Plan Association, to alleviate traffic congestion in New York City.[8]

Morris then proposed an elaborate scheme for the opera house, which integrated more fully a central plaza with a promenade leading up to it from Fifth Avenue (fig. 4). He also responded to the project's increasingly commercial mandate by introducing four taller, stepped-back skyscrapers.[9] He even proposed to landscape the setbacks of its low buildings, as Carol Krinsky observed.[10] The siting of towers surrounding the opera house employed Beaux-Arts composition in the service of civic art as well as an

aggregated plan. Ensemble planning had long served as an aesthetic standard in City Beautiful urban design. Morris' new study emphasized the economical use of land through concentration while taking advantage of New York City's 1916 zoning law, which allowed each tower to rise indefinitely on one quarter of the site.[11] This provision encouraged a trade-off between towers and open space. Although recent urban projects assembled high rises—among them Grand Central Terminal (1903–1913) with its viaduct (1919), adjacent hotels, and commercial towers, as well as Fred French's Tudor City (1925–1928), with its cluster of apartment towers, restaurants, shops, and private park—Rockefeller Center achieved an unprecedented composition of skyscrapers and spatial planning.[12]

The four components described—the formally landscaped plaza envisioned by Morris and Corbett, the promenade and multilevel terraces, the composed group of skyscrapers, and the superblock onto which these elements were grafted—would inform the final project. By late 1929 two events recalibrated the design. The first was the appointment of Reinhard and Hofmeister as project architects and, on the advice of Todd, the selection of Corbett and Raymond Hood as consultants. Todd was now manager of the Metropolitan Square Corporation, which would become Rockefeller Center in 1932.[13] Hood, who would soon take a decisive role in the design, was a strategic choice. During the 1920s he was considered the preeminent architect of skyscrapers in New York City. He had been previously recommended to the Rockefeller circle by its advisor William T. Aldrich as one of "the two most brilliant performers whom I know personally."[14] In his autobiography Todd described Hood as an "original thinker" who could bring "new ideas that were crowding architecture in the 20s into the practical life of New York." And he admired Hood's recent achievements, such as the Daily News Building (1928–1929; fig. 5). Hood also fit the narrow parameters of Todd's guarded profile: architects on

4. Benjamin Wistar Morris, study of Metropolitan Opera House and Square, aerial perspective by Chester B. Price, May 1929

Drawings Collection, Avery Architectural and Fine Arts Library, Columbia University

5. Raymond Hood with John Mead Howells and André Fouilhoux, Daily News Building (1928–1929), New York

Fay S. Lincoln Photograph Collection; courtesy of the Historical Collections and Labor Archives, Special Collections Library, The Pennsylvania State University

the project, he thought, should be neither "too much committed to the architectural past" nor "too much interested in wild modernism."[15]

A second event paired the withdrawal of the opera company with the departure of Morris from the project, paving the way for further commercial development while retaining the plaza. The Wall Street crash that fall made all the more imperative a definitive shift from a cultural to a commercial enterprise whose subsequent planning would be directed to "maximum income."[16] With the nation on the threshold of an economic depression, attention soon turned to marketing. As Todd later recalled, "ordinary buildings would not have rented," whereas the new buildings, distinguished by their height and enhanced by a public plaza, "made people sit up and take notice."[17] In early December 1929 plans focused on a central skyscraper envisioned as the "World's Tallest Tower," while retaining an overall goal of civic improvement, which had characterized the opera house project for Metropolitan Square.[18]

Modernity in the Urban Core: Hood's Contributions as *Auteur*

The *parti* or central idea that would determine the final design of Rockefeller Center, which historians consider the defining moment in its development, called for replacing the opera house with a central skyscraper (later the RCA Building). Moreover, four thirty-story office buildings (replacing the stepped-back towers) now stood perpendicular to the central skyscraper and all were sited around a plaza (fig. 6). Produced in January 1930, this scheme, with its abstract grouping of ground blocks and tall buildings, not only made efficient use of zoning provisions but also signaled Rockefeller Center's tilt toward modernity. Known as G-3, it was officially the work of Reinhard and Hofmeister, who had already been reported to be architects for the tower.[19] However, G-3 and subsequent schemes showed Hood's hand. Although he had been

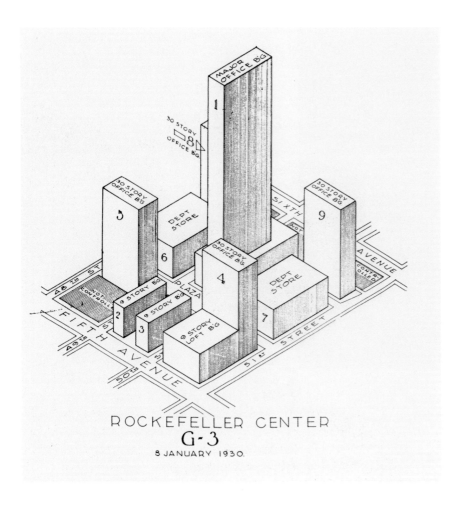

ROCKEFELLER CENTER
G-3
8 JANUARY 1930.

6. Reinhard and Hofmeister (and members of Associated Architects), Rockefeller Center, G-3 Scheme, January 8, 1930
Collection of The New-York Historical Society

appointed a consulting architect and would develop into a conscientious collaborator, he was by nature an *auteur* with ideas of his own, ones that would reconceptualize the design. Hood had been against the use of office towers to wall in a central building, as in Morris' 1929 scheme for the opera house (see fig. 4). According to Walter Kilham Jr., who worked in Hood's office from 1928 and would later become his first architectural biographer, Hood felt that the three-block area should be "concentrated in the center, looking out over low roofs in the north and south blocks," and thus open to and integrated with the city.[20]

In July 1930, six months after the G-3 proposal, Hood, with his partners, Frederick Godley and André Fouilhoux, formally joined two other groups—Reinhard and Hofmeister as well as Corbett and his partners, Wallace K. Harrison and William

MacMurray—to form the Associated Architects (fig. 7). Thereafter, rather than bearing the signatures of individuals, all plans were identified by the stamp of the Associated Architects, thus officially denoting a collaboration.[21] However, in order to understand the innovations that distinguish the various plans and the ideas that inform them as well as their origin and context, both local and transnational, it is useful to address the issue of authorship. In general, as Reinhard later confirmed, Corbett, Hood, and Harrison had been retained for their design skills, and their selection meant bringing on board their respective partners.[22] Moreover, Harrison later recalled, Corbett had taken the lead during the early years of the project's development, followed by Hood and Harrison himself.[23] Although Hood emphasized the collaborative nature of the project, he did acknowledge a "division of responsibility."[24] Astute critics looked beyond conventions. Writing for the *Nation*, Douglas Haskell suggested that formal elements in the Rockefeller Center design appeared "most like Hood's."[25] *New York Times* reporter H. I. Brock credited Hood with a fusion of utility and beauty in his "free handling of the severely functional modern formula."[26] More than any other member of the Associated Architects, Hood was given the responsibility of communicating the project's design principles, and it was to him that both support for and criticism of the project were most often directed.[27] All along it was Todd's strategy to "get the best out of individual effort and still not destroy the power of the group."[28] At the time of Hood's premature death in 1934, a consensus had begun to emerge among his colleagues, which Ely Jacques Kahn expressed when he wrote that the "Rockefeller work show[ed] the marks of his genius."[29]

In a new sequence of proposals for Metropolitan Square (the H series), executed in the spring and summer of 1930, the Associated Architects retained the central skyscraper, now with setbacks, as well as the adjacent lower towers, and the plaza (sometimes des-

7. Raymond Hood (left), Wallace Harrison (rear), and L. Andrew Reinhard with plaster model of Rockefeller Center, c. 1931

© *The Rockefeller Group Inc. / Rockefeller Center Archives 2008*

ignated a forum). An "oval building" was also proposed and, drawing on earlier studies, the transformation of 49th and 50th streets into "underground boulevards."[30] In response to the shift in the project's mission to one of uniting commerce and art, plans now called for the replacement of the opera house with an entertainment center especially devoted to the new electronic media of radio, film, and television. Presented to Rockefeller as "democratic rather than aristocratic," the new media center might still support his early aspirations to form a civic center linked to culture, reported the *New York Times*.[31] That summer Hood continued to experiment with massing models to unite the three blocks into a superblock and concentrate the buildings at the center, as he had in a project for Terminal Park, Chicago (1929), with John Holabird and Ralph Walker. Drawing the Rockefeller buildings away from the edge would strengthen the concept of a city center.

By March 1931 the project, then called Radio City, was sufficiently advanced in its design development for the Associated Architects to exhibit a plaster model of it.[32] This iteration retained the central tower of

the G-3 scheme, which, by virtue of its seventy stories and slender proportions, was soon characterized by the *New York Times* as a "slab."[33] The plan still featured an oval building prominently sited on Fifth Avenue, with a bank, shops, and restaurants within its fourteen stories. Although the figural building received a good deal of publicity, it was also the object of ridicule. This negative response led to a reconceptualization of the scheme. An axonometric drawing of the revised project (fig. 8) shows the retention of three components: a stepped-back central tower, adjacent towers, and a multilevel plan, revealing an underground shopping concourse. This "underground city," situated on two levels, was equipped with an extensive network of ramps and viaducts as well as concourses and corridors lined with businesses that connected the various units and would eventually lead pedestrians to a subway station on Sixth Avenue.[34] A landscaped promenade (later the Channel Gardens) and two low-rise structures on either side (later La Maison Française and the British Empire Building) replaced the oval one, thereby creating an unencumbered view of the plaza and central office tower from Fifth Avenue. The promenade was slated to join an underground road extending from 46th Street to Grand Central Terminal, whose arteries already connected to hotels and office buildings, the conjunction of which would offer the city an effective model of multilevel urban planning.[35]

The central tower continued to dominate the grouping of office buildings at Radio City. To prevent the building masses from obstructing light and air to one another, as Hood had cautioned, they were disposed in a "staggered" plan, suggesting a "five-spot card."[36] At a press conference in March 1931 Hood pointed out that individual buildings were designed and built "from the inside, not the outside," because of the need to solve technical problems such as space for elevator banks.[37] As Hood explained, the setbacks of the slabs were based on a module of twenty-seven feet of space from the

8. Associated Architects, Rockefeller Center, scheme for shopping
concourse

*Architectural Forum 54 (May 1931):
602*

for the "dissemination of information on political and civic topics at public gatherings."[40] Connecting the buildings effectively was still an issue, and Hood's concept of networking was simply pragmatic. If high-speed vertical transportation could make the corporate tower efficient, "mechanized horizontal transit" in the form of a "traveling platform," as Hood envisioned it, would transport pedestrians along arteries linked to adjacent units and metropolitan transit stations, an idea drawn from his preliminary master plan of 1929 for the Century of Progress International Exposition, discussed below.[41] Hood's commitment to a metropolis designed and understood in three dimensions, as well as to a cohesive assemblage of units and the networked spaces connecting them to the city, would continue to shape the development of Rockefeller Center and its emergence as an urban core.

To appreciate Hood's concept of urban grouping from the G-3 scheme forward and his contributions to the design of Rockefeller Center as a product of transition and synthesis—from Beaux-Arts to modern with European ideas infusing American practice—we need to probe the evolution and transatlantic character of Hood's intellectual formation and examine several of his earlier proposals for a city of towers aimed at solving problems associated with tall buildings in New York.

elevators to the windows, which was "the maximum to be allowed to provide adequate light and air to all parts of the building."[38] The abstract profile of the central tower (see also fig. 1), with its shallow, stepped-back ledges, bore a strong formal resemblance to Hood's Daily News Building (see fig. 5) only a few blocks away, even though the plan of its elevator core seemed closer to that of his earlier Chicago Tribune Building (with John Mead Howells; 1922).[39]

As the design of Radio City progressed, commentary on it helped reframe the local discourse on skyscrapers and their urban concentration. The future of the skyscraper in New York City was increasingly seen in terms of groups. Extending over several blocks and planned in relation to public space, the complex now assumed a civic dimension. It was broadly defined as a "civic and cultural center" with a forum

Raymond Hood's Visionary Planning

Trained at the École des Beaux-Arts before World War I and a confirmed Francophile, Hood kept abreast of European and especially French developments. His education and persuasion were similar to those of George Howe and several other progressive American architects who were open to the modern movement as it developed after World War I. In effect, Hood had one foot in the academic tradition and another in modernism. Among his American colleagues, he took the lead in championing the "originality" of the architecture of the 1925 Paris fair

(Exposition Internationale des Arts Décoratifs et Industriels Modernes) and encouraged American architects to distance themselves from historical precedents. "The American architect," Hood affirmed, "will no longer have to steal, borrow, copy or adapt inspiration from a prototype."[42] Hood subsequently visited Paris in 1926 as one of the organizers of the Architectural and Allied Arts Exposition, held at Grand Central Palace in New York (1927), which promoted the new architecture in the United States.[43] From the mid-1920s he had a special interest in modern European theory and design, notably the ideas of Auguste Perret (1874–1954) and Le Corbusier (born Charles-Édouard Jeanneret-Gris; 1887–1965). Fluent in French, he was conversant with Perret's work, had read Le Corbusier's *Vers une architecture* (1923), and from 1928 would come to know the latter's *Urbanisme* (1925) because, at his request, Kilham had loaned him his copy.[44] The visionary schemes of these architects, especially Le Corbusier's Plan Voisin for Paris (1925), which was exhibited at the Paris fair, held a powerful appeal for Hood.

Between 1924 and 1929 Hood made a number of proposals for the development of commercial towers in New York City that offered a critique of the city's 1916 zoning law. They reflected contemporary visionary ideas at home and abroad. Four of these would later inform his thinking about the Rockefeller Center design. In 1924 he published his proposal for a "City of Needles," illustrated with a rendering by Hugh Ferriss. What is important about Hood's scheme is that it rejected a stepped-back treatment in favor of a tower of nearly uniform width from bottom to top, a precursor to the slab, which would later appear in the RCA tower. "Set your fountain pen on end," instructed the *New York Times*, "and you will get a picture of something like the same proportions."[45] In 1926, when Hood published a description of his earlier project, he illustrated it with a more detailed drawing by Ferriss, which the renderer included in his *Metropolis of Tomorrow* (1929; fig. 9).[46] Hood said that

he sited the tall, freestanding columns of what he described as a "forest of towers" five hundred feet apart on elevated boulevards he called "four-mile covered bridges." Between the business towers, he designated "broad spaces, parks where workers can find rest, recreation, shade, peace, and where there will be wide avenues with light traffic." This multilevel plan situated shops one level below grade and beneath that a floor bed for high-speed transportation—subways and cars.[47] While such projects were specific to New York, they also reflected Hood's transatlantic engagement.

Hood's second project for a "City of Towers," a zoning study exhibited in 1927 at the Architectural and Allied Arts Exhibition, was similar to if less visionary than the 1924 project. It used none of the double-decked streets and elevated sidewalks of the earlier scheme. Hood said that the idea for his 1927 proposal—and, we may also assume, his 1924 project and Ferriss' renderings of 1924 and 1926—had come from a "French architect who, a number of years ago, when the project of demolishing the fortifications of Paris was under consideration, advocated … a space six or seven hundred feet wide running around the city [and] the building of apartments in the form of towers with gardens between them."[48] Hood's reference is to a project by Perret, which called for the concentration of housing in twenty-story towers aligned to a boulevard, a metropolitan infrastructure, and a green space on the periphery of Paris. A drawing of the Perret project by Jacques Lambert appeared in 1922 in the French revue *L'Illustration* (fig. 10).[49] Le Corbusier, who had worked for Perret before World War I and would have known the housing project before its publication, drew on it for the business towers of his Villes-Tours of 1921 (fig. 11), which he published in *Vers une architecture*. Le Corbusier claimed that the introduction of such towers in the centers of cities, surrounded by parks, would not only alleviate congestion and noise and promote the "purest air" but also afford an "uninterrupted view" from

9. Drawing by Hugh Ferriss for
Raymond Hood's "forest of
towers," 1926

Hugh Ferriss, Metropolis of Tomorrow *(New York, 1929), 87*

10. *Skyscrapers for Paris*, drawing
by Jacques Lambert inspired by
Auguste Perret's sketches, 1922

L'Illustration *160 (12 August 1922),
133*

their windows.[50] It is worth noting that the towers of Perret's and Le Corbusier's respective projects, shown rising above open space, were both based on American skyscrapers, giving evidence of the dynamics of transatlantic exchange in the arts around World War I.[51]

According to Kilham, Le Corbusier's 1927 project, as well as his book, with its machine-age rhetoric, and his concept of a city in three dimensions, greatly influenced Hood's thinking.[52] Hood's 1927 zoning study to relieve traffic congestion in New York, which drew on his 1924 project and Ferriss' two renderings of it (see fig. 9), was purported to offer advantages similar to Le Corbusier's Villes-Tours. Reconfiguring the New York City grid to accommodate towers on wider streets, Hood argued, would "solve

the problems of light, air and traffic."[53] His notation on one drawing of his 1927 plan estimated that the three skyscrapers occupying one block required no more space than did the fountains and obelisk on the Place de la Concorde. In asking the viewer to "imagine the next block built in the same manner," Hood projected his ambitions for New York as a city of towers, much as Le Corbusier had envisioned the center of Paris as a field of high rises in his Plan Voisin of 1925. Unlike the Parisian's proposal for large-scale redevelopment, however, Hood's project would be smaller in scale, built incrementally, and, therefore, more practical.[54]

With his third and fourth projects, both in 1929, Hood shifted the focus of his urban visions toward greater consolidation. His "City under a Single Roof" called for

11. Le Corbusier, Villes-Tours, 1921

Vers une architecture *(Paris, 1923),* 43; Plan FLC 31910; © 2008 Artists Rights Society (ARS), New York / ADAGP, Paris / FLC

12. Raymond Hood, model for "A City under a Single Roof," 1929

Thomas Adams, The Building of the City, *vol. 2 (New York, 1931), 189*

a mixed-use "unit building," configured as a monumental cruciform tower that occupied a three-block site (fig. 12). Based on a preference for increasing the width of the city street and thus providing open spaces, rather than merely restricting building heights, Hood's planning ideas as well as the project's formal character, especially its cruciform tower, drew on Le Corbusier's Villes-Tours (see fig. 11). According to Hood, such buildings would be "supported on columns [Le Corbusier's pilotis] which leave space beneath them open. Only the stairways and elevator entrances come down to the street." Multilevel planning would allow pedestrian and vehicular traffic to flow beneath. Hood's scheme also picked up on Le Corbusier's rationale for living and working in the city: long commutes would be eliminated, enabling city workers time for greater productivity and recreation.[55] But there were differences. Hood's mixed-use concept meant that workers could now shop, work, and live in the same tower: retail on lower floors, offices above, and apartments on the top floors. By contrast, Le Corbusier's Villes-Tours project sited its sixty-story business towers in the center of the city and its

13. Raymond Hood, "Manhattan 1950" business center, 1929
Architecture 61 (May 1930): 276

twelve-story *à redents* (indented) housing slabs at the city's edge. But both projects sought to eliminate waste by reducing building footprints and minimizing daily commutes for metropolitan office workers.

For his fourth city-of-towers project, called "Manhattan 1950" and published in 1930, Hood produced a suite of drawings. Superimposed on a map of Manhattan he envisioned more than twenty "apartment bridges" spanning the Hudson and East rivers. At the intersection of the island's major north–south arteries and on roads leading to bridges along the island's periphery, he imagined nearly forty clusters of office towers built over the entrances to subway and railroad lines. Hood's aerial view of one such intersection showed a "business center" in which four towers were connected to "overhead bridges" for traffic (fig. 13). Its multilevel planning and linkages to transportation were in sync with not only the early proposals of Morris and Corbett

for Rockefeller Center but also with the visionary schemes Le Corbusier was producing at the moment that Hood was brought on board the design team.[56] Through the intervention of Hood, therefore, Perret and Le Corbusier's demolition-based projects to transform an existing metropolitan quarter into a city of towers, with presumed economic benefits and salubrious conditions, merged with an ongoing North American discourse on skyscrapers and superblocks.[57]

Indeed, Hood was so committed to Le Corbusier's new urban vision that he extended two invitations to the Parisian architect. These would eventually result in Le Corbusier's first American lecture tour.[58] In his capacity as president of the Architectural League of New York (1929–1931), Hood invited Le Corbusier to participate in the league's annual exhibition and to give a series of lectures. Hoping to arrange a meeting in Paris, Hood wrote to him, "From the moment that I knew your work, I was a great admirer of it."[59] (It was not until 1935, the year after Hood's death, that Le Corbusier would make his first visit.)

Although Hood's ideas and plans were informed by the schemes of Perret and Le Corbusier, he was fundamentally no visionary. Most of Hood's contemporaries judged his design decisions to be pragmatic, driven by economic and utilitarian requirements, if also highly imaginative. As Hood himself professed, "Modern Architecture consists of studying our problems from the ground up, solving each point in the most logical manner." But by virtue of his Beaux-Arts training and intense interest in European, and especially French, developments, Hood maintained a transatlantic perspective that overturned the isolationist positions of many peers to create a "new style" deemed "distinctively American."[60]

Rockefeller Center Roof Gardens and the View from Above

One element of Corbusian design particularly resonated with Hood, perhaps because it had also entered American practice: roof

14. Associated Architects, Rocke-feller Center, "hanging gardens," 1931

Architectural Forum 56 (January 1932): 12; Avery Architectural and Fine Arts Library, Columbia University

not design the RCA tower as he would the McGraw-Hill Building (1931) with its logical and artistic expression of the steel frame. Featured in 1932 in *Modern Architecture: International Exhibition* at the Museum of Modern Art, McGraw-Hill was admired as a "turning point in skyscraper design" as well as a native example of the International Style.[63] On the other hand, like other modernists, Hood rejected "wasteful" historicist ornament. Instead, his solution called for skyscrapers decked with "modern hanging gardens."[64] In his *New York Times* article on the gardens, Hood picked up on the old metaphor of New York as the "new Babel." He recalled how its record skyscrapers around 1900 had been associated with the imagery and mythology of Babylon's tower.[65] Conflating hanging gardens and Persian carpets, Hood proposed "a garden pattern, or living rug, for each roof" (fig. 14).[66] Such landscapes served three functions. First, they offered Hood a way out of the dilemma of ornament in American modernism by animating buildings and public spaces with organic life, even though most of the gardens would be traditional ones. Second, in Hood's hands, "sky gardens" responded to a larger urban agenda to enrich the city and activate its increasingly three-dimensional character. Third, such landscapes would infuse the urban core with green roofs.

A 1931 rendering by John Wenrich of an elaborate sunken plaza and underground shopping concourse at the base of an office tower indicates Hood's aesthetic ambitions for Radio City (fig. 15).[67] A suite of subsequent Wenrich renderings envisioned Hood's ideas for cascading bridges connecting the rooftops. The setbacks and lower terraces would have "carpets" of parterres and trees. Although the Associated Architects had been working on the idea of bridges over 49th and 50th streets, Wenrich's drawings projected a truly visionary image, meant to publicize the scenic beauty of such gardens and green roofs (see essay frontispiece).[68]

But landscaped roofs signified more than mere ornamental or aesthetic embellish-

gardens. In the summer of 1931, as excavations were under way for the RCA tower, Hood suggested to Todd and his fellow architects that the formal landscapes of the promenade and sunken plaza could also extend to the rooftops. This would require a more robust steel structure to support the additional weight of the soil.[61] The gardens at Radio City would cover more than eight of its twelve acres. Even Corbett would later applaud Hood's "wild idea" to landscape the roofs of skyscrapers.[62]

Hood's rationale for the gardens oscillated between his practical agenda and his aesthetic and visionary ideals. On the one hand, under Todd's mandate Hood could

15. Associated Architects, Rocke-feller Center, plaza and sunken garden, drawing by John Wenrich, 1931

Courtesy of the Rockefeller Archive Center

ment. They were deeply embedded in the modernist sense of experiencing the city. For the "sky gardens," composed of hedges and flowerbeds, trees and fountains, would transform the landscape program from Corbett's two-dimensional plan (see fig. 3) and Morris' Beaux-Arts vision (see fig. 4) to Hood's audacious spatial projection and the resulting "garden pattern" on high terraces and rooftops (see fig. 14 and book frontis-piece). Hood's buildings would thereby assume a metropolitan character consonant with both modernist objectives and his own transatlantic aspirations. Endowed with a fourth "face," Hood argued, towers would now be seen fully in the round. They would also enhance the perception of office workers looking out on the great city or down to the roofs and terraces below, whether they inhab-ited the buildings of Radio City or those of neighboring blocks. The *New York Times* observed that Rockefeller Center would achieve "maximum sight lines from the win-dows of all towers."[69] And if replicated else-where in Manhattan, Hood speculated, these sight lines would be "lengthened as the roof-garden area spreads from block to block."[70]

"Rescuing the roof" by not merely weatherproofing it but enhancing it with a garden, Hood concluded, was the "aesthetic preoccupation of the urban architect."[71] Of course, the sky gardens at Rockefeller Cen-ter did help to insulate the buildings. But they also incorporated other principles of sustainable design. Gardens were outfitted with an underground system of irrigation. Their electric pumps recirculated water from the air-conditioning system as well as pools and fountains.[72] Even the gardens of the central plaza and promenade (later Channel Gardens) might be considered "green roofs" because they were built above their respec-tive basements.[73]

Hood's "wild idea" of designing land-scaped terraces for the Rockefeller Center roofs seems to have come from sources on both sides of the Atlantic. First, the ter-races recalled those of Le Corbusier's Con-temporary City for Three Million (Ville contemporaine) of 1922 (fig. 16), which were designated simply "roof gardens" and anticipated the theoretical formulation of the second of his "Five Points of a New Architecture" (1926). Hood would have seen drawings of the 1922 plan in *Urban-isme*.[74] And he probably knew of the roof garden at Le Corbusier's Maisons La Roche–Jeanneret in Paris (1923).[75] Hood's interest in sight lines may well have been drawn from the practical, optical, and poetic sig-nificance of Le Corbusier's urban vision: the importance of the "broad vista in the urban scene"; the roof as a "reclaimed surface, a superficial area of the city available for gar-dens or walks ... useful and ... beautiful"; the "profile of the town seen against the sky" as one of "pure line" and a "determining factor in our feelings."[76] His thinking may also have relied on Le Corbusier's own use of "hanging gardens" (*jardins suspendus*) to define the cellular units of housing slabs, which would give the urban worker a vital connection with nature.[77] The editors of the *New York Times* understood Le Corbusier's influence on the Rockefeller roofscapes. In support of Hood's model of providing Radio

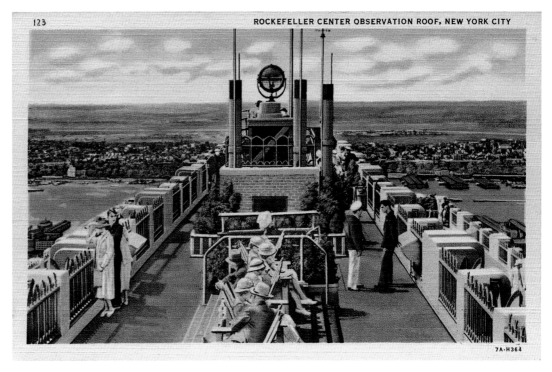

City office dwellers with landscaped terraces, they advocated restrictive legislation
to allow a Corbusian vision for the entire
metropolis: "great towers would rise like
trees in a garden or a park—only springing from a level a hundred feet … above
the street," as "Carbusier [*sic*] has given a
glimpse in his imagination of such a city,"
with Thomas Adams (general director of the
Regional Plan of New York) underscoring
the "relative areas of tower and garden."[78]
However, beyond Rockefeller Center the
city needed a development plan to "give the
high towers these garden spaces without

injustice to the owners of the lower buildings."[79] Indeed, the observation deck of the
RCA Building (fig. 17) was as much a tool for
advancing the scenographic potential of the
skyscraper as an evocation of Le Corbusier's
roof gardens.

Hood's thinking about lofty gardens was
also influenced by the ideas of his American
colleagues and collaborators, especially Ferriss' concept of the "spectacle of the city."
In *The Metropolis of Tomorrow* Ferriss
called for "hanging gardens" on "open terraces" and published a sequence of images
aimed at promoting the scenic values of

18. Raymond Hood, Century of Progress International Exposition, Chicago, plan, May 1929

RBA Digital File 197301, ColP_ RHood3, Edward H. Bennett Collection, Ryerson and Burnham Archives, The Art Institute of Chicago; reproduction © The Art Institute of Chicago

colossal skyscrapers he called "mountain peaks."[80] Ferriss' "mountains" invoked at once the concept of the sublime and John Ruskin's analogy between nature and buildings whose clifflike masses illuminated his "lamp of power."[81] In Ferriss' "imaginary metropolis," this was as true of the setback towers of the "business center" as those of the "art center."[82] Moreover, the integration of nature and architecture was Frank Lloyd Wright's obsession, especially evident in the roof terrace of the Larkin Building in Buffalo (1902–1906; demolished 1950), the promenades and outdoor terraces of both the Midway Gardens in Chicago (1913–1914; demolished 1929) and the Imperial Hotel in Tokyo (1912–1923; demolished 1968), and in the rooftop terraces of such projects as his "Skyscraper Regulation" scheme (1926) and his skyscraper apartments, St. Mark's-in-the-Bouwerie Towers in New York (1928–1930).

In accord with Ferriss and Wright, Hood was as preoccupied with the transfer of ideas from large-scale and visionary planning to actual construction as he was with the integration of landscaped terraces and tall buildings. Two projects of 1929 would illustrate this point. The first was Hood's master plan of May 1929 for the Century of Progress International Exposition in Chicago (1933), where he served as one of eight architects (along with Corbett) on the exposition's architectural commission. His monumental scheme, a revised version of an earlier one with an elevated moving sidewalk, featured an asymmetrical composition of elements around two central basins (fig. 18). A soaring skyscraper, with garden terraces capping the tops of setbacks, dominated one corner of a long basin and, at the opposite end, a water cascade flanked by rows of cross-shaped pylons.[83] Although Hood's skyscraper design drew on the abstract forms of both Dutch modernism and constructivism, it also looked to the visionary plans of Ferriss, while its stepped tower anticipate Wright's needlelike skyscrapers, beginning with Broadacre City (1929–1935).[84] Hood's second project of 1929 was a country club near Myrtle Beach, South Carolina. Elaborate drawings in a published prospectus indicate his use of landscaped terraces as ornament for a tall building, much as he would later prescribe them for Radio City.[85]

Gardens on the roofs and on the ledges of setbacks, Hood concluded, would encourage New Yorkers to experience the city from great heights and capture the view from above. "This transformation of our urban scene," Hood told readers of the *New York Times* in 1931, meant that the view from skyscrapers would be "more important than the view from the street." This was a heroic image of the city, one that Hood and Ferriss had already envisioned but that would be left to Norman Bel Geddes and other designers to exploit at the 1939 New York World's Fair.[86] Radio City would be an early test case. For the urban

19. RCA Building, La Maison Française, and British Empire Building,
Rockefeller Center, 1933

*Photograph Wurts Brothers; cour-
tesy of the Rockefeller Archive
Center*

Todd and the Rockefeller team now focused on the roof gardens, in the hope that they would draw the attention of both tenants and visitors to the new complex (fig. 19). Under Hood's direction, the gardens of the Promenade (Channel Gardens) and the Sunken Plaza were proceeding, and contracts had been let for the roof gardens on the seventh floor of the French and British Empire pavilions.[89] To refine, expand, and execute the planning, a landscape architect was brought on board. A number of candidates were considered, including Arthur Shurtleff of Boston and the French architect and landscape architect Jacques Gréber.[90] The Rockefeller team selected British horticulturalist Ralph Hancock, whose similar designs for the roof terraces of both the French and British Empire buildings featured trees, grass, clipped hedges, a rose garden, a fountain, a pool, and flagstone walks.[91] Hancock followed these in 1934 with the Garden of the Nations, which occupied a three-quarter-acre terrace on the eleventh floor of the RCA Building above the NBC Studios. Gardens representative of those in England, France, Italy, Spain, Holland, Japan, China, and Mexico joined a North American garden with wildflowers and native plants laid out with shrubs and dry walls. While most of the gardens were traditional and adhered to historical and national themes, a modern garden, which Hancock considered "very streamlined" and "original," deployed a zigzag mosaic of flower boxes in pastel shades of concrete (fig. 20). In 1936 Rockefeller Center held the record for having the "only large skyscraper gardens in the world." From May to November daily tours of "sky gardens" allowed visitors to experience these "modern hanging gardens" and the three-dimensional views of the metropolis from them.[92]

Transatlantic Reception and the Modernist Paradigm for the Urban Core

For all of its synthesis of formal elements, European and North American, Beaux-Arts

architect, Hood claimed, had a responsibility to "landscape" the roofs and terraces of office buildings, giving them what had formerly been the domain of private penthouses.[87] Embellishing the fourth "face" of skyscrapers with formal landscapes meant that adjacent offices could command higher rents because workers would have improved views. For developers of commercial buildings this feature contributed to optimal "cost and return."[88]

In 1933, with the completion of Radio City Music Hall, the RCA and RKO buildings, and La Maison Française and the British Empire Building on Fifth Avenue,

20. Garden of the Nations, RCA
Building, New York City, 1934
© *The Rockefeller Group Inc. /*
Rockefeller Center Archives 2008

and modern, the identity of Rockefeller Center was embedded in machine-age rhetoric. If the modern city concentrated "research, invention, design, organization, distribution and the division of the products of the machine age," as Hood suggested, then this complex of buildings with its privately owned public space would be New York City's locus.[93] But modernity was also a function of how buildings and spaces were perceived and experienced. This brings us to the transatlantic reception of Rockefeller Center and the feature that most captivated architects and critics: its public plaza. The unprecedented scale and complexity of the commercial development as well as the vitality of its modest open space suggested that Rockefeller Center could serve as a modernist paradigm for the urban core.

Initially Rockefeller Center met with a mixed critical reception. Proponents on both sides of the Atlantic praised it as a sign of progress in urban planning. Detractors questioned its materialism, density, and indifference to the neighborhood. At first, the social historian and critic Lewis Mumford vigorously opposed the project as it was presented in the spring of 1931. He faulted its tow-

ers for promoting "metropolitan disorder," "super-congestion," traffic, and waste, as he had skyscrapers in general in *The Brown Decades* (1931). But, given the resources of the Rockefellers, it was little wonder that Mumford chided their enterprise for skirting its "civic obligations" and the architects for failing to produce alternatives to both the skyscraper and the aggregated block as urban typologies.[94] (Frank Lloyd Wright concurred that it was a lost opportunity; Radio City was overscaled and its composition "haphazard," and its masonry materials were "falsifying" in concealing the nature of its construction.[95]) In a 1933 "Sky Line" column in the *New Yorker* Mumford pursued his critique, calling the project "planned chaos" and its RCA tower "a graceless hulk."[96] But by 1938 he reversed his position on the issue of urban order and endorsed Rockefeller Center as "the first attempt at a rational plan." Two years later he still thought the RCA tower, sunken plaza, and landscaped terraces were "blunders," but the "play of mass against mass" was nonetheless "exciting," and the newer mid-rise buildings introduced a more human scale.[97]

Among the partisans of European modernism, the view remained largely affirmative. They saw Rockefeller Center as a benchmark for their cause because its technical perfection, simplicity, and grouping of skyscrapers embodied the ideals they had long espoused. From the mid-1930s Europeans visited and reported on Rockefeller Center.[98] The French painter Fernand Léger endorsed its embodiment of "luxury with simplicity." However, this luxury was viewed not as elitist but as democratic and uniquely American. The concourses and public spaces at Radio City, Léger concluded, had created "social luxuriousness, luxury through which crowds circulate."[99] Le Corbusier also explored Rockefeller Center from bottom to top. He admired the RCA Building as a technical achievement, notwithstanding its excessively "narrow" profile and "cottage windows," at odds with its steel frame.[100] He was enthralled by this "rational, logically conceived, biologically normal" skyscraper with high-speed elevators and doors opened by electric eyes. Soaring to the sixty-fifth floor in an express elevator, Le Corbusier marveled, "your ears feel it a little at first, but not your heart, so perfect are these machines." The high performance of such skyscrapers, he thought, was due to American engineering, more specifically to the "flawless and rigorous division of responsibilities among technicians grouped in a team for the study and carrying out of these vast American constructions."[101] The development of reliable elevators now meant that the towers he envisioned for his urban projects, particularly the Radiant City of 1930, were not just aspirational but could become accepted practice on both sides of the Atlantic. Such skyscrapers could provide the amenities of modern city life, as Le Corbusier had advocated in his book *La Ville radieuse* (1935).[102] Walter Gropius, who visited Rockefeller Center in 1937, shared Le Corbusier's admiration for its technical efficiency and was especially curious about its operational functions. Gropius wanted to know all the facts: "what it cost, how it worked, whether it paid, how what got into it was delivered so that the streets and plaza were kept clear [and] what the parking arrangements were underground."[103] Aside from a demonstration of technical invention, Rockefeller Center evinced logical planning. But it was more than that. The large-scale grouping of the skyscrapers in relationship to one another was totally modern in the sense that it served the community, not just the individual; it was new, of the present, and transnational. It seemed the embodiment of a European vision. Indeed, Henry-Russell Hitchcock designated it the first expression of "the bold ideal of such European theorists of the skyscraper as Le Corbusier," even if the Parisian himself would have preferred towers of uniform height spread farther apart.[104]

Rockefeller Center as Civic Space

The possibility of civic expression was compelling to European protagonists of the Congrès Internationaux d'Architecture Moderne (CIAM), which called for the subordination of private interest to collective rights, efforts to decongest the dense centers of cities through the concentration of workers in towers, and the formation of communal space. To the Swiss historian Sigfried Giedion and the Catalonian architect José Luis Sert, both CIAM leaders, Rockefeller Center offered a paradigm of large-scale consolidation. It also showed that a patch of skyscraper city could be effectively inserted into an existing and, therefore, older urban order.

In his Norton Lectures at Harvard University in 1938 and 1939, later published in the book *Space, Time and Architecture* (1941), Giedion commended Rockefeller Center for introducing "for the first time into a contemporary city the large scale that is to be found in the parkways and great engineering works."[105] Its fourteen buildings of different heights, sited in relation to each other and to the plaza, rather than to city streets, signified to Giedion "open planning on the new scale," which Hood had earlier championed.[106] The placement of tall buildings in an open field surpassed the baroque concept of spatial planning, a development that even Mumford would come to appreciate.[107] The Time and Life Building at 1 Rockefeller Plaza (1937; fig. 21), approximating Building 5 in the G-3 scheme (see fig. 6), was sited at a ninety-degree angle to the RCA Building. Giedion identified this tensional shift as a "space-time" conception.[108] The aerial view confirms the logic of the plan. But walking among the buildings allowed Giedion to experience a more complex set of interrelations. From the ground the ensemble, "grasped from no single position nor embraced in any single view," was best understood through a photomontage.[109] The slabs, which he perceived as floating and hovering, had become "plastic elements" in the creation of new spatial organization.[110] Such demonstrations of the "visualization of movement," according to Stanislaus von Moos, characterized Giedion's work.[111] They helped him to uncover the "poetry of our time," an abiding theme in Le Corbusier's

oeuvre that Giedion also adopted as the principal objective of his Norton Lectures and subsequent book.[112]

During the 1930s and 1940s Europeans, among them Giedion and Sert, were especially drawn to Mumford's views on the social value of civic space.[113] Through his reading of Mumford's *The Culture of Cities* (1938) and other writings, Sert would deepen his understanding of the city as, in Mumford's characterization, "a geographic plexus, an economic organization, an institutional process, a theater of social action, and an esthetic symbol of collective unity."[114] The Catalonian would also draw on Mumford's concept of a "civic nucleus."[115] Sert's preparatory work in Europe and the United States on the CIAM book *Can Our Cities Survive?* (1942) involved him in a transatlantic dialogue with Giedion and others on both the urban core and civic identity, issues that he had raised at the CIAM 5 congress, held in

Paris in 1937 on the theme "Logis et loisirs" (dwellings and recreation).[116] CIAM protagonists were among the first to recognize the potential for Rockefeller Center to serve as a public forum, notwithstanding Mumford's early opposition to it.

A corollary to Giedion's space-time formulation, Sert's analysis of Rockefeller Center centered on town planning in three dimensions, namely height and density in relation to open spaces, a concept derived from earlier CIAM discourse.[117] His understanding of three-dimensional spatial composition on an urban scale would later join with Le Corbusier's planning concepts, which called for a grouping of building masses with different functions, on the model of such projects as the League of Nations (1926–1927). To Le Corbusier and other modernists, especially cubist artists and their followers, the increased magnitude and boundless character of space and its perception would suggest a fourth dimension. Such "ineffable space," Le Corbusier would later write, evoked "plastic emotion," a theme drawn from *Vers une architecture*.[118]

During the late 1930s, when the United States received Sert as well as Bauhaus émigrés Gropius, Marcel Breuer, Ludwig Mies van der Rohe, and other European architects, Giedion determined that the "circumstance" of the approaching war in Europe obliged the newly enriched country to take the lead in architectural production. Influenced by Mumford's writings, Giedion adopted a position, more tender than tough, when he cautioned the preeminent industrialized nation to bend its mass production "to the command of human needs."[119] After World War II Rockefeller Center remained at the crux of a debate between European modernists (notably Giedion and Sert) and Mumford. On the one hand, Giedion and Sert still supported Mumford's views, with Sert advancing Mumford's concept of the city as a spatial matrix for "collective drama" in the life of the community.[120] Moreover, they recognized that endowing the city with a core that offered a utilitarian, social, and symbolic space—in other words, what Mumford called a civic nucleus—would be the new responsibility for postwar architects and planners.[121] It represented a departure from an emphasis on "the functional city," which dominated such prewar congresses as CIAM 4 (1933), toward one that underscored the social structure of the urban core, expressed as the "Heart of the City" at the CIAM 8 congress (1951).[122] In his essay "Centres of Community Life," Sert explained that because "life has been leaving the old Cores" for the suburbs, the stability of the postwar city and its civic identity would depend on a "process of recentralisation" and the formation of new cores.[123] Indeed, Sert's adoption of Mumford's concept of the urban nucleus became a generative force in a series of postwar planning projects for Latin America. Sert designed a project for the Motor City (Cidade dos Motores), near Rio de Janeiro (1944–1947) and produced

a further refinement in his project for the Peruvian town of Chimbote (1946–1948) as civic enterprises in support of their respective postcolonial democratic states.[124]

Ironically, Giedion and Sert recognized what Mumford initially could not: that Rockefeller Center formed a vital nucleus in New York City. For, beyond their plastic expression of urban form and commercial functions, the buildings, plaza, concourses, promenades, and roof gardens embraced a locus of social activity on different levels. The new scale of the enterprise alone, Giedion maintained, conferred a civic dimension.[125] Thus, Rockefeller Center could offer the modern democratic state a model of open space for public assembly, in part because of alterations during the 1930s that enlivened its sunken plaza.[126] At the CIAM 8 congress, Giedion recalled his late wartime experience when a "New York crowd spontaneously took over" the plaza to celebrate the liberation of Paris, if prematurely (fig. 22).[127] Years later the memory of New Yorkers gravitating to that site still touched him: "I remember the gathering that collected at the tiny Rockefeller Center," he wrote, "when the voice of [the French-American opera singer] Lily Pons suddenly arose and gave expression to the emotion that moved the masses."[128] Of course, he understood the symbolism of the space, uniquely sited in relation to the twin French and British pavilions. For Giedion, Rockefeller Plaza would remain the vital central element in the city, offering a new experience of the poetry of forms in space.

Other European voices weighed in. If the architectural detailing of Rockefeller Center seemed "banal and trivial" to such modernists as Mies, it was overcome by the towering slab of the RCA Building, which recalibrated the spatial order of Manhattan. "Nowhere in New York do I see another building that really stands alone where you can see it," Mies remarked, like "a general standing on a hill looking at his army. Is he going to worry if the uniforms don't fit?"[129] Such monumentality, set off

22. New Yorkers celebrating news
of the liberation of Paris, Rockefeller Plaza, *Life*, September 4,
1944, 27

*Photograph Herbert Gehr; Getty
Images, Time & Life Pictures*

by an accessible open space, touched on a
postwar debate about the role of symbolic
and communitarian expression in modern
architecture and urbanism, which Giedion,
Sert, and Léger first explored in their 1943
essay, "Nine Points on Monumentality."[130]
To Giedion, Sert and other modernists,
Rockefeller Center embodied an aesthetic
experience of monumental forms in space
and the cohesive character of landscaped
promenades, as well as a social and civic
arena at the heart of the city. As Giedion
envisioned, these ideals would serve as a
model for the urban core in postwar planning and reconstruction.[131]

From the early postwar period the
American reception was relatively positive.
Giedion's vision of Rockefeller Center had
influenced even Mumford and his colleagues.
In her catalog for the Museum of Modern Art
exhibition *Built in USA, 1932–44*, Elizabeth
Mock picked up on Giedion's visual analysis
when she praised the "changing angles" of
its slabs as "one of the exciting urban experiences of our time."[132] Clarence Stein, Mumford's kindred spirit, recognized its "variety
of mass, height, and a common pooling of
open spaces" which resulted in "better lighting and ventilation" as well as "architectural
and civic beauty."[133] Even Jane Jacobs found

that Rockefeller Center "respects the street." She especially approved of the introduction of a cross street to scale down and enliven its long east-west blocks. But, as with Mumford, she was less sanguine about its "extreme density" which, she thought, obliged Rockefeller Center to "put the overflow of its street activity underground."[134] Like Mies, she valued the RCA slab, calling it a landmark. And, as with Giedion, she was particularly impressed with the plaza, whose four level changes, "ingenious variation," and "centering" made it a dramatic small square.[135] Subsequent assessments, however, focused on tensions between private enterprise and public control.[136]

From inception to reception the history of Rockefeller Center was deeply embedded in a transatlantic dialogue. The idea of a composed group of skyscrapers and open spaces, planned as a unit and dispersed on a twelve-acre site, joined formal Beaux-Arts planning with modernist ideas. Designed by the team of Associated Architects, it embodied the creative ideas of Raymond Hood, Harvey Wiley Corbett, and others. For his part, Hood looked to his own visionary schemes, which had been drawn on those of Auguste Perret and Le Corbusier, who in turn had taken ideas from the American discourse on skyscrapers earlier in the century. Rockefeller Center's modernism, therefore, was synthetic in the sense that it was conceived within a transatlantic culture of both rational and visionary thinking, a fusion of native and received ideas. Individual buildings were not defined by avant-garde design. However, the ensemble projected a new spatial order for the modern city by virtue of its tall buildings and tensional composition, its technical proficiency, its composition as an aggregated superblock (but with a cross street to reduce its scale), plaza, multilevel networked spaces, promenade, and green roofs. If its RCA tower launched electronic broadcasting as a new tool of communication in a democracy, its open plaza provided a space for democratic assembly. A product of midcentury private enterprise that engaged the public realm, Rockefeller Center offered a new paradigm for the urban core that drew international interest to its design and to its potential for enriching modern metropolitan life.

I thank Elizabeth Cropper and Therese O'Malley of the Center for Advanced Study in the Visual Arts at the National Gallery of Art as well as the conference chairs Stephen Mansbach and Joachim Wolschke-Bulmahn for giving me the opportunity to present this paper. Cynthia Ware, who contributed her expert editorial skills to the published essay, deserves special recognition. Bailey Skiles provided unfailing assistance in the preparation of the manuscript. I owe a debt of gratitude to Francesco Passanti for his close reading of the text and his insightful suggestions. Miles David Samson also provided very helpful comments on the manuscript. David Murbach, manager, Gardens Division, Rockefeller Center, Tishman Speyer Properties, generously shared his extensive knowledge of the gardens and their history. A number of institutions and their staff have made resources available and greatly facilitated my research. I thank Christine Roussel, archivist at the Rockefeller Center Archives / The Rockefeller Group Inc., New York City, and Michele Hiltzik, senior archivist at the Rockefeller Archive Center, Sleepy Hollow, New York, for sharing their knowledge of Rockefeller Center's history and of archival resources. I owe a great debt of thanks to Reto Geiser and to Daniel Weiss and Gregor Harbusch of gta Archiv in Zurich for their assistance with the Sigfried Giedion Papers. Mary Daniels and Inés Zalduendo of the Frances Loeb Library, Graduate School of Design, Harvard University, also deserve my appreciation. For their generous assistance with illustrations, I thank Michel Richard, Arnaud Dercelles and Léa Demillac (Fondation Le Corbusier, Paris); James P. Quigel Jr. (Historical Collections and Labor Archives, Special Collections Library, The Pennsylvania State University); Evelyn B. Lannon, and James P. Dorsey (Boston Public Library); Danielle N. Kramer (Ryerson and Burnham Archives, The Art Institute of Chicago); Miranda Schwartz and Jill Slaight (New-York Historical Society); and Janet Parks and Inna Guzenfeld (Avery Architectural and Fine Arts Library, Columbia University). I am most grateful to Christopher M. Leich for allowing me to reproduce drawings by Hugh Ferriss. I also thank Marta Gutman for assistance with a photographic source.

1. Carol Herselle Krinsky's *Rockefeller Center* (New York, 1978) remains the most authoritative study of the project's architecture and planning. Among other important studies are three by Winston Weisman: "The Way of the Price Mechanism: The Rockefeller Centre," *Architectural Review* 108 (December 1950): 399–405; "Who Designed Rockefeller Centre?," *Journal of the Society of Architectural Historians* (hereafter *JSAH*) 10 (March 1951): 11–17; and "The First Landscaped Skyscraper," *JSAH* 18 (May 1959): 54–59. See also William H. Jordy, "Rockefeller Center and Corporate Urbanism," in *American Buildings and Their Architects*, vol. 5, *The Impact of European Modernism in the Mid-Twentieth Century* (Garden City, 1972), 1–85; Walter H. Kilham Jr., *Raymond Hood, Architect* (New York, 1973); Arnold L. Lehman, "The New York Skyscraper: A History of Its Development, 1870–1939" (PhD diss., Yale University, 1974),

406–477; Alan Balfour, *Rockefeller Center: Architecture as Theater* (New York, 1978); Manfredo Tafuri, "The Disenchanted Mountain," in Giorgio Ciucci et al., *The American City: From the Civil War to the New Deal,* trans. Barbara Luigia La Penta (Cambridge, MA, 1979), 461–486; Robert A. M. Stern, Gregory Gilmartin, and Thomas Mellins, *New York 1930* (New York, 1987); and Daniel Okrent, *Great Fortune: The Epic of Rockefeller Center* (New York, 2003).

2. See Jerold S. Kayden, *Privately Owned Public Space: The New York City Experience* (New York, 2000).

3. On the financing, see Arthur C. Holden, "Technique of Urban Redevelopment: Part II; Combination and Large-Scale Initiative in Real Estate," *Journal of Land and Public Utility Economics* 20 (August 1944): 242.

4. Weisman 1951, 12.

5. In 1895 Morris attended the École des Beaux-Arts as a student in the atelier of Paul Blondel. Louis Thérèse David de Pénanrun, Edmond Augustin Delaire, and Louis François Roux, *Les Architectes élèves de l'École des Beaux-Arts, 1793–1907* (Paris, 1907), 354.

6. Weisman 1951, 12; Krinsky 1978, 28.

7. Reinhard and Hofmeister's plan appears in Weisman 1951, 13, fig. 4. Reinhard studied at the Beaux-Arts Institute of Design in New York City and in the 1920s worked for Benjamin Wistar Morris and Raymond Hood as well as the developer John R. Todd. Hofmeister subsequently worked in the office of Beaux-Arts-trained architects Warren and Wetmore.

8. Weisman 1959, 55–56. Harvey Wiley Corbett, "The Problem of Traffic Congestion, and a Solution," *Architectural Forum* 46 (March 1927): 200–208. On the competition, and specifically Corbett's entry (with partners Harrison and MacMurray), as well as Corbett's civic plans for the Regional Plan Association, see Krinsky 1978, 36–41, figs. 20, 21, 22.

9. Weisman 1951, 16.

10. Krinsky 1978, 39.

11. Raymond M. Hood, "Rockefeller Center," *Society of Beaux-Arts Architects 1933 Yearbook* (New York, 1933), 69.

12. For Hood's opinion on the importance of planned groups of skyscrapers, see George W. Gray, "The Future of the Skyscraper," *New York Times Magazine,* September 13, 1931, 5: 1.

13. Krinsky 1978, 44–45. On the change of name to Rockefeller Center, see Lehman 1974, 433, and Okrent 2003, 257–279.

14. Krinsky 1978, 36.

15. John R. Todd, *Living a Life* (New York, 1947), 88–90.

16. Weisman 1951, 12, 16; see also Krinsky 1978, 44–45, and Minutes of the Metropolitan Square Corporation, December 6, 1930, as quoted in Kilham 1973, 157.

17. Todd 1947, 95.

18. "Rockefeller's 'Midtown City' to be Speeded," *New York American*, December 7, 1929, folder 615, box 82, and Benjamin W. Morris to Colonel Arthur Woods, January 22, 1930, folder 802, box 107, both Business Interests series, Record Group 2 Office of Messrs. Rockefeller (OMR), Rockefeller Family Archives, Rockefeller Archive Center, Sleepy Hollow, New York (hereafter designated RAC).

19. Weisman 1950, 401; Weisman 1951, 17. The Radio Corporation of America signed a conditional agreement in 1930 and a final lease on October 29, 1931. See Raymond Hood, "The Design of Rockefeller City," *Architectural Forum* 61 (January 1932): 8.

20. Kilham 1973, 152.

21. Contracts for the three firms were signed on July 1, 1930. See Hood 1932, 8, and L. Andrew Reinhard, letter to the editor, *Architectural Forum* 88 (February 1948): 26, 30. Todd credits Reinhard with the suggestion that all firms be on an "equal footing." Todd 1947, 98.

22. L. Andrew Reinhard, letter, *Architectural Record* 102 (August 1947): 20.

23. William Jordy probed the issue of authorship, partly on the basis of his interview with Harrison. Jordy 1972, 38, 429 n. 14.

24. Hood 1933, 72; see also Hood 1932, 1.

25. Douglas Haskell, "Roxy's Advantage over God," *Nation*, January 4, 1933, 11.

26. H. I. Brock, "Our Greatest Show of Builder's Magic," *New York Times Magazine*, November 20, 1932, 7.

27. S. J. Woolf, "An Architect Hails the Rule of Reason," *New York Times*, November 1, 1931, 5: 6. When John D. Rockefeller Jr. faulted the design of the top of the RCA Building's north facade, he turned to Hood, who explained that it was a "frank expression of the interior." John D. Rockefeller Jr. to John R. Todd, March 31, 1933, folder 582, box 78, Business Interests series, RG 2 OMR, Rockefeller Family Archives, RAC. But Rockefeller endorsed Hood's decision to maintain the same height on the four Fifth Avenue buildings. John D. Rockefeller Jr. to Raymond Hood, February 3, 1934, folder 582, box 78, Business Interests series, RG 2 OMR, Rockefeller Family Archives, RAC. Nathaniel Owings later credited Hood as "the genius behind the Rockefeller Center project." Nathaniel Alexander Owings, *The Spaces In Between: An Architect's Journey* (Boston, 1973), 46.

28. Todd 1947, 103.

29. Ely Jacques Kahn, "Raymond Mathewson Hood, 1881–1934," *Architecture* 70 (October 1934): 194.

30. "Rockefeller Begins Work in the Fall on 5th Av. Radio City," *New York Times*, June 17, 1930, 1, 14. For an analysis of the H series, or "fling," proposals and Hood's models, see Krinsky 1978, 53–57; Weisman 1950, 401–402; and Kilham 1973, 158–161. On the objectives of the city center, see G.A.Y. [Grace Alexandra Young], "Raymond Hood's Skyline," *Arts and Decoration* 41 (October 1934): 43. As with the Daily News Building, Hood worked first, and best, from models. For a discussion of Hood's use of plasticine models as a design method in which "several *partis* may be tried out," see Rayne Adams, "Raymond Hood," *Architecture* 63 (March 1931): 134. See also "Raymond Hood," *Architectural Forum* 62 (February 1935): 131.

31. "Rockefeller Opens New Epoch for Radio," *New York Times*, June 16, 1930, 5. See also "A Radio City," *The Survey*, July 15, 1930, 355; and H. I. Brock, "Problems Confronting the Designers of Radio City," *New York Times*, April 5, 1931, 20: 3.

32. On March 5 the model was shown to members of the press and public at the office of Todd, Robertson & Todd: "Model of Radio City to Be Shown Tonight," *New York Times*, March 5, 1931, 27. A photograph of the model appeared in "Radio City to Create a New Architecture," *New York Times*, March 6, 1931, 3, and "Models Show 250,000,000, Radio City Plan," *New York Herald Tribune*, March 6, 1931, 1, 3. See also untitled article, *Pencil Points* 12 (May 1931): 387, and Henry H. Dean, "A New Idea in City Rebuilding," *American Architect* 139 (April 1931): 32.

33. Popular consensus fixes the number of stories at seventy. In 1932 Hood claimed sixty-six stories (Hood 1932, 5, 7); although editors at *Architectural Forum* added two more, Daniel Okrent and other historians allow only sixty-six; see Okrent 2003, xiii. An early, perhaps the earliest, use of the term "slab" to denote the central tower of the Rockefeller project appears in "Radio City to Create a New Architecture," *New York Times*, March 6, 1931, 3. H. I. Brock referred to the tower as a "slat" (Brock 1931, 3). Corbett explained that a tall building for a New York City block roughly 200 feet wide and 800 feet long "tends to become a slab," as reported in Gray 1931, 1. For Hood's use of the term "slab," see Hood 1933, 70. See also Douglas Haskell, "Architecture, the Rockefeller Necropolis," *Nation* 136 (May 31, 1933): 622. For a general discussion of the slab, see Winston Weisman, "Slab Buildings," *Architectural Review* 111 (February 1952), 119–123.

34. Brock 1931, 3; Roger Wade Sherman, "The Question of Radio City," *Architectural Forum* 54 (May 1931): 601–604. The underground concourse is discussed and illustrated in Carol Herselle Krinsky, "The Skyscraper Ensemble in Its Urban Context," in Roberta Moudry, ed., *The American Skyscraper* (New York, 2005), 206–208.

35. On the "underground city," see Arthur Warner, "Radio City to Rise in Scientific Plan," *New York Times*, March 15, 1931, science section, 4, and Dean 1931, 35. On the projected station, see also Hood 1932, 7, and "Rockefeller City Files Tunnel Plan," *New York Times*, August 5, 1932, 9. The subway station opened in 1940.

36. Hood 1932, 3–4; Hood 1933, 69. See also L. Andrew Reinhard, "What Is the Rockefeller Radio City?," *Architectural Record* 69 (April 1931): 281.

37. "Radio City to Create a New Architecture" 1931, 3.

38. Hood 1932, 5. For an elegant explanation of the setbacks as they were determined in the RCA tower, see also Jordy 1972, 45–46.

39. Kilham first noted the formal similarity between the RCA and Daily News buildings, comparing their plans with those of other skyscrapers. Walter H. Kilham Jr., "Tower Floor Plans of New York Skyscrapers Compared," *American Architect* 138 (October 1930): 30–31. See also Kilham 1973, 141.

40. On the civic center or "civic forum," see "Radio City," editorial, *New York Times*, March 7, 1931, 18, and "Radio City Adopts Wide Cultural Program: Civic Forum and Musicians' School Planned," *New York Times*, September 2, 1931, 1.

41. Gray 1931, 1.

42. "Changing Styles in Architecture," *New York Times*, February 21, 1926, 10: 2.

43. "Meet Foreign Architects," *New York Times*, October 10, 1926, 11: 19.

44. Le Corbusier-Saugnier [Charles-Édouard Jeanneret-Gris], *Vers une architecture* (Paris, [1923]); Le Corbusier, *Urbanisme* (Paris, 1925). Kilham recounts that when he approached Hood for a job in January 1928, Hood informed him that he had read *Vers une architecture* but had not yet read *Urbanisme*. Kilham 1973, 13–14. Walter Kilham, interview with Mardges Bacon, February 20, 1992, Cambridge, MA. On Hood's knowledge of French, see Raymond M. Hood, "A Vocabulary of Atelier French," pts. 1–7 (n.p., 1922).

45. Orrick Johns, "Architects Dream of a Pinnacle City," *New York Times Magazine*, December 28, 1924, 10. When the Ferriss rendering was republished in early 1926, it was identified as "based on a proposal of Raymond Hood, Architect." Frederic A. Delano, "Skyscrapers," *American City Magazine* 34 (January 1926): 9.

46. Raymond M. Hood, "New York's Skyline Will Climb Much Higher," *Liberty,* April 10, 1926, 19. Hugh Ferriss, *Metropolis of Tomorrow* (New York, 1929), 87. Carol Willis explored the history of Hood's visionary projects and their links to Rockefeller Center in "Towering Cities," *Skyline*, July 1982, 10–11, and in *Raymond Hood, City of Towers* (Whitney Museum of American Art at Philip Morris, New York, 1984).

47. Hood 1926, 19, 21–23. Hood endorsed a recent determination of the Regional Plan of New York, sponsored by the Russell Sage Foundation, that continued expansion of businesses would drive residential building off the island of Manhattan.

48. "A 'Tower City' Plan to Relieve Traffic," *New York Times*, February 13, 1927, 10: 2. Drawings of Hood's 1927 project appear in "Tower Buildings and Wider Streets," *American Architect* 132 (July 5, 1927): 67–68. See also Howard Robertson, "A City of Towers," *Architect and Building News*, October 21, 1927, 639–643.

49. *L'Illustration* 160 (August 12, 1922): 133. On the Perret project, see Francesco Passanti, "The Skyscrapers of the Ville Contemporaine," *Assemblage* 4 (October 1987): 56–57.

50. Le Corbusier-Saugnier 1923, 42–43. Quotations in English are from Le Corbusier, *Towards a New Architecture*, trans. Frederick Etchells (New York, 1927), 58, and Le Corbusier, *The City of Tomorrow and Its Planning*, trans. Frederick Etchells (New York, [1929]).

51. On American skyscrapers as models, see Passanti 1987, 56–60; Stanislaus von Moos, *Le Corbusier: Elements of a Synthesis* (Cambridge, MA, 1979), 190–191; and Mardges Bacon, *Le Corbusier in America: Travels in the Land of the Timid* (Cambridge, MA, 2001), 10–12.

52. Kilham interview 1922. Hood's city of towers of 1927 designated some of the buildings to be cruciform in plan. See his plan in "Tower Buildings and Wider Streets" 1927, 67. These cruciform towers looked to those of Le Corbusier's Villes-Tours (1921). A variant of the cruciform plan appeared in the buildings of the Hood-inspired scheme of 1931 by Associated Architects for the shopping concourse and towers at Rockefeller Center (see fig. 8). For an illustration of the "City of Towers" model, see Kilham 1973, 90.

53. "Tower Buildings and Wider Streets" 1927, 67.

54. G. Holmes Perkins, *The Architectural Archives, University of Pennsylvania* 2 (January 1983): 17.

55. Raymond M. Hood, "A City under a Single Roof," *Nation's Business* 17 (November 1929): 206. See also Thomas Adams, *The Building of the City*, vol. 2 (New York, 1931), 189. Rem Koolhaas publishes a more extensive view of the model in *Delirious New York* (New York, 1978), 146–147.

56. Unsigned, "Three Visions of New York," *Creative Arts* 9 (August 1931): 160–161. Hood produced three drawings for "Manhattan 1950." Signed by Hood and dated 1929, the project was shown in early 1930 at the Architectural League of New York exhibition during his tenure as the organization's president. See "A Pictorial Review of the Architectural League Exhibition," *Architecture* 61 (May 1930): 276. Arthur Tappan North's monograph on Hood illustrates the three drawings. See Arthur Tappan North, *Raymond Hood* (New York, 1931): cover, 86, 87.

57. See, for example, William Ward Walkin, "Impressions of Modern Architecture," pt. 3, *Pencil Points* 12 (July 1931): 529–530. On North American demolition-based planning and large-scale block development, see Bacon 2001, 168–169.

58. On Hood's initiatives in 1929 and 1930, see Bacon 2001, 27.

59. Raymond M. Hood to Le Corbusier, January 16, 1930, Fondation Le Corbusier (FLC) C3-5-270.

60. Raymond M. Hood, foreword to R[andolph] W[illiams] Sexton, *American Apartment Houses, Hotels and Apartment Hotels of Today* (New York, [1929]). Corbett held that Hood "understood the economic necessity of rational building but ever kept his

imagination free." Harvey Wiley Corbett, "Raymond Mathewson Hood," *Architectural Forum* 61 (September 1934): 15. See also Rayne Adams 1931, 130–131.

61. Todd 1947, 131.

62. Corbett 1934, 15.

63. Henry-Russell Hitchcock Jr., "Raymond Hood," in *Modern Architecture: International Exhibition* (Museum of Modern Art, New York, 1932), 131, 140.

64. Hood 1932, 5.

65. Raymond Hood, "Hanging Gardens of New York," *New York Times Magazine*, August 23, 1931, 1–3. For Hood's earlier invocation of "Babylonian hanging gardens," associated with his 1927 "City of Towers" project, see "A 'Tower City' Plan to Relieve Traffic" 1927, 10: 2.

66. Hood 1931, 1.

67. "The Rockefeller Building Project in Mid-town New York," *Pencil Points* 12 (October 1931): 777.

68. Hood 1932, 3, 5. John Wenrich's drawings are illustrated in *Rockefeller Center* (New York, 1932) and Balfour 1978, figs. 76, 87, 123, 124, 125.

69. H. I. Brock, "Radio City: A Monumental Enterprise Now Takes Shape," *New York Times*, May 8, 1932, 20: 3.

70. Hood 1931, 2.

71. Hood 1931, 3.

72. Benjamin F. Betts, interview with L. Andrew Reinhard, "Gardens on the Roofs of Radio City," *American Architect* 140 (November 1931): 35.

73. I thank David Murbach for this observation, May 20, 2008.

74. Le Corbusier published several perspective views of the project in *Urbanisme* (Le Corbusier 1925, 230–231, 232, 234–235, and foldout opposite page 168). See also Le Corbusier [1929], 238–239, 242–243, 245, 246–247, and foldout opposite page 176.

75. Two photographs of the roof garden appear in Charles-Edouard Jeanneret-Gris (Le Corbusier), *Almanach d'architecture moderne* (Paris 1926), 52–53.

76. Le Corbusier 1925, 220; Le Corbusier [1929], 232.

77. On *jardins suspendus*, see Le Corbusier-Saugnier 1923, 206–209; Le Corbusier 1927, 246–249. See also Le Corbusier 1925, 215.

78. "Tower and Garden," *New York Times*, August 23, 1931, 3: 1. The editorial was a response to Hood 1931.

79. "Tower and Garden" 1931, 1.

80. Ferriss 1929, 14, 19, 63, 94, 96, 119. On the history of Manhattan's roof gardens and terraces, see Carol Willis, "Pastoral Obsessions: The Garden in the Machine," *Skyline*, March 1983, 22–23, and "The Titan City," *Skyline*, October 1982, 26–27.

81. John Ruskin, *The Seven Lamps of Architecture* (London, 1849). The frontispiece to Ferriss 1929 suggests an analogy between the mountain and the sky-scraper. On the sense of awe associated with New York skyscrapers, see David E. Nye, "The Sublime and the Skyline," in Moudry 2005, 255–269.

82. For illustrations of the business center, see Ferriss 1929, 115, 119.

83. Lisa D. Schrenk, *Building a Century of Progress* (Minneapolis, 2007), 64–70.

84. On Wright's towers, see Hilary Ballon, "Frank Lloyd Wright: The Vertical Dimension," *Frank Lloyd Wright Quarterly* 15 (summer 2004): 4–13.

85. Raymond M. Hood, *Arcady* (New York, 1929), unpaged; Rosemarie Haag Bletter, "King Kong en Arcadie," *Archithese* 17, no. 20 (1976): 25–34.

86. Adnan Morshed, "The Aesthetics of Ascension in Norman Bel Geddes's Futurama," *JSAH* 63 (March 2004): 74–99.

87. Hood 1931, 1, 3.

88. Hood 1932, 2, 5.

89. Nelson Rockefeller to John D. Rockefeller Jr., September 12, 1933, folder 581, box 78, and John R. Todd to John D. Rockefeller Jr., November 18, 1933, folder 801, box 108, Business Interests series, RG 2 OMR, Rockefeller Family Archives, RAC.

90. Wallace Harrison recommended Gréber. John D. Rockefeller Jr. to John R. Todd, April 10, 1933, and John R. Todd to John D. Rockefeller Jr., April 13, 1933, folder 581, box 78, Business Interests series, RG 2 OMR, Rockefeller Family Archives, RAC.

91. For descriptions of the rooftop gardens of La Maison Française and the British Empire Building, see G.A.Y. [Grace Alexandra Young], "Common or Garden Talk: The Roof Gardens of Radio City," *Arts and Decoration* 39 (November 1933): 42–43.

92. Ralph Hancock, *When I Make a Garden* (London, [1936]), 12. *Rockefeller Center Sky Garden Tour*, privately printed brochure [1937]. For a description of the Rockefeller Center gardens on Easter Sunday 1934, see "Rockefeller Center" [press release], March 28, 1934, folder 801, box 108, Business Interests series, RG 2 OMR, Rockefeller Family Archives, RAC. On the Garden of Nations, see F. F. Rockwell, "Gardens of the World atop Radio City," *New York Times*, September 2, 1934, 10: 8; "M. L.," "Hancock Hangs the 'Hanging Gardens,'" *Rockefeller Center Weekly*, October 18, 1934, 8–9, 15. Hancock returned to Britain toward the end of 1935. A. M. van den Hoek succeeded him as horticulturalist. See also Weisman 1959 and Theodore Osmundson, *Roof Gardens: History, Design, and Construction* (New York, 1999), 132–134. In 1939 a tour of the "sky gardens" cost fifty cents: *New York City Guide* (New York, 1939), 333. Photographs and a section of Rockefeller Center appear in "Rockefeller Center," *Fortune* 14 (December 1936): 138–144, 146, 148, 150, 153.

93. Hood 1933, 69.

94. For Lewis Mumford's criticism, see "Notes on Modern Architecture," *New Republic* 66 (March 18, 1931): 121; reprinted in "Lewis Mumford on Radio

City," *Creative Art* 8 (April 1931): 303 (the source erroneously cited as *The Nation*).

95. Frank Lloyd Wright, "Architect Calls Radio City False, Frank Lloyd Wright Declares Plan Exaggerates Worst Elements, Sees Rentals Only Theme," *New York Evening Post*, June 30, 1931, 4; reprinted in Bruce Brooks Pfeiffer, ed., *Frank Lloyd Wright, Collected Writings 1931–1939*, vol. 3 (New York, 1993), 59–62.

96. "The Sky Line: Mr. Rockefeller's Center," *New Yorker*, December 23, 1933, 29.

97. Lewis Mumford, *Culture of Cities* (New York, 1938), [277]; "The Sky Line: Rockefeller Center Revisited," *New Yorker*, May 4, 1940, 73–74.

98. See, for example, Robert de Beauplan, "Une Moderne Babel au Centre de New York," *L'Illustration*, August 13, 1932, 472–476, and Dexter Morand, "Le 'Centre Rockefeller' à New York," *L'Architecture d'aujourd'hui* 7 (June 1936): 66–70.

99. Fernand Léger, "The New Realism," *Art Front* (1935), reprinted in Fernand Léger, *Functions of Painting*, trans. Harold Rosenberg (New York, 1973), 113.

100. H. I. Brock, "Le Corbusier Scans Gotham's Towers," *New York Times*, November 3, 1935, 10; Le Corbusier, *Quand les cathédrales étaient blanches: Voyage au pays des timides* (Paris, 1937), 94.

101. Le Corbusier 1937, 87–90, English translation from *When the Cathedrals Were White: A Journey to the Country of Timid People*, trans. Francis H. Hyslop Jr. (New York, 1947), 62, 64.

102. Le Corbusier, *La Ville radieuse* (Paris, 1935); English translation, *The Radiant City*, trans. Pamela Knight, Eleanor Levieux, and Derek Coltman (New York, 1967).

103. H. I. Brock explored Rockefeller Center with Gropius, as he had earlier toured it with Le Corbusier. See H. I. Brock, "A Modernist Scans Our Skyline," *New York Times Magazine*, April 11, 1937, 12, 24.

104. Henry-Russell Hitchcock, "The Architectural Future in America," *Architectural Review* 82 (July 1937): 1–2. Although Hitchcock knew Le Corbusier personally, and thus his urban theory first hand, he also read his books.

105. Sigfried Giedion, *Space, Time and Architecture: The Growth of a New Tradition* (Cambridge, MA, 1941), 570.

106. Giedion 1941, 574; Hood 1931, 1.

107. Mumford 1938, 124–128, 133, 135.

108. Giedion 1941, 576–577.

109. Giedion 1941, 575; the photomontage of Rockefeller Center also appears in Giedion 1941, 576, fig. 320.

110. Giedion 1941, 569–580.

111. Giedion 1941 and Siegfried Giedion, *Mechanization Takes Command* (Cambridge, MA, 1948). According to von Moos, Le Corbusier and his writings were recurring points of reference in Giedion's work.

See "Sigfried Giedion ou la deuxième découverte de l'Amérique," in Jean-Louis Cohen and Hubert Damisch, eds., *Américanisme et modernité* (Paris, 1993), 247–248. See also Stanislaus von Moos, "The Visualized Machine Age or: Mumford and the European Avant-Garde," in Thomas P. and Agatha C. Hughes, *Lewis Mumford: Public Intellectual* (New York and Oxford, 1990), 227–228.

112. Sigfried Giedion to Joseph Hudnut, February 1, 1938; Sigfried Giedion to Walter Gropius, February 6, 1938. See also Paul Sachs to Sigfried Giedion, February 17, 1938. Sigfried Giedion Papers, gta Archiv, Eidgenössische Technische Hochschule, Zurich.

113. On his concept of civic space, see Mumford 1938, 479, 481, 484. Mumford's influence on Giedion and Sert as well as the subsequent shift in the CIAM agenda toward a focus on the urban nucleus are discussed in Mardges Bacon, "Josep Lluís Sert's Evolving Concept of the Urban Core: Between Corbusian Form and Mumfordian Social Practice," in Eric Mumford and Hashim Sarkis, eds., *Josep Lluís Sert: The Architect of Urban Design, 1953–1969* (New Haven, 2008), 82–90.

114. Mumford 1938, 480.

115. On the "civic nucleus," see Mumford 1938, 133, 478.

116. José Luis Sert, *Can Our Cities Survive?* (Cambridge, MA, 1942). For Sert's transatlantic dialogue with Giedion and others, see Bacon 2008, 76–114. See also Martin Steinmann, ed., *CIAM: Dokumente 1928–1939* (Basel and Stuttgart, 1979), 192; CIAM, *Logis et loisirs, 5e Congrès CIAM, Paris, 1937* (Boulogne-sur-Seine, 1937), 35; Josep M. Rovira, *José Luis Sert* (Milan, 2000), 84–87; Eric Mumford, *The CIAM Discourse on Urbanism, 1928–1960* (Cambridge, MA, 2000), 104–116.

117. The concept of town planning based on "three dimensions" derived from the Town Planning Chart drafted at CIAM 4 (1933); see Sert 1942, 150, 249.

118. Le Corbusier, *New World of Space* (New York, 1948), 8; Le Corbusier-Saugnier 1923, vii, 3. See also Le Corbusier, "L'espace indicible," *L'Architecture d'aujourd'hui* 17 (November–December 1946): 9–17, and Linda Dalrymple Henderson, *The Fourth Dimension and Non-Euclidean Geometry in Modern Art* (Princeton, 1983).

119. Siegfried Giedion, "American Architecture Viewed from Europe," *Architect and Engineer* 36 (June 1939): 54. For echoes of Mumford's social principles in *The Culture of Cities*, see Giedion 1941, 430, 543.

120. Mumford 1938, 481. Josep Lluis Sert, "Centres of Community Life," in *The Heart of the City: Towards the Humanisation of Urban Life*, ed. Jaqueline Tyrwhitt, Josep Lluis Sert, and Ernesto N. Rogers, CIAM 8 (London, 1952), 8.

121. "Conversation at CIAM 8," in Tyrwhitt, Sert, and Rogers 1952, 36–40.

122. On CIAM 4 (1933), see Le Corbusier, *La Charte d'Athènes* (Paris, 1943); English translation: *The Athens Charter*, trans. Anthony Eardley (New York, 1973). On both CIAM 4 (1933) and 8 (1951), see Mumford 2000, 88–91, 201–215; see also Steinmann 1979 and Giorgio Ciucci, "The Invention of the Modern Movement," *Oppositions* 24 (spring 1981): 68–91.

123. Sert 1952, 4.

124. Bacon 2008, 76–114.

125. Giedion 1941, 579.

126. For discussions of the alterations, which included an underground shopping concourse with a network of corridors and access to the Sixth Avenue Subway, see Jordy 1972, 17, 20–22; Okrent 2003, 357–360.

127. The event was in September 1944, not in 1945, as Giedion wrote. Sigfried Giedion, "The Heart of the City: A Summing-up," in Tyrwhitt, Sert, and Rogers 1952, 161; see also pages vii, 4, 5.

128. Sigfried Giedion, *Architecture, You and Me* (Cambridge, MA, 1958), 126.

129. The quote is from William Turk Priestley, who had studied with Mies at the Bauhaus (Berlin) in the early 1930s. Priestley, interview with Ludwig Glaeser, September 3, 1976, Mies van der Rohe Archive, Museum of Modern Art, New York, tape 2, side 1, as quoted in Cammie McAtee, "Alien #5044325: Mies's First Trip to America," in *Mies in America* (Montreal and New York, 2001), 162, 190 n. 105.

130. Giedion published the text of "Nine Points on Monumentality" first in his book *Architektur und Gemeinschaft* (Hamburg, 1956), 40–42, and subsequently in Giedion 1958, 48–52.

131. Countering Giedion's "space-time" concept, the critic Douglas Haskell supported Hood's position that Rockefeller Center had a "pyramidal, Beaux-Arts composition redone in dominoes," which affirmed the "super block as core." See "Unity and Harmony at Rockefeller Center," *Architectural Forum* 124 (January 1966): 43.

132. Elizabeth Mock, ed., *Built in USA, 1932–1944* (New York, 1944), 102.

133. Clarence S. Stein, *Toward New Towns for America* (Chicago, 1951), 200.

134. Jane Jacobs. "Downtown Is for People," in *The Exploding Metropolis* (New York, 1957), 144. See also Jane Jacobs, *The Death and Life of Great American Cities* (New York, 1961), 181.

135. Jacobs 1961, 104. In spite of Jacobs' endorsement, her fellow urban sociologist William Whyte initially took issue with Rockefeller Center's sunken plaza and endorsed, instead, the amphitheater and railings above, which drew people to them. William H. Whyte, *The Social Life of Small Urban Spaces* (Washington, DC, 1980), 58.

136. To Manfredo Tafuri, Rockefeller Center signaled the hegemony of private enterprise over public control, commercial expediency over civic intention, realism over utopianism, and an aggregate of bland towers over a single ostentatious one. But in his view this model of rational planning and civic idealism failed to spawn similar nodes and thereby integrate fully into its urban fabric. Tafuri 1979, 483–484. In response to Tafuri, Reinhold Martin argued that the failure to replicate or integrate was due precisely to Rockefeller Center's success in casting "organic unity onto the disaggregated field of commerce." Reinhold Martin, *The Organizational Complex: Architecture, Media, and Corporate Space* (Cambridge, MA, 2003), 88.

Contributors

MARDGES BACON is Matthews Distinguished University Professor of Architecture Emeritus at Northeastern University. She is a specialist in modern and American architectural history with a focus on transatlantic exchange between Europe and the United States. Her publications include *Le Corbusier in America: Travels in the Land of the Timid* (2001) and *Ernest Flagg: Beaux-Arts Architect and Urban Reformer* (1986). She also served as editor and wrote a critical introduction to a volume of essays, *"Symbolic Essence" and Other Writings on Modern Architecture, Art, and American Culture by William H. Jordy* (2005).

SONIA BERJMAN is a landscape historian, preservationist, and consultant in Buenos Aires. She has been a senior fellow in the program of landscape studies at Dumbarton Oaks in Washington. She was a contributor to the Dumbarton Oaks symposium volume *Gardens and Cultural Change: A Pan-American Perspective* and is the author of more than a hundred publications, including twenty books on urban and landscape history, of which the most recent is *Los paseos públicos de Buenos Aires entre 1922 y 1946 y la labor de Carlos León Thays* (2014). She is an honorary member of the International Scientific Committee on Cultural Landscapes (ISCCL) of the International Council on Monuments and Sites (ICOMOS).

ANITA BERRIZBEITIA is professor of landscape architecture and director of the master in landscape architecture degree programs, Harvard University Graduate School of Design. Her research focuses on design theories of modern and contemporary landscape architecture, the productive aspects of landscapes, and Latin American cities and landscapes. She is coauthor, with Linda Pollak, of *Inside/Outside: Between Architecture and Landscape* (1999), which won a merit award from the American Society of Landscape Architects; author of *Roberto Burle Marx in Caracas: Parque del Este, 1956–1961* (2004), awarded the J. B. Jackson Book Prize in 2007 from the Foundation for Landscape Studies; and editor of *Michael Van Valkenburgh Associates: Reconstructing Urban Landscapes* (2009), which received an ASLA honor award.

SONJA DÜMPELMANN is associate professor of landscape architecture at the Harvard University Graduate School of Design. She has held research fellowships at the Ger-man Historical Institute and at Dumbarton Oaks in Washington. Her publications include a book on the Italian landscape architect Maria Teresa Parpagliolo Shephard (2004) and, most recently, *Flights of Imagination: Aviation, Landscape, Design* (2014) as well as the edited *Cultural History of Gardens in the Age of Empire* (2013) and the coedited *Greening the City: Urban Landscapes in the Twentieth Century* (2011).

LANCE HUMPHRIES is an independent scholar in Baltimore, Maryland. Much of his work focuses on the history of collecting in the United States and on eighteenth- and nineteenth-century visual culture of the Mid-Atlantic region. His publications include the two-volume *Daniel Garber: Catalogue Raisonné* (2006) and articles on the Peale family of painters, Baltimore painted furniture, and the Baltimore art collector and patron Robert Gilmor Jr. He is a founding board member of the Mount Vernon Place Conservancy, a nonprofit in Baltimore charged with restoring and maintaining this National Historic Landmark District comprising Robert Mills' first Washington Monument and the park squares surrounding it.

DOROTHÉE IMBERT is head of landscape architecture and the inaugural Hubert C. Schmidt '38 Chair in landscape architecture in the Austin E. Knowlton School of Architecture, Ohio State University. She previously taught landscape architecture at the Sam Fox School of Design and Visual Arts at Washington University in St. Louis and at the Harvard University Graduate School of Design. She has carried out extensive research on landscape modernism with an emphasis on Europe and California. Her books include *Between Garden and City: Jean Canneel-Claes and Landscape Modernism* (2009), *Garrett Eckbo: Modern Landscapes for Living* (1996), and *The Modernist Garden in France* (1993). She is the editor of the forthcoming *Food and the City: Histories of Culture and Cultivation* for Dumbarton Oaks.

MICHAEL G. LEE is the Reuben McCorkle Rainey Professor in the History of Landscape Architecture and associate professor of landscape architecture at the University of Virginia. He previously taught at the Harvard University Graduate School of Design, the Rhode Island School of Design, and Connecticut College and was a post-doctoral associate in garden and landscape studies at Dumbarton Oaks Research Library and Collection,

Washington. His research focuses on ideological constructions of nature at the intersection of philosophy, literature, and landscape design, with a special interest in garden history from the eighteenth to the twentieth century in Germany. He is coeditor, with Kenneth I. Helphand, of *Technology and the Garden*, Dumbarton Oaks Colloquium Series in the History of Landscape Architecture (2014); the author of *The German "Mittelweg": Garden Theory and Philosophy in the Time of Kant* (2007); and coeditor, with Mirka Beneš, of *Clio in the Italian Garden: Twenty-First-Century Studies in Historical Methods and Theoretical Perspectives* (2011).

KAREN M'CLOSKEY is associate professor of landscape architecture at the University of Pennsylvania and cofounder, with Keith VanDerSys, of an internationally recognized design practice, PEG office of landscape + architecture. Her writing focuses on contemporary landscape architecture, in particular the role of design methodology in terms of what particular representational techniques privilege and engender. Her recent publications include *Unearthed: the Landscapes of Hargreaves Associates* (2013) and "Synthetic Patterns: Fabricating Landscapes in the Age of 'Green,'" *Journal of Landscape Architecture* (spring 2013). M'Closkey was the recipient of the 2012–2013 Garden Club of America Rome Prize in landscape architecture.

STEVEN MANSBACH, professor of the history of twentieth-century art at the University of Maryland in College Park, focuses his research and teaching interests on the genesis and reception of "classical" modern art. Although his interests encompass all of Europe, his specific area of scholarly publication is the art of central and eastern Europe from the Baltic to the Adriatic. On this topic he has published numerous books, articles, exhibition catalogues, and essays, including *Riga's Capital Modernism* (2013), *Graphic Modernism: From the Baltic to the Balkans, 1910–1935* (2007), *Modern Art in Eastern Europe: From the Baltic to the Balkans, ca. 1890–1939* (1999), and *Standing in the Tempest: Painters of the Hungarian Avant-Garde* (1991). He has also taught this subject as a professor in Germany, Poland, Hungary, and South Africa, as well as at several American universities. In addition to holding fellowships and university professorships in the United States, Europe, and Africa, he served as associate dean of the Center for Advanced Study in the Visual Arts at the National Gallery of Art and as the founding dean and director of the American Academy in Berlin.

THERESE O'MALLEY is associate dean of the Center for Advanced Study in the Visual Arts, National Gallery of Art. Her publications concern the history of landscape architecture and garden design, primarily in the eighteenth and nineteenth centuries, focusing on the transatlantic exchange of plants, ideas, and people. Her recent publications include *Keywords in American Landscape Design* (2010); *The Art of Natural History: Illustrated Treatises and Botanical Paintings, 1400–1850*, coedited with Amy R. W. Meyers (Studies in the History of Art, vol. 69, 2008); and articles on the early profession of landscape design and the history of botanic gardens and treatises. She is a founding board member of the

Foundation for Landscape Studies and a board member of the Mount Vernon Place Conservancy, Baltimore. She also serves as an advisor to the United States Ambassadors Fund for the State Department. She has been president of the Society of Architectural Historians and chair of the Association of Research Institutes in the History of Art and was a senior fellow in landscape Studies at Dumbarton Oaks from 1989 to 1995. She lectures internationally and has been a guest professor at Harvard, Princeton, the University of Pennsylvania, and Temple University. In 2005 she was the guest curator and catalog author of *Glasshouses: The Architecture of Light and Air*, an exhibition at the New York Botanical Garden.

FRANCO PANZINI is a landscape architect and historian, and a guest lecturer at the Università IUAV di Venezia and the Università degli Studi di Roma Tre. He is a former fellow at Dumbarton Oaks, Washington. His scholarly interests center on the evolution of links between nature and the built environment. Among his publications are *Per i piaceri del popolo: L'evoluzione del giardino pubblico in Europa dalle origini al XX secolo* (1993), *Giardini delle Marche* (1998), and most recently *Projetar a natureza: Arquitetura da paisagem e dos jardins desde as origens até à época contemporânea* (2013).

ALAN POWERS is a curator and freelance writer and teaches at New York University, London. He was formerly a professor at the University of Greenwich. A specialist in twentieth-century architecture, art, and design, he has a long association with the Twentieth Century Society, a conservation charity for buildings in Britain after 1914, and coedits its journal, *Twentieth Century Architecture*, and a series of architectural monographs. His books include monographs on Serge Chermayeff and Eric Ravilious and a number of survey volumes, among them *Britain* (2007) in the series Modern Architectures in History, and, as principal contributor, *British Murals and Decorative Painting, 1920–1960: Rediscoveries and New Interpretations* (2013).

JOHANNES STOFFLER is a landscape architect in Zurich with a practice in historic garden research and restoration, as well as a lecturer on garden heritage conservation at Hochschule für Technik (HSR), Rapperswil, Switzerland. He is editor of the Schweizerische Gesellschaft für Gartenkultur yearbook *Topiaria Helvetica* and the author of numerous publications on the history of landscape architecture in Switzerland. His book *Gustav Ammann: Landschaften der Moderne in der Schweiz* appeared in 2008. His current research with the city of Zurich and HSR deals with conjectural replanting of public landscapes in Zurich, 1940–1970.

JOSÉ TITO ROJO is conservator of the botanical garden of the Universidad de Granada and a historian of gardens and ornamental plants. He is coauthor with Manuel Casares Porcel of *El jardín hispanomusulmán: Los jardines de Al-Andalus y su herencia* (2011) and coeditor with Luigi Zangheri and Michel Conan of *Histories of Garden Conservation: Case-Studies and Critical Debates*, Colloquio Internazionale sulla Storia della Conservazione dei Giardini (2005).

JOACHIM WOLSCHKE-BULMAHN is professor in the history of open-space planning and landscape architecture in the faculty of architecture and landscape, Leibniz Universität Hannover. From 1991 to 1996 he was director of landscape studies at Dumbarton Oaks, Washington. He is director and a founding member of the Zentrum für Gartenkunst und Landschaftsarchitektur, a research center of Leibniz Universität Hannover. He has published widely on garden history and the recent history of the profession of landscape architecture, including, as editor, *Travel Report: An Apprenticeship in the Earl of Derby's Kitchen Gardens and Greenhouses at Knowsley, England*, trans. Mic Hale, Ex Horto, Dumbarton Oaks Texts in Garden and Landscape Studies (2013), and, as coeditor with Hubertus Fischer and Sarah Ozacky-Lazar, *Environmental Policy and Landscape Architecture*, CGL-Studies (2014).

Index

Page numbers in *italics* indicate figures.

Huber, Engelbert, 42
Hünerwadel, Theodor, 56
Hunziker, Hans, 56
Huxley, Julian, *TVA: Adventure in Planning*, 90, 91, *91*
Hyères (France), Villa de Noailles, 208
hygiene, in Swiss swimming pool landscapes, 54, 58

I

Ibérica (periodical), *186*
Ibn al-'Awwām, 176
identity, Italian national cultural, 140, 144
IFLA. *See* International Federation of Landscape
    Architects
Illustration, L' (newspaper), 288
ilustración española y americana, La (journal), 172
Imperial Hotel (Tokyo), 295
Impington Village College (Cambridge), *85*, 85–86, *86*
indigenous plant species, garden design defined by use
    of, 6
industrialization, English cities as victims of, 75, 76
inglesa, jardín a la. See *jardín a la inglesa*
Institute of Landscape Architects, 73
Institute of Rural Reconstruction, 81
Internationale Kunst- und Grosse Gartenbau-
    Ausstellung (Mannheim), 37, *37*
International Federation of Landscape Architects
    (IFLA), 66
International Style, 292
Invierno, Jardines de (Buenos Aires), 236, *237*, *238*
Isabella II (queen of Spain), 171
Isabelline gardens, 171–172, 175, 176, 178
Italian cityscapes, trees in, 5, 117–134. *See also* Rome
    and African colonies, 120, 127–128, 131–133
    common species of, 125–128
    under Fascism, 120, 128–131
    symbolism of, 120, 125–128
Italian gardens, 5–6, 137–164. *See also specific gardens*
    as architecture, 139–140, 144–147
    as art, 140–142, 144
    conservation movement and, 139, 140–142, 144
    gender and, 147
    ideological purposes of, 140, 148–152
    as monuments, 140–141
    other countries inspired by, 139
    prescriptions for modern life in, 152–164
    publications on, twentieth-century, 141, 144–147
    regional styles in, 150
    stagnation and revival in design of, 139, 146
    vernacular, 139–140, 142–144
Italy. *See also specific cities*
    African colonies of, 120, 127–128, 131–133
    ambivalent relationship with history in, 119
    ancient history as shared history of, 119, 122–125, 150
    conservation movement in, 139, 140–142, 144
    countryside of
        under Fascism, 129
        historical lack of trees in, 120, 120–121, 152
    cultural nationalism in, 139, 144, 145, 148
    Fascist. *See* Fascist Italy

formation of modern state of, 120, 122–123, 140
gardens of. *See* Italian gardens
trees in cities of. *See* Italian cityscapes
vernacular architecture in, 142, 144

J

Jackson, Howard W., 273
Jackson, William Henry, *El Capitan, Yosemite Valley,*
    206
Jacobs, Jane, 301–302
Jäger-Pleger, Resi, 36
jardín a la inglesa
    definition of, 171
    domination of, 171–173, 176
    early publications on, 175, 176
    opposition to, 172–173, 178, 180–183
Jardin régulier, 12
Jeanneret, Pierre, 22, 153
Jefferson, Thomas, 210, 265
Jekyll, Gertrude, 61, 77, 156
    Cutting Heath-Turf, 78
Jellicoe, Geoffrey
    Caveman Restaurant in Cheddar Gorge, 86, *87*
    planning report on Broadway, 86, *88*
    in professionalization of landscape architecture, 73
    on Villa Gamberaia in Settignano, 154
Jenks, Jorian, 80
Joffre, Joseph, 252, 253
Johns Hopkins University, 252
Jones Falls (Baltimore), 257, 259, 269
June Garden (Junihave) at Svastika estate in Rungsted,
    17, *17–18*

K

Kahn, Ely Jacques, 285
Kansas Pacific Railway, 219
Kant, Immanuel, 36
Kastenbad, 54, *54*, 58
Key, Francis Scott, 249–250, 253
Kiley, Dan, 208
Kilham, Walter, Jr., 285, 288, 289
Kimball, Theodora, *An Introduction to the Study of*
    Landscape Design, x
kitchen gardens, in Weimar Germany, 34
Klee, Paul, 44
Klingberg (Germany), garden at residence of Maasz in,
    40, *40*
Köhler, Fritz, *Siedlung in Unterrath*, 34, *34*
kommende Garten. *See* coming garden/garden of the
    future
Koninck, Louis-Herman de, Canneel house in
    Auderghem, 20, *20*, *21*
Kotěra, Jan, 97
Kracauer, Sigfried, 44
Krall, Karl, 43, *43*
Krinsky, Carol, 283
Kropotkin, Peter, *Fields, Factories and Workshops*, 78

Studies in the History of Art
Published by the National Gallery of Art,
Washington

This series includes Studies in the History of
Art, collected papers on objects in the Gallery's
collections and other art-historical studies
(formerly Report and Studies in the History of
Art); Monograph Series I, a catalogue of stained
glass in the United States; Monograph Series II,
on conservation topics; and Symposium Papers
(formerly Symposium Series), the proceedings of
symposia sponsored by the Center for Advanced
Study in the Visual Arts.